MOUS *Essentials*

EXCEL 2000

MARIANNE FOX
BUTLER UNIVERSITY

LAWRENCE C. METZELAAR
BUTLER UNIVERSITY

Upper Saddle River, New Jersey

MOUS Essentials: Excel 2000

International Standard Book Number: 0-13-019104-3

Printed in the United States of America

03 02 01   4

Interpretation of the printing code: the rightmost double-digit number is the year of the book's printing; the rightmost single-digit number is the number of the book's printing. For example, a printing code of 00-1 shows that the first printing of the book occurred in 2000.

Trademark Acknowledgments

All terms mentioned in this book that are known to be trademarks or service marks have been appropriately capitalized. Prentice Hall cannot attest to the accuracy of this information. Use of a term in this book should not be regarded as affecting the validity of any trademark or service mark.

Microsoft and the Microsoft Office User Specialist Logo are registered trademarks of Microsoft Corporation in the United States and other countries. Prentice Hall is an independent entity from Microsoft Corporation and not affiliated with Microsoft Corporation in any manner. This publication may be used in assisting students to prepare for a Microsoft Office User Specialist Exam. Neither Microsoft Corporation, its designated review company, nor Prentice Hall warrants that use of this publication will ensure passing the relevant Exam.

Use of the Microsoft Office User Specialist Approved Courseware Logo on this product signifies that it has been independently reviewed and approved in complying with the following standards:

> *Acceptable coverage of all content related to the Core and Expert level Microsoft Office exams entitled "Excel 2000"; and sufficient performance-based exercises that relate closely to all required content, based on sampling of text.*

Screens reproduced in the book were created using Collage Plus from Inner Media, Inc., Hollis, NH.

Editor-in-Chief:
Mickey Cox

Acquisitions Editor:
Lucinda Gatch

Assistant Editor:
Jennifer Stagman

Managing Editor:
Monica Stipanov

Editorial Assistant:
Mary Toepfer

Technical Editor:
Lynda Fields

Director of Strategic Marketing:
Nancy Evans

Marketing Manager:
Kris King

AVP/Director of Production & Manufacturing:
Michael Weinstein

Production Manager:
Gail Steier de Acevedo

Project Manager:
Tim Tate

Manufacturing Buyer:
Natacha St. Hill Moore

Senior Manufacturing and Prepress Manager:
Vincent Scelta

Book Design:
Louisa Klucznik/Graphic World

Cover Design:
Pisaza Design Studio, Ltd.

Full Service Composition:
Graphic World

About the Authors

Marianne Fox is an Indiana CPA with BS and MBA degrees in Accounting from Indiana University. For more than 20 years, she has enjoyed teaching full-time—initially in Indiana University's School of Business; since 1988 in the College of Business Administration at Butler University. As the co-owner of an Indiana-based consulting firm, Marianne has extensive experience consulting and training in the corporate and continuing education environments. Since 1984, she has co-authored more than 35 computer-related books and made presentations on accounting, computer applications, and instructional development topics at a variety of seminars and conferences.

Lawrence C. Metzelaar earned a BS in Business Administration and Computer Science from the University of Maryland and an Ed.M and CAGS in Human Problem Solving from Boston University. Larry has more than 35 years experience with military and corporate mainframe and microcomputer systems. He has taught computer science and information systems at the University of Hawaii, Control Data Institute, Indiana University, Purdue University, and is currently on the faculty at Butler University. As the co-owner of an Indiana-based consulting firm, he has extensive experience consulting and training in the corporate environment. Since 1984, he has co-authored more than 35 computer-related books and made presentations on computer applications and instructional development topics at a variety of seminars and conferences.

Dedication

We would to dedicate this book to all who use it, in appreciation of your desire to learn how to learn, and your selection of our book to support those efforts.

Acknowledgments

We thank **J. Burdeane Orris**, Professor at Butler University and author of Excel 2000 Essentials Advanced, for major contributions to the macro, Goal Seek, Scenario, Solver, Report Manager, integrating applications, and collaboration sections of the text. We are grateful also for the support provided by our colleagues at Butler University, including our dean **Dr. Richard Fetter** and **Sondrea Ozolins**, Executive Director of Information Resources.

We want to express our appreciation to the entire MOUS Essentials 2000 team—other authors, editors, production staff, and those in marketing who start and end the process of developing and delivering a quality text. Special thanks go to those with whom we were most involved on a day-to-day basis, **Monica Stipanov** and **Tim Tate**. They earned our respect and gratitude for the prompt, professional, and always pleasant way in which they managed the creative process.

Contents at a Glance

Table of Contents

Introduction

Essentials courseware from Prentice Hall is anchored in the practical and professional needs of all types of students. Each title in the series reflects a "learning-by-doing" approach that encourages you to grasp application-related concepts as you expand your skills through hands-on tutorials.

The *MOUS Essentials* series has an added focus—preparing you for certification as a Microsoft Office User Specialist. The Specialist designation distinguishes you from your peers as knowledgeable in using Office products, which can also make you more competitive in the job market.

The Specialist program is available for many Office 2000 applications at both Core and Expert User levels. You can learn more about the Specialist program in Appendix B, "Preparing for MOUS Certification," and at the www.mous.net Web site.

How To Use this Book

You have selected a book providing a comprehensive approach to learning Excel, with emphasis on skill sets designated by Microsoft as *Core* or *Expert* for purposes of certification as a Microsoft Office User Specialist. Please take a few moments to familiarize yourself with the icons used in this book and its conventions. If you have questions or comments, visit the related Prentice Hall *MOUS Essentials* Web site: www.prenhall.com/mousessentials.

Each *MOUS Essentials* text consists of modular lessons that are built around a series of numbered step-by-step procedures that are clear, concise, and easy to review. Brief explanations are provided at the start of each lesson and, as needed, between steps. Many lessons contain additional notes and tips.

A *MOUS Essentials* book includes 15 to 21 projects, two appendixes and a glossary. Each project covers one area (or a few closely related areas) of application functionality, and is divided into lessons related to that topic. For example, a project on improving the appearance of a worksheet includes lessons on formatting numbers, aligning cell contents, changing font and font size, applying bold and italic, adding color, adding borders, using Format Painter and removing formatting. Each lesson presents a specific task or closely related set of tasks in a manageable chunk that's easy to assimilate and retain.

Each element in a *MOUS Essentials* title is designed to maximize your learning experience. Here's a list of the *MOUS Essentials* project elements and a description of how each element can help you:

- **Required MOUS Objectives Table**   These tables are organized into three columns: Objective, Required Activity for MOUS, and Exam Level. The objective column lists the general objectives of the project. The associated MOUS requirements for each objective are listed in the Required Activity for MOUS column. The particular exam levels of those activities—Core or Expert—are listed in the Exam Level column. Look over the objectives and MOUS requirements on the opening page of each project before you begin, and review them after completing the project to identify the main goals for each project.

- **Key Terms**   This book includes useful vocabulary words and definitions specific to the application. Key terms introduced in each project are listed in alphabetical order on the opening page of the project. These key terms then appear in bold italic within the text and are defined during their first occurence in the project. Definitions of key terms are also included in the glossary.

- **Why Would I Do This?** You are studying Excel to accomplish useful tasks in the real world. This brief section at the beginning of each project tells you why these tasks or procedures are important. What can you do with the knowledge? How can these application features be applied to everyday tasks?

- **MOUS Core Objective Icon** This icon indicates that a lesson relates to a specific MOUS Core-level skill. MOUS skills may be covered by a whole lesson or perhaps just a single step within a lesson.

- **MOUS Expert Objective Icon** This icon indicates that a lesson relates to a MOUS Expert-level skill. There may be a mix of Core and Expert objectives within a project. Some objectives are both Core and Expert, as well.

- **Lessons** Each lesson contains one or more tasks that correspond to an objective or MOUS requirement, which are listed on the opening page of the project. A lesson consists of step-by-step tutorials, associated screen captures, and the sidebar notes of the types described later. Though each lesson often builds on the previous one, the lessons have been made as modular as possible. For example, you can skip tasks that you've already mastered and begin a later lesson, if you choose.

- **Step-by-Step Tutorial** The lessons consist of numbered, bolded step-by-step instructions that show you how to perform the procedures in a clear, concise, and direct manner. These hands-on tutorials, which are the "essentials" of each project, let you "learn by doing." A short paragraph may appear after a step to clarify the results of the step. Screen captures are provided after key steps so that you can compare the results on your monitor. To review the lesson, you can easily scan the bold, numbered steps.

- **Exam Note** These sidebars provide information and insights on topics covered on MOUS exams. You can easily recognize them by their distinctive icon. It's well worth the effort to review these crucial notes again after completing a project.

- **Inside Stuff** Inside Stuff comments provide extra tips, shortcuts, alternative ways to complete a process, as well as special hints. You may safely ignore these for the moment to focus on the main task at hand, or you may pause to learn and appreciate these tidbits.

- **If You Have Problems...** These short troubleshooting notes help you anticipate or solve common problems quickly and effectively. Even if you don't encounter the problem at this time, do make a mental note of it so that you know where to look when you find yourself having difficulties.

- **Summary** This section provides a brief recap of the activities learned in the project. The summary often includes suggestions for expanding your knowledge.

- **Checking Concepts and Terms** This section offers optional true/false and multiple choice questions designed to check your comprehension and assess retention. If you need to refresh your memory, the relevant lesson number is provided after each question. For example, [L5] directs you to review Lesson 5 for the answer.

- **Skill Drill** This section enables you to check your comprehension, evaluate your progress, and practice what you've learned. The exercises in this section build on and reinforce what you have learned in each project. Generally, the Skill Drill exercises include step-by-step instructions. A Core or Expert icon indicates whether a MOUS required activity is introduced in a Skill Drill exercise.

- **Challenge**   This section provides exercises that expand on or relate to the skills practiced in the project. Each exercise provides a brief narrative introduction followed by instructions. Although the instructions are written in a step-by-step format, the steps are not as detailed as those in the Skill Drill section. Providing fewer specific steps helps you learn to think on your own.

- **Discovery Zone**   These exercises require advanced knowledge of project topics or application of skills from multiple lessons. Additionally, these exercises might require you to research topics in Help or on the Web to complete them. This self-directed method of learning new skills emulates real-world experience. A Core or Expert icon indicates if a MOUS required activity is introduced in a Discovery Zone exercise.

- **PinPoint Assessment**   Each project ends with a reminder to use MOUS PinPoint training and testing software to supplement the projects in the book. The software aids you in your preparation for taking and passing the MOUS exams. A thorough explanation of how to use the PinPoint software is provided in Appendix A, "Using the MOUS PinPoint Training and Testing Software."

Typeface Conventions Used in this Book

We have used the following conventions throughout this book so that certain items stand out from the rest of the text:

- Key terms appear in ***bold italic*** the first time they are defined.
- Monospace type appears frequently and looks `like this`. It is used to indicate 1) text that you are instructed to key in, 2) text that appears onscreen as warnings, confirmations, or general information, 3) the name of a file to be used in a lesson or exercise, and 4) text from a dialog box that is referenced within a sentence, when that sentence might appear awkward if the dialog box text were not set off.
- Hotkeys are indicated by underline. Hotkeys are the underlined letters in menus, toolbars, and dialog boxes that activate commands and options, and are a quick way to choose frequently used commands and options. Hot keys look like this: File, Save.

How To Use Student Data Files on the CD-ROM

The CD-ROM accompanying this book contains PinPoint as well as all the data files for you to use as you work through the step-by-step tutorials within projects and the Skill Drill, Challenge, and Discovery Zone exercises provided at the end of each project. The CD contains separate parallel folders for each project.

The names of the student data files correspond to the filenames called for in the textbook. Each filename includes six characters—an initial letter indicating the application, a dash, two digits indicating the project number, and two digits indicating the file number within the project. For example, the first file used in Excel Project 2 is named e-0201. The third file in Excel Project 14 is named e-1403. The Word document named `e-stufiles.doc` on the companion Web site (www.prenhall.com/mousessentials) provides a complete listing of data files by project, including the corresponding names used to save each file.

Please refer to the Readme file on the CD for instruction on how to use the CD-ROM.

Supplements

- *Instructor's Resource CD-ROM*—The Instructor's Resource CD-ROM includes the entire Instructor's Manual for each application in Microsoft Word format and also contains screen shots that correspond to the solutions for the lessons in the book. A computerized testbank is included to create tests, maintain student records, and to provide online practice testing. Student data files and completed solution files are also on the CD-ROM. PowerPoint slides, which elaborate on each project, are also included.

- *Companion Web Site (www.prenhall.com/mousessentials)*—For both students and instructors, the companion Web site includes all the ancillary material to accompany the MOUS Essentials series. Students can find additional test questions that evaluate their understanding of the key concepts of each application and also instant feedback on their results. Instructors will find the data and solution files, Instructor's Manual, and PowerPoint slides for each application.

Microsoft Excel 2000 MOUS Core and Expert User Skills

Each MOUS exam involves a list of required tasks you may be asked to perform. This list of possible tasks is categorized by skill area. The following tables list the skill areas and where their required tasks can be found in this book. Table A contains the Core-level tasks. Table B contains the Expert-level tasks.

 **Table A   Microsoft Excel 2000 Core MOUS Skills**

Skill Set	Required Activity for MOUS	Project	Lesson(s)	Page(s)
Working with cells				
	Use Undo and Redo	1	2	6
	Clear cell content	1	2	6
	Enter text, dates, and numbers	1	2	6
		5	7	112
	Edit cell content	1	2	6
	Go to a specific cell	1	1	2
	Insert and delete selected cells	8	1	176
	Cut, copy, paste, paste special and move	2	2, 5, 7	32, 37, 40
	selected cells, use the office Clipboard	4	4	79
	Use Find and Replace	8	2	178
	Clear cell formats	3	8	63
	Work with series (AutoFill)	2	3	34
	Create hyperlinks	17	5-7	379-382
Working with files				
	Use Save	1	3	9
	Use Save As (different name, location, format)	4	8	87
	Locate and open an existing workbook	2	1	30
	Create a folder	1	3	12
	Use templates to create a new workbook	8	8	188
	Save a worksheet/workbook as a Web Page	7	8	165
	Send a workbook via email	8	7	187
	Use the Office Assistant	1	4	12
		10	1	220
		11	3	248
		13	1	284
Formatting worksheets				
	Apply font styles (typeface, size, color, and styles)	3	3-5	56-58
	Apply number formats (currency, percent, dates, comma)	3	1	52
	Modify size of rows and columns	1	2	6
	Modify alignment of cell content	3	2	54
	Adjust the decimal place	3	1	52
	Use the Format Painter	3	7	62
	Apply AutoFormat	8	4	182
	Apply cell borders and shading	3	5-6	58-60
	Merging cells	3	2	54
	Rotate text and change indents	3	2	54
		8	2	178
	Define, apply, and remove a style	8	5	184

Core Level Mouse Skills (continued)

Skill Set	Required Activity for MOUS	Project	Lesson(s)	Page(s)
Page setup and printing				
	Preview and print worksheets & workbooks	1	7	19
		7	7	163
	Use Web Page Preview	7	8	165
	Print a selection	1	7	19
	Change page orientation and scaling	1	6	16
	Set page margins and centering	1	6	16
	Insert and remove a page break	12	7	272
	Set print, and clear a print area	1	6	16
	Set up headers and footers	1	6	16
	Set print titles and options (gridlines, print quality, row & column headings)	1	6	16
Working with worksheets & workbooks				
	Insert and delete rows and columns	2	4	36
	Hide and unhide rows and columns	4	6	84
	Freeze and unfreeze rows and columns	4	5	81
	Change the zoom setting	4	2	75
	Move between worksheets in a workbook	7	2	154
	Check spelling	2	8	42
	Rename a worksheet	7	2	154
	Insert and delete worksheets	7	2	154
	Move and copy worksheets	7	2	154
		8	6	186
	Link worksheets & consolidate data	7	5	159
	using 3D References	14	1	308
Working with formulas & functions				
	Enter a range within a formula by dragging	4	2	75
	Enter formulas in a cell and using the formula bar	1	5	15
		4	2	75
	Revise formulas	4	3-4	77-79
		7	6	161
	Use references (absolute and relative)	2	7	40
	Use AutoSum	2	6	39
	Use Paste Function to insert a function	5	2-6, 8	99-110, 114
	Use basic functions (AVERAGE, SUM, COUNT,	5	1	98
	MIN, MAX)	5	Skill Drill 1, 3	118
	Enter functions using the formula palette	7	6	161
	Use date functions (NOW and DATE)	5	7	112
	Use financial functions (FV and PMT)	5	2-4	99-106
	Use logical functions (IF)	5	5-6	108-110
Using charts and objects				
	Preview and print charts	6	8	143
	Use chart wizard to create a chart	6	2-3, 5	127-131, 135
	Modify charts	6	4, 6-7	133, 137-141
	Insert, move, and delete an object (picture)	9	7	209
	Create and modify lines and objects	9	1-6	198-208

Table B   Microsoft Excel 2000 Expert MOUS Skills

Skill Set	Required Activity for MOUS	Project	Lesson(s)	Page(s)
Importing and exporting data	Import data from text files (insert, drag, and drop)	18	6	399
	Import from other applications	7	1	152
		18	8	402
	Import a table from an HTML file (insert, drag and drop – including HTML round tripping)	18	7	401
	Export to other applications	18	1-5	390-396
Using templates	Apply templates	8	8	188
	Edit templates	8	8	188
	Create templates	8	8	188
Using multiple workbooks	Using a workspace	14	8	318
	Link workbooks	14	2	309
Formatting numbers	Apply number formats (accounting, currency, number)	3	1	52
	Create custom number formats	8	3	180
	Use conditional formatting	7	6	161
Printing workbooks	Print and preview multiple worksheets	7	7	163
	Using the Report Manager	14	5-7	314-317
Working with named ranges	Add and delete a named range	11	1	244
	Use a named range in a formula	11	1	244
	Use Lookup Functions (HLOOKUP or VLOOKUP)	5	8, Discovery Zone 2	114, 122
Working with toolbars	Hide and display toolbars	9	1	198
	Customize a toolbar	1	1	2
		15	Challenge 3	344
	Assign a macro to a command button	15	7	337
Using macros	Record macros	15	1, 2, 4	328, 330, 332
	Run macros	15	3, 5	331, 334
	Edit macros	15	6	335
Auditing a worksheet	Work with the auditing toolbar	12	6-7	271-272
		16	1-3	348-352

Expert Level Mouse Skills (continued)

Skill Set	Required Activity for MOUS	Project	Lesson(s)	Page(s)
Auditing a worksheet (continued)	Trace errors (find and fix errors)	12 16	6-7 1	271-272 348
	Trace precedents (find cells referred to in a specific formula)	16	2-3	350-352
	Trace dependents (find formulas that refer to a specific cell)	16	2-3	350-352
Displaying and Formatting Data	Apply conditional formats	7	6	161
	Perform single and multi-level sorts	10	2-3	222-224
	Use grouping and outlines	14	3-4	312-313
	Use data forms	10	7-8	233-235
	Use subtotaling	7	4	157
	Apply data filters	10	4-6	226-231
	Extract data	17	4	377
	Query databases	18	8	402
	Use data validation	12	1-5, 8	264-270, 275
Using analysis tools	Use PivotTable AutoFormat	13	7	294
	Use Goal Seek	16	4	353
	Create pivot chart reports	13	6	292
	Work with Scenarios	16	6	357
	Use Solver	16	7	360
	Use data analysis and PivotTables	13 16	2-5 5	285-292 355
	Create interactive PivotTables for the Web	13	8	297
	Add fields to a PivotTable using the Web browser	13	8	297
Collaborating with workgroups	Create, edit and remove a comment	11	2	246
	Apply and remove worksheet and workbook protection	11	4-6	249-252
	Change workbook properties	11	7	253
	Apply and remove file passwords	11	8	254
	Track changes (highlight, accept, and reject)	17	1-2	372-373
	Create a shared workbook	17	3	375, 382
	Merge workbooks	17	3	375

Getting Started with Excel 2000

Key terms introduced in this project include

- arithmetic operator
- AutoComplete
- cell
- cell address
- column letter
- current (or active) cell
- default
- Formatting toolbar
- formula

- formula bar
- landscape orientation
- long label
- menu bar
- mouse pointer
- name box
- Office Assistant
- portrait orientation
- row number

- scrollbars
- spreadsheet
- Standard toolbar
- status bar
- title bar
- workbook
- worksheet
- worksheet frame
- worksheet window

Objectives	Required Activity for MOUS	Exam Level
➤ Explore the Excel Work Area	Go to a specific cell	Core
➤ Enter Text and Numbers	Enter text, dates, and numbers; edit cell content; use Undo and Redo	Core
➤ Save a Workbook	Use Save	Core
➤ Get Help	Use the Office Assistant	Core
➤ Enter a Formula	Enter formulas in a cell and using the formula bar	Core
➤ Prepare a Worksheet for Printing	Change page orientation and scaling; set page margins and centering; set up headers and footers; set print titles and options (gridlines, print quality, and row and column headings)	Core
➤ Print a Worksheet	Preview and print worksheets and workbooks; print a selection	Core
➤ Create a Folder	Create a folder	Core
➤ Close a File and Exit Excel		

Why Would I Do This?

lectronic spreadsheets, such as Microsoft Excel, are versatile tools for both personal and business use, designed primarily for organizing and analyzing numeric data.

A **spreadsheet**—called a **worksheet** in Excel—is composed of rows and columns. Each intersection of a row and column forms a **cell**. You can enter text, a number, or a formula in a cell.

This project shows you how spreadsheets work and what you can do with them. After you start the program, you explore the Excel work area, enter data, and learn how to access onscreen Help. You also save and print a partially completed worksheet. You begin by exploring the Excel work area.

Lesson 1: Exploring the Excel Work Area

An Excel screen consists of a **title bar** and six additional sections: the **menu bar**, one or more toolbars, the **name box**, the **formula bar**, the **worksheet window**, and a **status bar**. The additional sections form the Excel work area (see Figure 1.1).

Figure 1.1
A worksheet window occupies most of the Excel work area.

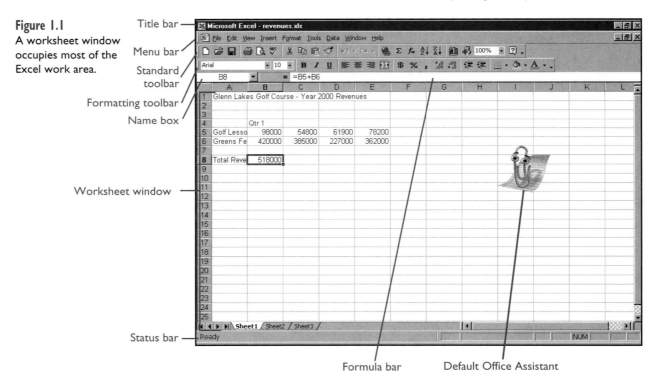

Title bar
Menu bar
Standard toolbar
Formatting toolbar
Name box
Worksheet window
Status bar
Formula bar
Default Office Assistant

In the sample work area, the **Formatting toolbar** displays below the **Standard toolbar** (refer to Figure 1.1). In Excel 2000, the Standard and Formatting toolbars share one row unless you turn that setting off. The figures in this book show separate toolbars.

The default Office Assistant appears on the screen unless that feature has been turned off. In this context, **default** refers to a setting that a program uses unless you specify another setting. **Office Assistant** is a component of onscreen Help in the form of an animated graphic image. The default Office Assistant is a paper clip called Clippit. You learn how to use this feature and how to show or hide it in Lesson 4. Subsequent figures in this book do not display the Office Assistant unless its use is part of a lesson.

Explanations of Excel's screen elements are provided in a table at the end of this lesson. For now, launch Excel and explore the work area.

To Start Excel and Explore the Excel Work Area

1 **Move the mouse pointer to the Start button at the left edge of the Windows Taskbar, and then click the left mouse button.**
The Start button's pop-up menu displays.

2 **Move the mouse pointer to the <u>P</u>rograms menu item.**
You see a listing of the available programs on your system.

3 **Move the mouse pointer to Microsoft Excel, and click the left mouse button.**

> **X** ***If You Have Problems...***
> If you don't see Microsoft Excel on the <u>P</u>rograms submenu, move the mouse pointer over the Microsoft Office folder and click the Microsoft Excel icon from the Microsoft Office submenu.
>
> If a shortcut icon for Excel displays on your Windows desktop, you can also start Excel by double-clicking it. (If Windows has been configured to use the Active Desktop, you can single-click the shortcut icon.)
>
> Many systems automatically display the Microsoft Office Shortcut bar on the Windows desktop. This bar contains buttons you can use to launch Microsoft Office programs, including Excel.

Excel is loaded into the computer's memory and a blank worksheet displays (see Figure 1.2).

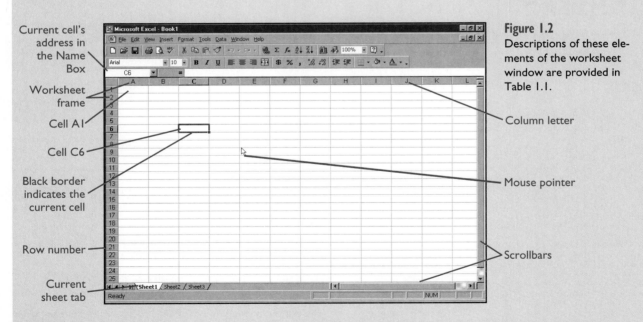

Current cell's address in the Name Box

Worksheet frame

Cell A1

Cell C6

Black border indicates the current cell

Row number

Current sheet tab

Column letter

Mouse pointer

Scrollbars

Figure 1.2
Descriptions of these elements of the worksheet window are provided in Table 1.1.

4 **Move the mouse pointer to cell C6 in the worksheet, and click the left mouse button.**

continues ▶

To Start Excel and Explore the Excel Work Area (continued)

 If You Have Problems...
The first time you start Excel, the Office Assistant might appear on your screen. If comments display next to the Office Assistant when you start Excel, click the Begin working in Excel right away button and click cell C6.

Clicking a cell selects it. An outline appears around the cell to indicate it is the *current cell* (also called the *active cell*). The cell address C6 appears in the name box to let you know which cell is selected (refer to Figure 1.2). The *cell address* refers to the column and row that intersect to form the cell—in this case, column C and row 6. Typing data or executing a new action takes place at the current cell address.

5 Press ⬇, and then press ➡.
Pressing an arrow key shifts the active cell by one cell in the direction indicated on the key.

6 Press End, and then press ⬇.
The active cell is in row 65536, the last row in the worksheet.

7 Press End, and then press ➡.
The active cell is IV65536, the lower-right corner of the worksheet.

 8 Press F5.
The Go To dialog box opens. A flashing cursor appears in the Reference area.

9 Type aa300 in the Reference area, and press ←Enter or click OK.
Cell AA300 is the current cell.

10 Press the two-key combination Ctrl + Home.
Pressing Home while you hold down Ctrl makes cell A1 the current cell. Leave the blank worksheet open for the next lesson, in which you enter data.

In this lesson, you have been introduced to a number of spreadsheet basics. Table 1.1 lists and describes the screen elements used in this lesson.

Table 1.1 Parts of the Microsoft Excel Screen

Element	Description
Cell	The intersection of a column and a row.
Cell address	Describes which column and row intersect to form the cell; for example, A1 is the address for the first cell in the first column (column A) and the first row (row 1).
Column letter	Lettered A through Z, AA through AZ, and so on through IV; up to 256 columns.
Current (or active) cell	The cell surrounded by a thick black border. The next action you take, such as typing, affects this cell.
Formatting toolbar	Provides, in button form, shortcuts to frequently used commands for changing the appearance of data. Formatting and Standard toolbars share one row unless that setting is turned off.

Element	Description
Formula bar	Displays the contents of the current or active cell.
Menu bar	Contains common menu names that, when activated, display a list of related commands. The File menu, for example, contains such commands as Open, Close, Save, and Print.
Mouse pointer	Selects items and positions the insertion point (cursor).
Name box	Displays the cell address of the current cell or the name of a range of cells.
Office Assistant	A component of onscreen Help in the form of an animated graphic image that can be turned on or off; brings up a list of subjects related to a question you type.
Row number	Numbered 1 through 65,536.
Scrollbars	Enable you to move the worksheet window vertically and horizontally so that you can see other parts of the worksheet.
Sheet tab	A means for accessing each sheet in a workbook. Click a sheet tab to quickly move to that sheet.
Standard toolbar	Provides, in button form, shortcuts to frequently used commands, including Save, Print, Cut (move), Copy, and Paste. Standard and Formatting toolbars share one row unless that setting is turned off.
Status bar	Provides information about the current operation or work area, such as displaying CAPS if you turn on [Caps Lock].
Title bar	Displays the name of the software and the name of the active workbook—either a default name, such as Book1, or a saved file.
Workbook	An Excel file that contains one or more worksheets.
Worksheet frame	The row and column headings that appear along the top and left edge of the worksheet window.
Worksheet window	Contains the current worksheet—the work area.

Inside Stuff: **ScreenTips**

To find out what a toolbar button does, position the mouse pointer over the button and wait a moment or two until a ScreenTip appears with the button's description. If the ScreenTip feature is not active, you can enable it by clicking View on the menu bar, pointing at the Toolbars command, clicking Customize, selecting the Options page tab in the Customize dialog box, and then clicking the Show ScreenTips on toolbars check box.

Exam Note: **Tips on Exam Pacing**

Become familiar with Excel, the parts of the worksheet windows, and how to move around the worksheet. MOUS exams are timed exams. They test your productivity as well as your competency. The longer it takes you to complete a task, the less time you have to complete all the activities in the exam, which affects your score. You are allowed to use Help during an exam, but the time you spend using Help slows you down.

Lesson 2: Entering Text and Numbers

Now that you know the parts of the Excel work area and how to move around a work-sheet, it's time to enter data. Excel accepts two broad types of cell entries: **constants** and **formulas**. Constants can be text values (also called labels), numeric values (numbers), or date and time values. Constants do not change unless you edit them.

A formula produces a calculated result, usually based on a reference to one or more cells in the worksheet. The results of a formula change if you alter the contents of a cell refer-enced in the formula.

In this lesson, you begin creating a worksheet. As you type, notice that sometimes Excel seems to anticipate what you are going to enter into a cell. For example, you might start typing text and Excel automatically completes the word or phrase you have begun. This is a feature called **AutoComplete**, which compares text you are typing with text already entered in the same column. For example, if text in a cell begins with Golf and you start typing G into another cell in the same column, Excel assumes you are entering Golf again. If Excel is correct, this saves you some typing. If not, just keep typing.

To Enter Text and Numbers

❶ If necessary, start Excel and display a blank worksheet.

❷ Click cell A1.
A thick black border surrounds cell A1, indicating that it is the current cell. Now, enter the worksheet title.

❸ Type Glenn Lakes Golf Course-Year 2000 Revenues **and press** **.**

> ✗ **If You Have Problems...**
> If you make a mistake as you enter the text, you can make corrections the same way you do in a word processing program; press ⟦Del⟧ or ⟦←Backspace⟧ to delete the error and continue typing. Use ⟦Del⟧ to erase text to the right of the cursor and press ⟦←Backspace⟧ to erase text to the left of the cursor.
>
> If you discover a mistake after you move to another cell, click the mouse or use the arrow keys to select the cell that contains the mis-take, double-click the cell to change to edit mode, and then use ⟦←Backspace⟧ or ⟦Del⟧ to correct the mistake. If you want to replace the en-tire contents of the cell, select the cell and begin typing; the new data you enter replaces the cell's previous contents.
>
> If you start to edit a cell and change your mind, press ⟦Esc⟧ to cancel the revisions in progress.

Excel enters the text you typed into cell A1, and cell A2 becomes the current cell. The text appears to be in cells A1 through E1 of the worksheet.

❹ Click cell A1 and look in the formula bar (see Figure 1.3).
The formula bar indicates that the entire worksheet title is stored in cell A1. Text that exceeds the width of its cell is sometimes referred to as a **long label**. Overflow text displays if the adjacent cells are blank. Therefore, it is not necessary to widen column A at this time.

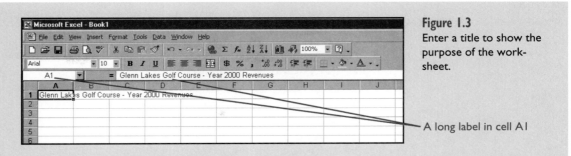

Figure 1.3
Enter a title to show the purpose of the worksheet.

A long label in cell A1

5 **Click cell B4, type Qtr 1, and press ⏎Enter.**
Qtr 1 appears left-aligned in cell B4 and cell B5 becomes the current cell.

6 **Enter the following text in the cells indicated:**

Cell A5	Golf Lessons
Cell A6	Greens Fees
Cell A8	Total Revenue

7 **Click cell B5, type 98000, and press ⏎Enter.**
The number 98000 displays right-aligned in cell B5. The last two letters of the Golf Lessons label that extended into cell B5 no longer display (see Figure 1.4). Column A needs to be widened to accommodate the labels in rows 5 through 8.

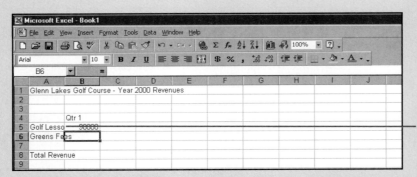

Figure 1.4
Part of the entry in cell A5 is not visible.

Because the adjacent cell is not blank, the text display is limited to the width of cell A5

8 **Position the mouse pointer between column letters A and B in the worksheet frame; click and hold down the left mouse button (see Figure 1.5).**
The pointer changes to a bi-directional arrow. Drag right to increase the width of column A; drag left to reduce the width of column A.

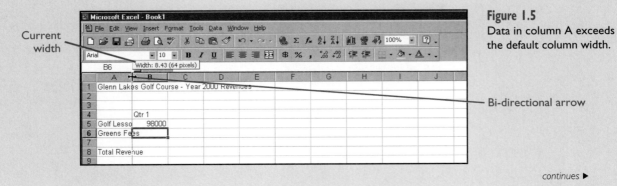

Current width

Figure 1.5
Data in column A exceeds the default column width.

Bi-directional arrow

continues ▶

To Enter Text and Numbers   (continued)

9 **Drag the pointer to the right until the column is wide enough to display the Total Revenue label in cell A8. (Hold down the mouse button while you check your work against Figure 1.6.)**

The thin, vertical, dotted line that extends from the pointer to the bottom of the worksheet makes it easy to see the distance you must drag to expand the column to the desired width.

Figure 1.6
Clicking between column letters displays a bidirectional arrow. Dragging the bidirectional arrow changes the width of the leftmost column.

Drag right until the vertical dotted line clears the Total Revenue label

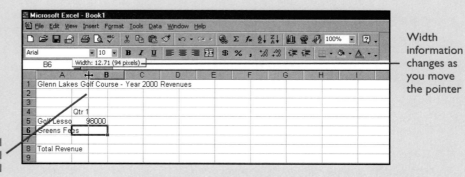

Width information changes as you move the pointer

10 **Release the mouse button.**

Column A widens to display Total Revenue within the boundaries of cell A8.

  If You Have Problems...

You can click the Undo toolbar button or select Excel's <u>U</u>ndo command on the <u>E</u>dit menu to reverse an action. If you change the width of the wrong column, for example, you can use the <u>U</u>ndo command to restore the original column width.

11 **Enter the following numbers in rows 5 and 6 in the cells indicated. (Pressing ⏎ enters the number and moves the cell pointer to the next cell in a row.)**

Cell C5	54800
Cell D5	61900
Cell E5	78200
Cell B6	420000
Cell C6	385000
Cell D6	227000
Cell E6	362000

12 **Check that your entries match those shown in Figure 1.7.**

The text entries in column A describe the content of rows 5, 6, and 8. Cells B5 through E6 contain numbers.

Leave the partially completed worksheet open and continue to the next lesson, in which you save your work.

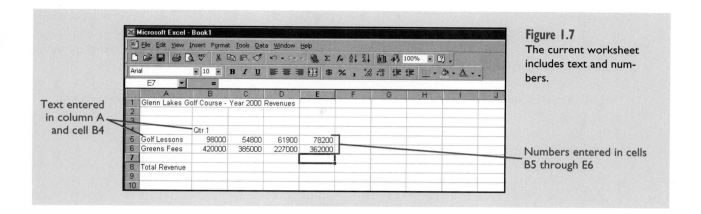

Figure 1.7
The current worksheet includes text and numbers.

Text entered in column A and cell B4

Numbers entered in cells B5 through E6

Inside Stuff: Changing Column Width
Click the mouse pointer between two columns in the worksheet frame and drag left or right to narrow or widen the leftmost column to a width you specify. Double-clicking between column letters automatically narrows or widens the column to the longest entry in that column. You can also choose <u>C</u>olumn from the F<u>o</u>rmat menu and set a specific width or automatically change column width to fit cell contents. You learn to choose menu commands in the next lesson.

Exam Note: Undo and Redo
Undo reverses the last command or deletes the last typed entry. You can reverse more than one action at a time by clicking the arrow next to the Undo button and clicking the actions on a drop-down list that you want to undo. The command changes to Can't Undo if you cannot reverse the last action.

Redo reverses the action of the Undo command. You can redo more than one action at a time by clicking the arrow next to the Redo button and clicking the actions you want to redo on the drop-down list. You can reverse a Redo action by choosing Undo.

Lesson 3: Saving a Workbook

Up to this point, none of the data you entered has been safely stored for future use. At the moment, your worksheet and the workbook that contains it are stored in the computer's random-access memory (RAM). If your computer were to crash or shut down for any reason, you would have to re-create the workbook. For this reason, it is important to save your work frequently. When you save a workbook or file, you assign the file a name and location on a disk.

You can type any name that complies with Windows' file-naming rules. The name can include up to 255 upper- and lowercase characters and spaces, but not the symbols \ / : * ? " < > or |. Excel automatically stores the file in the default Excel file format and adds the .xls (Excel spreadsheet) file extension.

You save a file by executing a <u>F</u>ile, <u>S</u>ave command or a <u>F</u>ile, Save <u>A</u>s command. As in other Windows programs, you can execute a command by clicking a command on the menu bar and then clicking the command you want from the submenu.

With Excel 2000 you can choose to use short or full menus. The short menu displays an abbreviated list of commonly used commands (see Figure 1.8). The full menu includes all available commands (see Figure 1.9). By default, the short menu displays first; then after a momentary delay, the full menu displays.

Figure 1.8
The short menu displays initially when you choose a command . . .

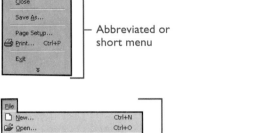

Abbreviated or short menu

Figure 1.9
. . . but Excel provides quick access to the full menu after a few seconds delay.

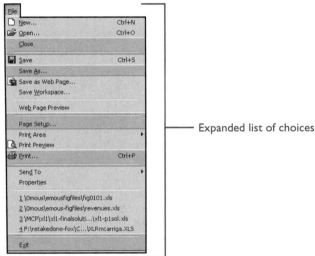

Expanded list of choices

Use the menu bar now to save your partially completed Sheet1 in a workbook named Revenues.

To Save the Current Workbook

❶ Click File on the menu bar.
The short File menu appears first, followed by the long File menu after a momentary delay (refer to Figures 1.8 and 1.9). The menus on your screen might not appear exactly like those shown in the book. Excel 2000 adapts the screen display to your work patterns. This means that the program shows the commands at the top of each drop-down menu that you use most frequently. Because the program automatically customizes the menus to the way you work, your menus probably display slightly different commands (or in a different order) from those shown in the figures.

❷ In the File submenu, click Save As.
The Save As dialog box appears (see Figure 1.10). You specify the filename and select the file type near the bottom of the dialog box. You specify the storage location in the Save in box near the top of the dialog box. Notice that Book1.xls appears as the filename. This is the temporary filename that Excel assigns to your workbook.

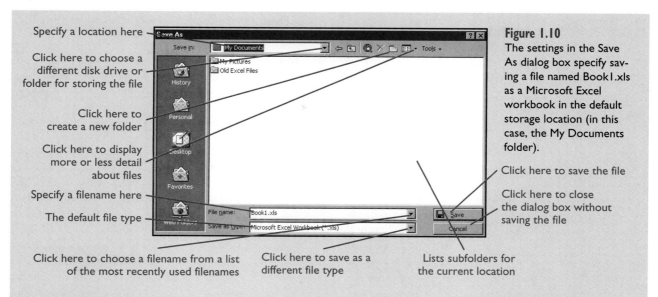

Specify a location here

Click here to choose a different disk drive or folder for storing the file

Click here to create a new folder

Click here to display more or less detail about files

Specify a filename here

The default file type

Click here to choose a filename from a list of the most recently used filenames

Click here to save as a different file type

Lists subfolders for the current location

Click here to save the file

Click here to close the dialog box without saving the file

Figure 1.10
The settings in the Save As dialog box specify saving a file named Book1.xls as a Microsoft Excel workbook in the default storage location (in this case, the My Documents folder).

❸ Change Book1 to revenues in the File name box.
The name you type replaces the temporary name assigned by Excel.

❹ Click the down arrow at the right end of the Save in box.
The display in the Save in drop-down list reflects the drives, folders, and files on your system. In the Save As dialog box, Excel automatically proposes to save the workbook on the current drive and in the default folder.

❺ Select the drive and folder where you want to save your current workbook.
Figure 1.11 shows the settings for saving to a 3-1/2 inch disk in drive A. You might prefer to store your work on a hard disk, a zip disk, or a network drive, depending on the drives supported by your system. If you want to save the file in a different folder, select the folder from the Save in list, or click the Create New Folder button to create and name a new folder. Ask your instructor if you are not sure about the location for saving the files you create during this course.

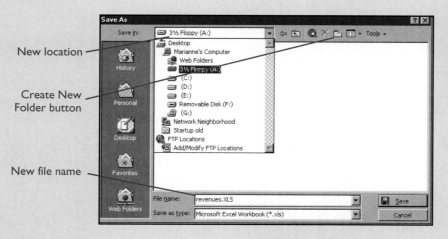

New location

Create New Folder button

New file name

Figure 1.11
The selections in the dialog box specify saving a file named revenues as a Microsoft Excel workbook on a disk in drive A.

continues ▶

To Save the Current Workbook   (continued)

6 **After checking your settings for location, filename, and file type, click the Save button in the lower-right corner of the dialog box.**
Leave the Revenues workbook open for the next lesson, in which you learn to use onscreen Help.

 Exam Note: Comparing Save and Save As
If you have not yet saved a new workbook, you can click the Save button on the Standard toolbar to display the Save As dialog box. However, if you have already saved a workbook, clicking the Save button immediately resaves the current file under its current name without displaying a dialog box.

If you haven't yet saved a new workbook and you choose Save instead of Save As from the File menu, Excel automatically displays the Save As dialog box.

  Exam Note: Another Way to Create a Folder
Excel's Save As dialog box includes a Create New Folder button (see Figure 1.10). You can also click the drive or folder in Windows Explorer where you want to create the new folder and choose the menu sequence File, New, Folder. Type a name for the new folder and press ꜀Enter꜀.

 ## Lesson 4: Getting Help

You have entered text and numbers in Sheet1 of your Revenues workbook. Now, you want to enter a formula, but you need more information about formulas and how to enter them.

Excel provides a number of onscreen Help options. For example, you can use the Office Assistant to find the answer to a specific question. You can use Contents to scroll through topics and related subtopics or Index to search for a keyword. You can also use the What's This? pointer to display a description of any feature on the screen.

In this lesson, you use Help's Office Assistant and Contents to learn about formulas.

To Get Help

1 **If the Office Assistant does not appear on your screen, click Help on the menu bar and choose Show the Office Assistant.**
The currently selected Assistant appears (Clippit is the default setting).

2 **Left-click the Office Assistant to display a balloon.**
The balloon includes a white text box above the Options and Search buttons. The balloon might also include a list of topics from the most recent use of the Office Assistant.

3 **Type learn about math operators in the text box, and click the Search button.**
Office Assistant displays a new balloon that lists related topics, as shown in Figure 1.12. You can select a topic, type a different question, display more topics, and display tips or options. Click outside the balloon to close it.

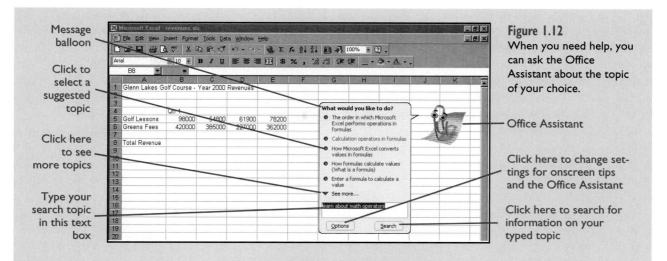

Message balloon

Click to select a suggested topic

Click here to see more topics

Type your search topic in this text box

Figure 1.12
When you need help, you can ask the Office Assistant about the topic of your choice.

Office Assistant

Click here to change settings for onscreen tips and the Office Assistant

Click here to search for information on your typed topic

4 **Select the topic Calculation operators in formulas and read the information about Arithmetic operators.**

The Excel Help program starts, and a Help Topics window displays on your screen, as shown in Figure 1.13. Don't be concerned that the Help window displays on top of your Excel application window and that the screen looks a bit cluttered. These effects disappear when you close the Help window.

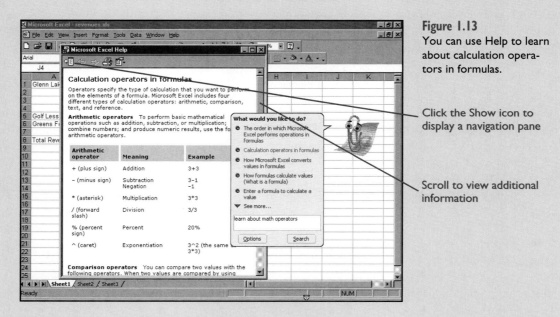

Figure 1.13
You can use Help to learn about calculation operators in formulas.

Click the Show icon to display a navigation pane

Scroll to view additional information

5 **Click the Show icon near the upper-left corner of the Help window.**

Clicking the Show icon displays a navigation pane to the left of the current Help topic pane. The navigation pane includes Contents, Answer Wizard, and Index tabs.

6 **Click the Contents tab in the navigation pane.**

Excel displays a list of topics, each of which is preceded by a closed book icon.

continues ▶

To Get Help   (continued)

7 **Double-click the topic Creating Formulas and Auditing Workbooks.**
The icon preceding the selected topic changes to an open book, and Excel displays a list of related subtopics.

8 **Double-click the subtopic Entering Formulas.**
A Help icon—a question mark—precedes each additional subtopic under Entering Formulas.

9 **Select the subtopic The order in which Microsoft Excel performs operations in formulas.**
The Help topic shown in Figure 1.14 appears. Notice, for example, that Excel performs multiplication and division before addition and subtraction. Also note that you can change the order of evaluation by enclosing the part of the formula to be calculated first in parentheses.

Figure 1.14
You can use Help to learn about the order in which Microsoft Excel performs operations in formulas.

Click the Hide icon to remove the navigation pane from view

Click Contents to select among general Help topics

Click Answer Wizard to type your request for help

Click Index to search by keyword

Navigation pane

Close button

Help topic pane

The order in which Microsoft Excel performs operations in formulas

If you combine several operators in a single formula, Microsoft Excel performs the operations in the order shown in the following table. If a formula contains operators with the same precedence — for example, if a formula contains both a multiplication and division operator — Excel evaluates the operators from left to right. To change the order of evaluation, enclose the part of the formula to be calculated first in parentheses. For more information about calculation operators, click [image].

Operator	Description
: (colon)	Reference operators
(single space)	
, (comma)	
–	Negation (as in –1)
%	Percent
^	Exponentiation
* and /	Multiplication and division
+ and –	Addition and subtraction
&	Connects two strings of text (concatenation)

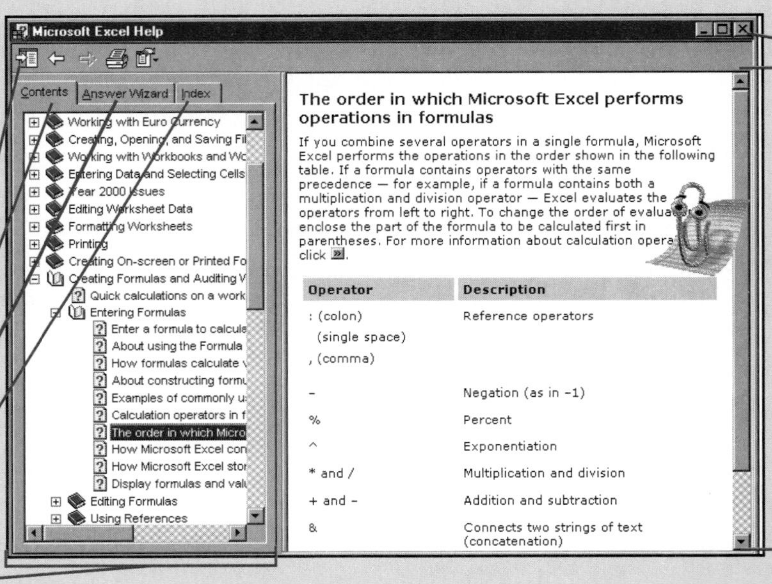

10 **Click the Close button in the upper-right corner of the Help window.**
Help closes and you return to the worksheet. Now, you have the information you need to continue to the next lesson and enter a formula.

Exam Note: **Tips on Using Help**

To open the Office Assistant, you can press F1 at any time or click the Microsoft Excel Help button on the Standard toolbar. If the Office Assistant icon is onscreen, simply click it to open the balloon, in which you can type a question.

If the Office Assistant can't find topics related to the question you type, a balloon appears, telling you so. Check to be sure that you typed the question correctly, or try being more specific and click Search again.

To change the icon used to represent the Office Assistant, click the Options button in any Office Assistant balloon, choose the Gallery tab, and click Next to display a series of available icons. Select from The Dot, The Genius, Mother Nature, and so on. When you have found an Office Assistant you like, click OK.

Help's Index tab includes an alphabetical listing of topics (or keywords) that you can use to find related topics. For example, if you enter the keyword `Print`, Excel finds more than 80 topics related to the word and displays them in the Help window. You can double-click a topic to select it and display its associated Help screen.

To print the contents of a Help Topics window, click the Print button. You can print the current page or print everything contained in the current heading.

To use the What's This? pointer to display a ScreenTip about an item on the screen, choose Help, What's This?, or press Shift+F1. When the pointer resembles a question mark with an arrow, point at the item about which you need information.

In the Help program, keywords and phrases that appear in a different color and underlined are hypertext links. When you point at a hypertext link, the mouse pointer changes to a hand with a pointing finger. When you click a hypertext link, Excel displays additional information.

If you can't find the information you need within Excel, you can access resources that are available on the World Wide Web. Assuming that you have Internet access, you can choose Help, Office on the Web to view information on Microsoft's Web site for Excel.

Lesson 5: Entering a Formula

The true power of a spreadsheet program resides in formulas. In Excel, starting an entry with an equal sign (=) identifies it as a formula rather than data to be entered in the cell.

Generally, a formula consists of arithmetic operators and references to cells. **Arithmetic operators** include +, -, *, and / (to add, subtract, multiply, and divide, respectively). The order of the elements in a formula determines the final result of the calculation. Excel evaluates a formula from left to right, according to the order of operator precedence. For example, multiplication and division take place before addition and subtraction.

In this lesson, you type a simple formula to add the contents of two cells. You work with more complex formulas and other ways to enter them in Project 4 "Entering Formulas in Well-Designed Worksheets."

To Enter a Formula

❶ Click cell B8 in Sheet1 of the Revenues workbook.

❷ Type =B5+B6 and press ⏎Enter.

You entered a formula to add the contents of cell B6 to the contents of cell B5 and display the result in cell B8.

❸ Click cell B8 and look in the formula bar.

The formula displays in the formula bar, and the results of the formula display in cell B8 (see Figure 1.15).

Figure 1.15
Excel stores a formula in a cell, but displays the results of the formula.

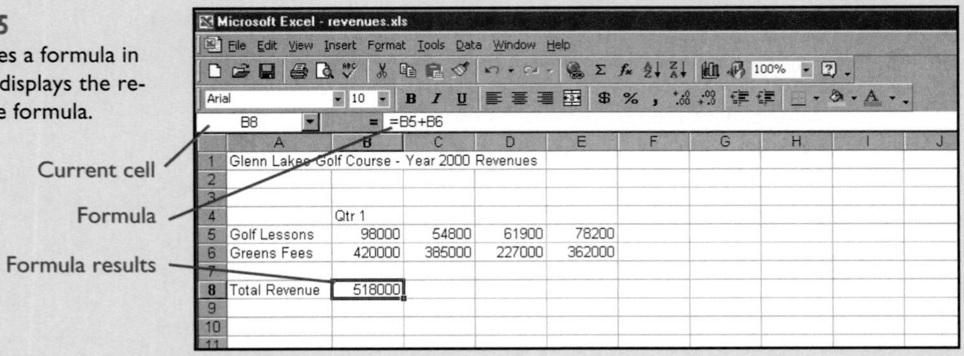

Current cell

Formula

Formula results

❹ Click the Save button on the Standard toolbar.

Your latest changes to the Revenues workbook are saved. Keep the workbook open for the next lesson, which focuses on printing your work.

Lesson 6: Preparing a Worksheet for Printing

With Excel, you can quickly print a worksheet by using the default page setup—portrait orientation, 100 percent of normal size, 8–by–11–inch paper, with 1–inch top and bottom margins and 0.75 inch left and right margins. **Portrait orientation** produces a printed page that is longer than it is wide.

You can also change settings to meet your requirements for printed output. For example, you can switch to **landscape orientation**, which produces a printed page that is wider than it is long. You can add a header or footer to help identify the contents of the printed page, adjust the page margins, or turn on the printing of grid lines and row-and-column headings. A **header** contains text or graphics that repeat at the top of each page in a multipage printout; a **footer** contains text or graphics that repeat at the bottom of each page.

Now, use Excel's Page Setup feature to review current settings and to turn on the display of gridlines and row-and-column headings.

To Prepare a Worksheet for Printing

1 **Select Sheet1 in the Revenues workbook, click File in the toolbar and choose Page Setup.**

The Page Setup dialog box with four tabs displays. Use this dialog box to adjust the page setup before you print your worksheet.

2 **Click the Page tab, if necessary (see Figure 1.16).**

Click here to change default margins

Click here to specify text or graphics to appear at the top (header) or bottom (footer) of every printed page

Enlarge or reduce the print size here

Click here to switch to automatic scaling (also set the number of pages wide and number of pages tall)

Click here to specify a different paper size

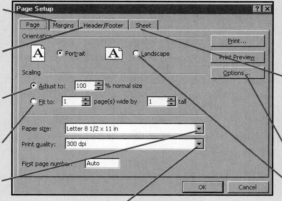

Figure 1.16
The Page tab is one of four available in the Page Setup dialog box.

Click here to specify other setup options, including gridlines and row and column headings

Click here to change printer-specific options

Click here to switch orientation

Click here to specify a different print quality

3 **Click the Margins tab in the Page Setup dialog box.**

The Margins options display. The default top and bottom margins are 1 inch. The default left and right margins are 0.75 inch.

4 **Click the Header/Footer tab in the Page Setup dialog box, and click the Custom Footer button in the middle of the dialog box.**

The Footer dialog box displays (see Figure 1.17). Directions to enter the contents of the footer appear in the upper-left corner of the dialog box. You can type text, such as your name in the Center section. You can also use buttons to insert predefined contents, such as the current date in the Left section and the filename in the Right section.

Directions to enter the contents of a footer

Font

Page number

Total pages

Current date

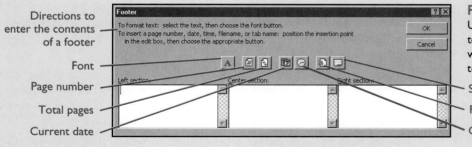

Figure 1.17
Use the Footer dialog box to specify text that you want to print at the bottom of each page.

Sheet (tab) name

Filename

Current time

5 **Click within the Left section of the Footer dialog box and click the current date button (refer to Figure 1.17).**

The code &[Date] is left-aligned in the Left section.

continues ▶

To Prepare a Worksheet for Printing   (continued)

6 **Click within the Center section of the Footer dialog box, and type your first and last names.**
Your full name is centered in the Center section. Entering your name in a header or footer makes it easy to identify your work if you share a printer with others.

7 **Click within the Right section of the Footer dialog box, and click the filename button (see Figure 1.17).**
The code &[File] is right-aligned in the Right section.

8 **Click OK.**
Excel accepts your settings, and the Footer dialog box closes. The settings you specified appear in the Footer window on the Header/Footer tab.

9 **Click the Sheet tab in the Page Setup dialog box, and click the check box in front of Gridlines.**
A check mark appears in the Gridlines box, indicating the feature is turned on. This setting prints the lines that border cells.

10 **Click the check box in front of Row and column headings.**
A check mark appears in the Row and column headings box, indicating the feature is turned on. This setting prints the worksheet frame.

11 **Click OK.**
The Page Setup dialog box closes. You have finished setting up the worksheet page for printing.

12 **Click the Save button on the Standard toolbar.**
Excel saves the changes you made to the Revenues workbook. Leave the workbook open for the next lesson, in which you learn how to preview and print the current worksheet.

 Exam Note: **Using Other Page Setup Options**
The Page Setup dialog box includes four tabs: Page, Margins, Header/Footer, and Sheet. You have already applied several settings using this dialog box. The following paragraphs summarize other commonly used options you can set before printing. When you save a file, Excel also saves the current page setup specifications.

Use the Page tab to select orientation (portrait or landscape), scaling, paper size, and print quality in terms of dpi (density per inch). Excel provides two scaling options: Adjust to (a user-specified higher or lower percentage of original size) or Fit to (a user-specified number of pages wide by number of pages tall). Predefined paper sizes include Letter, Legal, Executive, and Envelope.

Use the Margins tab to center printed output as well as change margins. Click the Horizontally check box to center printed output from left to right. Click the Vertically check box to center printed output from top to bottom.

The Sheet tab includes four sections: Print area, Print titles, Print and Page order. You can specify a range to print by entering the upper-left and lower-right cells in the range separated by a colon, such as B5:H25, in the Print area box. It is helpful to set a print area when there is a specific portion of a large worksheet that you print frequently.

Set a Print title to specify worksheet rows and/or columns to repeat on each page of a multi-page printout. You can specify one or more rows, such as $1:$3 for rows one through three, in the Rows to repeat at top box. You can also specify one or more columns, such as $A:$A for column A, in the Columns to repeat at left box.

You have already worked with two options in the Print section—turning on or off display of Gridlines and turning on or off the display of Row and column headings (the worksheet frame). Two other check boxes are included in this section, one to print Black and White, and the other to print Draft quality.

The Page order section enables you to control which pages of a multipage printout are printed first. The default setting for Page order is Down, then over. You can change that setting to Over, then down.

Lesson 7: Printing a Worksheet

Now that you have adjusted the page setup and saved your changes, you can print a copy of your worksheet for your files or to review while you are away from the computer.

It's a good idea to save documents immediately before printing them, as you did in Lesson 6. It's also a good idea to preview on your screen the way the worksheet will look when it is printed. That way, you can make adjustments to the page setup before you print. Now, preview and print the first sheet in your Revenues workbook.

To Print a Worksheet

1 **Make sure that the printer is turned on, has paper, and is online.**
You can't print if the printer is not turned on, the printer is out of paper, or the printer is not online. Printers often have a light that shows whether the printer is online or receiving commands from the computer. If the printer is not online, Excel displays an error message.

2 **Select Sheet1 in the Revenues workbook, and then choose File, Print.**
The Print dialog box appears, as shown in Figure 1.18.

3 **Click the Preview button in the Print dialog box.**
The worksheet displays in the Print Preview window, which enables you to see how the entire worksheet will look when printed (see Figure 1.19). In Print Preview, you can see the effects of the changes you made to the page setup, including the footer, gridlines, and worksheet frame.

4 **Click anywhere in the worksheet.**
Your view of the worksheet becomes enlarged, so you can easily read it, but you can't see the entire page.

5 **Click the worksheet again.**
The view of the whole page is restored. If you decide you want to make a change in the worksheet before you print it, click the Close button to close the view and return to the worksheet in Excel, or click the Setup button to open the Page Setup dialog box.

continues ▶

To Print a Worksheet (continued)

Figure 1.18
You can change any of the options in the Print dialog box.

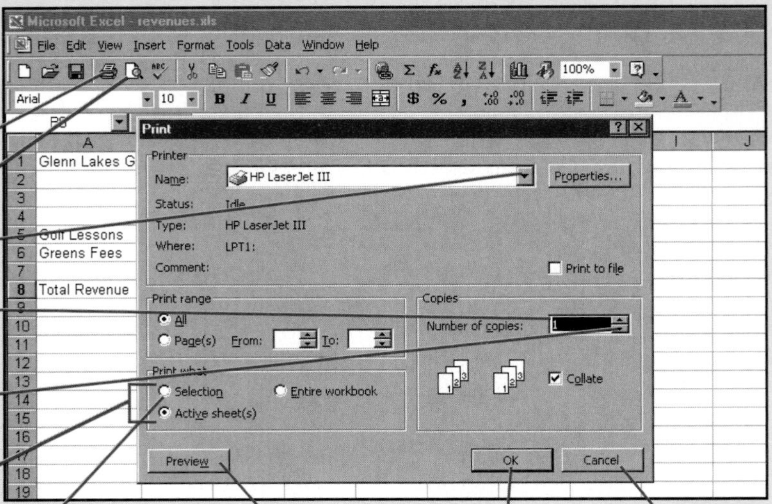

Print button

Print Preview button

Click to select a different printer

Specify printing more than one copy here

Use the up and down arrows to change the value in preset increments

Specify what to print here

Click here to print only the selected range

Click here to preview the worksheet before printing

Click here to print

Click here to close the dialog box without printing

Figure 1.19
View the worksheet as it will look when printed to decide whether you need to make changes.

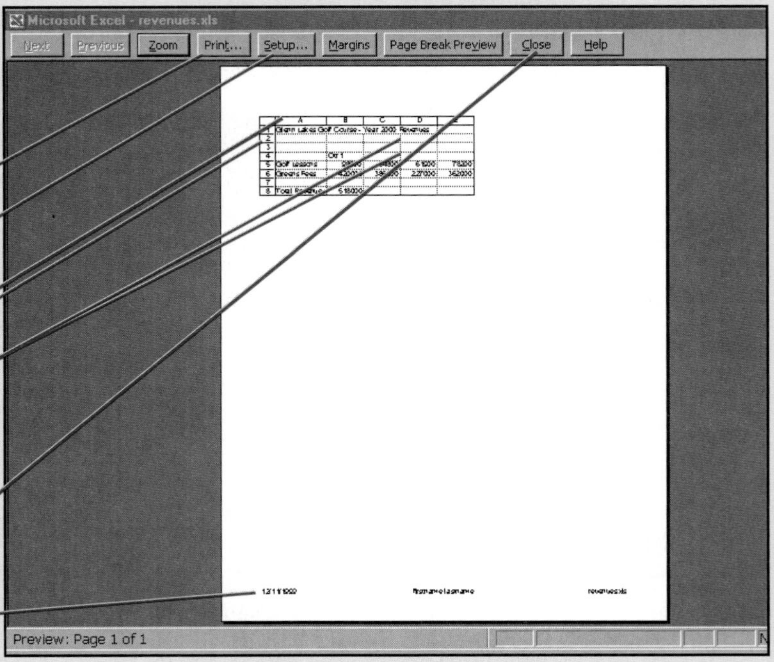

Click here to print

Click here to open the Page Setup dialog box

Row and column headings (worksheet frame)

Gridlines

Click to close Print Preview

Footer

6 **Click the Print button (or click Close to exit Print Preview without printing).**
Excel sends a copy of your worksheet to the printer. In the next lesson, you learn how to close the Revenues workbook and exit the program.

Exam Note: Using Toolbar Buttons to Preview and Print
To print the current worksheet without opening the Print dialog box, click the
Print button on the Standard toolbar.

To change to Print Preview without opening the Print dialog box, click the Print
Preview button on the Standard toolbar, or choose <u>F</u>ile, Print Pre<u>v</u>iew from the
menu.

Lesson 8: Closing a File and Exiting Excel

Before you turn off your computer, you should first close the file you created and then
exit Excel, so that you don't lose any of your work. Complete this project by closing your
file and exiting the Excel software.

To Close a File and Exit Excel

❶ Choose <u>F</u>ile, <u>C</u>lose.
If you haven't saved your work, Excel displays a dialog box—or a balloon if
the Assistant is active—that asks whether you want to save your work.
Choosing Yes saves the file and closes it. Choosing No closes the file and
erases any work you have done since the last time you saved.

❷ Choose <u>F</u>ile, E<u>x</u>it.
Excel closes. If there are any files left open, Excel displays a dialog box that
asks whether you want to save your work. Choosing Yes saves all open files
and closes the program. Choosing No closes the program without saving the
files; any work you have done since the last time you saved is erased. After
you close Excel, the Windows desktop appears if no other software applications are running.

This concludes Project 1. You can reinforce and extend the learning experience by working through the end-of-project activities that follow.

Summary

This project began with an introduction to the components of the Excel work area, ac-
companied by explanations of a variety of terms. After you learned the language of
spreadsheets, you began to develop a small worksheet to sum two sources of revenue.
After entering text and numbers in cells, you put the extensive onscreen Help system to
work, so you could understand how formulas calculate and how to construct them. Saving
and printing your work completed the Project 1 learning experience.

After you know the basics, you can quickly expand your skills through a read-and-do approach. You read when you make the use of onscreen Help an integral part of your learning strategy. You convert knowledge to a skill when you apply what you have learned in
the worksheets you create.

Checking Concepts and Terms ✓

True/False

For each of the following, check *T* or *F* to indicate whether the statement is true or false.

__T __F **1.** To quickly print the current worksheet without opening the Print dialog box, you can click the Print button on the toolbar. [L7]

__T __F **2.** Select Portrait orientation if you want to produce a printed page that is wider than it is long. [L6]

__T __F **3.** The only way to move around a worksheet is by using the mouse. [L1]

__T __F **4.** There are more than 65,000 rows in an Excel worksheet. [L1]

__T __F **5.** If you have already saved a worksheet, clicking the Save button on a toolbar gives you the opportunity to change the file's name or storage location. [L3]

Multiple Choice

Circle the letter of the correct answer for each of the following.

1. Which of the following describes an Excel feature that automatically completes the word or phrase as you type a cell entry? [L2]

a. AutoFinish

b. AutoComplete

c. the Repeat button on a toolbar

d. none of the above; not an Excel feature

2. Which of the following is a valid cell address? [L1]

a. b-12

b. B:12

c. B12

d. B/12

3. Assume that the following data is entered in the cells A1 through A3. The result of entering the formula =A1-A2*A3 in cell B1 would be _____. [L5]

Cell A1	15
Cell A2	3
Cell A3	2

a. 9

b. 20

c. 24

d. some other result

4. Which of the following is an example of an Excel formula? [L5]

a. =B2+B3+B4

b. $240

c. C1+C2

d. both a and c

5. In Excel, the arithmetic operator for multiplication is _____. [L5]

a. ×

b. @

c. %

d. none of the above

Skill Drill

Skill Drill exercises reinforce project skills. Each skill reinforced is the same, or nearly the same, as a skill presented in the project. Detailed instructions are provided in a step-by-step format.

Several exercises in this project direct you to access a new blank workbook. Starting Excel displays a new blank workbook. If you have been working on another file, you can display a new workbook by clicking the New button at the left end of the Standard toolbar.

Each exercise is independent of the others, so you can perform the exercises in any order. If you need a paper copy of a completed exercise, enter your name centered in a header before printing.

1. Changing Column Width

You are compiling a list of selected state names and postal codes, and you want to adjust the default column widths.

To enter data and change column widths:

1. Start Excel and access a new blank workbook.

2. Click cell A1, type **Selected State Codes**, and press ⏎**Enter**).

3. Click cell A3, type **Indiana**, and press ⏎**Enter**).

4. Enter the remaining text, as shown in Figure 1.20 (do not change the width of a column yet).

Figure 1.20
You change the widths of columns A and B after entering the data.

5. Position the mouse pointer between A and B in the worksheet frame; click and hold down the left mouse button.

6. Drag the pointer to the right a short distance until some white space displays between the word Minnesota and the right edge of cell A5 (see Figure 1.20), and then release the mouse button.

7. Position the mouse pointer between B and C in the worksheet frame; click and hold down the left mouse button.

8. Drag the pointer to the left to narrow column B (refer to Figure 1.20), and then release the mouse button.

9. Choose File, Save As.

10. Change Book1 to **states** in the File name box.

11. Select the drive and folder where you want to save the workbook, and click the Save button in the lower-right corner of the dialog box.

12. Choose File, Close (or choose File, Exit to quit Excel and close the workbook).

2. Using the Subtract Operator in a Formula

Your supervisor has asked you to prepare a report that summarizes sales and sales returns for the year. You decide to include a calculation of the net sales as well.

To enter text, numbers, and a formula:

1. Start Excel and access a new blank workbook.

2. Click cell A1, type `Year 2000 Summary`, and press `⏎Enter`.

3. Enter the remaining text and numbers, as shown in Figure 1.21 (text in cells A3, A4 and A5; numbers in cells B3 and B4).

Figure 1.21
After entering labels in column A and numbers in cells B3 and B4, you enter a formula in B5.

4. Click cell B5, type `=B3-B4`, and press `⏎Enter`.

Ensure that 9800 appears in cell B5—the result of subtracting the contents of cell B4 (200) from the contents of cell B3 (10000).

5. Choose File, Save As.

6. Change Book1 to **sales** in the File name box.

7. Select the drive and folder where you want to save the workbook, and click the Save button in the lower-right corner of the dialog box.

8. Choose File, Close (or choose File, Exit to quit Excel and close the workbook).

3. Using the Division Operator in a Formula

You want to compute your share of a rental fee, assuming that the cost is shared equally. You plan to enter the number of people in a separate cell and label it, so the calculation works for any fee and any number of people sharing the cost.

To enter text, numbers, and a formula:

1. Start Excel and access a new blank workbook.

2. Click cell A1, type `Calculating Cost per Person`, and press `⏎Enter`.

3. Enter the remaining text and numbers, as shown in Figure 1.22 (numbers in cells A3 and A4; text in cells B3, B4, and B5).

Figure 1.22
After entering text and numbers, you enter a formula in cell A5.

4. Click cell A5, type `=A3/A4`, and press `⏎Enter`.

5. Ensure that 41.66667 appears in cell A5—the result of dividing the contents of cell A3 (500) by the contents of cell A4 (12).

6. Choose File, Save As.

7. Change Book1 to **share** in the File name box.

8. Select the drive and folder where you want to save the workbook, and click the Save button in the lower-right corner of the dialog box.

9. Choose File, Close (or choose File, Exit to quit Excel and close the workbook).

Challenge

Challenge exercises expand on or are somewhat related to skills presented in the lessons. Each exercise provides a brief narrative introduction, followed by instructions in a numbered step format that are not as detailed as those in the Skill Drill section.

Each exercise is independent of the others, so you can complete the exercises in any order. If you need a paper copy of the completed exercise, enter your name centered in a header before printing.

1. Calculating a Monthly Rental Fee

You rent a copy machine, for which the rental company charges a fixed amount for the month plus an amount for each copy. Create a worksheet to calculate the amount due for any month. Test your results by changing one or more variables—the rental fee per month, the charge per copy, or the number of copies made in a month.

To enter text, numbers, and a formula containing two arithmetic operators:

1. Start Excel and access a new blank workbook.
2. Enter the text and numbers shown in Figure 1.23.

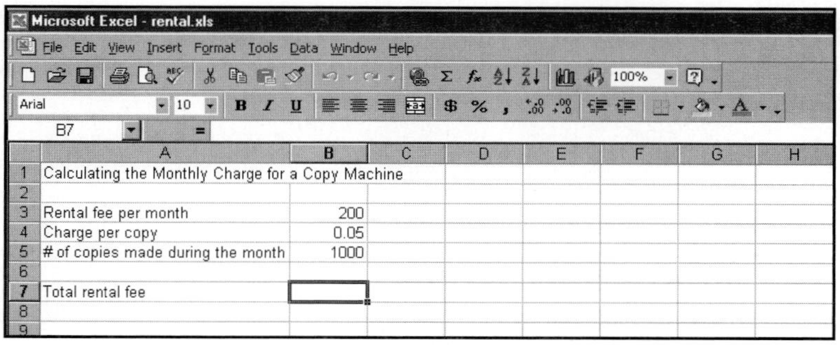

Figure 1.23
After entering text and numbers, you enter a formula in cell B7.

3. In cell B7, enter the formula to calculate Total rental fee. (*Hint:* Multiply the number of copies by the charge per copy, and add the result to the rental fee per month; use cell references instead of numbers in the formula.)

   Make sure 250 displays as the total rental fee in cell B7.

4. In cell B5, change the number of copies to **2000**.

   Check that 300 displays as the total rental fee in cell B7. Doubling the number of copies increased the total rental fee by 50 dollars. Now, find out how much you would pay if you could negotiate a charge of 4 cents a copy.

5. In cell B4, change the charge per copy to **0.04**.

   Check that 280 displays as the total rental fee in cell B7. You save 20 dollars if you pay one cent less on each of 2000 copies.

6. In the drive and folder of your choice, save the workbook as **rental**.
7. Close the workbook (also exit Excel if you want to end your work session).

2. Calculating Your New Rate of Pay per Hour

You have put in a request for a raise. Create a worksheet to calculate the new wage rate per hour. Test your results by changing one or both variables—the original wage rate per hour and the percent increase.

To enter text, numbers, and a formula containing two arithmetic operators:

1. Start Excel and access a new blank workbook.

2. Enter the text and numbers shown in Figure 1.24.

Figure 1.24

After entering text and numbers, you enter a formula in cell B5.

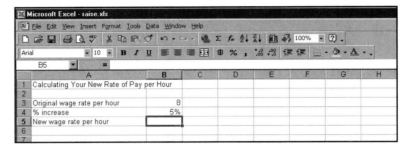

3. In cell B5, enter the formula to calculate New wage rate per hour. (*Hint:* Multiply the original wage rate by the percent increase, and add the result to the original wage rate; use cell references instead of numbers in the formula.)

    Check that 8.4 displays as the new wage rate per hour in cell B5. (You learn to change the display to $8.40 in Project 3, "Improving the Appearance of a Worksheet.")

4. In cell B3, change the wage rate per hour to **10**.

    Check that 10.5 displays as the new wage rate in cell B5.

5. In cell B4, change the percent increase to **10%**.

    Check that 11 displays as the new wage rate in cell B5.

6. In the drive and folder of your choice, save the workbook as **raise**.

7. Close the workbook (also exit Excel if you want to end your work session).

3. Preparing to Print a Worksheet

You know that you'll be creating a worksheet slightly larger than can fit on one page, printed with one-inch margins in landscape orientation. You want to print the worksheet periodically by clicking the Print button on the toolbar, so you set up the print specifications now.

To set up a worksheet to print:

1. Start Excel and access a new blank workbook.

2. Access the File menu and display the Page Setup dialog box.

3. Select the Page tab and specify landscape orientation.

4. Set scaling to fit to one page wide by one page tall.

5. Select the Margins tab and set all margins to one inch.

6. Close the Page Setup dialog box and save your workbook as **print**.

7. Close the workbook (also exit Excel if you want to end your work session).

Discovery Zone

Discovery Zone exercises require advanced knowledge of topics presented in *MOUS Essentials* lessons, application of skills from multiple lessons, or self-directed learning of new skills. Each exercise is independent of the others, so you can complete the exercises in any order.

1. Using the What's This? Feature of Onscreen Help

You are entering a custom footer to print at the bottom of every page and you don't remember what several of the buttons mean. You try to access What's This? by choosing Help, What's This? and by pressing (◆Shift)+(F1). Neither produces the information you need. Sometimes, clicking the right mouse button produces results, such as displaying information or a menu of frequently used commands. Try this method to find out what the buttons mean.

1. Start Excel and access a new blank workbook.

2. Choose File, Page Setup.

3. Click the Header/Footer tab in the Page Setup dialog box, and click the Custom Footer button.

4. Click Help in the menu bar.

   The feature is not active in the Footer dialog box.

5. Point to the first button above the Center section (the button with the letter A).

⊠ *If You Have Problems...*

If you click the button with the letter A instead of pointing to it, the Font dialog box opens. Click Cancel to close the Font dialog box and repeat Step 5.

---

6. Press (◆Shift)+(F1).

   Information about entering text in the Left section appears, instead of an explanation of the first button.

7. Point to the first button again, and click the right mouse button.

   The What's This? button appears.

8. Click the What's This? button.

   An explanation of the button appears.

9. Point to another button above the Center section and click the right mouse button; then click the What's This? button.

10. Repeat the previous step to view explanations of the other buttons, as desired.

11. Click Cancel to close the Footer dialog box, and then click Cancel to close the Page Setup dialog box.

12. Continue working in Excel or choose File, Exit.

2. Getting Help on AutoComplete and Footers

After working through this project, you have questions about two features—AutoComplete and footers. You have heard that many features in Excel can be turned on or off to suit your work preferences. Use one or more of Excel's Help options to find out how to turn off AutoComplete. For example, you can type your search topic in the message balloon provided by the Office Assistant. You can also display Help's Index and specify your search topic as a keyword.

You also want to know whether you can have more than one custom footer in a worksheet, and whether you can enter more than one line of text in a footer. Use Excel's on-screen Help to find the answers to your questions. For example, you might look in Contents for subtopics related to printing.

PinPoint Assessment

You have completed the project and its associated lessons, and have had an opportunity to assess your skills through the end-of-project questions and exercises. Now use the PinPoint software Evaluation Mode to further assess your comprehension of the specific exam activities you have just learned. You can also use the PinPoint Trainer Mode and the Show Me tutorials to practice these exam activities.

Modifying a Worksheet

Key terms introduced in this project include

- absolute reference
- AutoCorrect
- AutoFill
- AutoSum

- Clipboard
- fill handle
- function
- range

- relative reference
- select
- shortcut menu
- Spelling checker

Objectives	Required Activity for MOUS	Exam Level
➤ Open an Existing Workbook	Locate and open an existing workbook	Core
➤ Select Worksheet Items	Cut, copy, paste, paste special, and move selected cells	Core
➤ Use AutoFill	Work with series (AutoFill)	Core
➤ Insert and Delete Rows and Columns	Insert and delete rows and columns	Core
➤ Copy and Move Cell Contents	Cut, copy, paste, paste special, and move selected cells, using the Office Clipboard	Core
➤ Use AutoSum	Use AutoSum	Core
➤ Copy a Formula with Relative References	Use references (absolute and relative)	Core
➤ Spellcheck a Worksheet	Check spelling	Core

Why Would I Do This?

Now that you are familiar with the Excel screen and the basics of entering data and saving files, it's time to work with some of Excel's more powerful editing tools. In Project 1, "Getting Started with Excel," you learned how to create a simple worksheet in the Revenues workbook. In this project, you expand the worksheet to include data for three more quarters. For each revenue source—Greens Fees, Golf Lessons, and Pro Shop Sales—you also calculate the total revenue for each quarter and for the year.

 ## Lesson 1: Opening an Existing Workbook

After you create and save a workbook, you can reopen the workbook and resume working with its data. In this lesson, you open a variation of the Revenues workbook you created in Project 1. The initial sheet in this workbook has been expanded to include revenue amounts for the second, third, and fourth quarters.

To Open an Existing Workbook

❶ **Start Excel if it is not already running, and choose File in the menu bar.**
The File menu opens to display a number of commands.

 ❷ **Choose the Open command.**
The Open dialog box displays. You can also click the Open button on the Standard toolbar to display the Open dialog box.

❸ **Click the down arrow at the right end of the Look in box (see Figure 2.1).**
The Look in drop-down list shown in Figure 2.1 reflects the drives, folders, or files on a specific computer. (The drives, folders, and files on your system may be different, depending on the software and hardware you have installed.)

Figure 2.1
Use the Open dialog box to open an existing file.

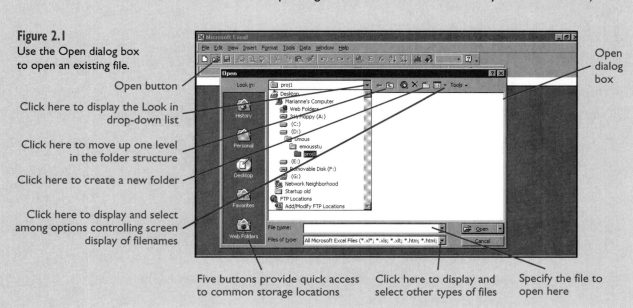

Open button
Click here to display the Look in drop-down list
Click here to move up one level in the folder structure
Click here to create a new folder
Click here to display and select among options controlling screen display of filenames

Open dialog box

Five buttons provide quick access to common storage locations
Click here to display and select other types of files
Specify the file to open here

Select the drive and folder containing the student files for this book, and click the e-0201 file icon to select the file.

If you don't see e-0201 in the list, open another folder from the Look in drop-down list or look on another drive. The file may be stored in a different location on your system. If you can't find the file on your computer, ask your instructor for the location of the data files you will use with this book.

X ***If You Have Problems...***

If, when you click the file to select it, the characters in the filename are highlighted instead of the entire filename, it means you changed to Rename mode. In Rename mode, you can change the name of an existing file or folder. To select the file, make sure that you click its icon.

---

5 **Click the Open button in the lower-right corner of the Open dialog box.**

The partially completed worksheet, shown in Figure 2.2, displays. Now, use the Save As command to save a copy of this sample file under a more descriptive filename. The original data file will be stored intact.

Name of the currently active file

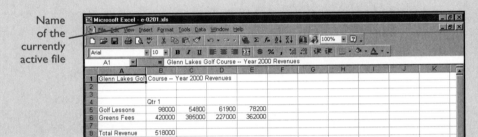

Figure 2.2
Save the sample file e-0201 as Revenues to use in this project.

6 **Choose File again, and choose the Save As command.**
The Save As dialog box displays.

7 **In the File name text box, type Revenues to replace e-0201.**
Revenues is the workbook filename that is used throughout this project.

8 **From the Save in drop-down list, select the appropriate drive and folder for saving the new file.**
If necessary, ask your instructor where you should save the new workbook file.

9 **Choose Save.**

 If You Have Problems...

If you save to the same location as you did for Lesson 1, a message displays, telling you that the Revenues file already exists. Click Yes to replace the file you previously created with this expanded version.

Excel saves the workbook as Revenues and adds the extension .xls to the filename. The name of the file changes to Revenues.xls in the title bar at the top of the screen. Keep the workbook open for the next lesson, or close the workbook and exit Excel.

continues ▶

To Open an Existing Workbook (continued)

The two files, the original student data file named e-0201.xls and the new file, Revenues.xls, are identical. Throughout this book you will modify copies of student data files. Each original file remains intact if you want to rework a project.

 Exam Note: **Opening a File**

To open a file quickly from the Open dialog box, double-click the file's icon in the list of files. If you double-click the filename, you might end up in Rename mode.

 # Lesson 2: Selecting Worksheet Items

To build a worksheet, you must learn how to select items in the worksheet. When you ***select*** an item, you highlight that item so you can make changes to it. You select a cell, for example, so you can copy the cell's content into another cell. You select a column so you can change the column's width or delete the column.

In this lesson, you learn how to select items in the Revenues workbook.

To Select Worksheet Items

❶ Open the Revenues workbook, if necessary, and click cell A5 in Sheet1.

You selected cell A5 by clicking it. After you select a cell, the cell's border is highlighted in bold, the cell's address appears in the name box of the formula bar, and the cell's content appears in the contents area of the formula bar. In addition, the letter heading of the column and the number heading of the row in which the cell is located appear in bold.

❷ Click cell A5, press and hold down the left mouse button, and drag the mouse pointer to cell E5. Release the left mouse button when the mouse pointer is in cell E5.

Several adjacent cells—called a ***range***—are now selected (see Figure 2.3). In Excel, a range can be a cell or a rectangular group of adjacent cells. As you drag the mouse, the name box on the formula bar shows you how many rows and columns you are selecting. After you finish selecting the range, the entire range of selected cells is highlighted.

❸ Click column heading B in the worksheet frame.

The entire worksheet column B is highlighted. The previously selected range A5 through E5 is no longer highlighted.

❹ Click row heading 8 in the worksheet frame.

Column B is deselected, and the worksheet row 8 is selected.

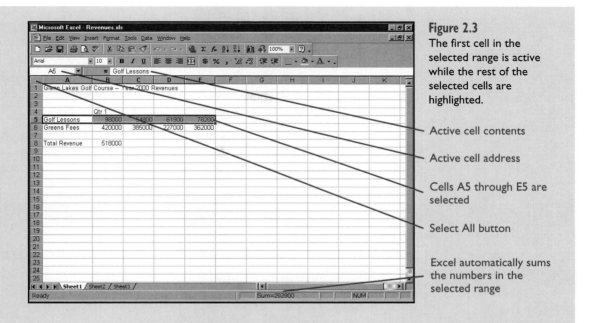

Figure 2.3
The first cell in the selected range is active while the rest of the selected cells are highlighted.

Active cell contents

Active cell address

Cells A5 through E5 are selected

Select All button

Excel automatically sums the numbers in the selected range

⑤ Click the Select All button—the rectangle in the top-left corner of the worksheet frame.

Row 8 is deselected, and the entire worksheet is selected.

⑥ Click any cell to deselect the worksheet.

Keep the workbook open for the next lesson, or close the workbook and exit Excel.

 Exam Note: **Selecting Cells and Cell Contents**

In Excel, the standard notation for identifying ranges is to list the first cell in the range, a colon, and the last cell in the range. For example, A5:E5 refers to the range of cells in row 5 from column A through column E.

You can select adjacent cells by clicking the first cell, and then pressing and holding down ⬆Shift while you click the last cell. For example, to select all cells in column A from row 3 through row 50, you can click cell A3, press and hold down ⬆Shift, click cell A50, and then release ⬆Shift. Excel highlights all cells in the range A3:A50.

To select nonadjacent cells, click the first cell, press and hold Ctrl, and click additional cells. The last cell that you click is the active cell, but the others remain selected.

To select only the content or part of the content of a cell, you can double-click in the active cell to display the I-beam mouse pointer, and drag the I-beam across any part of the text or data in the cell or the formula bar to select it. For example, you might want to boldface only a selected portion of the text in a long label.

Lesson 3: Using AutoFill

Currently, Sheet1 in the Revenues workbook has values for two sources of revenue over four quarters. Before the worksheet is complete, however, a few items need to be changed. For example, row 4 should have column headings for each quarter of revenues you track. Using Excel's **AutoFill** feature, you can easily fill in a series of numbers, dates, or other items in a specified range.

In this case, by selecting the cell containing the label Qtr 1 and then selecting a range of cells, you can automatically add a sequence of quarter labels (Qtr 2, Qtr 3, and Qtr 4) to the range you select.

To Use AutoFill

❶ Open the Revenues workbook, if necessary, and click cell B4 in Sheet1.
The *fill handle*, a small black square, displays in the lower-right corner of cell B4. Dragging the fill handle copies the contents of the current cell or selected range to adjacent cells. Now drag the fill handle to create a series of consecutive quarter labels.

❷ Move the mouse pointer to the lower-right corner of cell B4 until the pointer changes to a thin black cross.
When the mouse pointer changes to a black cross, Excel is ready to select a range of cells to be filled (see Figure 2.4).

Figure 2.4
Drag the fill handle right to create the remaining quarter labels.

Black cross

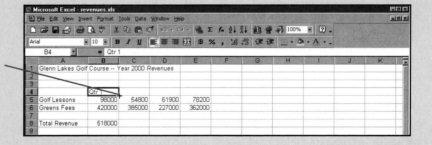

❸ Press the left mouse button, drag right to cell E4, and release the mouse button.
The range B4 through E4 is selected. When you release the mouse button, Excel fills the selected range with quarter labels (starting with Qtr 2 and increasing by one quarter for each cell in the range), as shown in Figure 2.5.

Figure 2.5
The AutoFill command is used here to create a series of quarter labels.

④ Click any cell.

The range is deselected. From here, you can take the next step to build your worksheet—inserting and deleting columns and rows.

⑤ Click the Save button on the Standard toolbar.

Keep the Revenues workbook open for the next lesson, or close the workbook and exit Excel.

  If You Have Problems...

When using AutoFill, if you select cells that contain data, Excel overwrites the data in the cells. You can reverse the fill action and restore original data by choosing Edit, Undo.

  Exam Note: **Fill Effects**

You can fill columns as well as rows. To fill in increasing order, drag down or to the right. To fill in decreasing order, drag up or to the left.

If you want to create a sequence of consecutive entries, you can provide an example in one or two cells, select the cell(s) containing the example, and drag the lower-right corner of the selection. The sequences can be text, numbers, or a combination of text and numbers, such as Qtr 1. For example, if you enter Jan in a cell, and then use the Fill handle to drag right or down eleven more cells, Excel automatically enters Jan, Feb, . . . through Dec in the sequence of twelve cells. If you enter January in a cell as the example to start a sequence, Excel enters January, February, March . . . through December.

If a fill sequence is to be a set of numbers incrementing by the same amount, provide a pattern in two adjacent cells, such as the number 10 in one cell and the number 20 in the next. If you select both cells and drag right or down, Excel fills the copy range with numbers incrementing by 10 (10, 20, 30, 40, and so on).

You can also use the AutoFill feature to enter a series of dates. If you fill a range of dates based on the contents of one cell, each additional date increments by one. For example, applying AutoFill to a cell containing 1/1/2000 produces a series of dates 1/1/2000, 1/2/2000, 1/3/2000 and so forth. If you desire a different sequence, such as the last day of each month, provide a pattern in two cells. For example, if you enter 1/31/2000 in one cell and 2/29/2000 in the next cell, and select and drag those cells, Excel continues the sequence with 3/31/2000, 4/30/2000 and so forth.

Inside Stuff: **Other Ways to Specify a Series**

If you specify a start value in one cell, and click and drag with the right mouse button instead of the left, a shortcut menu displays with predefined increments including days, weekdays, months, and years if the start value is a date.

Excel also provides a Series dialog box that you can access by choosing Edit, Fill, Series. A variety of options are available that vary with the type of data set up as the start value.

Lesson 4: Inserting and Deleting Rows and Columns

If you decide to add more data within an existing worksheet, you can insert rows and columns. Inserting a row is a two-step process: select any cell in a row, and choose Insert, Rows. Inserting a column involves a similar process: select any cell in a column, and choose Insert, Columns. Excel always inserts a new row above the row you select, and inserts a new column to the left of the column you select.

Sometimes, you no longer want to include an entire row or column of data. Deleting a row or column can be done in two steps: select a row heading or a column heading in the worksheet frame, and choose Edit, Delete.

In this lesson, you insert a row in the first sheet of the Revenues workbook and enter another revenue category called Pro Shop Sales.

To Insert a Row

1 **Open the Revenues workbook, if necessary, and click any cell in row 6 of Sheet1.**

2 **Choose Insert, Rows.**
The content of row 6 and all rows below it move down one row. A new, blank row is inserted as the new row 6 (see Figure 2.6). Excel automatically renumbers the rows beneath the new row 6.

Figure 2.6
A new, blank row 6 is inserted into Sheet1 of the Revenues workbook.

Inserted row

Contents move down

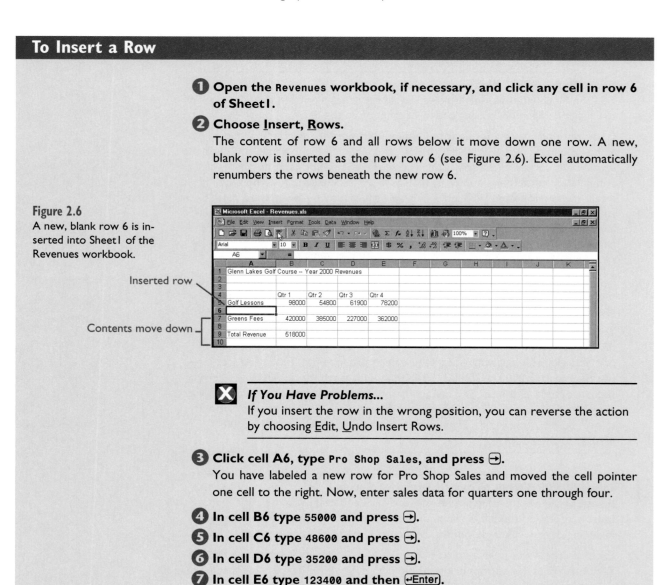

X *If You Have Problems...*
If you insert the row in the wrong position, you can reverse the action by choosing Edit, Undo Insert Rows.

3 **Click cell A6, type Pro Shop Sales, and press →.**
You have labeled a new row for Pro Shop Sales and moved the cell pointer one cell to the right. Now, enter sales data for quarters one through four.

4 **In cell B6 type 55000 and press →.**

5 **In cell C6 type 48600 and press →.**

6 **In cell D6 type 35200 and press →.**

7 **In cell E6 type 123400 and then ↵Enter.**
Your worksheet should now look similar to Figure 2.7.

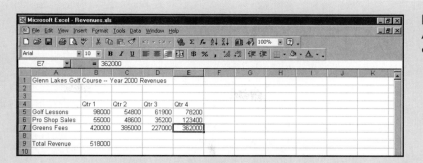

Figure 2.7
A third source of revenue
displays in the new row 6.

8 **Save your changes to the Revenues workbook.**

Keep the `Revenues` workbook open for the next lesson, or close the workbook and exit Excel.

 Exam Note: **Inserting or Deleting Rows and Columns**

If you want to insert more than one row or column at a time, select as many adjacent rows or columns as you need blank rows or columns, and choose Insert, Rows or Insert, Columns. For example, if you want to insert five new rows beginning at row 4, select rows 4 through 8, and choose Insert, Rows.

If you want to delete more than one row or column at a time, select the row or column headings in the worksheet frame, and choose Edit, Delete.

If you select a row heading or a column heading in the worksheet frame, and then choose Delete on the Edit menu, Excel immediately removes the selected row or column. Additional options are available if you click any cell in a row or column instead of the worksheet frame, and choose Edit, Delete. Excel displays the Delete dialog box with four options: Shift cells left, Shift cells up, Entire row, and Entire column. Use the first two options to delete a cell's contents and shift adjacent data to fill the blank cell.

You can use a shortcut menu to insert or delete columns, rows, and cell contents. A *shortcut menu* pops up in the worksheet area and displays common commands. Select the item you want to insert or delete, move the mouse pointer to it, click the right mouse button to display the shortcut menu, and choose the appropriate command.

Lesson 5: Copying and Moving Cell Contents

By adding a row, you made an important change to Sheet1 of your Revenues workbook. As you look at the three sources of revenue, however, you decide to change the order by listing the primary revenue source first. Although you could insert a new row 5 and retype the Greens Fees label and associated amounts, copying or moving data is generally much quicker than typing it a second time.

You can copy or move text, numbers, and formulas from one cell to another, from one worksheet to another, and from one file to another. After a copy operation, the selected cell contents appear in two places—the original location and the new location. After a move (cut) operation, the selected cell contents appear in only the new location.

Both operations involve a four-step process: select the cell(s) to copy or move; choose either Copy or Cut from the Edit menu; position the cell pointer on the upper-left cell of the target range; and choose Edit, Paste.

In this lesson, you insert a blank row, move selected cell contents to the new row, and delete the blank row formerly holding the moved data.

To Move Cell Contents

① Open the Revenues workbook, if necessary, and click any cell in row 5 of Sheet1.

② Choose Insert, Rows.
A new blank row appears above the renumbered row 6 that contains Golf Lessons data.

③ Select the Greens Fees label and data (the range A8:E8).
The range A8:E8 appears highlighted.

④ Click the Cut button on the Standard toolbar (or choose the menu sequence Edit, Cut).
A copy of the selected cells' contents is placed in the Windows Clipboard. The *Clipboard* stores data that you want to copy or move to another location. A flashing dotted line appears around the selected cells.

⑤ Click cell A5, the first cell in the new blank row.
The location you want the cut cell contents to appear is selected. You do not have to select a range that is the same size as the range you are moving; Excel automatically fills in the data, starting with the cell you select.

⑥ Click the Paste button on the Standard toolbar (or choose the menu sequence Edit, Paste).
The contents of selected cells disappear from the range A8:E8 and appear in cells A5 through E5, as shown in Figure 2.8. As indicated by the commands you have chosen, this move process (called cutting and pasting) is a very common procedure in Windows applications.

Figure 2.8
The first source of revenue is now Greens Fees.

Pasted data ———

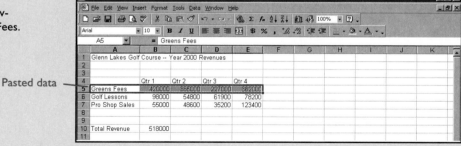

⑦ Click the row heading for row 8.
The blank row 8 is selected (highlighted).

⑧ Choose Edit, Delete.
The extra blank row before the Total Revenue row is removed.

⑨ Click cell B9.
The formula =B5+B6 appears in the formula bar. You must edit the formula to include the third source of revenue in cell B7.

⑩ Click in the formula bar at the end of the current formula, type +B7, and press ⏎Enter.

⑪ Click cell B9 again.

The formula =B5+B6+B7 appears in the formula bar and the result of the calculation appears in cell B9 (see Figure 2.9).

Current cell

Formula stored in cell B9

Calculated result

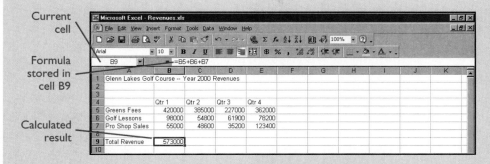

Figure 2.9
The formula in cell B9 sums the three sources of Qtr I revenue.

⑫ Save your changes to the current worksheet.

Keep the Revenues workbook open for the next lesson, or close the workbook and exit Excel.

 Exam Note: Copy and Paste

Executing a copy-and-paste operation differs from a cut-and-paste operation in only the second step of the four-step process. After selecting the cells to copy, click the Copy button on the Standard toolbar instead of the Cut button (or select the menu sequence Edit, Copy instead of Edit, Cut).

 Inside Stuff: Shortcut Menus and Move By Dragging

You can use Excel's shortcut menus to perform many common commands, including cut, copy, and paste. To open a shortcut menu, move the mouse pointer to the cell or area you want to affect, and right-click.

A handy way to move one or more cells of data quickly is to select the cells and position the mouse pointer on any border of the cells so the cell pointer changes to a white arrow. Click and drag the white arrow to the new location. An outline of the cells that you are moving appears as you drag, and a ScreenTip shows you the current active cell where the information will appear if you release the mouse button. When you release the mouse button, the cells' contents appear in the new location. If the new location already contains information, a dialog box appears, asking whether you want to replace the contents of the destination cells.

Lesson 6: Using AutoSum

You have entered all labels and numbers in Sheet I of the Revenues workbook. Now you want to enter formulas to total revenues for the year by type of revenue and for each quarter. Excel provides an **AutoSum** feature that you can use to insert a formula to sum a range of cells automatically. Excel suggests a formula, which you can accept or edit.

The suggested formula is a Sum function that includes Excel's suggestion for a range of cells to sum. A **_function_** is a predefined formula in Excel (Project 5, "Working with Functions," provides in-depth coverage of functions).

Now, use the AutoSum feature to calculate the total Greens Fees in the Revenues workbook.

To Calculate Using AutoSum

1 **Open the Revenues workbook, if necessary, and click cell F4 in Sheet1.**
The current cell is just to the right of the label Qtr 4. Enter a label to describe the new entries in column F.

2 **Type Annual and press ⏎Enter.**
The word Annual displays left-aligned in cell F4. The current cell is F5.

Σ

3 **Click the AutoSum button on the toolbar.**
AutoSum evaluates the cells above and to the left of the current cell. Upon finding an adjacent set of consecutive cells containing values, AutoSum automatically displays the suggested range to sum (see Figure 2.10).

Figure 2.10
Clicking the AutoSum
button automatically
inserts a Sum function.

AutoSum button

Dashed line forms a border
around the suggested range

Formula suggested by AutoSum

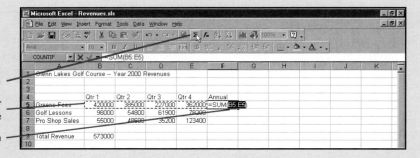

4 **Press ⏎Enter.**
Excel enters the function =SUM(B5:E5) in cell F5 and displays 1394000 as the calculated result.

5 **Save your changes to the current worksheet.**
Keep the Revenues workbook open for the next lesson, or close the workbook and exit Excel.

Lesson 7: Copying a Formula with Relative References

The Year 2000 Revenues worksheet is nearly complete. All that remains is to copy two formulas to adjacent cells. Refer to Figure 2.10. Total Revenue for each quarter is calculated by adding the contents of cells in rows 4, 5, and 6. Only the column designation changes from one formula to the next. Figure 2.10 also shows that the remaining formulas in column F must perform the same calculation—adding the contents of cells in columns B through E. Only the row designation changes from one formula to the next.

When row and/or column cell references change as a formula is copied, each reference to a cell in the formula is a **relative reference**. If you don't want Excel to adjust a reference to a cell when you copy a formula, use an **absolute reference**. You can create an absolute reference by placing a dollar sign ($) in front of the part(s) of the cell reference you do not want to change during the copy operation.

Now, copy the two formulas in Sheet1 of the Revenues workbook.

To Copy a Formula with Relative References

① Open the Revenues **workbook, if necessary, and click cell F5 in Sheet1.**

② Position the mouse pointer on the lower-right corner of cell F5 **(Figure 2.11).**

The cursor changes to a thin, black cross.

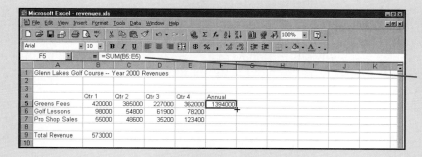

Figure 2.11
Copy the formula in cell F5 to cells F6 and F7.

Formula with relative cell references

③ Press the left mouse button, drag down to cell F7, and release the **mouse button.**

The formula in cell F5 is copied to cells F6 and F7 (see Figure 2.12). The copied formula did not contain any absolute cell references, so the formulas in cells F6 and F7 adjust to the appropriate row reference: row 6 for the formula in cell F6 and row 7 for the formula in cell F7.

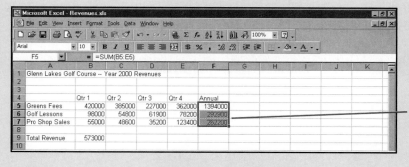

Figure 2.12
The copied formulas calculate annual revenues from Golf Lessons and Pro Shop Sales.

Results of copying a formula

④ Click cell B9 and position the mouse pointer on the lower-right corner of the cell.

continues ▶

To Copy a Formula with Relative References (continued)

5 **Press the left mouse button, drag right to cell F9, and release the mouse button.**

The formula in cell B9 is copied to cells C9 through F9 (see Figure 2.13). The copied formula did not contain any absolute cell references, so the formulas in cells C9 through F9 adjust to the appropriate column reference.

Figure 2.13
The copied formulas calculate total revenue for remaining quarters and for the year.

Results of copying another formula

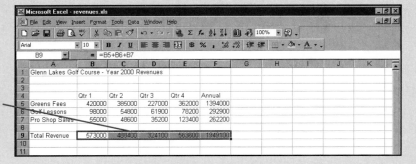

6 **Click any cell—such as cell A1—to deselect the highlighted range, and save your changes to the Revenues workbook.**

 ## Lesson 8: Spell-Checking a Worksheet

Microsoft Excel includes an **AutoCorrect** feature that can correct common errors as you type, such as changing adn to and. The program also includes a **Spelling checker** that highlights words that are not in its dictionary. You have the option to change or ignore any highlighted word. If a highlighted word, such as a person's name or a technical term, is spelled correctly and you use the word frequently, you can add it to a dictionary file called CUSTOM.DIC.

The Spelling checker doesn't catch all errors. You should still read text entries carefully to see if words are missing or used incorrectly, such as "affect" when you mean "effect."

In the following steps, you enter a misspelled word and correct it using the Spelling checker.

To Check Spelling in a Worksheet

1 **Open the** Revenues **workbook, if necessary, and click cell A2 in Sheet1.**

2 **Type** Prepaired by: **and press** ⏎Enter **(make sure you type the entry as shown, including the spelling error).**

3 **Click cell A1.**

The spell check is set to begin at the top of the worksheet.

 4 **Click the Spelling button on the Standard toolbar.**

The Spelling dialog box opens. The Spelling checker highlights the first occurrence of a word not found in its dictionary (see Figure 2.14).

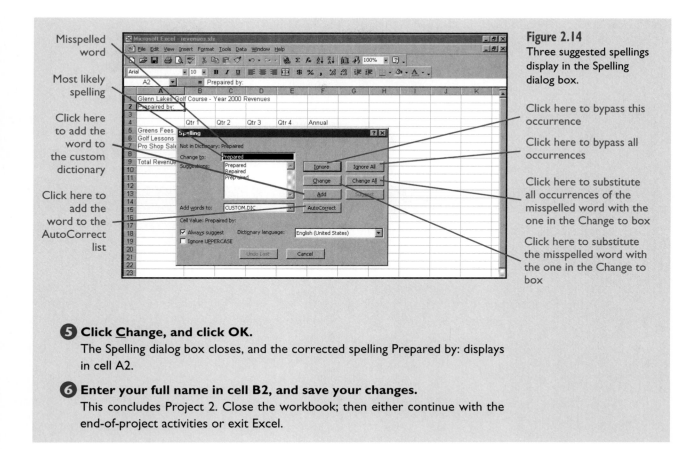

Misspelled word

Most likely spelling

Click here to add the word to the custom dictionary

Click here to add the word to the AutoCorrect list

Figure 2.14
Three suggested spellings display in the Spelling dialog box.

Click here to bypass this occurrence

Click here to bypass all occurrences

Click here to substitute all occurrences of the misspelled word with the one in the Change to box

Click here to substitute the misspelled word with the one in the Change to box

5 **Click Change, and click OK.**
The Spelling dialog box closes, and the corrected spelling Prepared by: displays in cell A2.

6 **Enter your full name in cell B2, and save your changes.**
This concludes Project 2. Close the workbook; then either continue with the end-of-project activities or exit Excel.

Inside Stuff: **Tips on Using the Spelling Checker**
A check of spelling begins at the current worksheet cell and continues to the end of the worksheet. If you do not start the Spelling checker at the beginning of the worksheet, Excel asks whether you want to continue checking from the beginning. Choose Yes to continue a check of the entire worksheet, or choose No to close the Spelling checker.

If the Spelling dialog box does not suggest alternatives to a highlighted word, check to be sure that the Always Suggest check box is selected in the Spelling dialog box.

Summary

In this project, you learned several essential tasks to develop a worksheet with a minimum of effort. Your experiences included using AutoFill to enter a sequence of labels, using AutoSum to enter a function that adds the contents of adjacent cells, and entering a formula once and copying it to other cells. You also learned basic editing techniques: selecting worksheet items, inserting or deleting rows and columns, executing a four-step process to move or copy cell contents, and spell-checking a worksheet.

You can extend your learning by practicing variations of techniques presented in these steps. For example, in Lesson 3, you used AutoFill to enter a series of quarter labels. In a blank worksheet, try using AutoFill to enter the months of the year, the days of the week, and a series of numbers that increment by a set amount (for example, 1, 2, 3 . . . or 10, 20, 30 . . .). Reinforce the skills presented in Lesson 5 by moving and copying the ranges that you created by using AutoFill. You inserted a row in Lesson 4. On your own, try to insert a column and delete a column or row. Be sure to browse the extensive onscreen Help for related topics.

Checking Concepts and Terms

True/False

For each of the following, check *T* or *F* to indicate whether the statement is true or false.

__T __F **1.** You use the <u>F</u>ile, <u>O</u>pen command to re-trieve a file that has been previously saved. [L1]

__T __F **2.** Select the entire worksheet by clicking the sheet tab. [L2]

__T __F **3.** When you use AutoFill, if you select cells that already contain data, Excel overwrites the data in the cells. [L3]

__T __F **4.** To lessen the likelihood of losing data, Excel enables you to delete only one row at a time. [L4]

__T __F **5.** Excel always inserts a new row below the row you select. [L4]

Multiple Choice

Circle the letter of the correct answer for each of the following.

1. What function is used to add the values in a range of cells? [L6]

   a. TOTAL

   b. SUM

   c. PLUS

   d. ADD

2. Which of the following is a true statement? [L2]

   a. In Excel, a range can be a single cell.

   b. In Excel, a range can be a rectangular group of adjacent cells.

   c. Both a and b are true statements.

   d. Neither a nor b is a true statement.

3. Which of the following statements is false? [L5]

   a. The move process is called cutting and pasting, a common procedure in Windows applications.

   b. Using Excel, you can copy or move text, numbers, and formulas from one worksheet to another.

   c. After a cut operation, the selected cell contents appear in two places—the original location and the new location.

   d. You can use buttons on a toolbar or choose menu options to copy or move worksheet contents.

4. When row and/or column cell references change as a formula is copied, what is each reference to a cell in the formula called? [L7]

   a. relative reference

   b. absolute reference

   c. static reference

   d. none of the above

5. Excel uses different cursors to indicate the current operation. What does a small, thin black cross indicate? [L5]

   a. You can move cell contents by dragging.

   b. You can copy cell contents by dragging.

   c. You can insert one or more rows.

   d. none of the above

Skill Drill

Skill Drill exercises reinforce project skills. Each skill reinforced is the same, or nearly the same, as a skill presented in the project. Detailed instructions are provided in a step-by-step format.

Each exercise is independent of the others, so you can complete the exercises in any order. Be sure to save the workbook after completing each exercise. If you need a paper copy of one or more completed exercises, enter your name centered in a header before printing. Other print options have already been set to print compressed to one page, and to display the filename, sheet name, and current date in a footer.

Before beginning your Project 2 Skill Drill exercises, complete the following steps:

1. Open the file named **e-0202** and save it as **e2drill**.

The workbook contains an overview sheet and three exercise sheets labeled #1-DeleteCol, #2-Move, and #3-AutoSum.

2. Click the Overview sheet to view the organization and content of the Project 2 Skill Drill Exercises workbook.

Be sure to save your changes and close the workbook if you need more than one work session to complete the desired exercises. Then, continue working on **e2drill** instead of starting over on the original e-0202 file.

1. Deleting a Column

Your initial design for summarizing volunteer hours included a column for summing hours after the first and second quarters. Now you want to present only the annual totals for each organization.

To delete a column:

1. If necessary, open the **e2drill** workbook; then click the #1-DeleteCol sheet tab.

2. Click any cell in column D, such as D7, which holds the label 1/2 Year.

3. Choose Edit, Delete to display the Delete dialog box.

4. Click Entire column, and click OK.

5. Save your changes to the e2drill workbook.

2. Moving Cell Contents

You decide to change the original location of a title and subtitle on a worksheet that summarizes volunteer hours.

To move cell contents:

1. If necessary, open the **e2drill** workbook; then click the #2-Move sheet tab.

2. Select the range E1:E2.

   The worksheet's title and subtitle are selected. These titles display across several columns, but are stored in the two cells in column E.

3. Click the Cut button on the Standard toolbar (or choose Edit, Cut).

4. Click cell A3 to select the first cell in the destination range.

5. Click the Paste button on the Standard toolbar (or choose Edit, Paste).

6. Save your changes to the e2drill workbook.

3. Using AutoSum and Copy with Relative Cell References

You entered labels and numbers in a worksheet to keep track of volunteer hours. Now, use AutoSum to enter a function summing hours for the first organization and copy the formula to compute total hours for other organizations.

To use AutoSum and copy the formula suggested by AutoSum:

1. If necessary, open the **e2drill** workbook; then click the #3-AutoSum sheet tab.

2. Click cell F7, the first cell under the Annual label.

3. Click the AutoSum button on the Standard toolbar.

4. Press ⏎Enter to accept the suggested function =SUM(B7:E7).

5. Position the cell pointer on the lower-right corner of cell F7.

6. Click and drag the fill handle to cell F9, and release the mouse button.

7. Save your changes to the e2drill workbook.

Challenge

Challenge exercises expand on or are somewhat related to skills presented in the lessons. Each exercise provides a brief narrative introduction, followed by instructions in a numbered step format that are not as detailed as those in the Skill Drill section.

Each exercise is independent of the others, so you can complete the exercises in any order. If you need a paper copy of the completed exercise, enter your name centered in a header before printing. Other print options have already been set to print compressed to one page and to display the filename, sheet name, and current date in a footer.

Before beginning your first Project 2 Challenge exercise, complete the following steps:

1. Open the file named **e-0203** and save it as **e2challenge**.

   The workbook contains four sheets: an overview, and exercise sheets named #1-Flowers, #2-Flowers, and #3-% Change.

2. Click the Overview sheet to view the organization of the Project 2 Challenge Exercises workbook.

Be sure to save your changes and close the workbook if you need more than one work session to complete the desired exercises. Then, continue working on **e2challenge** instead of starting over on the original e-0203 file.

1. Adding Labels and Formulas to a Sales Data Worksheet

Among your responsibilities as the sales manager of Flowers Your Way is the preparation of a five-year analysis of sales. You have already entered data for sales by type: in-store sales, phone/fax orders, and Web sales. Within each type, you show sales to corporations separately from sales to individuals. Now, you want to complete the worksheet by adding labels and formulas.

To add labels by using AutoFill, add a formula by using AutoSum, and copy formulas:

1. If necessary, open your **e2challenge** workbook; then click the #1-Flowers sheet tab.

2. Use AutoFill to enter the years 1996 through 2000 in the range B6:F6.

3. Click cell B10 and use AutoSum to enter the function =SUM(B8:B9).

4. Drag the fill handle to copy the formula in cell B10 to the range C10:F10.

   You copied by dragging a formula with relative cell addresses to a range of adjacent cells. Now, copy a formula to nonadjacent cells.

5. Click cell B10 again and click the Copy button on the Standard toolbar.

6. Select the range B15:F15, hold down **Ctrl**, and select the range B20:F20.

7. Click the Paste button on the Standard toolbar.

   In each of the highlighted cells in B15:F15 and B20:F20, Excel enters a formula to sum the contents of the two cells above the formula.

8. Select cell B22, and enter a formula to add cells B10, B15, and B20.

9. Copy the formula in B22 to the range C22:F22.

10. Save your changes to the e2challenge workbook.

2. Changing the Order of Data Using Insert, Move, and Delete

Among your responsibilities as the sales manager of Flowers Your Way is the preparation of a five-year analysis of sales. You have categorized sales by type: in-store sales, phone/fax orders, and Web sales. Now, you decide to list Web sales first rather than last. You can make the switch by inserting rows, moving the Web sales data, and deleting extra blank rows.

To move cell contents including formulas:

1. If necessary, open your **e2challenge** workbook; then click the #2-Flowers sheet.

2. Select the range A7:A11, and choose Insert, Rows.
   Blank rows 7 through 11 appear above the label In-Store Sales.

3. Select the Web sales data in the range A22:F25, and click the Cut button on the Standard toolbar.

4. Click cell A7, and click the Paste button on the Standard toolbar.
   The Web sales data is moved to the blank rows 7 through 10.

5. Select the range A22:A26, and choose Edit, Delete.

6. Select Entire row in the Delete dialog box, and click OK.

7. Save your changes to the e2challenge workbook.

3. Calculating the Percentage Change from One Year to the Next

You are one of the managers in a small firm and are responsible for monitoring the following assets: Cash, Accounts Receivable, Inventory, and Supplies. At the moment, you are interested in finding out how the amounts in these accounts at the end of the year compare to the amounts in these accounts at the beginning of the year. You'd like to show the percentage increase or decrease in each account.

To enter and copy a formula:

1. If necessary, open your **e2challenge** workbook; then click the #3-% Change sheet tab.

2. Select cell D6 and enter a formula to compute the percentage change in Cash.

3. Check that the formula produces the correct percentage change results.
   The drop in Cash from $10,000 at 1/1/00 to $8,000 at 12/31/00 is a 20 percent decrease (a minus sign displays in front of 20.0% in cell D6).

 If You Have Problems...
You want to know how the end-of-year $8,000 compares to having $10,000 in cash at the beginning of the year. The percent change is calculated by finding the difference between the two amounts and dividing the result by the amount at the beginning of the year. Excel performs calculations within parentheses first. You need to be sure that you find the difference between the two amounts before the division takes place. Use onscreen Help if you do not remember which math operator indicates division.

---

4. Correct the formula, if necessary, and copy the formula down to compute the percentage change in the other three accounts.

5. Ensure that the copied formulas produce the correct percentage change results. Accounts Receivable, for example, increased by 12.5 percent.

6. Save your changes to the e2challenge workbook.

Discovery Zone

Discovery Zone exercises require advanced knowledge of topics presented in *MOUS Essentials* lessons, application of skills from multiple lessons, or self-directed learning of new skills. Each exercise is independent of the others, so you can complete the exercises in any order.

Be sure to save the workbook after completing each exercise. If you need a paper copy of the completed exercise, enter your name centered in a header before printing. Other print options have already been set to print compressed to one page and to display the filename, sheet name and current date in a footer.

Before beginning your first Project 2 Discovery Zone exercise, complete the following steps:

1. Open the file named **e-0204** and save it as **e2discovery**.
   The workbook contains three sheets: an overview and two exercise sheets named #1-Shortcut and #2-Expenses.

2. Click the Overview sheet to view the organization of the Project 2 Discovery Zone Exercises workbook.

Be sure to save your changes and close the workbook if you need more than one work session to complete the desired exercises. Continue working on **e2discovery** instead of starting over on the original e-0204 file.

1. Using AutoFill's Shortcut Menu

You want to know more about Excel's AutoFill feature. Use the Office Assistant to search for information on using AutoFill. Select the topic **Automatically fill in data based on adjacent cells,** and select the topic **Fill in a series of numbers, dates, or other items.** In the Notes area, read the information about using the right mouse button to drag a fill range. Apply what you learn by using AutoFill to enter the series of dates indicated in columns B though E of the #1-Shortcut worksheet (fill each column to row 20).

2. Modifying an Office Expenses Worksheet

It's July, and your supervisor asked you to look into ways to reduce the expense of running the office. Before you make any suggestions, you want a clear idea of what those office-related expenses were during the first six months of the year. You've already started to develop an Excel worksheet to show the individual expenses and totals for each month.

At this point, the worksheet contains only a few expense names (see the #2-Expenses sheet in your e2discovery workbook). Modify the worksheet in the following ways: Use AutoFill to enter the names of the months Jan through June across row 4. Change the order of expenses by putting those related to utilities (electricity, water, and phone) in adjacent cells in column A. Add at least three other expenses related to maintaining an office (insurance, cleaning, and so on). Insert a column between March and April, and enter a **Qtr 1** label. Set up a column for Qtr 2 data to the right of the June data. Enter and copy formulas, as necessary, to complete the worksheet. Add sample data to test formula results.

PinPoint Assessment

You have completed this project and its associated lessons, and have had an opportunity to assess your skills through the end-of-project questions and exercises. Now use the PinPoint software Evaluation Mode to further assess your comprehension of the specific exam activities you have just learned. You can also use the PinPoint Trainer Mode and the Show Me tutorials to practice these exam activities.

Improving the Appearance of a Worksheet

Key terms introduced in this project include

- border
- font
- format
- pattern
- point
- typeface

Objectives	Required Activity for MOUS	Exam Level
➤ Format Numbers	Apply number formats (currency, percent, dates, comma); Adjust the decimal place	Core
➤ Align Cell Contents	Modify alignment of cell content	Core
➤ Change Font and Font Size	Apply font styles (typeface, size, color, and styles)	Core
➤ Apply Bold, Italic, and Underline		
➤ Add Color	Apply cell borders and shading; Apply font styles (typeface, size, color, and styles)	Core
➤ Add Borders	Apply cell borders and shading	Core
➤ Use Format Painter	Use the Format Painter	Core
➤ Remove Formatting	Clear cell formats	Core

Why Would I Do This?

After you create a worksheet, you may want to format it to make it more readable and attractive. When you *format* a worksheet, you apply attributes to cells that alter the display of cell contents. For example, you can format a worksheet by italicizing text and displaying a border around a cell or group of cells. Figure 3.1 illustrates the formats you apply in this project, which begins with formatting numbers.

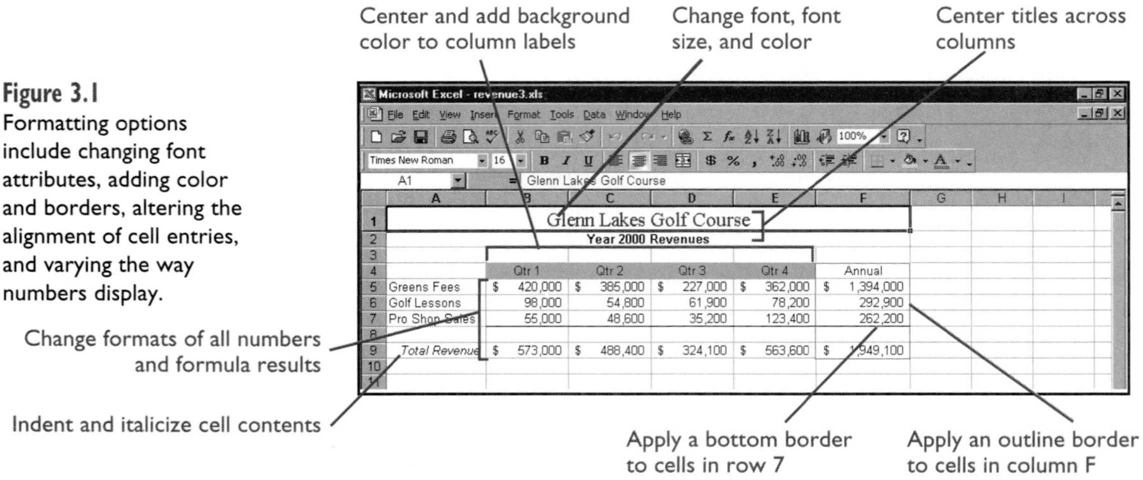

Center and add background
color to column labels

Change font, font
size, and color

Center titles across
columns

Figure 3.1
Formatting options
include changing font
attributes, adding color
and borders, altering the
alignment of cell entries,
and varying the way
numbers display.

Change formats of all numbers
and formula results

Indent and italicize cell contents

Apply a bottom border
to cells in row 7

Apply an outline border
to cells in column F

Lesson 1: Formatting Numbers

When you enter a number or a formula into a cell, the entry may not appear as you hoped it would. You might type **5**, for example, but want it to look like $5.00. You could type the dollar sign, decimal point, and zeros; or you can have Excel automatically format the number for you. When you want to apply a standard format to a number, you format the cell in which the number is displayed.

In Excel, you can format numbers in many ways by using the Number tab of the Format Cells dialog box (see Figure 3.2). You usually format numbers as currency, percentages, dates, or times of day.

Figure 3.2
You can choose among
Number, Alignment, Font,
Border, Patterns, and
Protection tabs in the
Format Cells dialog box.

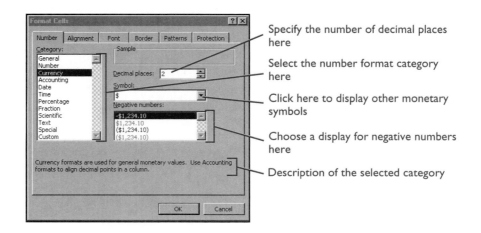

Specify the number of decimal places
here

Select the number format category
here

Click here to display other monetary
symbols

Choose a display for negative numbers
here

Description of the selected category

Toolbar buttons are provided for three common number formats: Currency Style, Percent Style, and Comma Style. In this lesson, you use the Currency Style and Comma Style buttons on the toolbar to format the number display in the Revenues workbook.

To Format Numbers

1 **Open the file e-0301 and save it as Revenue3.**
The workbook is a duplicate of the one you created in Project 2. Saving it with the number 3 in the filename helps you to remember that the file reflects the changes introduced in Project 3.

2 **Select cells B5 through F5 in the first sheet.**
You want to format the first row of numbers to display in a currency format.

3 **Click the Currency Style button on the Formatting toolbar.**
The selected cells display the default currency format, as shown in Figure 3.3.

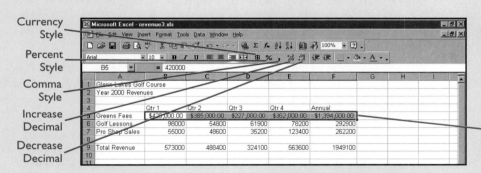

Figure 3.3
Select cells, and click the appropriate button on the toolbar.

Selected numbers formatted in currency style

4 **With cells B5:F5 still selected, click the Decrease Decimal button twice.**
Each time you click the Decrease Decimal button, Excel removes one decimal place. Clicking the button twice causes the amounts in row 5 to appear with no decimal places.

5 **Select cells B6:F7, and click the Comma Style button.**

6 **Click the Decrease Decimal button twice.**
The amounts for Golf Lessons and Pro Shop Sales in rows 6 and 7 display with commas to indicate thousands and zero decimal places.

7 **Select cells B9:F9, click the Currency Style button, and click the Decrease Decimal button twice.**
The amounts for Total Revenue in row 9 display the currency format with zero decimal places (see Figure 3.4, which shows the results of all changes in number formatting).

8 **Click the Save button.**
Excel saves your changes to the Revenue3 workbook. Keep the workbook open for the next lesson, or close the workbook and exit Excel.

continues ▶

To Format Numbers (continued)

Figure 3.4
You can specify currency and comma number formats by using toolbar buttons or the Format Cells dialog box.

Rows displaying currency format

Rows displaying comma format

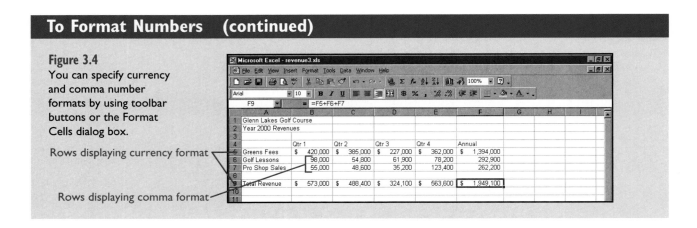

 Exam Note: Applying Number Formats

Excel rounds the display of values to fit the specified number of decimal places. For example, if you enter 235.75 in a cell that is set to display zero decimal places, the number 236 displays. However, the actual value stored in the cell—in this case, 235.75—is used in any calculations.

When you apply any kind of formatting, you apply it to the worksheet cell, not to specific cell contents. Therefore, if you change the content of a cell, the formatting still applies. You can even format empty cells, so that when data is entered, the data automatically displays with the correct format.

You can apply a percent style format as you enter the data. Simply type the number followed by a percent sign, for example 12.5%. If you'd rather use the Percent Style button on the toolbar, first enter the data as a decimal, for example .125.

 If You Have Problems...

You might enter a number or formula, and find that the display is not consistent with the data. For example, suppose you enter a formula to subtract an order date of 6/15/99 from a date shipped of 6/24/99. You want the number 9 to appear as the result of the formula, indicating the number of days it took to ship the order. Instead, you are likely to see 1/9/00 (for January 9, 1900—the date represented by the number 9). In this case, the formula is correct; the display is not. To fix the display problem, apply a non-date format, such as general or comma to the problem cell(s).

 ## Lesson 2: Aligning Cell Contents

When you enter data into a cell, text aligns with the left side of the cell; and numbers, dates, and times automatically align with the right side of the cell. You can change the alignment of data at any time. For instance, you might want to fine-tune the appearance of column headings by centering all the information in the column.

You can use the Merge and Center toolbar button to align data across several columns in one step. (For Merge and Center to work correctly, the text must be in the leftmost cell of the selected range.) You can also wrap data onto multiple lines and rotate text within the cell.

In this lesson, you center the worksheet title and subtitle across six columns, center column headings within cells, and indent text in a cell (see Figure 3.5).

Align Right
Center
Align Left
Merge and Center
Decrease Indent
Cell contents indented

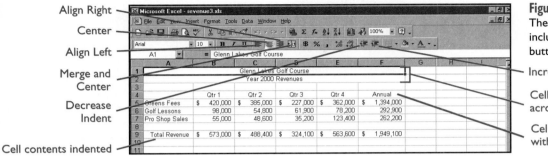

Figure 3.5
The Formatting toolbar includes six alignment buttons.

Increase Indent

Cell contents centered across columns

Cell contents centered within cells

To Align Text

1 **Open the Revenue3 workbook, if necessary, and select cells A1 through F1.**
You want the title in A1 centered over the width of the worksheet.

2 **Click the Merge and Center button on the toolbar.**
Excel merges the selected cells into one cell, and centers the title Glenn Lakes Golf Course across the width of the worksheet (refer to row 1 in Figure 3.5). Even though the worksheet title is centered across the worksheet, it is still located in cell A1. If you want to select the text for further formatting or editing, you must select cell A1.

3 **Select cells A2 through F2, and click the Merge and Center button.**
Excel merges the selected cells into one cell, and centers the subtitle Year 2000 Revenues across the width of the worksheet (refer to row 2 in Figure 3.5).

4 **Select cells B4 through F4.**
The cells containing the column headings you want to center are selected.

5 **Click the Center button on the toolbar.**
Excel centers the Qtr and Annual labels (refer to row 4 in Figure 3.5).

6 **Click cell A9.**
The cell containing the label you want to indent is selected.

7 **Click the Increase Indent button.**
Excel indents the Total Revenue label (refer to cell A9 in Figure 3.5).

8 **Click the Save button.**
Excel saves your changes to the Revenue3 workbook. Keep the workbook open for the next lesson, or close the workbook and exit Excel.

Exam Note: Other Alignment Options

Toolbar buttons are provided for only the six most common alignment options. You can access all alignment options by selecting F<u>o</u>rmat, C<u>e</u>lls and choosing the Alignment tab in the Format Cells dialog box.

A label describing data often takes up more space than its associated data. For example, a column heading might be Days to Ship, while the data in cells below comprise no more than two characters (it assumes no higher than 99 days to ship an order). Several options on the Alignment tab of the Format Cells dialog box enable you to keep columns narrow and still display longer labels. You can choose <u>W</u>rap Text when you want to enter more than one line of text within a cell. As you type, the text automatically wraps to the next line in the cell. You can choose Shrin<u>k</u> to Fit when you want to reduce the appearance of text to fit within the displayed column width.

Excel also supports aligning text vertically within a cell, such as at the top or centered rather than at the bottom. You can also rotate text or display text vertically, one character above the next.

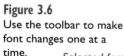 ## Lesson 3: Changing Font and Font Size

You can dramatically improve the appearance of your worksheet by using different fonts. Used as a general term, **font** refers to the type style, type size, and type attributes that you apply to text and numbers. As a specific command in Excel, font refers to the **typeface**—a style of print such as Arial, Courier, or Times New Roman. The default font in an Excel worksheet is Arial.

Type size is measured in points. A **point** is a unit of measurement that is used in printing and publishing to designate the height of type. An inch has roughly 72 points. The default type size in a worksheet is 10 points.

Toolbar buttons let you quickly apply a single formatting characteristic, such as a different font or font size. You can also change typeface, type size, and type attributes by using the Font dialog box, which enables you to preview and apply many formatting characteristics at one time.

In this lesson, you use toolbar buttons to change the font and font size of the worksheet title Glenn Lakes Golf Course, as shown in Figure 3.6.

Figure 3.6
Use the toolbar to make font changes one at a time.

Selected font for the current cell

Click here to view available fonts

Selected font size for the current cell

Click here to view available font sizes

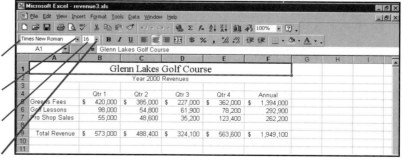

To Change Font and Font Size

1 **Open the** Revenue3 **workbook, if necessary, and click cell A1.**

This selects the cell containing the title Glenn Lakes Golf Course, even though the title displays in cells C and D.

2 **Click the down arrow to the right of the current font (see Figure 3.6).**

3 **In the Font drop-down list, select Times New Roman.**

The typeface you want to apply to the active cell is selected. You might have to use the scroll arrows to scroll through the list of fonts to get to Times New Roman.

4 **Click the down arrow to the right of the current font size on the toolbar.**

5 **In the Size drop-down list, select 16.**

The font size increases to 16 points. Notice that the row height automatically adjusts to accommodate the new font size.

6 **Check that the title in your worksheet reflects the changes in font and font size shown in Figure 3.6, and click the Save button on the toolbar.**

Excel saves your changes to the Revenue3 workbook. Keep the workbook open for the next lesson, or close the workbook and exit Excel.

Inside Stuff: **Selecting Fonts**

To open the Format Cells dialog box quickly, right-click the active cell and choose Format Cells from the shortcut menu. Click the Font tab to see additional font options. The fonts available in the Font list vary, depending on the software installed on your computer and the printer(s) you use.

To scroll through the Font drop-down list quickly, start typing the name of the font you want to apply. Excel locates the fonts alphabetically.

Lesson 4: Applying Bold, Italic, and Underline

You can use buttons on the toolbar to apply three common font attributes—**bold**, *italic*, and underline. To change attributes (called **font styles** in Excel), simply select the cells that you want to format, and click the relevant button on the Formatting toolbar. To remove an attribute, click its button again.

In this lesson, you bold the subtitle Year 2000 Revenues and apply italic to another label, as shown in Figure 3.7.

Figure 3.7
Bold the subtitle in cell
A2 and italicize the label
in cell A9.

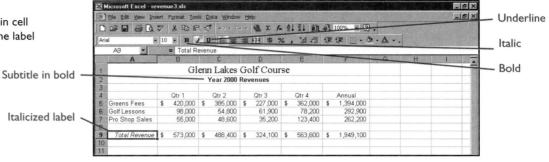

Underline

Italic

Bold

Subtitle in bold

Italicized label

To Apply Bold and Italic

1 **Open the** Revenue3 **workbook, if necessary, and click cell A2.**
The cell containing the subtitle Year 2000 Revenues is selected, even though
the subtitle displays in cells C2 and D2.

B

2 **Click the Bold button on the toolbar.**

3 **Click cell A9.**
The cell containing the label Total Revenue is selected.

I

4 **Click the Italic button on the toolbar.**

5 **Check that the subtitle in cell A2 and the label in cell A9 reflect the
changes in font style shown in Figure 3.7, and click the Save button
on the Standard toolbar.**
Excel saves your changes to the Revenue3 workbook. Keep the workbook
open for the next lesson, or close the workbook and exit Excel.

 Exam Note: **Applying Formats**
The Font tab in the Format Cells dialog box includes a Bold Italic option. You
can also apply color and select among a variety of underline styles (Single,
Double, Single Accounting, Double Accounting) and special effects
(Strikethrough, Superscript, Subscript).

You can also apply font styles to individual characters within a cell rather than
the entire cell's contents. To do so, double-click the cell, drag to select the
characters you want to format, apply the format, and press ⏎Enter.

 ## Lesson 5: Adding Color

The selective use of color can enhance the appearance of a worksheet. You can apply
color to cell contents, to the background of a cell, or to a border surrounding cells. In this
lesson, you display the worksheet title in blue and apply a green background to the column headings for quarters, as shown in Figure 3.8.

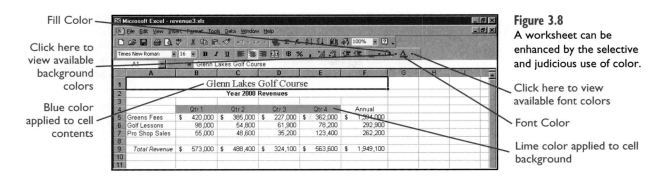

Fill Color

Click here to view available background colors

Blue color applied to cell contents

Figure 3.8
A worksheet can be enhanced by the selective and judicious use of color.

Click here to view available font colors

Font Color

Lime color applied to cell background

To Add Color

1 **Open the Revenue3 workbook, if necessary, and click cell A1.**
The cell containing the title Glenn Lakes Golf Course is selected, even though the title displays in the range B1:E1.

2 **Click the down arrow to the right of the Font Color button on the toolbar.**
A palette of 40 colors displays. If you position the mouse pointer on a color square and pause, you see the name assigned to that color.

3 **Click the Blue square in the Font color palette.**
The title Glenn Lakes Golf Course displays blue, as shown in Figure 3.8.

X *If You Have Problems...*
If the background displays in blue instead of the text, you used Fill Color instead of Font Color. Click Undo on the toolbar to reverse the incorrect action.

---

4 **Select cells B4 through E4.**
The column headings for quarters 1 through 4 are selected.

5 **Click the down arrow to the right of the Fill Color button on the toolbar.**
A palette of 40 colors displays.

6 **Click the Lime square in the Fill Color palette, and click cell A1.**
The backgrounds of cells B4 through E4 display lime green, as shown in Figure 3.8.

7 **Check that the colors applied to your worksheet match those shown in Figure 3.8, and click Save.**
Excel saves your changes to the Revenue3 workbook. Keep the workbook open for the next lesson, or close the workbook and exit Excel.

Exam Note: **Applying Patterns**

You can draw attention to selected worksheet cells by shading with a pattern. A *pattern* repeats an effect, such as a horizontal, vertical, or diagonal stripe. To apply a pattern, select the Patterns tab in the Format Cells dialog box, and display the Patterns drop-down list. Choose one of 18 predefined settings that include crosshatch and stripe patterns as well as various percentages of gray. The default pattern color is black, but you can select from a palette of colors.

 Inside Stuff: **Color Concerns in Printed Worksheets**

You can apply more than one color setting to a cell, such as blue text, yellow background, and red border. However, overuse of color may be distracting. Also color may be an effective enhancement when viewing a worksheet on-screen, but its use can produce printed output that is hard to read, especially if you are not printing on a color printer. For best results when printing, keep the choices of colors and patterns simple.

 # Lesson 6: Adding Borders

A *border* is a solid or dashed line that is applied to one or more sides of a cell or range of cells. You can use a border as a divider between cell entries. Selective use of borders can also help to focus a user's attention on a specific section of a worksheet.

You can use the Borders button on the toolbar to select among twelve common border styles. Additional options—including one to apply color to a border—are available on the Borders tab of the Format Cells dialog box.

In this lesson, you set up two borders (see Figure 3.9): one using the toolbar and the other using the Format Cells dialog box.

Figure 3.9
The selective use of borders can improve readability.

Red outline border applied to the range F4:F9

Bottom border applied to the range B7:F7

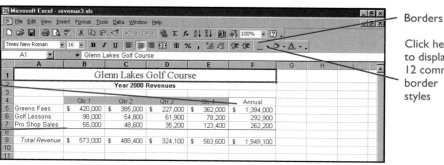

Borders

Click here to display 12 common border styles

To Add a Border

❶ **Open the Revenue3 workbook, if necessary, and select the range B7:F7.**

The cells containing numbers and a formula related to Pro Shop Sales are selected.

2 **Click the down arrow to the right of the Borders button on the toolbar.**
A palette of 12 border styles displays.

3 **Position the mouse pointer on the second border style in the first row—the style named Bottom Border (see Figure 3.10).**

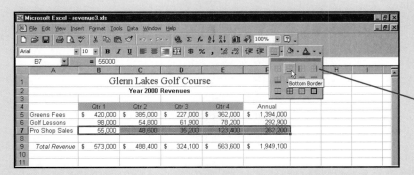

Figure 3.10
Clicking a border style applies it to the selected cells.

Palette of common border styles

4 **Click the border style named Bottom Border.**
Excel applies a solid black single-line border to the bottom edges of the selected cells (refer to row 7 in Figure 3.9).

5 **Select cells F4 through F9.**

6 **Choose Format, Cells.**
The Format Cells dialog box displays.

7 **Click the Border tab.**

8 **Click the down arrow to the right of the Color box and choose Red.**
The selected color displays in the color window (see Figure 3.11).

Creates a border surrounding selected cells

Click here to remove a border

Current settings display in the preview diagram

Applies the selected border style to the bottom of the cell(s)

Use buttons below, and to the left of, the preview diagram to apply the selected style in the direction indicated on the button

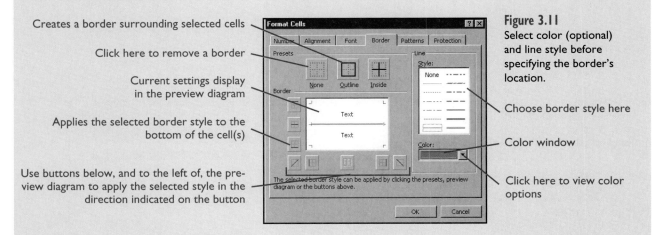

Figure 3.11
Select color (optional) and line style before specifying the border's location.

Choose border style here

Color window

Click here to view color options

9 **Click the Outline button in the Presets area, and click OK.**

10 **Deselect the range and check that the borders applied to your worksheet match those shown in Figure 3.9.**

11 **Make changes, if necessary, and click Save.**
Excel saves your changes to the Revenue3 workbook. Keep the workbook open for the next lesson, or close the workbook and exit Excel.

Exam Note: Applying a Border

The order in which you select options from the Border tab in the Format Cells dialog box is important. If you select border style and/or border color after selecting the border's position, Excel ignores the style and color settings. If the desired settings do not display in the preview diagram, select the style and color again and then specify location.

 Lesson 7: Using Format Painter

Excel provides a Format Painter button that you can use to copy formatting applied to worksheet cells. The Format Painter makes it possible to apply existing formats without opening dialog boxes or making multiple selections from toolbars. In this lesson, you copy the color and alignment settings for the quarterly column headings to the row descriptions of revenue sources (see Figure 3.12).

Figure 3.12
The formats applied to B4 are copied to the range A5:A7.

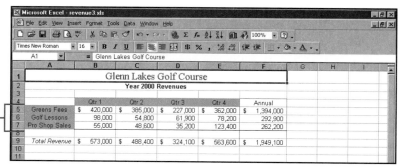

Copied formats: center alignment and lime fill color

To Copy Formats Using Format Painter

1 Open the Revenue3 workbook, if necessary, and click cell B4.

2 Click the Format Painter button on the toolbar.
A flashing dotted line displays around the selected cell (see Figure 3.13).

Figure 3.13
Formats to be copied include center alignment and lime fill color.

Format Painter is active

Format Painter copies the formats applied to the selected cell(s)

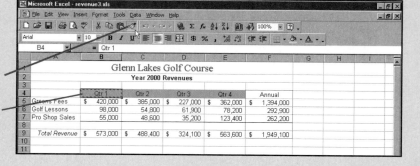

3 Move the mouse pointer towards cell A5.
The pointer changes to a white block cross. A paintbrush displays to the right of the cross.

4 **Select cells A5 through A7, release the mouse button, and deselect the range.**

Excel applies center alignment and a lime fill color to the specified cells in column A.

5 **Check that the formats applied to your worksheet match those shown in Figure 3.12, and click Save.**

Excel saves your changes to the Revenue3 workbook. Keep the workbook open for the last lesson in this project, or close the workbook and exit Excel.

Exam Note: **Using Format Painter**

If you single-click the Format Painter button to start a copy operation, the feature automatically turns off as soon as you select the target range. If you want to copy formatting to more than one location, double-click the Format Painter button to start the copy. The feature remains active until you click the Format Painter button again.

Inside Stuff: **Copying Column Widths**

You can use Format Painter to copy a column width. Select the heading of a column that is already set to the desired width, click the Format Painter button, and click the heading of the column you want to change.

Lesson 8: Removing Formatting

The quickest way to remove all applied formats is to select the cell(s) and choose Edit, Clear, Formats. If you want to remove some, but not all, of the formats applied to a cell, you must remove the effects one at a time. In most cases, you start the process to apply the format, and then select an option to restore the default setting (such as Automatic to remove color or None to remove a border). Some effects can be removed by choosing a related button on the toolbar, such as Left Align to remove centering, Decrease Indent to remove indenting, or one of the Decimal buttons to adjust number of decimal places.

In this lesson, you remove one format (a border), and then remove multiple formats with a single command (centering and fill color).

To Remove Formatting

1 **Open the Revenue3 workbook, if necessary, and select the range F4:F9.**

The cells surrounded with a red border are selected.

2 **Choose Format, Cells and select the Border tab.**

3 **Click None in the Presets area, and click OK.**

Excel removes the single-line red border surrounding the range F4:F9. Now, remove multiple formats with a single command.

continues ▶

To Remove Formatting (continued)

4 Select the range A5:A7; then choose Edit, Clear.

Four options display on the Clear menu (see Figure 3.14). The first option re-moves both contents and formats. Choose the second option to remove only formats.

Figure 3.14
Use the Edit, Clear menu if you want to remove only formats or both formats and contents.

Removes contents and formats

Removes only formats

Removes only contents

Removes comments

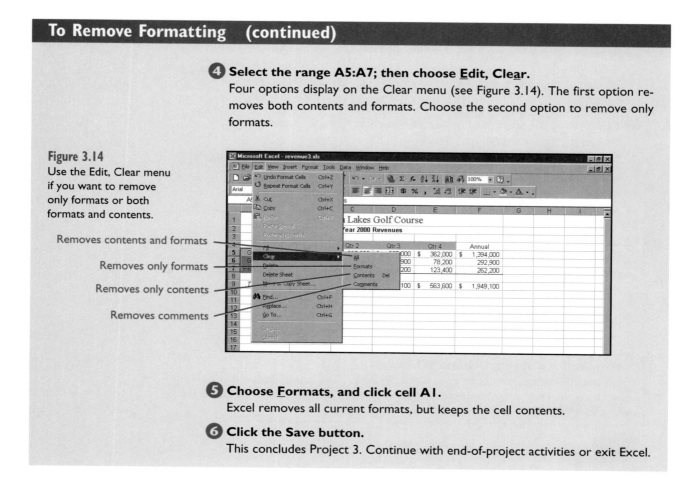

5 Choose Formats, and click cell A1.

Excel removes all current formats, but keeps the cell contents.

6 Click the Save button.

This concludes Project 3. Continue with end-of-project activities or exit Excel.

Summary

In this project, you learned how to apply the most basic formatting options. Your experiences focused primarily on using toolbar buttons to apply effects to selected cell(s) quickly. You formatted numbers in currency and comma styles, centered cell contents across columns and within cells, indented text, changed font style, increased font size, applied bold and italics, added color and borders, copied formats using Format Painter, and removed formats.

You can extend your learning by practicing variations of the techniques presented in the lessons. Experiment with different number formats, including date and percent. Explore different options in the Format Cells dialog box, such as discovering the difference between Double underline and Accounting Double underline. Use onscreen Help to get information and try out Excel's AutoFormat and Conditional Formatting features.

Checking Concepts and Terms ✓

True/False

For each of the following, check *T* or *F* to indicate whether the statement is true or false.

__T __F   **1.** Numbers can be formatted only as dates, currency, and general numbers. [L1]

__T __F   **2.** By default, when you enter data into a cell, numbers align to the left side of a cell and text aligns to the right side of a cell. [L2]

__T __F   **3.** When you apply formatting, it applies to the worksheet cell—not to the text, number, or formula entered in the cell. [L1]

__T __F   **4.** You can apply combinations of font styles such as bold, italic, and underline to the same cell. [L4]

__T __F   **5.** Excel removes formats and contents if you select a range of cells and press the Del key. [L8]

Multiple Choice

Circle the letter of the correct answer for each of the following.

1. Which of the following is a font style rather than a typeface? [L3]

   a. Italic

   b. Times New Roman

   c. Arial

   d. Courier

2. Which of the following number formats cannot be applied by using a toolbar button? [L1]

   a. currency

   b. percent

   c. date

   d. comma

3. Which of the following is true about the use of color in a worksheet? [L5]

   a. You can click the Font Color button to apply a color to the background of a cell.

   b. You can click the Patterns button to apply one of 18 predefined patterns.

   c. Excel supports applying color three ways—to cell contents, to the backgrounds of cells, and to borders around cells—but you cannot apply more than one technique to a cell.

   d. None of the above are true.

4. Which of the following best describes the effect(s) of increasing font size? [L3]

   a. Row height automatically adjusts, but column width does not.

   b. Column width automatically adjusts, but row height does not.

   c. Both row height and column width automatically adjust.

   d. Neither row height nor column width automatically adjust.

5. Which of the following is not a form of alignment supported by Excel? [L2]

   a. justify

   b. merge and center

   c. indent

   d. All of the above are supported by Excel.

Skill Drill

Skill Drill exercises reinforce project skills. Each skill reinforced is the same, or nearly the same, as a skill presented in the project. Detailed instructions are provided in a step-by-step format.

Each exercise is independent of the others, so you can complete the exercises in any order. Be sure to save the workbook after completing each exercise. If you need a paper copy of the completed exercise, enter your name centered in a header before printing. Other print options have already been set to print compressed to one page and to display the filename, sheet name, and current date in a footer.

Before beginning your first Project 3 Skill Drill exercise, complete the following steps:

1. Open the file named **e-0302** and save it as **e3drill**.

The Community Volunteer Corps (CVC) workbook contains four sheets: an overview, and exercise sheets named #1-Format, #2-Border, and #3-Remove.

2. Click the Overview sheet to view the organization of the Project 3 Skill Drill Exercises workbook.

If you need more than one work session to complete the desired exercises, continue working on **e3drill** instead of starting over on the original e-0302 file.

1. Formatting Numbers

Having completed a simple worksheet to summarize volunteer hours at the Community Volunteer Corps, you decide to add some enhancements to make the data more readable. You want to display volunteer hours without decimal places by using the comma as a thousands separator. You also realize that the date in the worksheet doesn't display in a common date format. You want the date represented by the number to display in the form mm/dd/yyyy (for example 2/25/2000).

To make the desired formatting changes:

1. If necessary, open the **e3drill** workbook; then click the sheet tab named #1-Format.

2. Select the range B9:F12.

3. Click the Comma Style button on the toolbar.

4. Click the Decrease Decimal button twice.

5. Select cell F5.

6. Choose Format, Cells, and click the Number tab.

7. Select the Date category.

8. Select the mm/dd/yyyy format near the bottom of the list of date formats.

2. Adding Borders

To enhance the appearance of your worksheet by separating data from labels and totals, you decide to add a border around cells containing volunteer hours.

To add a gold, double-line border:

1. If necessary, open the **e3drill** workbook; then click the sheet tab named #2-Border.

2. Select the range B9:E11.

3. Choose Format, Cells, and select the Border tab in the Format Cells dialog box.

4. Select the double-line style.

5. Display the drop-down palette of colors, and select Gold.

6. Click Outline in the Presets area, and click OK.

3. Removing Formats

You have applied several formats to the Community Volunteer Corps worksheet and now you want to remove one or more of them. You decide you don't like the underline effect you applied to offset data from total hours. You also plan to remove all formatting applied to the names of volunteer organizations.

To remove formats:

1. If necessary, open the **e3drill** workbook; then click the sheet tab named #3-Remove.

2. Select the range B11:F11.

3. Choose Format, Cells, and select the Font tab in the Format Cells dialog box.

4. Click the down arrow at the right end of the Underline window, select None from the list of Underline options, and click OK.

5. Select the range A9:A11, which contains 12-point right-aligned labels with a light green background.

6. Choose Edit, Clear, Formats.

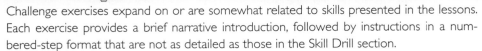

Challenge

Challenge exercises expand on or are somewhat related to skills presented in the lessons. Each exercise provides a brief narrative introduction, followed by instructions in a numbered-step format that are not as detailed as those in the Skill Drill section.

Each exercise is independent of the others, so you can complete the exercises in any order. Be sure to save the workbook after completing each exercise. If you need a paper copy of the completed exercise, enter your name centered in a header before printing. Other print options have already been set to print compressed to one page and to display the filename, sheet name, and current date in a footer.

Before beginning your first Project 3 Challenge exercise, complete the following steps:

1. Open the file named **e-0303** and save it as **e3challenge**.

   The e3challenge workbook contains five sheets: a scenario, an overview, and exercise sheets named #1-Format, #2-Indent, and #3-Pattern.

2. Click the Scenario and Overview sheets to view the context and organization of the Project 3 Challenge Exercises workbook.

If you need more than one work session to complete the desired exercises, continue working on **e3challenge** instead of starting over on the original e-0303 file.

1. Formatting Numbers and Dates

You have received the five-year trend analysis for Flowers Your Way, Inc. and it is now your job to improve the appearance of the worksheet for the next meeting of the managers. You don't like the formatting that someone else applied. You decide to correct the date format and remove other formatting (but not the data).

To remove formatting and change the date format:

1. If necessary, open your **e3challenge** workbook; then click the sheet tab named #1-Format.

2. Select the cell range A9:F24.

3. Choose an option on the Edit menu to remove all formatting in the selected range (don't remove the contents).

If You Have Problems...
If you accidentally clear the contents of the range, use Undo to reverse the action and try again.

4. Select cell E6, containing a number that displays in a comma format with two decimal places instead of as a date.

5. Apply the long date format (in the form of March 14, 1998) to cell E6.

   Recall that dates are numbers—when ####### appears in a cell, it means that the cell contents are too long to display in the cell.

6. Display the full date by centering the contents of cell E6 across the two cells E6 and F6.

7. Apply the Comma Style (zero decimal places) to Total Sales amounts in row 24.

2. Indenting Cell Contents

As you look for ways to improve the readability of the Flowers Your Way worksheet, you decide to offset each occurrence of the labels Corporate and Individual a few characters from the left edge of their respective cells. You decide to indent the labels describing totals for each of the three sources of sales even further (In Store, Phone/Fax, and the Web).

You want to apply these changes as quickly and efficiently as possible. Therefore you plan to use a combination of selecting nonadjacent cells and clicking the Increase Indent button once or twice.

To apply indenting to multiple, nonadjacent cells:

1. If necessary, open your **e3challenge** workbook; then click the sheet tab named #2-Indent.

2. Hold down Ctrl and select the following cell ranges: A10:A11, A15:A16, and A20:A21.

3. Click the Increase Indent toolbar button.

4. Select the nonadjacent cells that label the totals for the three sources of sales (cells A12, A17, and A22) and double-indent cell contents.

3. Applying a Pattern Instead of a Color

You know how to apply a color background to a cell or range of cells by using the Color Fill button on the toolbar. You also know that additional options for shading cells can be found on the Font tab of the Format Cells dialog box. Assume that you do not have access to a color printer, and experiment with applying a black and white pattern instead of color to enhance the appearance of the printed output.

To apply a pattern:

1. If necessary, open your **e3challenge** workbook; then click the sheet tab named #3-Pattern.

2. Select the column headings and data for the years 1996, 1998, and 2000 (the ranges B8:B24, D8:D24, and F8:F24).

3. Display the Patterns tab in the Format Cells dialog box.

4. Display the Pattern options by clicking the arrow at the right end of the Pattern window located in the lower-left corner of the dialog box.

5. Move the mouse pointer back and forth over the 18 options at the top of the pattern drop-down list (the first three rows, six samples per row).

Resting the mouse pointer on a sample displays its description, such as 6.25% Gray for the upper-right sample.

6. Select 12.5% Gray, and click OK.

7. Deselect the cells to view the results, and look at the pattern effect by using Print Preview.

8. Print the worksheet (optional).

You will probably find that the pattern effect is much clearer on the printed output than it appeared to be onscreen.

Discovery Zone

Discovery Zone exercises require an advanced knowledge of the topics presented in *MOUS Essentials* lessons, application of skills from multiple lessons, or self-directed learning of new skills.

Each exercise is independent of the others, so you can complete the exercises in any order. Be sure to save the workbook after completing each exercise. If you need a paper copy of the completed exercise, enter your name centered in a header before printing. Other print options have already been set to print compressed to one page and to display the filename, sheet name, and current date in a footer.

Before beginning your first Project 3 Discovery Zone exercise, complete the following steps:

1. Open the file named `e-0304` and save it as `e3discovery`.

The e3discovery workbook contains four sheets: a scenario, an overview, and two exercise sheets named #1-AutoFormat and #2-Text Orientation.

2. Click the Scenario and Overview sheets to view the context and organization of the Project 3 Discovery Zone Exercises workbook.

If you need more than one work session to complete the desired exercises, continue working on `e3discovery` instead of starting over on the original e-0304 file.

1. Using AutoFormat to Improve the Appearance of a List

You are looking for ways to enhance the appearance of the Telemarketing Sales data for Flowers Your Way, Inc. You heard about a feature called AutoFormat, which enables you to choose among a variety of predefined formats, and now you want to try it out.

Before you begin, use onscreen Help to learn how to apply an AutoFormat. When you are ready, select an AutoFormat for the data in the range A5:F16 on the sheet named #1-AutoFormat in your e3discovery workbook. Adjust column width, as necessary. Undo the initial AutoFormat, and experiment with applying number formats before and after applying an AutoFormat. Why would it be best to apply a number format, such as comma, before applying an AutoFormat? Before you save your final version, apply some of the other enhancements that you learned in Project 3.

2. Changing the Text Orientation of Column Headings

You have an idea in mind of how to align column headings, as shown in Figure 3.15.

Figure 3.15
**Creating eye-catching
column headings.**

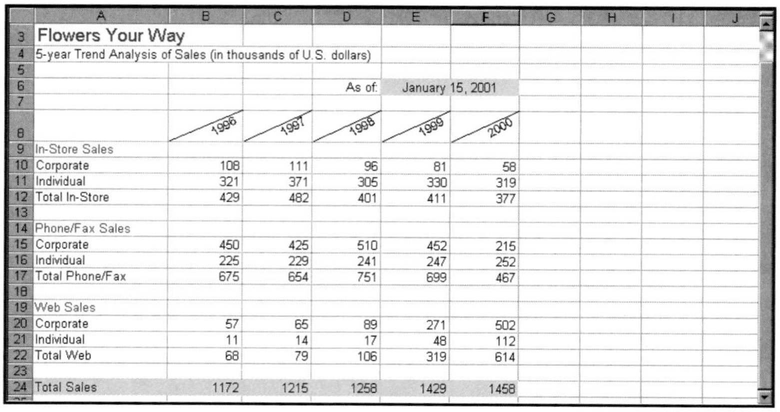

	A	B	C	D	E	F	G	H	I	J
3	Flowers Your Way									
4	5-year Trend Analysis of Sales (in thousands of U.S. dollars)									
5										
6				As of:	January 15, 2001					
7										
8		1996	1997	1998	1999	2000				
9	In-Store Sales									
10	Corporate	108	111	96	81	58				
11	Individual	321	371	305	330	319				
12	Total In-Store	429	482	401	411	377				
13										
14	Phone/Fax Sales									
15	Corporate	450	425	510	452	215				
16	Individual	225	229	241	247	252				
17	Total Phone/Fax	675	654	751	699	467				
18										
19	Web Sales									
20	Corporate	57	65	89	271	502				
21	Individual	11	14	17	48	112				
22	Total Web	68	79	106	319	614				
23										
24	Total Sales	1172	1215	1258	1429	1458				

Learn all you can about changing the orientation of text by using onscreen Help. Also, study the orientation options on the Alignment tab of the Format Cells dialog box. When you are ready, modify the worksheet named #2-Text Orientation in your e3discovery workbook to include the text orientation and other enhancements shown in Figure 3.15.

PinPoint Assessment

You have completed this project and its associated lessons, and have had an opportunity to assess your skills through the end-of-project questions and exercises. Now use the PinPoint software Evaluation Mode to further assess your comprehension of the specific exam activities you have just learned. You can also use the PinPoint Trainer Mode and the Show Me tutorials to practice these exam activities.

Entering Formulas in Well-Designed Worksheets

Key terms introduced in this project include

- comparison operator
- concatenation operator
- order of precedence
- reference operator

Objectives	Required Activity for MOUS	Exam Level
➤ Work with Operators and Order of Precedence		
➤ Use Type-and-Point to Enter Formulas	Enter formulas in a cell and using the formula bar	Core
➤ Compare Absolute and Relative Cell References	Use references (absolute and relative)	Core
➤ Create and Copy Formulas with Absolute and Relative Cell References	Use references (absolute and relative); Use AutoSum	Core
➤ Freeze and Split the Worksheet Display	Freeze and unfreeze rows and columns	Core
➤ Hide and Unhide Rows and Columns	Hide and unhide rows and columns	Core
➤ Display Formulas Instead of Formula Results		
➤ Use Save As to Change File Name, File Type, or Storage Location	Use Save As (different name, location, format)	Core

Why Would I Do This?

n previous projects, you created a simple worksheet containing one formula. By copying that formula, you were able to expand the worksheet quickly. Through those experiences, you acquired the basic skills needed to develop larger and more complex worksheets.

Multiple formulas add complexity to a worksheet. Larger worksheets exceed the viewing area on the screen and require multiple-page printouts. Excel provides a variety of ways to create and copy formulas, display formulas, and view more than one area of a worksheet at a time.

You should plan the layout of each worksheet in a workbook before you begin to enter constants and formulas. In this project, you create the worksheet shown in Figure 4.1. The worksheet contains monthly and annual data.

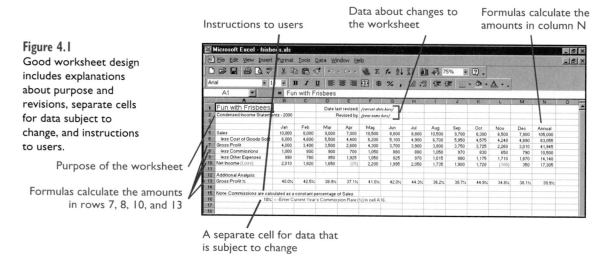

Instructions to users

Data about changes to the worksheet

Formulas calculate the amounts in column N

Figure 4.1
Good worksheet design includes explanations about purpose and revisions, separate cells for data subject to change, and instructions to users.

Purpose of the worksheet

Formulas calculate the amounts in rows 7, 8, 10, and 13

A separate cell for data that is subject to change

Lesson 1: Working with Operators and Order of Precedence

The terms formula and arithmetic operator were introduced in Project 1, "Getting Started with Excel 2000." You used the arithmetic operator (+) to add the contents of two cells. While learning about onscreen Help, you used the Help feature to read about the order in which Excel performs calculations—sometimes referred to as the **order of precedence**. For example, you learned that multiplication and division take place before addition and subtraction.

The terms AutoSum and function were introduced in Project 2, "Modifying a Worksheet." In that project, you used AutoSum to enter the function =SUM(B5:E5). The colon (:) connected the first and last cells of the range to be summed. The colon is an example of a **reference operator**, which is used to combine cell references in calculations.

Excel provides two other types of operators: comparison and concatenation. A **comparison operator** is used to test the relationship between two items, such as finding out whether the items are equal or if one is greater than the other. A **concatenation operator** joins one or more text entries to form a single entry.

This lesson provides a more in-depth look at operators and the order of calculations than was provided in Projects 1 and 2. If you understand the order of precedence and how to modify that order by using parentheses, you have the minimum skills required to create and edit formulas and functions.

To Work with Operators and Order of Precedence

1 **Open the file** e-0401 **and save it as** Frisbees.

2 **Click the sheet tab named Operators.**

The Operators worksheet displays four categories of operators: arithmetic, comparison, text concatenation, and reference (see Figure 4.2). The symbol to type for each operator appears in red.

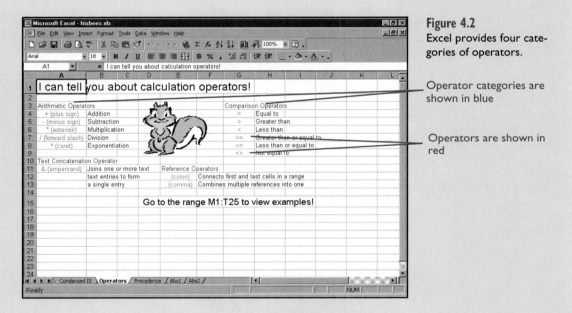

Figure 4.2
Excel provides four categories of operators.

Operator categories are shown in blue

Operators are shown in red

3 **After studying the categories of operators, display columns M through T on the screen, starting with row I.**

This area of the worksheet contains one example for each operator category (see Figure 4.3).

4 **Click cell N6.**

A formula that contains the arithmetic operator for multiplication (*) appears in the formula bar.

5 **Click cell N11.**

An IF function that contains the comparison operator for greater than or equal to (>=) appears in the formula bar. The operator tests whether the contents of cell N9 (Actual Net Income) are greater than or equal to the contents of cell N10 (Target Net Income) and displays one of two messages, depending on whether the comparison is true or false. You work with IF functions in Project 5, "Working with Functions."

continues ▶

To Work with Operators and Order of Precedence (continued)

Figure 4.3
An arrow points to each cell that contains an operator in the formula.

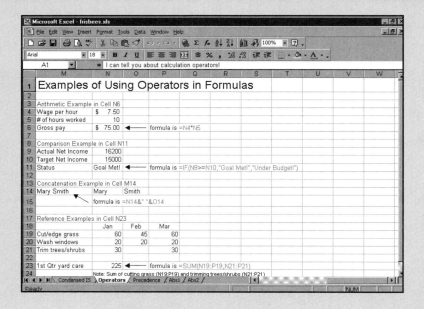

6 Click cell M14.

A formula that contains the concatenate operator (&) appears in the formula bar. The formula joins the contents of cells N14 and O14 and adds a space between the first and last names. Quotation marks surround literal text in a formula. Literal text is text that does not change—in this case, the blank space.

7 Click cell N23.

A formula that contains the reference operators colon (:) and comma (,) appears in the formula bar. The colon marks the beginning and ending cells in a range; the comma separates the ranges in the formula.

8 Click the sheet tab named Precedence.

A text box containing the question What is 5 plus 3 times 2? appears near the top of the worksheet. How would you answer the question?

9 Click cell D8.

The formula =5+3*2 appears in the formula bar; the formula result displays in cell D8. Excel first multiplies 3*2, and then adds the result (6) to the number 5.

10 Click cell D12.

The formula =(5+3)*2 appears in the formula bar; the formula result displays in cell D12. Operations within parentheses take precedence over those not encased in parentheses. In this case, Excel first adds the numbers 5 and 3, and then multiplies the result (8) by 2.

11 After studying the two examples, display columns M through R on the screen, starting with row 1.

This area of the worksheet lists the order of Excel operations in formulas (see Figure 4.4). Keep this order in mind as you construct your own formulas.

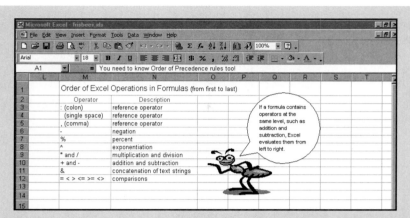

Figure 4.4
Order of precedence refers to the order in which Excel performs calculations, based on a formula containing multiple operators.

This concludes the overview of operators and the order in which Excel performs calculations. Now that you have a better understanding of operators and order of calculations, you are ready to enter the five formulas needed to complete the condensed income statements for Fun with Frisbees. Keep the Frisbees workbook open for the next lesson, or close the workbook and exit Excel.

Lesson 2: Using Type-and-Point to Enter Formulas

You can complete the design of the Condensed IS worksheet for Fun with Frisbees by entering five formulas and copying them to related cells. One of the formulas involves addition—computing annual sales as the sum of sales for each month. Calculations performed by the other formulas include subtraction, multiplication, and division.

You can easily create a basic formula by typing an equation into a cell, as you did in Project 1 to add the contents of two cells. You can also enter a cell or range of cells in a formula by clicking the cell or selecting the range of cells in the worksheet. This simplifies the process of creating a formula and also helps to ensure that you enter the correct cell addresses.

In this lesson, you use the type-and-point method to create a Gross Profit formula. This is the first of five formulas needed to complete the Condensed Income Statements for Fun with Frisbees.

To Use Type-and-Point to Enter Formulas

1 **Open the Frisbees workbook, if necessary, and click the sheet tab named Condensed IS.**

2 **Click cell B7, and click the equal button on the formula bar.**
Excel displays the formula palette and inserts an equal sign in the formula bar (see Figure 4.5).

To Use Type-and-Point to Enter Formulas (continued)

Figure 4.5
The first element of a formula is an equal sign.

Click here to display the most recently used functions

Click here to cancel the formula being constructed

Click here to enter the formula being constructed

Click here to start a formula and display the formula palette

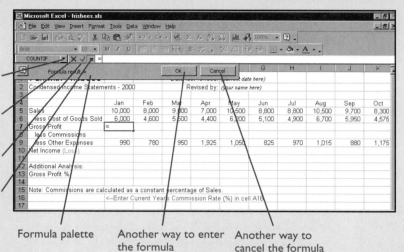

Formula palette   Another way to enter the formula   Another way to cancel the formula

3 **Click cell B5.**
=B5 appears in the formula bar and in cell B7.

4 **Type a minus sign, and click cell B6.**
Excel enters –B6 into the formula (see Figure 4.6). A flashing dotted line appears around cell B6 to remind you that it is the cell you selected for the formula. The result of the formula also appears in the formula palette.

Figure 4.6
The formula under construction appears in its worksheet cell and in the formula bar.

A dotted line surrounds the most recently selected cell

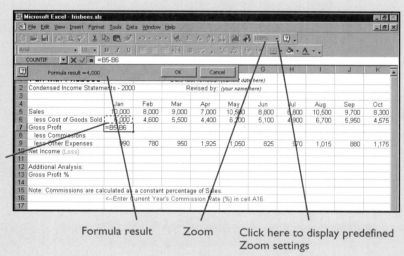

Formula result   Zoom   Click here to display predefined Zoom settings

5 **Click OK in the formula palette.**
You can also click the Enter button on the formula bar (a green check mark) or press ⏎Enter in place of Step 5. Excel enters the formula to calculate January's Gross Profit in cell B7 and closes the formula palette. Now, set Zoom to 75% and copy the formula to calculate Gross Profit for the other months.

6 **Display the drop-down list of predefined Zoom percentages (refer to the toolbar in Figure 4.6) and select 75%.**
All months—January through December—display.

7 **Click cell B7 and position the mouse pointer on the lower-right corner of the cell.**

8 **Press the left mouse button, drag the fill handle right to cell M7, and release the mouse button.**

Excel fills the range C7:M7 with the formula and displays the results of the formula in each cell (see Figure 4.7). The copied formulas are relative to their locations: =C5–C6 in column C, =D5–D6 in column D, =E5–E6 in column E, and so forth.

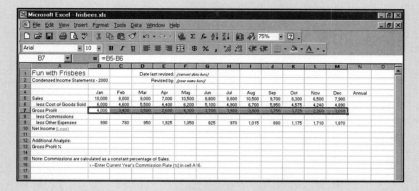

Figure 4.7
You can enter the gross profit formula for January and copy it to calculate gross profit amounts for the other months.

9 **Click any cell to deselect the highlighted range.**

10 **Save your changes to the Frisbees workbook.**

You entered and copied the first of five formulas needed to complete the condensed income statements for Fun with Frisbees. The next formula requires an understanding of when to use absolute cell references and how to create them. Keep the `Frisbees` workbook open for the next lesson, or close the workbook and exit Excel.

Lesson 3: Comparing Absolute and Relative Cell References

As explained briefly in Project 1, each reference to a cell in a formula is a relative reference if the row and/or column cell references change as a formula is copied. If you don't want Excel to adjust a reference to a cell when you copy a formula, use an absolute reference to that cell in the formula.

You may find it easier to understand the concept of relative and absolute cell references if you compare the effects of copying with and without absolute cell references. In this lesson, you view results of copying a formula that is similar to the one needed for the Fun with Frisbees workbook. In the first example, copying a formula with only relative cell references produces errors. In the second example, changing one cell reference to absolute—by placing a dollar sign ($) in front of both the column letter and row number—produces correct results.

To Compare Absolute and Relative Cell References

1 **Open the `Frisbees` workbook, if necessary, select the sheet tab named Abs1, and click cell B9.**

Case 1 displays, showing errors after copying the Commissions formula =B8*A4 from B9 to C9:E9.

2 **Click cell C9.**

In cell C9, #VALUE! displays, indicating an error in the formula =C8*B4. The formula tells Excel to multiply Qtr 2 Sales by the contents of cell B4. Excel cannot multiply an amount by a label.

3 **Click cell D9.**

The number 0 displays in cell D9, indicating an error in the formula =D8*C4. The formula tells Excel to multiply Qtr 3 Sales by the contents of cell C4, which is blank. Multiplying a value by zero produces zero as the result.

4 **Read the analysis provided in the Problem text box, select the sheet tab named Abs2, and click cell B9.**

Case 2 displays, showing the correct results after copying the Commissions formula =B8*$A$4 from B9 to C9:E9 (see Figure 4.8).

Figure 4.8
Using an absolute cell reference corrects the errors in copy results.

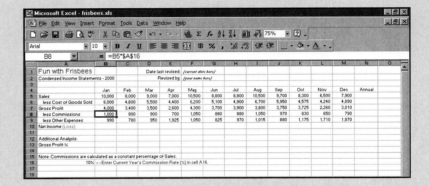

5 **Click cells C9, D9, and E9, one after the other. After selecting each cell, look at the associated formula in the formula bar.**

Formula results are consistent with the explanation provided in rows 11 through 16.

Keep the workbook open for the next lesson, or close the workbook and exit Excel.

 Exam Note: Using Mixed Cell References

You already know that you can mix relative and absolute cell references in a formula. For example, the previous Case 2 showed the effects of copying the formula =B8*$A$4. In that formula, the reference to cell B8 is relative and the reference to cell A4 is absolute. You can also mix relative and absolute settings within a single cell reference, if needed to produce the desired copy results.

Inside Stuff: **Using F4 to Make Cell References Absolute**
Excel can enter the dollar sign(s) to make one or more parts of a cell reference absolute. While you create or edit a formula, click within a cell reference and press F4 until you get the desired result (such as =$B$8, =B$8, =$B8, or =B8).

Lesson 4: Creating and Copying Formulas with Absolute or Relative Cell References

Now that you have a better understanding of the effects on copying with absolute references in formulas, you can enter the remaining formulas in the Condensed IS worksheet of the Frisbees workbook.

To Enter and Copy Formulas with Absolute or Relative Cell References

1 **Open the Frisbees workbook, if necessary, and click cell A16 in the Condensed IS worksheet.**
The cell in which to enter the current year's commission rate is selected.

2 **Type 10% and press Enter.**

3 **Click cell B8, and enter the formula =B5*$A$16.**
The formula multiplies January Sales (B5) by the current commission rate (A16).

4 **Drag the formula to fill the range C8:M8, and click any cell to deselect the range.**
The copied formulas multiply February Sales through December Sales by the commission rate in A16 (see Figure 4.9).

Formula to copy

Check formula results in row 8

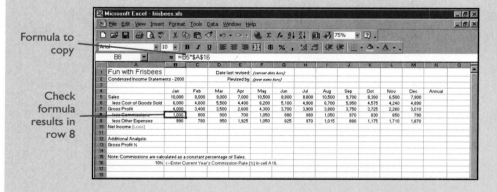

Figure 4.9
Calculated commission amounts appear in row 8.

 If You Have Problems...
If your calculated results in row 8 do not match those shown in Figure 4.9, you may have an incorrect or missing percentage in cell A16 or an error in the formula in cell B8, or you may have had trouble copying the formula. Check your work, correct any mistakes, and try the copy operation again.

continues ▶

To Enter and Copy Formulas with Absolute or Relative Cell References (continued)

5 **Click cell B10, and enter =B7-B8-B9 by typing the entire formula or by using the type-and-point technique.**

The formula =B7–B8–B9 in cell B10 calculates the 2,010 January Net Income by subtracting the contents of cells B8 (Commissions) and B9 (Other Expenses) from the amount in cell B7 (Gross Profit).

6 **Copy the formula in cell B10 to the range C10:M10 (see Figure 4.10).**

A negative amount indicates a net loss instead of net income (see cells E10 and L10). The cells in row 10 were previously formatted to display negative numbers in red within parentheses. (You learn about conditional formatting in Project 7, "Developing a Multiple-Sheet Workbook.")

Figure 4.10
Net income or net loss amounts appear in row 10.

Formula to copy

Check formula results in row 10

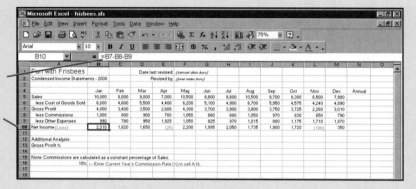

7 **Click cell N5, and click AutoSum on the toolbar.**

The formula =SUM(B5:M5) appears in the formula bar.

8 **Press ⏎Enter to accept the suggested range of cells to sum.**

Excel adds the contents of cells B5 through M5 and displays 105,000 as Annual Sales.

9 **Copy the formula in cell N5 to the range N6:N10, and deselect the range.**

Annual totals for other line items in the condensed income statement display in column N (see Figure 4.11).

Figure 4.11
Annual totals appear in column N.

Formula to copy

Check formula results in column N

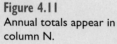
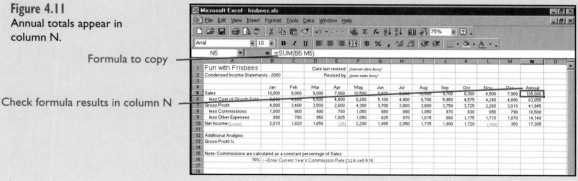

⑩ Click cell B13, and enter =B7/B5 by typing the entire formula or by using the type-and-point technique.

The formula =B7/B5 in cell B13 calculates the 40.0% January gross profit percentage by dividing the contents of cell B7 (gross profit) by the amount in cell B5 (sales).

⑪ Copy the formula in cell B13 to the range C13:N13, and deselect the range.

Gross profit percentages display in row 13 for each month and for the year (see Figure 4.12).

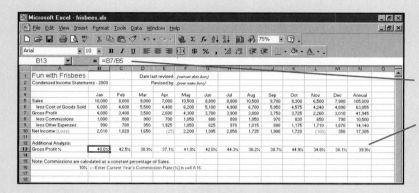

Figure 4.12
Gross profit percentages display in row 13.

Formula to copy

Check formula results in row 13

⑫ Save your changes to the Frisbees workbook.

The Condensed IS worksheet is complete. Keep the workbook open for the next lesson, in which you learn techniques to view large worksheets, or close the workbook and exit Excel.

Lesson 5: Freezing and Splitting the Worksheet Display

The combination of screen size, screen resolution, font size, and zoom level determines the amount of a worksheet that you can view on one screen. Font size and zoom level settings are controlled within Excel. As a general guideline, do not alter font sizes just to view a larger area of a worksheet, because changes in font size are also reflected on printed output. Changing the zoom level on the toolbar increases or decreases your view of one area of a worksheet without affecting your printed output.

If you want to view different sections of a worksheet at one time, Excel provides two features that you can use alone or in combination. You can split the worksheet window into two or four panes and scroll to any area of the worksheet in any pane. You can also freeze selected rows and/or columns on the screen. Freezing enables you to keep row and column headings in view as you scroll right and left to view other columns, or scroll up and down to view other rows.

In this lesson, you use both features to view different sections of the Condensed IS worksheet.

To Freeze and Split the Worksheet Display

1 If necessary, open the `Frisbees` workbook and click the sheet tab named **Condensed IS.**

2 Change the Zoom level to 100% if another setting is active.

3 Click cell B5 to make it the current cell.

The current cell determines which rows and columns are affected by a freeze command. Excel freezes rows above the current cell and columns to the left of the current cell.

4 Choose **Window, Freeze Panes.**

Horizontal and vertical lines intersect at the upper-left corner of the current cell B5 (see Figure 4.13).

Figure 4.13
Horizontal and vertical lines indicate that Freeze Panes is active.

Columns to the left of the vertical line remain in view as you scroll to other columns

Rows above the horizontal line remain in view as you scroll to other rows

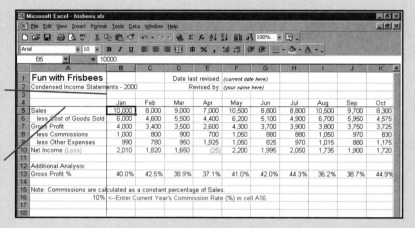

5 Scroll right until column G displays next to column A.

Columns B through F disappear from view, but the labels in Column A remain on the screen (see Figure 4.14).

Figure 4.14
As you scroll to any part of the worksheet, Column A and rows 1 through 4 remain in view.

Columns B through F disappear

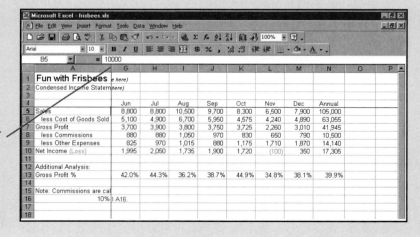

6 **Choose Window, Unfreeze Panes.**

The horizontal and vertical lines disappear, and columns B through F reappear. Panes are no longer frozen on the screen.

7 **Display cell A1 in the upper-left corner of the worksheet window, and click cell E1.**

Cell E1 becomes the current cell. Excel splits a worksheet into panes above and to the left of the current cell.

8 **Choose Window, Split.**

Because the current cell is at the top of the worksheet, Excel can split the worksheet into only left and right panes (see Figure 4.15). You can scroll around the worksheet in either pane.

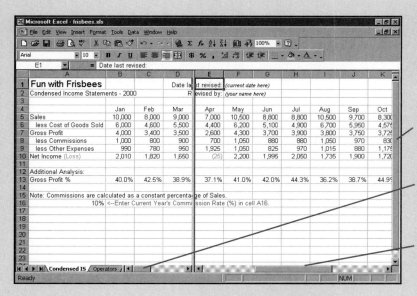

Figure 4.15
Excel splits a worksheet into panes to the left of and above the current cell.

Use this vertical scrollbar to shift the screen display up or down in both panes

Use this horizontal scrollbar to shift the worksheet display left or right in the left pane

Use this horizontal scrollbar to shift the worksheet display left or right in the right pane

9 **Scroll the worksheet display in either pane as desired, and choose Window, Remove Split.**

10 **Make cell A1 the current cell and save your changes to the Frisbees workbook.**

Keep the workbook open for the next lesson, or close the workbook and exit Excel.

 Inside Stuff: **Editing When Split Panes are Active**

When a worksheet is split into panes, it's possible to see the same section of a worksheet in multiple panes. This effect relates only to screen display; the command does not create duplicate cells. Therefore you can edit the contents of a cell in one pane and the changes immediately appear in any other pane that displays the same cell.

Lesson 6: Hiding and Unhiding Rows and Columns

For privacy or other reasons, there may be rows or columns in a worksheet that you do not want to display at the moment. Perhaps you'd like to generally keep a column containing employees' salary data hidden, displaying it only when you want to edit an entry. Or you may want to temporarily hide twelve columns that store monthly data so you can concentrate on reviewing annual amounts.

When you hide rows or columns in a worksheet, the data in those hidden parts is removed from view but not deleted. If you print the worksheet, the hidden parts do not print.

In this project, you hide twelve columns and three rows, view the results in Print Preview, and then restore the display of hidden columns and rows.

To Hide and Unhide Rows and Columns

1 **If necessary, open the** Frisbees **workbook, click the sheet tab named Condensed IS, and set the Zoom level to 75%.**

2 **Click the B column heading in the worksheet frame, and drag right until columns B through M are selected.**

3 **Choose F̲ormat, C̲olumn, H̲ide.**
Excel hides columns B through M (see Figure 4.16). A thick border displays between columns A and N. The border disappears when you move the cell pointer.

Figure 4.16
Hidden columns do not display on the screen, or print.

Columns between A and N are hidden

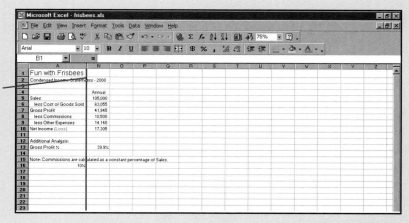

4 **Click the row heading 12 in the worksheet frame, and drag down until rows 12 through 14 are selected.**

5 **Choose F̲ormat, R̲ow, H̲ide.**
Excel hides rows 12 through 14. A thick border displays between rows 11 and 15.

6 **Choose F̲ile, Print Preview (see Figure 4.17).**

7 **Click the Close button to exit Print Preview.**

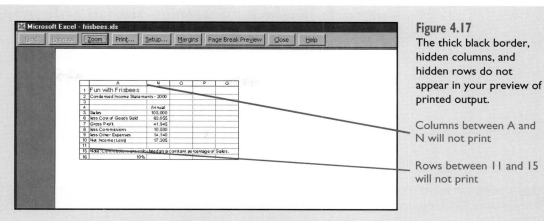

Figure 4.17
The thick black border, hidden columns, and hidden rows do not appear in your preview of printed output.

Columns between A and N will not print

Rows between 11 and 15 will not print

8 **Click the A column heading in the worksheet frame, and drag right until column N is also selected.**
By selecting at least one column heading or cell on each side of the hidden columns, you are selecting the hidden columns.

9 **Choose Format, Column, Unhide.**
Excel restores the display of columns B through M.

10 **Click row 11 in the worksheet frame, and drag down until row 15 is also selected.**
By selecting at least one row heading or cell on each side of the hidden rows, you are selecting the hidden rows.

11 **Choose Format, Row, Unhide.**
Excel restores the display of rows 12 through 14.
This concludes Project 6. You can continue with the next project or exit Excel.

Exam Note: Unhiding Column A or Row 1
If the first column or row in a worksheet is hidden, you can select it by choosing Edit, Go To and specifying A1 in the Reference box. After clicking OK to exit the Go To dialog box, point to either Row or Column on the Format menu and click Unhide.

Inside Stuff: Hiding Worksheets and Workbooks
You can also hide and unhide workbooks, and worksheets within workbooks. To hide the current worksheet, choose Format, Sheet, Hide. To hide a workbook, open it and choose Window, Hide.

To unhide a worksheet, choose Format, Sheet, Unhide and select from a list of hidden sheets in the Unhide dialog box. To unhide a workbook, choose Window, Unhide, and select from a list of hidden workbooks.

Lesson 7: Displaying Formulas Instead of Formula Results

As you create larger, more complex worksheets, you may find it useful to check your work by displaying formulas instead of formula results. Viewing or printing a worksheet in this display mode can help you understand the calculations performed by the worksheet. Printed copy can also be a valuable resource if disk versions are damaged or missing, and you have to reconstruct the worksheet.

In this lesson, you set the worksheet display to show the formulas in the Condensed IS worksheet, and then you turn the setting off.

To Display Formulas Instead of Formula Results

1 If necessary, open the Frisbees workbook and click the sheet tab named Condensed IS.

2 Check that Zoom level is set to 75%; and choose **T**ools, **O**ptions.
The Options dialog box appears with eight tabs: View, Calculation, Edit, General, Transition, Custom Lists, Chart, and Color.

3 Click the View tab if it is not the active tab.

4 In the Window options section, click the check box to the left of For̲mulas (see Figure 4.18).

Figure 4.18
Use the View tab in the Options dialog box to alter display settings.

The active tab

Turning display of formulas on

Click here to accept the current settings and close the dialog box

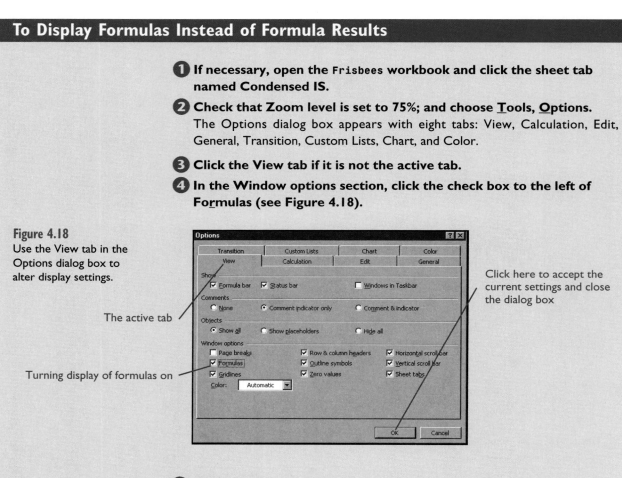

5 Click OK.
Excel doubles the width of each column and displays what is stored in each cell (see Figure 4.19).

6 Choose **T**ools, **O**ptions.

7 Click the View tab if it is not the active tab.

8 In the Window options section, click the check mark in the box to the left of For̲mulas.
The check mark disappears, which indicates that Formulas view is turned off.

9 Close the workbook without saving your changes.
This concludes Lesson 7. You can continue with the last lesson in this project or exit Excel.

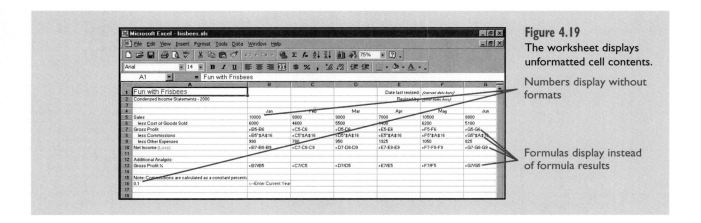

Figure 4.19
The worksheet displays unformatted cell contents.

Numbers display without formats

Formulas display instead of formula results

Lesson 8: Using Save As To Change Filename, File Type, or Storage Location

Clicking the Save button on the toolbar immediately resaves the current workbook under its current name and in its current storage location. If you want to change the name or storage location, or save the workbook as another file type, use the Save As option on the File menu to display the Save As dialog box (see Figure 4.20).

Click here to display the drives and folders for your system

Scroll down to display additional file type options

Click here to display options to change file type

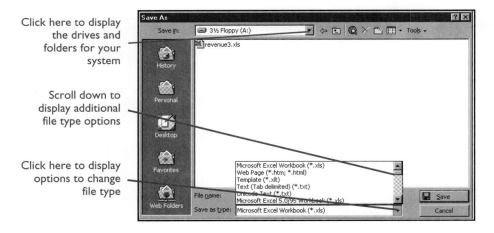

Figure 4.20
The selections in the dialog box specify saving a file as a Microsoft Excel workbook (.xls extension) on a disk in drive A.

Always check that you have specified the desired settings in three areas of the dialog box—Save in, File name, and Save as type—before clicking the Save button.

At the bottom of the Save As dialog box is a Save as type list box. Clicking the list box arrow displays predefined file types. For example, you can save as a Web page (Project 7 "Developing a Multiple-Sheet Workbook"); save as a template (Project 8 "Working with Custom Formats, AutoFormats, Styles, and Templates"); save as an earlier version of Excel, such as 5.0/95; and save as a (Lotus) 1-2-3, Quattro Pro, or dBASE IV file.

In this lesson, you change the name of a workbook as you save it, delete several worksheets in the workbook, and then resave.

To Change a Filename and Delete Sheets

1 **If necessary, open the `Frisbees` workbook and click the sheet tab named Condensed IS.**

2 **Choose File, Save As.**
The Save As dialog box displays (see Figure 4.20).

3 **Check that the entry in the Save in text box at the top of the dialog box is the desired location in which to save the file (for example, the A drive in Figure 4.20).**

4 **Click within the File name text box and change the filename from Frisbees to `demoabsolute.xls` (see Figure 4.21).**

Figure 4.21
Filename is one of three specifications to set before clicking the Save button in the lower-right corner of the dialog box.

Click here to move up one level in the folder structure

Click here to create a new folder

New filename

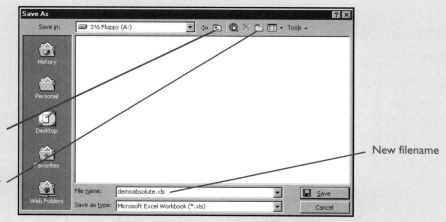

5 **Click the Save button.**
The dialog box closes and the new name demoabsolute.xls displays in the title bar at the top of the screen.

6 **Click the Condensed IS sheet, if necessary, and display the Edit menu.**

7 **Choose Delete Sheet and click OK.**
The Condensed IS worksheet is permanently deleted from the demoabsolute workbook. Now try an alternative way to delete a sheet.

8 **Right-click the Operators sheet tab.**
A shortcut menu displays (see Figure 4.22).

9 **Choose Delete from the shortcut menu, and click OK.**
The Operators worksheet is permanently deleted from the demoabsolute workbook.

10 **Delete the Precedence worksheet from the demoabsolute workbook.**
The Precedence worksheet is permanently deleted from the demoabsolute workbook. The remaining two sheets demonstrate the wrong and right ways to use absolute cell addressing.

11 **Save your changes to the demoabsolute workbook.**
This concludes Project 4. You can continue with end-of-project exercises, start another project, or exit Excel.

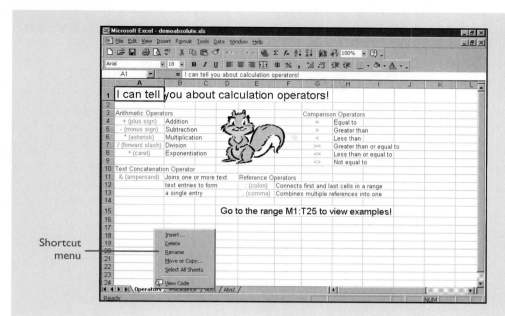

Shortcut
menu

Figure 4.22
Right-clicking a sheet tab
displays a shortcut menu
of actions you can apply
to the selected sheet(s).

 Inside Stuff: **Recovering a Deleted Sheet**
You cannot use Excel's Undo feature to restore a deleted sheet. As a precaution, save a workbook immediately before applying any action that cannot be undone. If the results are not what you want, such as deleting the wrong sheet, close the current workbook without saving the most recent change. You can then open the workbook, which includes the sheet deleted in error, and continue to edit.

Summary

This project began with an introduction to basic worksheet design techniques, with an emphasis on providing adequate documentation and using cell references instead of numbers in formulas. As you worked through subsequent lessons, you learned how operators and the order of precedence affect formulas. You also used the type-and-point method to enter formulas and copied formulas containing absolute cell references. As a natural extension of a focus on formulas, the remaining lessons presented features for viewing and saving your work—freezing panes or splitting the screen display into multiple windows, hiding and unhiding rows and columns, showing formulas instead of formula results, saving under different filenames or file types, and saving to another location.

You can extend your learning by viewing related Help topics. You'll find numerous subtopics under Creating Formulas and Auditing Workbooks using Help's Contents tab. Take advantage also of the many opportunities to enter and copy formulas provided in the end-of-project exercises.

Checking Concepts and Terms

True/False

For each of the following, check *T* or *F* to indicate whether the statement is true or false.

__T __F **1.** A colon (:) is an example of a concatenation operator. [L1]

__T __F **2.** You can hide worksheets as well as columns and rows within worksheets, but you cannot hide workbooks. [L6]

__T __F **3.** To make a cell reference in a formula absolute, you can click within the cell reference in the formula bar and press F5. [L3]

__T __F **4.** The Save As command enables you to change filename, file type, or storage location. [L8]

__T __F **5.** If you edit the contents of a cell in one pane, the change immediately appears in any other pane that displays the same cell. [L5]

Multiple Choice

Circle the letter of the correct answer for each of the following.

1. Assume that numbers are entered in three cells as follows: 50 in cell A1, 20 in cell B1, and 10 in cell C1. The formula =A1+B1/C1 is stored in cell D1. What result displays in cell D1? [L1]

a. 7

b. 52

c. 0

d. some other value

2. Which of the following is an arithmetic operator? [L1]

a. $ (dollar sign)

b. @ (at sign)

c. ^ (caret)

d. ? (question mark)

3. Which is not a valid relational operator? [L1]

a. >

b. <=

c. *

d. <>

4. Which window option enables you to display two or four panes on the screen? [L5]

a. Freeze Panes

b. Arrange

c. Split

d. New Window

5. Which symbol(s) is/are used to change the order of operations in a formula? [L1]

a. =

b. ()

c. []

d. ^

Skill Drill

Skill Drill exercises reinforce project skills. Each skill reinforced is the same, or nearly the same, as a skill presented in the project. Detailed instructions are provided in a step-by-step format.

Each exercise is independent of the others, so you can complete the exercises in any order. Be sure to save the workbook after completing each exercise. If you need a paper copy of the completed exercise, enter your name centered in a header before printing. Other print options have already been set to print compressed to one page, and to display the filename, sheet name, and current date in a footer.

Before beginning your first Project 4 Skill Drill exercise, complete the following steps:

1. Open the file named **e-0402** and save it as **e4drill**.
   The workbook contains four sheets: an overview and exercise sheets named #1-Point, #2-Absolute, and #3-Split.

2. Click the Overview sheet to view the organization of the Project 4 Skill Drill Exercises workbook.

If you need more than one work session to complete the desired exercises, continue working on **e4drill** instead of starting over on the original e-0402 file.

1. Using the Type-and-Point Method to Enter Formulas

You are developing a simple worksheet model to calculate the sales tax due on one purchase. You designed the model to work with any specified sales tax rate. Now you are ready to enter the two formulas—one to calculate the amount of tax; the other to add the tax to the original purchase amount. You know that you are less likely to make mistakes if you point to cell references instead of typing them.

To use the type-and-point method to enter formulas:

1. Open the **e4drill** workbook, and select the sheet tab named #1-Point.

2. Click cell B8, and type an equal sign (=).
   This starts the formula to calculate sales tax.

3. Click cell B7, and type an asterisk (*).
   The partially completed formula =B7* displays in the formula bar.

4. Click cell B5, and click the Enter button (the green check mark) in the formula bar.
   The formula =B7*B5 displays in the formula bar. The formula result (Sales tax of 1.00) displays in cell B8.

5. Click cell B9, and type an equal sign (=).
   This starts the formula to calculate total due on the purchase.

6. Click cell B7, and type a plus sign (+).

7. Click cell B8, and click the Enter button in the formula bar or press ⏎Enter.
   The formula =B7+B8 results in 20.95 as the total due on the purchase.

8. Test the model by entering other combinations of the sales tax rate in cell B5 and the purchase amount in cell B7.

2. Creating and Copying a Formula with an Absolute Cell Reference

You are in charge of putting price tags on ten products, all of which are to be marked up by the same percentage on cost. You are nearly finished with a worksheet that will do the necessary calculations. The final step involves entering a formula to compute the selling price of the first item and copying it to calculate the selling price for the other products. The formula must include an absolute reference to the cell containing the current markup on cost percentage.

To create and copy the formula:

1. Open the **e4drill** workbook and select the worksheet named #2-Absolute.

2. Click cell C6, and type an equal sign (=).
   This starts the formula to calculate Selling Price for Product A.

3. Click cell B6, and type an asterisk (*).

4. Click cell D4.
   The partially completed formula =B6*D4 appears in the formula bar.

5. Press F4
   The formula =B6*$D$4 appears in the formula bar.

6. Type a plus sign (+), and click cell B6.
   The formula =B6*$D$4+B6 appears in the formula bar.

7. Click the Enter button in the formula bar or press ↵Enter.
   The formula =B6*$D$4+B6 results in 10 as the Selling Price (marked up 25 percent over its $8.00 cost). Excel performs the multiplication first—using B6*$D$4 to compute the increase of two dollars over cost—and then adds the increase to the cost.

8. Click the lower-left corner of cell C6 and drag the formula to the other cells in the range C7:C15.

9. Test the model by entering other markup percentages in cell D4.

3. Splitting the Screen into Top and Bottom Panes

You are under consideration for a promotion that would involve a move to another city. While you are waiting for a decision, you continue to collect information through the World Wide Web on homes available in selected areas. Now that the list is getting too long to fit on one screen, you want to split the screen into two panes of about equal size. Doing so enables you to view different parts of the worksheet on one screen.

To split the screen into top and bottom panes:

1. Open the e4drill workbook and select the worksheet named #3-Split.

2. Select cell A13.

3. Choose Window, Split.

4. Click any cell in either pane and use the scrollbar(s) to shift worksheet display.

Challenge

Challenge exercises expand on or are somewhat related to the skills presented in the lessons. Each exercise provides a brief narrative introduction, followed by instructions in a numbered-step format that are not as detailed as those in the Skill Drill section.

Each exercise is independent of the others, so you can complete the exercises in any order. Be sure to save the workbook after completing each exercise. If you need a paper copy of the completed exercise, enter your name centered in a header before printing. Other print options have already been set to print compressed to one page and to display the filename, sheet name, and current date in a footer.

Before beginning your first Project 4 Challenge exercise, complete the following steps:

1. Open the file named e-0403 and save it as e4challenge.
   The e4challenge workbook contains four sheets: an overview and three exercise sheets (#1-Sale Price, #2-Rental Fee, and #3-Overtime).

2. Click the Overview sheet to view the organization of the Project 4 Challenge Exercises workbook.

If you need more than one work session to complete the desired exercises, continue working on e4challenge instead of starting over on the original e-0403 file.

1. Entering a Formula to Compute Adjusted Selling Price

Even though you've only been using Excel for a short time, you realize that its power lies in performing calculations. You're interested in developing your ability to set up formulas so that the worksheet can still be used if the data changes. You are currently developing a simple worksheet to calculate the amount due if an item is on sale at a reduced percent. For example, if an item with an original cost of $30.00 is now on sale at 25 percent off, the pretax sale price is $22.50.

The labels are already in place.

To enter and test a formula to compute adjusted selling price:

1. Open your **e4challenge** workbook and select the worksheet named #1-Sale Price.
2. Enter a sample original price, such as **30**, in cell B5.
3. Enter a sample percent discount, such as **25%**, in cell B6.
4. Enter a formula in cell B7 to compute the pretax sale price.
   If the formula in cell B7 is correct, 22.5 is the pretax sale price that displays in cell B7.
5. Test the formula again by changing the sample numbers to **100** in cell B5 and **10%** in cell B6.
   If the formula in cell B7 is correct, 90 is the pretax sale price that displays in cell B7.

2. Designing a Worksheet to Calculate Rental Fees

You must make a decision soon on buying or renting a copy machine. As part of the decision process, you are evaluating three pricing structures from firms that rent copy machines. All have a two-part rental plan—a monthly charge plus an amount per copy. You spent a few minutes yesterday setting up a worksheet to evaluate the rental options. Now, you need to finish the design and test the model with various assumptions about the numbers of copies made in a month.

To design a worksheet to calculate rental fees:

1. Open your **e4challenge** workbook and select the worksheet named #2-Rental Fee.
2. Think about the elements that affect the total rental fee—two are set by the rental companies (monthly fee and charge per copy) and the other is related to actual usage (number of copies).
3. Enter the appropriate labels in cells A8, A9, and A10 to describe each of the three elements of the total rental fee.
4. For the rows described as monthly fee and charge per copy, enter the appropriate numbers in columns B, C, and D that are related to the three rental options:

   Option A   Monthly Fee **$500**, Charge per Copy **$0.03**

   Option B   Monthly Fee **$200**, Charge per Copy **$0.04**

   Option C   Monthly Fee **$800**, Charge per Copy **$0.015**
5. Enter **10,000** as the initial number of copies for all three options.
6. Enter a formula in cell B12 to compute the total rental fee, and copy the formula to cells C12 and D12.

7. Check the accuracy of your results and make changes in formulas, as necessary. At the 10,000-copy level, the total rental fees are as follows: Option A, $800; Option B, $600; Option C, $950. Assuming that service arrangements are comparable, you would probably select Option B as the most attractive pricing structure.

8. Change the number of copies to **20,000**.

9. Below row 12, type a note in the worksheet that summarizes the best option if copies per month are likely to average 20,000.

10. Change the number of copies to **30,000**.

11. Below your previous note, type another note that summarizes the best option if copies per month are likely to average 30,000.

3. Designing a Worksheet To Calculate Gross Pay

You started a full-time job recently, and for the first time you work for a firm that pays overtime (the usual rate of 1.5 times your regular pay rate per hour, which is applied to every hour worked over 40 hours). You want to be sure that your pay is computed correctly each week, so you are designing a worksheet to calculate your weekly pay before any deductions for taxes and benefits.

To design a worksheet to calculate gross pay:

1. Open your **e4challenge** workbook and select the worksheet named #3-Overtime.

2. To avoid using a number instead of a cell reference in a formula, enter the label **Overtime premium rate** in cell A8 and the number **1.5** in cell B8.

3. Select cell B15 and enter a formula to compute the total gross pay for the week. The formula you enter should reflect the fact that your pay has two components: regular hours at regular pay (a maximum of 40 hours) and overtime hours (hours in excess of 40) at 1.5 times your regular pay. Remember to use cell references instead of numbers in your formula.

4. Test the formula by entering simple numbers in the input cells: **40** in B11, **1** in B12, and **10** in B13.
   If the formula in B15 is correct, the total gross pay for the week is $415—40 hours at $10 an hour (or $400), plus $15 for the one overtime hour.

5. Test that the formula computes correctly if there are no overtime hours: enter **38** in B11, **0** in B12, and **12** in B13.
   If the formula in B15 is correct, the total gross pay for the week is $456—38 hours at $12 per hour.

6. Test the overtime calculation again, assuming that the total hours worked are 45 and the pay per hour does not change.
   The total gross pay for the week is $570—40 hours at $12 per hour, plus 5 hours at $18 an hour.

 Inside Stuff: **Using One Function for Gross Pay**
In Project 5 "Working with Functions," you use a function to calculate gross pay. The function calculates one way if the hours worked in a week total 40 or fewer; it calculates a different way if the hours exceed 40. The calculation is harder to set up, but you only have to enter the total hours worked in one cell, instead of separating your total hours into overtime hours and regular hours.

Discovery Zone

Discovery Zone exercises require an advanced knowledge of the topics presented in *MOUS Essentials* lessons, application of skills from multiple lessons, or self-directed learning of new skills.

Each exercise is independent of the others, so you can complete the exercises in any order. Be sure to save the workbook after completing each exercise. If you need a paper copy of the completed exercise, enter your name centered in a header before printing. Other print options have already been set to print compressed to one page and to display the filename, sheet name, and current date in a footer.

Before beginning your first Project 4 Discovery Zone exercise, complete the following steps:

1. Open the Excel file named `e-0404` and save it as `e4discovery`.

   The e4discovery workbook contains three sheets: an overview and two exercise sheets (#1-Improve Design, and #2-Find and Fix).

2. Click the Overview sheet to view the organization of the Project 4 Discovery Zone Exercises workbook.

If you need more than one work session to complete the desired exercises, continue working on `e4discovery` instead of starting over on the original e-0404 file.

1. Improving Worksheet Design and Documentation

You are the owner and manager of a small firm with ten employees. In a few weeks, you will announce an increase in wages per hour for all employees. This year everyone has been working hard, and you plan to give the same percentage increase to all employees.

Open the `e4discovery` workbook and select the worksheet named #1-Improve Design. The worksheet reflects your initial attempt to have Excel calculate each employee's proposed new rate. Now, you want to modify the worksheet to incorporate good design techniques, including sufficient documentation. One improvement you have in mind is to put the percent in a separate cell, so you can easily change just that one cell and immediately see the results of using a different percentage in the calculation of each employee's proposed pay per hour.

2. Finding and Fixing Errors in Calculations

A coworker asked you to review a worksheet designed to report monthly and annual income. You already verified that the data are correct—the current commission rate and amounts reported for Sales, Cost of Goods Sold, and Other Expenses. Now you need to check the accuracy of the calculations.

Open the **e4discovery** workbook and select the worksheet named #2-Find and Fix. Find any errors that affect calculations, and type a brief description of each error below the Net Income row. Make the corrections needed to produce accurate results.

Hint: Display formulas instead of formula results, and check for inconsistencies in the ranges used in formulas. Try a percentage commission rate that is easy to verify visually, such as 1 percent.

PinPoint Assessment

You have completed this project and its associated lessons, and have had an opportunity to assess your skills through the end-of-project questions and exercises. Now use the PinPoint software Evaluation Mode to further assess your comprehension of the specific exam activities you have just learned. You can also use the PinPoint Trainer Mode and the Show Me tutorials to practice these exam activities.

Project 5

Working with Functions

Key terms introduced in this project include

- annuity
- argument
- AVERAGE function
- FV function
- HLOOKUP function

- IF function
- MAX function
- MIN function
- NOW function
- PMT function

- variable data
- VLOOKUP function
- worksheet model

Objectives	Required Activity for MOUS	Exam Level
➤ Use AVERAGE, MAX, and MIN Functions	Use basic functions (AVERAGE, SUM, COUNT, MIN, MAX)	Core
➤ Calculate a Payment Using PMT	Use financial functions (FV and PMT); Use Paste Function to insert a function	Core
➤ Create a Loan Payment Table		
➤ Evaluate Investment Plans with FV	Use financial functions (FV and PMT)	Core
➤ Use IF to Display Messages	Use logical functions (IF)	Core
➤ Use IF to Calculate	Use logical functions (IF)	Core
➤ Use NOW to Display the Current Date	Use date functions (NOW and DATE)	Core
➤ Use VLOOKUP to Convert Data	Use lookup functions (HLOOKUP and VLOOKUP)	Expert

Why Would I Do This?

Excel provides hundreds of functions to help you with tasks, such as adding a list of values and determining loan payments. Functions are presented in 11 categories: Database and List Management, Date and Time, DDE and External, Engineering, Financial, Information, Logical, Lookup and Reference, Math and Trigonometry, Statistical, and Text. In this project, you glimpse the power of functions by working with one or more functions from five categories: statistical, financial, logical, date and time, and lookup and reference.

Lesson 1: Analyzing Data with AVERAGE, MAX, and MIN

A function is a predefined formula that calculates by using arguments in a specific order. An **argument** is a specific value in a function, such as a range of cells. For example, the function =AVERAGE(B5:M5) has one argument—the range of cells from B5 through M5.

You can enter functions in more than one way. If you know the name and structure of the function you want to use, you can type it into the cell in which you want the results to appear or you can type it into the formula bar. You can also use the formula palette or the Paste Function dialog box to select from a list of functions.

Excel provides a substantial number of statistical functions, including AVERAGE, MAX, and MIN. The **AVERAGE function** calculates the average of specified values. Use the **MAX function** to display the largest value among specified values. The **MIN function** calculates the smallest value among specified values.

In this lesson, you use the three statistical functions AVERAGE, MAX, and MIN to analyze sales. Each function has the same structure—equal sign, function name, and range of cells within parentheses.

To Analyze Data with AVERAGE, MAX, and MIN

1 **Open the e-0501 workbook, and save the file as Functions1.**
The workbook contains one sheet named Condensed IS.

2 **Set Zoom level to 75% and click cell B16.**

3 **Type =AVERAGE(and select the range B5:M5 (that is, click cell B5 and drag the pointer to cell M5).**
The nearly complete function appears in the formula bar and in cell B16 (see Figure 5.1).

4 **Type the closing parenthesis to complete the function, and click the green check mark in the formula bar.**
The function =AVERAGE(B5:M5) appears in the formula bar. The function result $8,750 displays in cell B16.

 If You Have Problems...
If you pressed ↵Enter instead of the green check mark in the formula bar, the cell below cell B16 is the current cell. Click cell B16 to see the AVERAGE function in the formula bar.

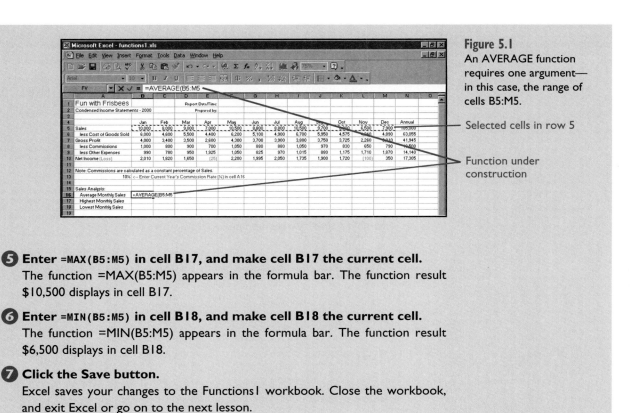

Figure 5.1
An AVERAGE function requires one argument—in this case, the range of cells B5:M5.

Selected cells in row 5

Function under construction

5 **Enter** =MAX(B5:M5) **in cell B17, and make cell B17 the current cell.**
The function =MAX(B5:M5) appears in the formula bar. The function result $10,500 displays in cell B17.

6 **Enter** =MIN(B5:M5) **in cell B18, and make cell B18 the current cell.**
The function =MIN(B5:M5) appears in the formula bar. The function result $6,500 displays in cell B18.

7 **Click the Save button.**
Excel saves your changes to the Functions1 workbook. Close the workbook, and exit Excel or go on to the next lesson.

Lesson 2: Calculating a Loan Payment with PMT

The **PMT function** calculates the payment due on a loan, assuming equal payments and a fixed interest rate. In this lesson, you use the Paste Function button to select the PMT function, and enter its arguments on the formula palette. The worksheet you use is set up as a model. A **worksheet model** generally contains labels and formulas, but the cells that hold variable data are left blank. **Variable data** consists of amounts that are subject to change, such as interest rate or the amount borrowed in a loan situation.

The PMT function requires that you specify three arguments in order—the annual interest rate adjusted for the number of payments within a year, the total number of payments, and the amount borrowed. If a minus sign (–) precedes the amount borrowed, the function result is a positive number. If a minus sign does not precede the amount borrowed, the function result is a negative number. You determine the display you want; either way, the dollar amount is the same.

To Calculate a Loan Payment with PMT

1 **Open the** e-0502 **workbook and save it as** Functions2.
The workbook includes six worksheets: Intro PMT, Single PMT, Create PMT, Multiple PMT, Intro FV, and Compare FV. You use this file for lessons 2, 3, and 4.

2 **Click the sheet tab named Intro PMT and read its contents to learn about uses for the PMT function.**

continues ▶

To Calculate a Loan Payment with PMT (continued)

3 **Select the Single PMT worksheet, and click cell B10.**

The function =PMT(B6/B7,B8,-B5) appears in the formula bar. The function result displays in cell B10 (see Figure 5.2). The monthly payment on an 8.5%, 4-year, $8,000 loan is $197.19.

Figure 5.2
This PMT function has three arguments, separated by commas.

Argument 1: The annual interest rate, adjusted to a monthly basis

Argument 2: The number of payments (periods)

Argument 3: The amount borrowed

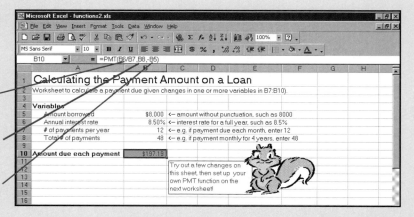

4 **Click cell B8, and enter 36 instead of 48 as the total number of payments.**

The function recalculates by using the revised number of payments. Reducing the loan term to 36 months raises the monthly payment on an 8.5%, $8,000 loan to $252.54. You now enter a PMT function by using the Paste Function button on the toolbar.

5 **Select the Create PMT worksheet.**

A worksheet similar to the Single PMT worksheet displays. Because the worksheet is set up to be a model for any combination of loan terms, a note about an error message has been set up in a text box.

6 **Click cell B12, and click the Paste Function button in the toolbar.**

The Paste Function dialog box displays. If the dialog box covers the cells in column B, click the title bar in the dialog box and drag the box to the right (see Figure 5.3). The most recently used function category and function name appear as selected. (These may vary from the selections on your screen.)

7 **Select the Financial function category and the PMT function, as shown in Figure 5.3, and click OK.**

The PMT formula palette displays. If the palette covers the cells in column B, click a blank area of the palette and drag the palette to the right.

8 **Click in the Rate text box of the PMT formula palette, and click cell B8.**

Excel displays B8 in the Rate text box, and =PMT(B8) in cell B12 and the formula bar.

9 **Type / (the symbol for division), and click cell B4.**

The specification of the first argument, the annual interest rate adjusted to a monthly basis, is complete. Excel displays B8/B4 in the formula palette, and =PMT(B8/B4) in cell B12 and the formula bar (see Figure 5.4).

First part of
the function

Paste
Function
dialog box

Selected
function
category

Scroll to
view other
categories

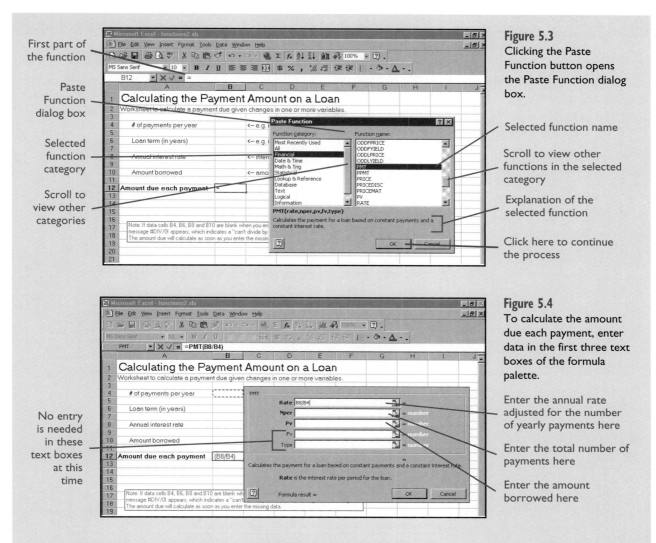

Figure 5.3
Clicking the Paste
Function button opens
the Paste Function dialog
box.

Selected function name

Scroll to view other
functions in the selected
category

Explanation of the
selected function

Click here to continue
the process

No entry
is needed
in these
text boxes
at this
time

Figure 5.4
To calculate the amount
due each payment, enter
data in the first three text
boxes of the formula
palette.

Enter the annual rate
adjusted for the number
of yearly payments here

Enter the total number of
payments here

Enter the amount
borrowed here

10 **Click in the Nper (number of periods) text box of the formula
palette.**

11 **Click cell B6, type an asterisk (*), and click cell B4.**
The specification of the second argument, the number of payments, is complete. This argument calculates the total payments as the number of years for
the loan, multiplied by the number of payments each year. Excel displays
B6*B4 in the formula palette, and =PMT(B8/B4,B6*B4) in cell B12 and the formula bar.

12 **Click in the Pv (Present value) window of the formula palette, and
click cell B10.**
The specification of the third argument, which is the amount borrowed, is
complete. Check that the display in your formula bar matches that shown in
Figure 5.5 and make changes in the PMT formula palette, as necessary.

13 **Click OK, and click the Save.**
Excel enters the function, closes the PMT formula palette, and saves the
worksheet shown in Figure 5.6. You can now use this worksheet to calculate
the monthly payment due for any combination of loan terms and amount borrowed.

continues ▶

To Calculate a Loan Payment with PMT   (continued)

Figure 5.5
To specify the Rate argument in a PMT function, divide the annual interest rate by the number of payments in a year.

Function constructed by using the PMT formula palette

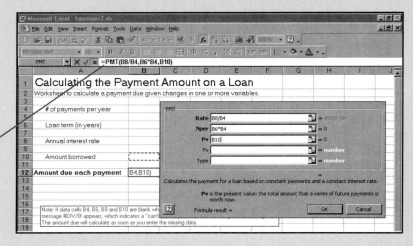

Figure 5.6
To calculate a loan payment, enter data in cells B4, B6, B8, and B10.

Message that appears until values are entered in cells B4, B6, B8, and B10

Note explaining the error message in cell B12

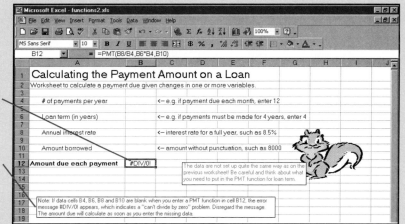

⓮ **Use the model by entering the data to compute the loan payment on a 4-year, 8.5%, $8,000 loan assuming monthly payments: 12 in cell B4, 4 in cell B6, 8.5% in cell B8 and 8000 in cell B10.**
The payment amount ($197.19) displays in cell B12. The parentheses indicate a negative number. If you prefer that the result be expressed as a positive number, precede the third argument in the PMT function with a minus sign.

⓯ **Try other combinations of the four variables, and close the workbook without saving your changes to the data.**
You saved the labels and the PMT function in Step 13. By closing without saving your changes to cells containing loan-specific data, the model is ready to use with another set of loan terms. You can now exit Excel or continue with the next lesson.

Inside Stuff: **Other Financial Functions**

Excel provides a variety of financial functions for business and personal use. Some relate to the time value of money, such as PMT (payment), FV (future value), and IRR (internal rate of return). Others provide investment information (such as TBILLPRICE and TBILLYIELD, both of which relate to treasury bills). Some functions calculate depreciation under a variety of methods, including SL (straight line), DDB (double-declining balance), and SYD (Sum-of-the-Years Digits).

Lesson 3: Creating a Loan Payment Table

Calculating a loan payment due, based on one set of loan terms, has limited use. You understand how to set up and copy formulas containing absolute and relative cell references, so you decide to create a table of payments at varying interest rates, loan terms, or amounts borrowed.

In this lesson, you create a table that shows the payments due on loans of varying length. You also set up two additional columns for summary information over the life of the loan—one for total payments and the other for total interest.

To Create a Loan Payment Table

① **Open the** `Functions2` **workbook, if necessary, and select the work-sheet named Multiple PMT.**

The partially completed Multiple PMT worksheet is designed to provide three items of information over multiple loan terms: the amount of a payment on a loan (column C), the total payments on a loan (column D), and the total interest on a loan (column E). Loan terms in half-year increments are listed in column A, and formulas in column B calculate the corresponding number of months. After the appropriate formulas are entered in columns C through E, you can quickly generate information by varying the interest rate in cell B7 or amount borrowed in cell D7.

② **Click cell C11 and click the Paste Function button in the toolbar.**

This action starts the process of entering a PMT function in the first cell below the Amount of Each Payment column heading.

③ **Select the Financial function category; select the PMT function, and click OK.**

The PMT formula palette displays. If the palette covers row 7 or cell C11, drag the palette to the right.

④ **Enter the three arguments shown in Figure 5.7.**

You can type each formula in its window: `$B$7/$C$7` in the Rate window, `B11` in the Nper window, and `-$D$7` in the Pv window. You can also use a combination of typing the arithmetic operators and pointing to (clicking) the cell references, followed by changing all but one cell reference to an absolute reference. To convert a relative cell reference to absolute, click it in the PMT formula palette, and press (F4).

continues ▶

To Create a Loan Payment Table (continued)

Figure 5.7
Good spreadsheet design requires the use of cell references instead of numbers in PMT function arguments.

Enter both cells as absolute cell references

Enter as a relative cell reference

Enter a minus sign before the absolute cell reference

Preview the solution here

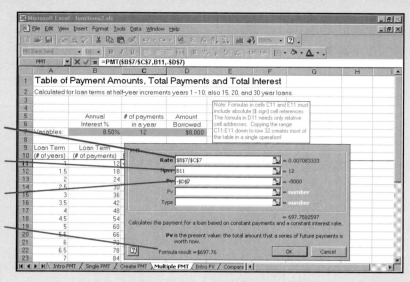

5 **Click OK.**

The function, =PMT($B$7/$C$7,B11,–$D$7), appears in the formula bar. The function result, $697.76, displays in cell C11. Now, enter formulas to calculate total payments and total interest for the first loan term of 12 months.

6 **Click cell D11, and enter the formula =B11*C11.**

This formula calculates the total payments as the number of payments multiplied by the amount of each payment. If you copy the function down the column, Excel correctly calculates total payments for other loan terms because both cell references are relative.

7 **Click cell E11, and enter the formula =D11-$D$7 (see Figure 5.8).**

This formula calculates the total interest on the loan as the total of the payments minus the original amount borrowed. If you copy the function down the column, Excel correctly calculates total interest for other loan terms because the reference to the amount borrowed is absolute.

8 **Select the range C11:E11, and position the mouse pointer on the lower-right corner of cell E11.**

9 **Press and hold down the left mouse button, drag the fill handle down to include row 32, release the mouse button, and click any cell to deselect the highlighted range.**

Excel fills the range C12:E32 with the formula heading each column and displays the results of the formulas in each cell. You can scroll down to view the end of the table (see Figure 5.9).

10 **Save your changes to the Functions2 workbook.**

Now, you can use the Multiple PMT worksheet to perform a what-if analysis, such as calculating the monthly payment for a home mortgage.

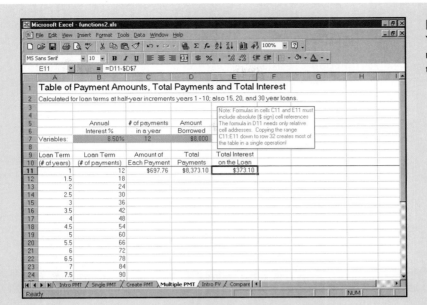

Figure 5.8
You can copy the three new formulas to create the rest of the table.

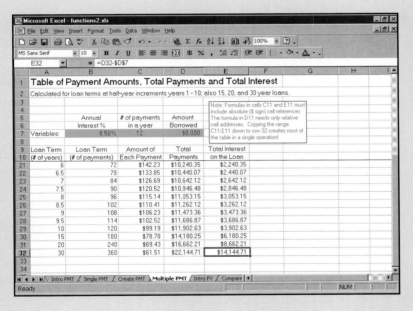

Figure 5.9
The correct mix of relative and absolute cell references in formulas enabled you to create the rest of the table with a single copy operation.

⑪ Change the amount borrowed to 150000 in cell D7.

The monthly payment on a $150,000, 8.5% loan for 30 years is approximately $1,153 (see the formula results in row 32). Over the life of the loan, you would pay $415,213 to retire a $150,000 loan. The monthly payment on a $150,000, 8.5% loan for 15 years is approximately $1,477 (see the formula results in row 30). Over the life of the loan, you would pay about $265,880 to retire a $150,000 loan—nearly $149,333 less than for the 30-year loan.

⑫ Try other combinations of interest rates and amounts borrowed as desired.

This concludes Lesson 3. Keep the workbook open for the next lesson, or close the workbook and exit Excel.

Lesson 4: Evaluating Investment Plans with the FV Function

The **FV function** calculates the future value of an investment based on fixed payments (deposits) earning a fixed rate of interest across equal time periods. Excel refers to such fixed payments at equal intervals as an **annuity**, a term used in explanations of the function's arguments.

The FV function requires that you specify three arguments in order—the annual interest rate adjusted for the number of payments within a year, the total number of payments, and the amount of each periodic payment. If a minus sign (–) precedes the amount of the periodic payment, the function result is a positive number.

In this lesson, you enter and copy an FV function that calculates future value based on a variety of interest rates. Let's begin with an introduction to future value.

To Evaluate Investment Plans with FV

① **Open the Functions2 workbook if necessary, and click the sheet tab named Intro FV.**
The worksheet shows two ways to calculate future value of a 10-year investment plan—computing interest earned each year (the range A9:E19) and an FV function (cell G8).

② **Click a variety of cells within the range B10:E19 to learn how formulas in that area calculate future value (principal plus interest) one year at a time.**

③ **Click cell G8.**
The function =FV(D4,D5,-D6) appears in the formula bar. The function result displays in cell G8 (see Figure 5.10). The future value of a series of equal deposits at year's end earning 8% interest is $14,486.56.

Figure 5.10
The FV function has three arguments, separated by commas.

Argument 1: The annual interest rate

Argument 2: The total number of payments (deposits)

Argument 3: The amount of each payment

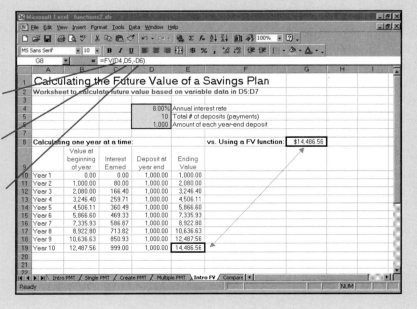

4 **Click cell D4, and enter 9% instead of 8% as the annual interest rate.**
The function recalculates by using the revised interest rate. An increase of 1% in the interest rate increases the future value to $15,192.93. Now it's your turn to enter a FV function.

5 **Select the Compare FV worksheet.**
This worksheet is designed to calculate future value at various levels of interest rates. If you use the correct combination of absolute and relative addressing when you enter a FV function in cell B9, you can compute future value at other interest rates by copying the function across row 9.

6 **Click cell B9; click the Paste Function button in the toolbar, and select the FV function.**
The FV formula palette displays. If the palette covers the cells in column B, drag the palette below row 9.

7 **Enter the FV arguments shown in Figure 5.11 (B8 in the Rate text box, $B$6 in the Nper text box, and -$B$5 in the Pmt text box).**

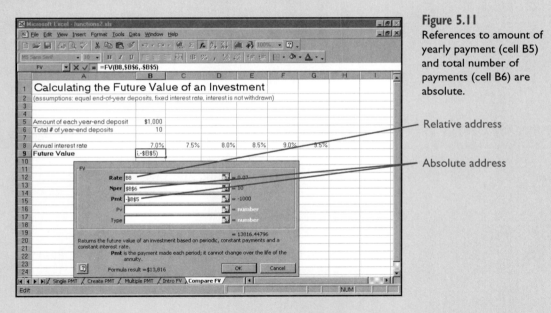

Figure 5.11
References to amount of yearly payment (cell B5) and total number of payments (cell B6) are absolute.

Relative address

Absolute address

8 **Click OK; copy the function to the range C9:G9, and click cell G9 (see Figure 5.12).**

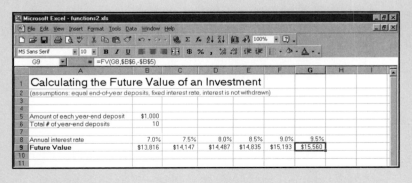

Figure 5.12
Future values based on a variety of interest rates display in row 9.

continues ▶

To Evaluate Investment Plans with FV   (continued)

⑨ Enter 2000 in cell B5.

Values in row 9 reflect doubling the payment amount. For example, the future value of investing $2,000 at the end of each year for 10 years earning 9% is $30,386.

⑩ Save your changes, and close the functions2 workbook.

This concludes Lesson 4. Continue with the next lesson, or exit Excel.

Lesson 5: Using IF to Display Messages

You have heard that you can use a logical function named IF to implement different actions, depending on whether a condition is true or false. If the condition is true, Excel displays one result; if the condition is false, Excel displays a different result. The **IF function** requires that you specify three arguments in order: the logical test, the value if true, and the value if false.

You can use this feature to display a Met goal! message if an individual's sales for the month meet or exceed the target sales. Otherwise, you don't want any message to display.

To Use IF to Display a Message

① Open the e-0503 workbook, and save the file as Functions3.

A partially completed Sales Force Monthly Earnings Report for Fun with Frisbees displays on the IF-duo sheet.

② Click cell C11, and click the Paste Function button.

③ Select the Logical function category in the Paste Function dialog box, and select the IF function (see Figure 5.13).

Figure 5.13
The description near the bottom of the Paste Function dialog box tells you that the IF function returns one value if a condition you specify evaluates to TRUE; another value if it evaluates to FALSE.

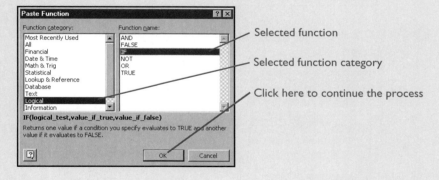

Selected function

Selected function category

Click here to continue the process

④ Click OK.

The IF formula palette displays. If cell contents in rows 1 through 11 are not visible, drag the palette below row 11.

5 Click in the Logical_test window of the IF formula palette; click cell B11, and type >= (greater-than symbol followed by an equal sign).

6 Click cell A7, and press F4 to make the reference absolute.

The first argument in the IF function, which tests whether sales for the first salesperson are greater than or equal to the sales target for the month, is entered (see Figure 5.14). Excel displays B11>=$A$7 in the formula palette and =IF(B11>=$A$7) in cell C11 and the formula bar.

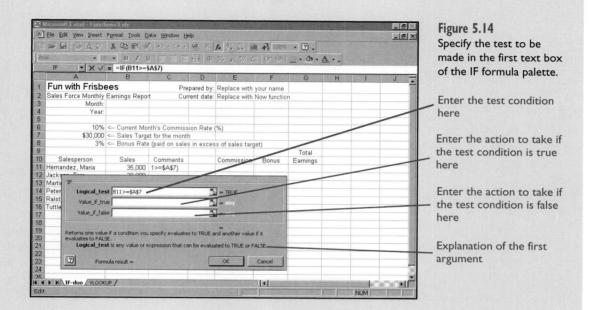

Figure 5.14
Specify the test to be made in the first text box of the IF formula palette.

Enter the test condition here

Enter the action to take if the test condition is true here

Enter the action to take if the test condition is false here

Explanation of the first argument

7 Click in the Value_if_true window, and type Met Goal!

8 Click in the Value_if_false window, and enter " " (type a quotation mark, press Spacebar, and type another quotation mark).

Make sure that your specifications for the three arguments match those shown in Figure 5.15, and edit as necessary. If you do not enter a second argument, Excel displays the word TRUE if the test condition is met. If you do not enter a third argument—in this case, a space between quotation marks that makes a cell appear blank—Excel displays the word FALSE if the test condition is not met.

9 Click OK.

The phrase Met Goal! displays in cell C11. The sales amount in cell B11 (35,000) exceeds the target sales amount in cell A7 ($30,000).

10 Click cell C11, and drag the fill handle down to copy the IF function to the range C12:C16.

The phrase Met Goal! displays in three more cells: C14, C15, and C16. No message appears in cells C12 and C13 because the corresponding sales amounts in column B are less than the target sales in cell A7.

continues ▶

To Use IF to Display a Message   (continued)

Figure 5.15
The function in the formula bar reflects the specifications in the IF formula palette.

Current function, based on entries in the IF formula palette

Explanation of the third argument

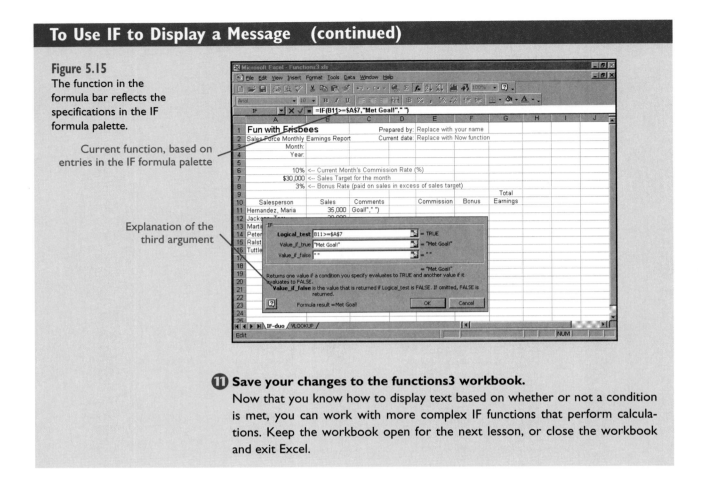

⑪ **Save your changes to the functions3 workbook.**
Now that you know how to display text based on whether or not a condition is met, you can work with more complex IF functions that perform calculations. Keep the workbook open for the next lesson, or close the workbook and exit Excel.

 ## Lesson 6: Using IF to Calculate

As you continue to develop the Sales Force Monthly Earnings Report for Fun with Frisbees, you realize that you can use an IF function to calculate bonuses. Only those members of the sales staff whose sales exceed the sales target for the month earn a bonus, currently calculated as 3% of sales in excess of target sales. If sales are equal to or below the target sales, the bonus is zero.

In this lesson, you enter and copy two formulas and one logical function. The first formula calculates each salesperson's commission on sales at the current rate of 10%. The IF function calculates the bonus, if applicable. The second formula computes total earnings by adding commission and bonus.

To Use IF to Calculate

❶ **Open the Functions3 workbook, if necessary, and click cell E11 in the IF-duo sheet.**

❷ **Type =B11*$A$6, press ↵Enter, and click cell E11.**
The formula =B11*$A$6 displays in the formula bar and the formula results (3,500) display in cell E11.

3 **Drag the fill handle for cell E11 down to copy the formula to the range E12:E16.**

Ensure that the commissions for the other members of the sales force compute correctly at 10% of sales. For example, Tom Jackson's commission is 2,800; Susan Tuttle's commission is 4,100.

 If You Have Problems...

If your results are not consistent with the previous examples, make sure that the reference to cell A6 is absolute in the commission formula (a dollar sign should precede both the column letter A and the row number 6).

4 **Click cell F11 and click the Paste Function button on the toolbar.**

5 **Select the Logical function category in the Paste Function dialog box; select the IF function, and select OK.**

The IF formula palette displays. If cell contents in rows 1 through 11 are not visible, drag the palette below row 11.

6 **Click in the Logical_test text box of the IF formula palette; click cell B11, and type > (greater-than symbol).**

7 **Click cell A7, and press F4 to make the reference absolute.**

The first argument in the IF function, which tests whether sales for the first salesperson are greater than the sales target for the month, is entered.

8 **In the Value_if_true text box, enter (B11-$A$7)*$A$8.**

The second argument in the IF function, which subtracts target sales from actual sales, and multiplies the difference by the current bonus percentage, is entered.

9 **In the Value_if_false text box, enter 0 (zero).**

The third argument in the IF function is entered. Ensure that your specifications for the three arguments in the IF formula palette match those shown in Figure 5.16, and edit as necessary. In this case, you decide to enter a zero if no bonus is earned, instead of leaving the cell blank.

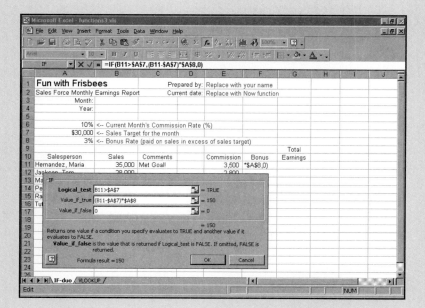

Figure 5.16
The specifications to calculate a bonus, if any, display in the IF formula palette.

continues ▶

To Start PowerPoint   (continued)

⑩ Click OK, and copy the function in cell F11 down to the range F12:F16.

Four members of the sales force earn bonuses and two do not (see Figure 5.17).

Figure 5.17
Copying the formula in cell F11 calculates the bonuses, if any, due to other salespeople.

IF function

IF function result (test condition is met)

IF function result (test condition is not met)

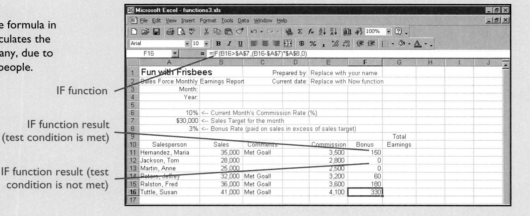

⑪ Click cell G11, and enter the formula =E11+F11.

⑫ Copy the formula in cell G11 to the range G12:G16, and click the Save button.

The Sales Force Monthly Earnings Report is nearly finished. Keep the workbook open for the next lesson, or close the workbook and exit Excel.

 Inside Stuff: **Nesting Functions within Functions**
You can use a function as one of the arguments of another function. For example, nesting more IF statements within an IF statement enables you to calculate the price of a ticket if the ticket price is dependent on age—one price for seniors, another for adults, yet another for children. Use onscreen Help to learn more about nesting functions within functions.

 ## Lesson 7: Using NOW to Display the Current Date

You are nearly finished designing the Sales Force Monthly Earnings Report for Fun with Frisbees. You plan to update and print this report monthly, and you want to enter a date so that it displays the current date each time you open the report workbook.

Excel stores dates as sequential (also called serial) numbers. For example, a 1900 date system assigns the number 1 to January 1, 1900 and the number 2 to January 2, 1900. For each succeeding day, the assigned number increments by one. Under this system, the numbers 36161 and 36526 are assigned to January 1, 1999 and January 1, 2000 respectively. Onscreen Help provides extensive information on how Microsoft Excel stores dates and interprets two-digit years.

A variety of Date and Time functions are available, including DATE, NOW, and TODAY. For example, the **NOW function** enters the serial number of the current date and time; numbers to the left of a decimal point represent the date, and numbers to the right of the decimal point represent the time. Before or after you enter a NOW function, you can apply a variety of date and/or time formats to the cell.

In this lesson, you enter a NOW function and experiment with several ways to display the current date or time. You also finish documenting the worksheet by entering your name, and the month and year to which the report applies.

To Use NOW to Display the Current Date

1 **If necessary, open the** Functions3 **workbook, and click cell E2 on the IF-duo sheet.**

2 **Type** =NOW() **and press** ⏎Enter.
Number signs (########) fill cell E2, indicating that the cell is too narrow to display numeric content. Before you widen the column, check to see whether applying the desired date and/or time format fixes the problem.

3 **Click cell E2, and choose F̲ormat, C̲ells.**

4 **Choose the Number tab; select Date in the C̲ategory window, and select the setting in the T̲ype window that displays only a date in the form 3/14/1998.**
Make sure that your selections match those displayed in Figure 5.18, and make changes as necessary.

Select the category of number format here —

Select the display type within the selected category here

Scroll to view other date and time formats —

General instructions for date and time formats

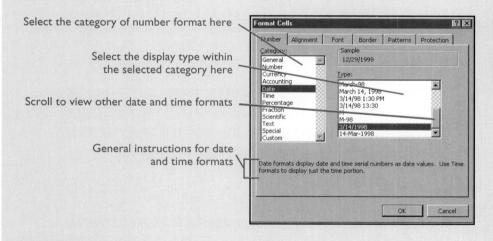

Figure 5.18
Use the Number tab in the Format Cells dialog box to select among a wide variety of date formats.

5 **Click OK.**
The current date displays in cell E2 in the form *mm/dd/yyyy*.

6 **Enter your full name in cell E1.**

7 **Make cell A1 the current cell, and save your changes to the** functions3 **workbook.**
Keep the workbook open for the last lesson, or close the workbook and exit Excel.

***Inside Stuff:*   Entering a Date That Doesn't Change**
If you do not want the date to update each time you open a workbook, just type the date without using a function. If you type the date in a common format, such as 12/31/99, you can still use the Format Cells dialog box to apply a different date style.

***Exam Note:*   Using the DATE Function in a Formula**
Excel 2000 includes 20 functions in the Date and Time category. One function commonly used in formulas is the DATE function, which generates the serial number representing a specified date. For example, the function =DATE(2010,1,1) enters the serial number 40179, indicating that January 1, 2010 is the 40,179th day since 1/1/1900.

The DATE function is most useful in a formula. For example, the formula =DATE(2010,1,1)-NOW() calculates the days between the current date and January 1, 2010.

 Lesson 8: Using VLOOKUP to Convert Data

Excel provides several functions that you can use to create data by converting numbers to text and text to numbers. You can also use these functions to expand coded data, such as displaying the term Accounting each time the code AC is found. If the data you want to look up is stored vertically in a table—that is, in columns— use the ***VLOOKUP function***. If the data is stored horizontally—that is, in rows—use the ***HLOOKUP function***.

In this lesson, you use the VLOOKUP function to convert numeric data to text. You are analyzing survey data completed by customers who recently rented vehicles from Indy 500 Motor Works. When you print a report showing satisfaction ratings, you want descriptions to appear instead of the numeric codes 1 through 5. Figure 5.19 illustrates the important components of the VLOOKUP function you create in this lesson.

Figure 5.19
You enter a VLOOKUP function in cell K18 that looks in the first column of the table for a match to the data in cell J18.

The value to look up must be in the leftmost column of the table

Data in the leftmost column must be in ascending order

Column 2 in the table

The first value to look up in the table

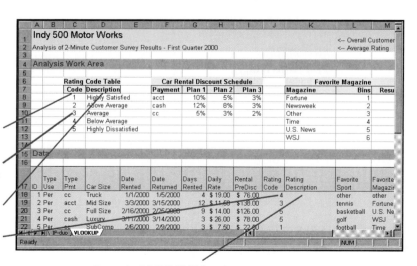

Enter the VLOOKUP function to convert a number (the rating code 4) to text (Below Average)

To Use VLOOKUP to Convert Data

1 **Open the `functions3` workbook if necessary; select the VLOOKUP sheet, and click cell K18.**

2 **Click the Paste Function button; select Lookup & Reference as the function category; select VLOOKUP as the function name, and click OK.**

The VLOOKUP formula palette appears on your screen. If you prefer to select ranges with a mouse instead of typing them, drag the formula palette away from the cells you need to select.

3 **Enter J18 in the Lookup_value text box.**

4 **Enter $C$8:$D$12 in the Table_array text box.**

In this case, the range C8:D12 is an array constant, which means a group of constants arranged in a special way and used as an argument in a formula. Specifying dollar signs makes the reference to the table absolute. This is necessary because you are going to copy the VLOOKUP function.

5 **Enter 2 in the Col_index_num text box (see Figure 5.20).**

Col_index_num tells the VLOOKUP function that when it finds the appropriate value in the table, it should select the corresponding value from the second column in the Table_array.

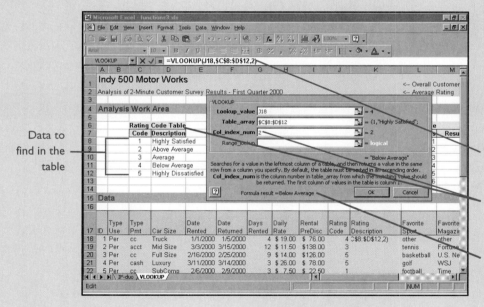

Data to find in the table

Figure 5.20
You can type the function shown in the formula bar, or you can specify the components of the function using the VLOOKUP formula palette.

The VLOOKUP function displays in the formula bar

Look in column 2 for the description to enter in K18

Result of the VLOOKUP function to be entered in cell K18

6 **Click OK to close the formula palette.**

Below Average displays in cell K18 as the description for rating code 4.

> **X** **If You Have Problems...**
> When cell K18 is selected, =VLOOKUP(J18,$C$8:$D$12,2) should display in the formula bar. Edit the formula as needed. Be sure to include the dollar signs that make the reference to the range C8:D12 absolute before you copy the function in the next step.

continues ▶

To Use VLOOKUP to Convert Data   (continued)

7 Copy the function in cell K18 to the range K19:K47.

The copied VLOOKUP functions produce code descriptions in the range K19:K47. Excel looks up each value in the Rating Code column J and enters the corresponding rating description in column K. For example, the rating code in cell J22 is 1. Excel found that value in the first column of the table_array (C8:D12), looked up the corresponding label Highly Satisfied in the second column of the table_array, and placed that label in cell K22.

8 Save your changes to the functions3 workbook.

This concludes Project 5. You can continue with end-of-project activities or exit Excel.

 Exam Note: **Finding an Exact Match with the VLOOKUP Function**

An optional fourth component to the VLOOKUP function is named Range_lookup. If you specify the logical value TRUE for this component, or omit it as in the previous illustration, the function uses the largest value that is less than or equal to the lookup_value. For example, if the rating code being looked up is 2.5, which is not one of the whole number choices in the leftmost column of the table, the function selects the description for rating code 2. However, if you specify False as the Range_lookup, only exact matches satisfy the lookup.

Summary

This project presented a small sample of the hundreds of predefined formulas that Excel provides. By working with AVERAGE, MAX, and MIN, you added to your knowledge of statistical functions. (SUM was presented in a previous project.) You had a rather in-depth experience with one financial function—first by using PMT to calculate a single monthly payment and then by constructing a table of monthly payments and other data. The FV scenario provided you the opportunity to see the effects of varied interest rates on the future value of a savings plan.

You glimpsed the power of an electronic worksheet over a calculator when you used the logical IF function to vary results, depending on whether a test condition was met or not. After you learned how Excel stores dates, you used the date and time NOW function to enter a date that automatically updates to the current system date. You also viewed a variety of date and time formats before applying one to the cell containing the NOW function. The project ended with the creation of text data from numbers using the VLOOKUP function.

You can extend your learning by viewing related Help topics. The Contents tab includes the topic Creating Formulas and Auditing Workbooks. Subtopics include Using Functions and Worksheet Function Reference. Also take advantage of the many opportunities to work with functions in the end-of-project exercises.

Checking Concepts and Terms

True/False

For each of the following, check *T* or *F* to indicate whether the statement is true or false.

__T __F   **1.** The PMT function is one of the statistical functions provided by Excel. [L2]

__T __F   **2.** Nearly all functions have one or more arguments. [L1]

__T __F   **3.** If data you want to look up is stored vertically in a table—that is, in columns—use the HLOOKUP function. [L8]

__T __F   **4.** Use the NOW function to display the current system date. [L7]

__T __F   **5.** The Paste Function dialog box provides a description of the selected function. [L2]

Multiple Choice

Circle the letter of the correct answer for each of the following.

1. Which of the following is a function that returns different results, depending on whether a specified condition is true or false? [L5]

   a. OR

   b. IF

   c. EITHER

   d. none of the above

2. Which of the following characters separates the arguments in a function? [L2]

   a. $ (dollar sign)

   b. : (colon)

   c. / (forward slash)

   d. none of the above

3. Which of the following is a valid function, assuming that the range B5:B15 includes numbers? [L1]

   a. =AVG(B5:B15)

   b. =SUM(B5:B15)

   c. both a and b

   d. none of the above

4. Assume that you plan to use an IF function to display the message Over Budget, if the actual costs in cell A3 exceed the budgeted costs in cell B3, and to display the message Within Budget, if actual costs are equal to or less than budgeted costs. Which of the following would be a valid test condition in the IF function? [L5]

   a. A3<B3

   b. A3<=B3

   c. A3>B3

   d. b or c could be used as the test condition

5. Which of the following are used to encase the arguments in a function? [L1]

   a. quotation marks

   b. parentheses

   c. square brackets

   d. none of the above

Skill Drill

Skill Drill exercises reinforce project skills. Each skill reinforced is the same, or nearly the same, as a skill presented in the project. Detailed instructions are provided in a step-by-step format.

Each exercise is independent of the others, so you can complete the exercises in any order. Be sure to save the workbook after completing each exercise. If you need a paper copy of the completed exercise, enter your name centered in a header before printing. Other print options have already been set to print compressed to one page and to display the filename, sheet name, and current date in a footer.

Before beginning your first Project 5 Skill Drill exercise, complete the following steps:

1. Open the file named `e-0504` and save it as `e5drill`.

   The workbook contains four sheets: an overview sheet, and exercise sheets named #1-Stats, #2-Text-IF, and #3-COUNT.

2. Click the Overview sheet to view the organization of the Project 5 Skill Drill Exercises workbook.

If you need more than one work session to complete the desired exercises, continue working on `e5drill` instead of starting over on the original e-0504 file.

1. Analyzing Data with SUM, AVERAGE, MIN, and MAX

You manage a sales force of 10, and it's time to analyze last month's data on commissions earned.

To perform simple statistical analysis:

1. Open the `e5drill` workbook, and select the sheet tab named #1-Stats.

2. Click cell E11, and enter the function `=SUM(C11:C20)`.

3. Click cell E12, and enter the function `=AVERAGE(C11:C20)`.

4. Click cell E13, and enter the function `=MAX(C11:C20)`.

5. Click cell E14, and enter the function `=MIN(C11:C20)`.

2. Using IF to Display a Message

Your firm's annual sales meeting is next month, and you are in charge of identifying those members of the sales force who will receive the Super Star Award. You already have a worksheet that lists names alphabetically, along with the amount of sales and commissions earned. Now, you want to add a column in which the phrase Super Star appears for those whose sales meet or exceed the minimum sales for the award. You also decide to display the phrase Keep Trying for those who didn't reach the award minimum.

To use an IF function to produce the desired results:

1. Open the `e5drill` workbook, and select the sheet tab named #2-Text-IF.

2. Click cell D10, and click the Paste Function button on the toolbar.

3. Select the Logical function category in the Paste Function dialog box; select the IF function, and click OK.

   The IF formula palette displays. If the cells in rows 1 through 10 are not visible, drag the palette below row 10.

4. Click in the Logical_test text box of the IF formula palette; click cell B10, and type >= (greater than symbol, followed by an equal sign).

5. Click cell D5, and press F4.

   The first argument in the IF function, which tests whether sales for the first salesperson are greater than or equal to the sales needed for the award, is entered.

6. Click in the Value_if_true text box, and type **Super Star**.

7. Click in the Value_if_false text box, and type **Keep Trying**.

8. Click OK, and check that the phrase Keep Trying displays in cell D10.

9. Click cell D10, and drag the fill handle down to copy the IF function to the range D11:D19.
   The phrase Super Star displays for Jessica Keller, Shea Lewis, and Sarah Tyler if the function has been entered and copied correctly.

3. Analyzing Data with COUNT and COUNTIF

You already know how to use the SUM, AVERAGE, MAX, and MIN functions in data analysis. Now, you want to see whether there are functions that count—such as counting all cells containing sales numbers, and counting only those cells that contain sales greater than a specified amount. The Paste Wizard dialog box lists four related statistical functions: COUNT (cells that contain numbers), COUNTA (all cells), COUNTBLANK (blank cells), and COUNTIF (cells that meet specified criteria).

To analyze data by using COUNT and COUNTIF:

1. Open the **e5drill** workbook, and select the worksheet named #3-COUNT.

2. Click cell A4, and enter the function **=COUNT(B13:B22)**.
   Excel displays 10 as the count of cells containing numbers in the range B13:B22.

3. Click cell A8, and enter **25000** as the target sales.

4. Click cell A6, and click the Paste Function button on the toolbar.

5. Select the Statistical function category in the Paste Function dialog box; select the COUNTIF function, and select OK.
   The COUNTIF formula palette displays. If the cell contents in columns A and B are not visible, drag the palette to the right of column B.

6. Click in the Range text box of the COUNTIF formula palette, and select the range B13:B22.

7. Click in the Criteria text box, type > (greater than), and click cell A8.
   You think the arguments have been entered correctly, but the message Formula Result = at the bottom of the COUNTIF formula palette does not show an answer.

8. Click OK.
   The results are not correct. Cell A6 displays a count of 0. The problem relates to the >A8 portion of the COUNTIF function. Excel encases the stated criteria >A8 in quotation marks (see the formula bar), which keeps the contents of cell A8 from being treated as number data.

9. Click cell A8, and edit the entry to read >25000 instead of 25000.

10. Click cell A6, and edit the function to delete the greater than sign (>) and the quotation marks.
    The results are now correct. The function =COUNTIF(B13:B22,A8) returns a count of 7 in cell A6.

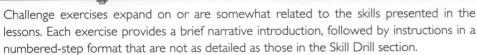

Challenge

Challenge exercises expand on or are somewhat related to the skills presented in the lessons. Each exercise provides a brief narrative introduction, followed by instructions in a numbered-step format that are not as detailed as those in the Skill Drill section.

Each exercise is independent of the others, so you can complete the exercises in any order. Be sure to save the workbook after completing each exercise. If you need a paper copy of the completed exercise, enter your name centered in a header before printing. Other print options have already been set to print compressed to one page and to display the filename, sheet name, and current date in a footer.

Before beginning your first Project 5 Challenge exercise, complete the following steps:

1. Open the file named **e-0505** and save it as **e5challenge**.

   The e5challenge workbook contains four sheets: an overview sheet, and three exercise sheets named #1-NewData, #2-Overtime, and #3-Schedule.

2. Click the Overview sheet to view the organization of the Project 5 Challenge Exercises workbook.

If you need more than one work session to complete the desired exercises, continue working on the **e5challenge** workbook instead of starting over on the original e-0505 file.

1. Using Functions to Create New Data

You enjoy tracking daily average temperatures each month. For the current month, you want to use functions to calculate the average temperature for the month and to find the highest and lowest temperatures in the month. You also want to display the message Below Freezing each day that the average temperature was 32 degrees Fahrenheit or less.

To use functions to create this new data:

1. Open your **e5challenge** workbook, and select the worksheet named #1-NewData.

2. In cell F9, enter a function to display the highest temperature stored in column B.

3. In cell F10, enter a function to display the lowest temperature stored in column B.

4. In cell F11, enter a function to calculate the average of the temperatures stored in column B.

5. In cell C6, enter a function to display the message Below Freezing if the average temperature for the first day of the month is less than the freezing temperature stored in cell E5. Cell C6 should appear blank if the average temperature for Day 1 is equal to or above the freezing temperature.

   Use good worksheet-design techniques. Do not use raw numbers in formulas!

6. Copy the function down column C to all cells adjacent to the temperatures for days 1 through 31.

7. Check that the results are accurate and make changes as necessary.

2. Using IF to Calculate Gross Pay Including Overtime

You want to calculate gross pay, including overtime, by using the minimum number of columns for data and formulas. At the present time, your firm follows a common policy of paying one-and-a-half times the base wage rate for each hour worked over 40. The overtime premium and number of hours to work are subject to change, though, and you want to set up a worksheet model that still works if there are changes in policy. Your worksheet model to calculate weekly gross pay is almost finished.

To use an IF function to calculate weekly gross pay:

1. Open your **e5challenge** workbook, and select the worksheet named #2-Overtime.

2. Select cell D10; display the Paste Function dialog box, and select the logical function IF.

3. Enter appropriate arguments in the IF formula palette.
   Remember to use cell references (not numbers) in formulas and to check whether a cell reference needs to be absolute before copying.

4. Check that the function in cell D10 correctly computes the $550 weekly gross pay for Jordan Fields, and make corrections to the function as needed.

5. Copy the function to compute the weekly gross pay for the other employees.

3. Using NOW in a Worksheet Tracking Project Deadlines

You are the Project Manager for Jordan Construction Company's Projects 1 through 4. For planning purposes, you like to be able to display the months or years remaining on very long-term projects. You want this data to update each day.

To use NOW in a worksheet tracking project deadlines:

1. Open your **e5challenge** workbook and select the worksheet named #3-Schedule.

2. In cell D4, enter a function to display the current system date. The format of the date should be the same as that applied to the other cells displaying dates.

3. In cell C9, enter a formula to calculate the months remaining from now until the target completion date for the first project.
   Remember that the results should be expressed in months, not days.

4. In cell D9, enter a formula to calculate the years remaining from now until the target completion date for the first project.
   Remember that the results should be expressed in years, not days. Excel provides a YEARFRAC function that might be of use here, but you do not need it to produce the correct results.

5. Verify that formulas are correct, and copy the formulas to compute the months and years remaining for the other projects.

Discovery Zone

Discovery Zone exercises require an advanced knowledge of topics presented in *MOUS Essentials* lessons, application of skills from multiple lessons, or self-directed learning of new skills.

Each exercise is independent of the others, so you can complete the exercises in any order. Be sure to save the workbook after completing each exercise. If you need a paper copy of the completed exercise, enter your name centered in a header before printing. Other print options have already been set to print compressed to one page and to display the filename, sheet name, and current date in a footer.

Before beginning your first Project 5 Discovery Zone exercise, complete the following steps:

1. Open the Excel file named **e-0506** and save it as **e5discovery**.
   The e5discovery workbook contains three sheets: an overview sheet, and two exercise sheets named #1-Design-IF and #2-HLOOKUP.

2. Click the Overview sheet to view the organization of the Project 5 Discovery Zone Exercises workbook.

If you need more than one work session to complete the desired exercises, continue working on **e5discovery** instead of starting over on the original e-0506 file.

1. Using IF to Calculate Customer Discounts

Your firm recently implemented a program to allow customers a 2 percent discount on the amount due if the payment is received within 10 days of the billing date. Both the percent discount and the restriction on the number of days are subject to change. You are in the process of creating a worksheet that calculates the correct discount after checking to see whether the payment was made within the required time period.

Open the **e5discovery** workbook and select the worksheet named #1-Design-IF. You already entered data on eight sample customers. Now, you are ready to set up the necessary calculations and enter sufficient documentation so that others can easily use the model. You plan to incorporate good worksheet-design techniques, which include not using raw numbers in formulas.

2. Using HLOOKUP to Convert Text to Numbers

You would like to analyze data on contributions you have made to a variety of agencies and organizations. You have the agency names entered in a row above the data. Now you want to convert the agency names to unique numeric codes, so that you can generate a frequency distribution. Because the names to convert are entered across a row instead of down a column, use HLOOKUP instead of VLOOKUP.

Open the **e5discovery** workbook and select the #2-HLOOKUP worksheet. The names of the agencies or organizations that have received your contributions are already in alphabetical order across row 3 in the range A3:J3. Enter the numbers 1 through 10, one to a cell, in the range A4:J4—that is, the number 1 in cell A4, the number 2 in cell B4, and so forth. Enter a HLOOKUP function in cell D12 that will display the number code if the lookup value is Church. Copy the function in cell D12 to the range D13:D45. Check the accuracy of number assignments in the Agency Code column D. For example, verify that the number 4 displays in cell D20 and the number 8 displays in cell D30.

PinPoint Assessment

You have completed this project and its associated lessons, and have had an opportunity to assess your skills through the end-of-project questions and exercises. Now use the PinPoint software Evaluation Mode to further assess your comprehension of the specific exam activities you have just learned. You can also use the PinPoint Trainer Mode and the Show Me tutorials to practice these exam activities.

Creating and Modifying Charts

Key terms introduced in this project include

- chart
- clustered column chart
- column chart
- combination chart
- data series

- embedded chart
- legend
- line chart
- pie chart
- sizing handles

- stacked column chart
- X-axis
- Y-axis

Objectives	Required Activity for MOUS	Exam Level
➤ Identify Common Chart Types and Features		
➤ Create an Embedded Pie Chart	Use Chart Wizard to create a chart	Core
➤ Create an Embedded Column Chart	Use Chart Wizard to create a chart	Core
➤ Change the Chart Type	Modify charts	Core
➤ Chart Nonadjacent Data Series	Use Chart Wizard to create a chart	Core
➤ Modify Chart Formats	Modify charts	Core
➤ Add, Reorder, and Delete a Data Series	Modify charts	Core
➤ Create and Print a Combination Chart	Preview and print charts	Core

Why Would I Do This?

After you create a worksheet, you may want to show the information to someone else. You can print the worksheet if you need only numerical detail. You can also transform information in the worksheet into a **chart**, a graphical representation of data that makes it easy for users to see trends and make comparisons.

This project shows you how to create an **embedded chart**, which is a graphical representation of data created within the worksheet instead of as a separate worksheet. You create several charts based on sample data. You also learn how to enhance various types of charts and modify chart features.

Lesson 1: Identifying Common Chart Types and Features

You can create a variety of chart types by using Excel. Chart features include titles and labels that explain the graphed data, and enhancements, such as gridlines and color that improve readability or add visual appeal.

In this lesson, you view examples of common chart types and features. You apply this knowledge in the remaining lessons as you create and modify charts similar to those shown in the examples.

To Identify Common Chart Types and Features

1 **Open the file e-0601 and save it as Sample charts.**
This is a workbook with seven sheets, the first of which is named Charts. The remaining sheets illustrate three common types of charts: pie (sheets Pie1 and Pie2), line (sheets Line1 and Line2), and column (sheets Column1 and Column2).

2 **Click the Pie1 sheet tab.**
The sample embedded pie chart shown in Figure 6.1 appears. A **pie chart** is a circular chart, in which each piece (wedge) shows a data segment and its relationship to the whole. A pie chart is limited to one **data series**, which is a set of related values that are entered in a row or column of the worksheet. The chart displays the percentage of Greens Fees earned in each quarter, based on the amounts in row 5. The corresponding text entries in row 4 (Qtr 1, Qtr 2, and so on) appear as data labels for the pie slices.

3 **Click the Pie2 sheet tab.**
The chart embedded in the Pie2 worksheet displays the percentage contribution that each revenue source made toward the total revenues for the year. The data series for this chart is a set of values entered in a column instead of a row. In this sample pie chart, a legend appears to the right of the pie. (A **legend** displays the colors, patterns, or symbols that identify data categories.)

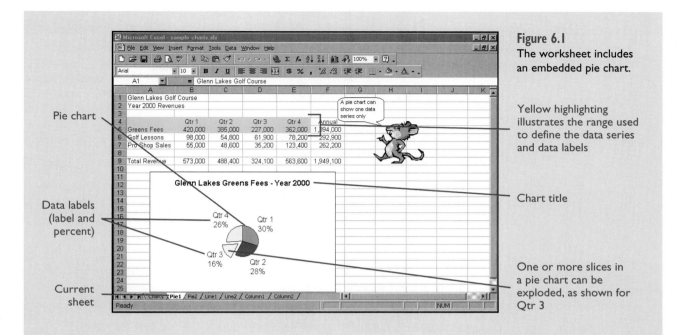

Figure 6.1
The worksheet includes an embedded pie chart.

Pie chart

Yellow highlighting illustrates the range used to define the data series and data labels

Chart title

Data labels (label and percent)

Current sheet

One or more slices in a pie chart can be exploded, as shown for Qtr 3

4 **Click the Line1 sheet tab.**

A *line chart* plots one or more data series as connected points along an axis, as shown in Figure 6.2. The chart illustrates total revenue for each quarter in the year 2000. Data points for each quarter are arranged above the *X-axis*, the horizontal axis of a chart that generally appears at the bottom edge. Each quarterly amount is reflected in the height of its data point in relation to the scale shown on the *Y-axis*, a vertical axis of a chart that usually appears at the left edge.

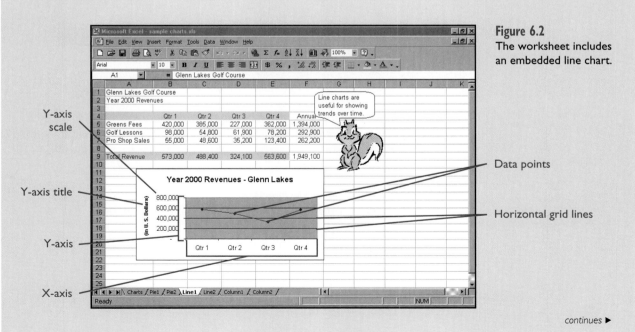

Figure 6.2
The worksheet includes an embedded line chart.

Y-axis scale

Y-axis title

Y-axis

X-axis

Data points

Horizontal grid lines

continues ▶

To Identify Common Chart Types and Features (continued)

5 **Click the Line2 sheet tab.**

The sample line chart embedded in sheet Line2 includes three data series: Greens Fees, Golf Lessons, and Pro Shop Sales. A unique symbol marks each data point in a series, such as the diamond shape assigned to Greens Fees. The legend displays the symbols that identify each data series.

6 **Click the Column1 sheet tab.**

The sample embedded column chart shown in Figure 6.3 appears. In a **column chart**, each data point is reflected in the height of its column in relation to the scale shown on the Y-axis. In this chart, columns are grouped along the X-axis by *quarter*—a result achieved by specifying that data series are organized in *rows*.

Figure 6.3
The worksheet includes an embedded column chart.

First data series in row 5

Second data series in row 6

Third data series in row 7

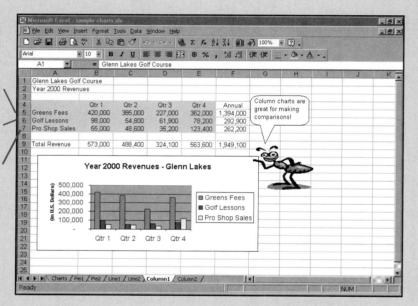

7 **Click the Column2 sheet tab.**

Yellow highlighting indicates the range used to define the column chart, which is the same range used to produce the chart in the Column1 sheet. In this chart, however, columns are grouped along the X-axis by *type of revenue*—a result achieved by specifying that data series are organized in *columns*.

8 **Close the Sample charts file.**

Leave Excel open if you want to continue with the next Lesson.

Exam Note: Printing a Chart

The steps to print a worksheet and its embedded chart(s) are the same as those for printing a worksheet without charts; that is, specify the desired settings in the Page Setup and Print dialog boxes. To print just a chart in Excel without printing the entire worksheet, select the chart by clicking any blank area inside the chart; then choose File, Print to open the Print dialog box. Click the Selected Chart option button in the Print What area, and click OK.

There are advantages to printing a chart instead of viewing it onscreen. Printing lets you view the worksheets you create, even when you are away from your computer. A printed copy of a chart, combined with the worksheet data, makes a very effective presentation.

Lesson 2: Using Chart Wizard to Create an Embedded Pie Chart

To create a chart, you select the data you want to use in the chart and choose Insert, Chart or click the Chart Wizard button on the Standard toolbar. The Chart Wizard provides step-by-step assistance, through a series of dialog boxes, for choosing a chart type and specifying chart options. It automatically creates the chart from the selected data and places it in a box (frame). You can then move, size, change, or enhance the chart. Now, try creating an embedded pie chart that shows the percentage of Year 2000 Greens Fees earned in each quarter.

To Create an Embedded Pie Chart

1 **Open the file e-0602 and save it as mycharts.**
A workbook opens with seven sheets, the first of which is named Pie.

2 **Select the range A4:E5 in the Pie worksheet; then click the Chart Wizard button in the toolbar.**
The Chart Type dialog box opens (Chart Wizard–Step 1 of 4), as shown in Figure 6.4.

3 **In the Chart type list, click Pie.**

4 **Make sure that the selected subtype is Pie, the picture in the upper-left corner.**

5 **Click the Next button at the bottom of the dialog box.**
The Chart Source Data dialog box opens (Chart Wizard—Step 2 of 4), as shown in Figure 6.5.

6 **Make sure that the direction of the data series is Rows, and click Next.**
The Chart Options dialog box opens (Chart Wizard—Step 3 of 4). When the chart type is Pie, the dialog box displays three tabs: Titles, Legend, and Data Labels.

7 **Click the Titles tab, if necessary, to display the dialog box shown in Figure 6.6.**

continues ▶

To Create an Embedded Pie Chart   (continued)

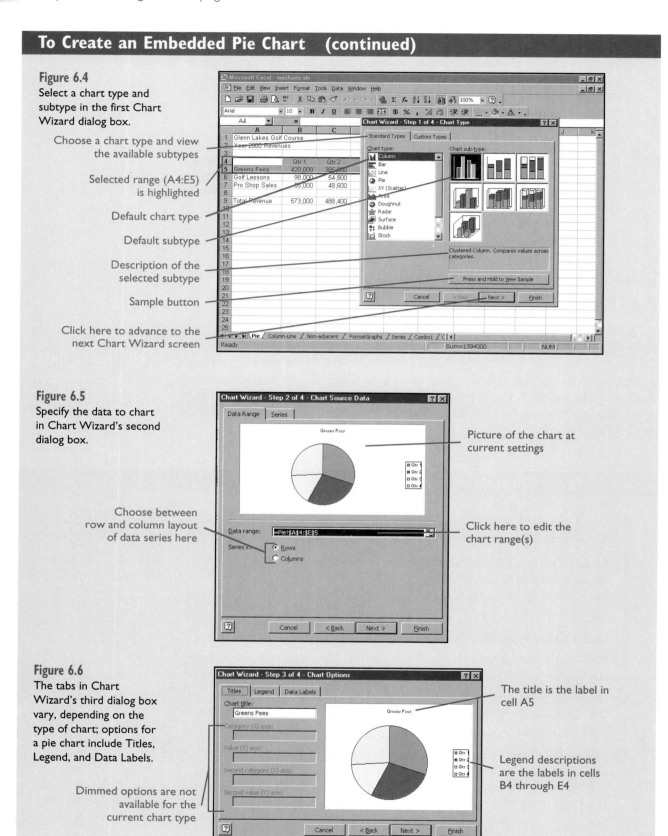

Figure 6.4

Select a chart type and subtype in the first Chart Wizard dialog box.

Choose a chart type and view the available subtypes

Selected range (A4:E5) is highlighted

Default chart type

Default subtype

Description of the selected subtype

Sample button

Click here to advance to the next Chart Wizard screen

Figure 6.5

Specify the data to chart in Chart Wizard's second dialog box.

Choose between row and column layout of data series here

Picture of the chart at current settings

Click here to edit the chart range(s)

Figure 6.6

The tabs in Chart Wizard's third dialog box vary, depending on the type of chart; options for a pie chart include Titles, Legend, and Data Labels.

Dimmed options are not available for the current chart type

The title is the label in cell A5

Legend descriptions are the labels in cells B4 through E4

8 **Click within the Chart <u>T</u>itle text box; edit the title to read** `Year 2000` `Revenues-Greens Fees.`

After a short delay, the revised title automatically appears in the sample chart that fills the right half of the Chart Options dialog box.

 If You Have Problems...

If you press `↵Enter` after editing the title, the Chart Location dialog box appears (Chart Wizard—Step 4 of 4). Press the <u>B</u>ack button to return to the Chart Options dialog box.

9 **Click the Legend tab in the Chart Options dialog box; then click the <u>S</u>how Legend check box to remove the check mark.**

The legend no longer appears on the pie chart.

10 **Click the Data Labels tab in the Chart Options dialog box; then click the** `Show label` **<u>a</u>nd** `percent` **option.**

Quarter labels and associated percentages appear by their respective pie slices, as shown in Figure 6.7.

The sample chart reflects changes in title, legend, and labels.

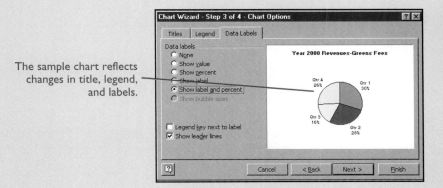

Figure 6.7
The Chart Options dialog box includes a sample chart, illustrating the current settings.

11 **Click Next.**

The Chart Location dialog box appears (Chart Wizard—Step 4 of 4). Select the default option, As <u>o</u>bject in, if you want to see the chart displayed next to its source data. Select the option As new <u>s</u>heet if you prefer to work with the chart separately on its own sheet.

12 **Make sure that the current setting is to place the chart as an object in Pie; then click <u>F</u>inish.**

Excel creates the chart and displays it with eight black squares, called *sizing handles*, at the corners and midpoints of the border surrounding the box. The handles indicate that the chart is an object that can be moved and sized. To move a selected object, click within the object and drag it to its new location. To size a selected object, click a handle and drag it in the desired direction.

 If You Have Problems...

Your screen might display a floating chart toolbar after you click <u>F</u>inish to exit the Chart Wizard. If there is a floating toolbar, and it displays on the chart you are about to move, click the Close button (the X in the upper-right corner of the toolbar).

continues ▶

To Create an Embedded Pie Chart   (continued)

13 **Click inside the chart area (in any blank area) and drag the chart so that the upper-left corner is positioned near the middle of cell A11.**

As you drag the chart, the pointer changes to a four-headed arrow.

14 **Click outside the chart to deselect it.**

The content and layout of the pie chart in your worksheet should resemble the one shown in Figure 6.8. If there are slight differences in chart height, width, or location, you can size or move the chart as desired.

Figure 6.8
The embedded pie chart displays below the data on which it is based.

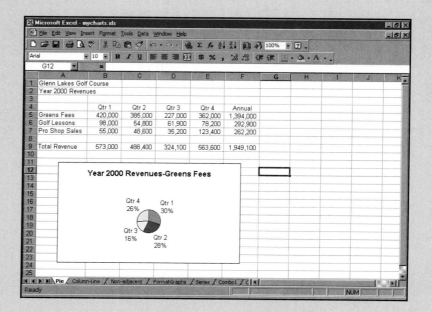

15 **Click the Save button.**

The embedded pie chart is saved in the Pie worksheet. Keep the workbook open for the next lesson, or close the workbook and exit Excel.

 Exam Note: Deleting and Resizing a Chart

If you want to delete a chart, simply select the chart and press Del.

When you resize a chart by dragging a handle on the middle of one side of the box, you change the size horizontally or vertically. When you drag a corner handle, you change the vertical and horizontal dimensions at the same time. If you hold down ⬆Shift while dragging a corner handle, you maintain the original proportions of the chart.

Lesson 3: Using Chart Wizard to Create an Embedded Column Chart

A pie chart is limited to one data series, and the data charted must be components of a whole. Excel provides a variety of other types, including a column chart, suitable for charting multiple data series. You can use the Chart Wizard to construct all chart types. Now, try creating an embedded column chart that compares Year 2000 quarterly revenues from three sources: greens fees, golf lessons, and pro shop sales.

To Create an Embedded Column Chart

1 **Open the file Mycharts, if necessary; then click the Column-Line sheet tab.**
The Column-Line sheet, like the previous Pie sheet, contains the Year 2000 revenue data for Glenn Lakes Golf Course.

2 **Select the range from A4 through E7; then click the Chart Wizard button on the Standard toolbar.**

3 **Click Column in the Chart type list, if it isn't already selected.**

4 **Make sure that the Clustered Column subtype from the Chart subtype list is selected.**

5 **Point to the Press and Hold to View Sample button, and click and hold down the left mouse button.**
A sample of the chart displays in the Sample box, as shown in Figure 6.9.

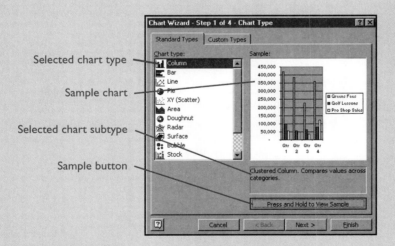

Figure 6.9
The Chart Type dialog box includes a sample of the selected chart type.

Selected chart type

Sample chart

Selected chart subtype

Sample button

6 **Release the mouse button, and click Next.**
The Chart Source Data dialog box appears (Chart Wizard—Step 2 of 4).

7 **Make sure that the data range is $A$4:$E$7 in the Column-Line worksheet and the data series is in Rows, and click Next.**
The Chart Options dialog box appears (Chart Wizard—Step 3 of 4). When the chart type is Column, the dialog box displays six tabs: Titles, Axes, Gridlines, Legend, Data Labels, and Data Table.

continues ▶

To Create an Embedded Column Chart   (continued)

8 **Click the Titles tab, if necessary, and enter the chart title and X-axis title shown in Figure 6.10.**

Figure 6.10
Use titles to explain the data.

Company name and type of data

Time period

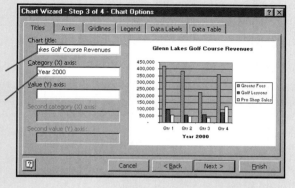

9 **Click Finish, and move the embedded column chart below the worksheet data, as shown in Figure 6.11.**
Clicking Finish bypasses the Chart Location dialog box (Chart Wizard—Step 4 of 4). Excel automatically creates an embedded chart, as opposed to a chart on a separate sheet, unless you specify otherwise.

Figure 6.11
The embedded column chart shows revenues by category.

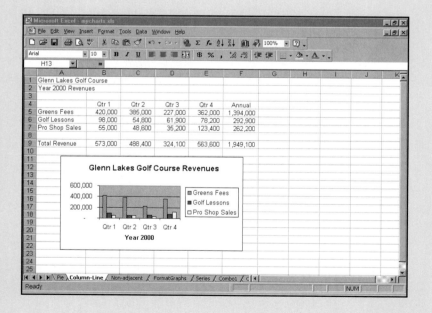

10 **Click the Save button.**
The embedded column chart is saved in the Column-Line worksheet. Keep the workbook open for the next lesson, or close the workbook and exit Excel.

Inside Stuff: **Comparing Clustered and Stacked Column Charts**
A ***clustered column chart*** subtype presents multiple data series as side-by-side columns (refer to Figure 7.11). If you select ***stacked column*** as the chart sub-type, multiple data series appear as stacked components of a single column in-stead of side-by-side columns. The stacked column subtype is appropriate if the multiple data series total a meaningful number. For example, stacking three rev-enue amounts—greens fees, golf lessons, and pro shop sales—in a single column for each quarter is meaningful because it shows the contribution of each rev-enue source to the total revenue for the quarter.

Lesson 4: Changing the Chart Type

It is important to select a chart type that can help you display the information in the most dramatic, appropriate, and meaningful manner possible. For example, you can usually spot trends more easily with a line chart, whereas a pie chart is best for showing parts of a whole.

After you create a chart, you may decide that you do not like the type of chart that you selected or you may want to compare different chart types by using the same data series. Excel enables you to change the chart type without re-creating the entire chart.

Now, make a copy of the embedded column chart and change the type of the copied chart to Line.

To Change the Chart Type

1 **Open the file** `Mycharts`**, if necessary, and click the Column-Line sheet tab.**
The Column-Line sheet includes the embedded column chart that you created in the previous lesson.

2 **Click inside the chart area (in any blank area) to select the entire chart, and click the Copy button.**
A moving dashed line appears inside the chart border. The chart is copied to the Windows Clipboard.

3 **Select a cell below the lower-left corner of the original column chart, and click the Paste button.**
Two identical column charts appear in the Column-Line worksheet, one below the other.

4 **Right-click in any blank area of the second column chart.**
A shortcut menu with chart options appears, as shown in Figure 6.12.

5 **Choose Chart** **T**y**pe on the shortcut menu, and choose Line.**
The default line chart is Line with markers displayed at each data value, as shown in Figure 6.13.

continues ▶

To Change the Chart Type   (continued)

Figure 6.12
Handles on the chart border indicate that the entire chart is selected.

Shortcut menu with chart options

Original column chart

Copy of the column chart

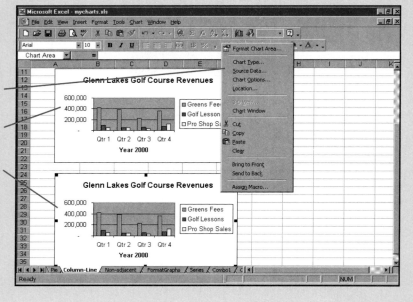

Figure 6.13
You can choose between seven line chart subtypes.

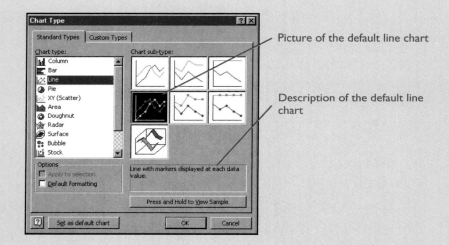

Picture of the default line chart

Description of the default line chart

6 **Click the OK button in the Chart Type dialog box, and click outside the line chart to deselect it.**

Data series are presented in lines instead of columns, as shown in Figure 6.14.

7 **Click the Save button.**

The embedded column and line charts are saved in the Column-Line worksheet. Keep the workbook open for the next lesson, or close the workbook and exit Excel.

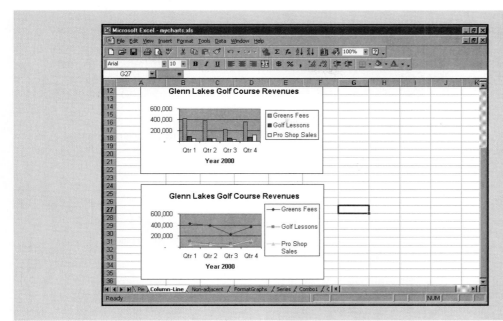

Figure 6.14
The embedded line chart shows revenues by category.

Inside Stuff: **Choosing an Appropriate Chart Type**

In this lesson, you learned the steps to change the chart type. You need to know which chart type(s) to select, given the nature of the data. If you are not familiar with the purpose of one or more chart types, you can display the Office Assistant, search the phrase `chart types`, and select the topic Examples of chart types. This Help topic provides an illustration and description of the standard chart types: area, column, bar, line, pie, doughnut, stock, xy (scatter), bubble, radar, surface, cone, cylinder, and pyramid.

Exam Note: **Other Ways to Change Chart Types**

You can display the Chart Type dialog box after you select the chart you want to change in several ways. You can choose Chart, Chart Type; or click the Chart Wizard button.

You can also change a chart to one of 18 predefined types by using the Chart toolbar. If this toolbar does not automatically appear when you select a chart, choose View, Toolbars, and select Chart. The drop-down list for the Chart Type button on this toolbar is a 3x6 display of chart icons. Click the icon that depicts the type of chart you want.

Lesson 5: Charting Nonadjacent Data Series

You can select nonadjacent sets of numbers to be charted by holding down Ctrl while dragging over numbers in the various areas of the worksheet. Make sure that the sets of numbers selected represent the same data series.

Now, try creating an embedded column chart that compares Year 2000 Greens Fees (the data series in row 5) to Total Revenue (the data series in row 9).

To Chart Nonadjacent Data Series

① **Open the file Mycharts, if necessary, and click the Non-adjacent sheet tab.**
The Non-adjacent sheet contains a copy of the data used in the previous sheets, Pie and Column-Line.

② **Select the range A4 through E5, and press and hold down Ctrl.**

③ **Select the range A9 through E9, and release Ctrl.**
Only the ranges A4 through E5 and A9 through E9 are highlighted.

> **X** *If You Have Problems...*
> Only the first five cells in rows 4, 5, and 9 should be highlighted. If any other cells are selected, click outside the selected areas to deselect them, and repeat Steps 2 and 3.

④ **Click the Chart Wizard button, and make sure that the Standard Types tab is selected in the Chart Type dialog box.**

⑤ **Select Column as the chart type and Clustered Column as the chart subtype, and click Next.**
The Chart Source Data dialog box (Chart Wizard—Step 2 of 4) appears, as shown in Figure 6.15.

Figure 6.15
The column chart compares Greens Fees (the data in row 5) with Total Revenue (the data in row 9).

First data series

Second data series

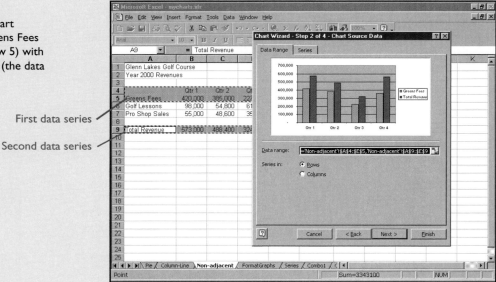

⑥ **Make sure that the Series in setting is Rows, and click Next.**
The Chart Options dialog box appears (Chart Wizard—Step 3 of 4).

⑦ **On the Titles tab, type Impact of Greens Fees on Revenue in the Chart title text box.**

⑧ **Type Glenn Lakes Golf Course – Year 2000 in the Category (X) axis text box, and click Finish.**

9 **Move the newly created chart below its associated worksheet data, as shown in Figure 6.16.**

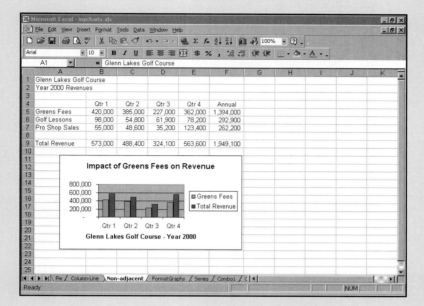

The embedded column chart compares revenue from Greens Fees to Total Revenue for each of four quarters.

10 **Click the Save button.**

The embedded column chart is saved in the Non-adjacent worksheet. Keep the workbook open for the next lesson, or close the workbook and exit Excel.

Lesson 6: Modifying Chart Formats

After you create a chart, you can make changes that improve readability or enhance visual appeal. For example, you can display dollar signs in front of the numbers in a Y-axis scale, italicize a title, add a textured background, and change the color of a data series. The chart in Figure 6.17 reflects these enhancements. You can make these changes yourself now.

Figure 6.17
Changes in the format of chart elements can improve readability and visual appeal of the chart.

Bold, italic, 11-point font

Textured background

$ precedes Y-axis values

Color of the Greens Fees data series is changed to green

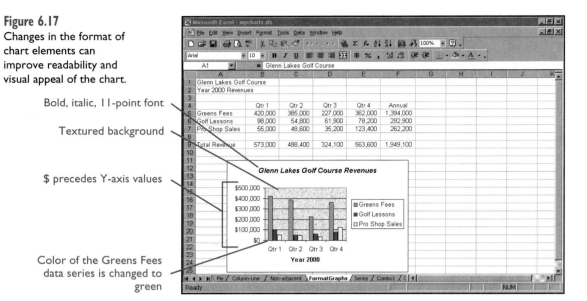

To Modify Chart Formats

1 **Open the file Mycharts, if necessary, and click the FormatGraphs sheet tab.**
The FormatGraphs sheet contains an embedded column chart below the worksheet data.

2 **Position the pointer on any value in the Y-axis scale, and right-click.**
A pop-up menu appears with two options, Format Axis, and Clear. Two small square sizing handles at the top and bottom of the Y-axis indicate that the Y-axis is selected.

3 **Choose Format Axis.**
The Format Axis dialog box opens.

4 **Click the Number tab, and click Currency in the Category list (see Figure 6.18).**

5 **Specify the settings for Decimal places, Symbol and Negative numbers (shown in Figure 6.18), and click OK.**
The Format Axis dialog box closes, and dollar signs appear in front of the Y-axis numbers. The Y-axis remains selected.

6 **Position the pointer anywhere on the chart title, and right-click.**
A shortcut menu appears with two options: Format Chart Title, and Clear. Sizing handles at the corners and midpoints of the border surrounding the title indicate that the title is selected. The sizing handles on the Y-axis disappear, indicating that a selected area of a chart is deselected as soon as another area is selected.

7 **Choose Format Chart Title, and click the Font tab in the Format Chart Title dialog box.**

Preview a sample

Categories of number formats

Top and bottom handles indicate that the Y-axis is selected

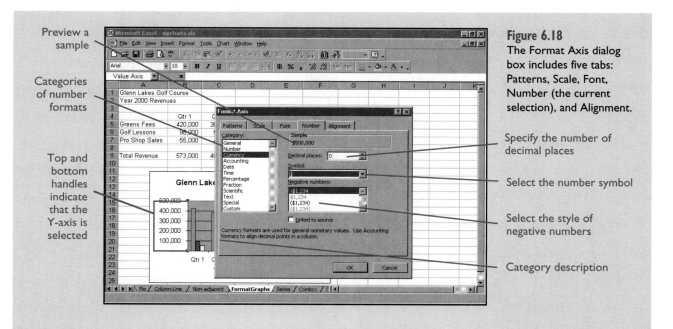

Figure 6.18
The Format Axis dialog box includes five tabs: Patterns, Scale, Font, Number (the current selection), and Alignment.

Specify the number of decimal places

Select the number symbol

Select the style of negative numbers

Category description

8 **Select Bold Italic in the Font style list; select 11 in the Size list, and click OK.**

The Format Chart Title dialog box closes, and the 11-point chart title displays in boldface and italic. The title remains selected.

9 **Position the pointer on a blank area between gridlines in the chart, and right-click.**

A shortcut menu appears with multiple options, the first and last of which are Format Plot Area, and Clear. Sizing handles at the corners and midpoints of the gray shaded area indicate that the plot area is selected.

10 **Choose Format Plot Area.**

The Format Plot Area dialog box opens.

11 **Click the Fill Effects button, and click the Texture tab in the Fill Effects dialog box (see Figure 6.19).**

Scroll to view additional textures

Name of the selected texture

Click here to view other texture options

Sample of the selected texture

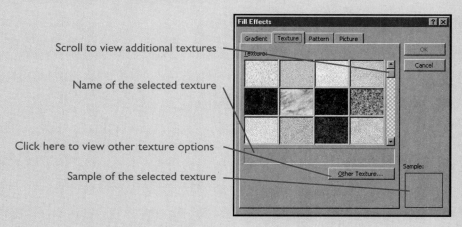

Figure 6.19
The Fill Effects dialog box includes four tabs: Gradient, Texture (the current selection), Pattern, and Picture.

continues ▶

To Modify Chart Formats   (continued)

⓬ **Click the first style in the upper-left corner of the display to select the Newsprint texture, and click OK twice to close, in sequence, the Fill Effects and Format Plot Area dialog boxes.**

A textured background (fill) replaces the solid gray background. The plot area remains selected.

⓭ **Position the pointer on any of the blue columns that represent the quarterly Greens Fees, and right-click.**

A shortcut menu appears with the options shown in Figure 6.20. The small black square in each blue column indicates that the Greens Fees data series is selected.

Figure 6.20
The most common commands applied to a data series display in the shortcut menu.

Name of the selected data series

Contents of the selected data series

Black squares indicate that the data series is selected

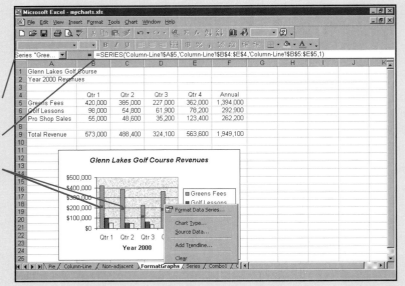

⓮ **Choose Format Data Series, and click the Patterns tab in the Format Data Series dialog box.**

The Patterns tab includes three sections: Border and Sample on the left, and Area on the right.

⓯ **Click the bright green-colored square (the fourth color square in the fourth row) in the Area section, and click OK.**

The color of the Greens Fees data series changes from blue to bright green. The data series remains selected.

⓰ **Click in any blank area to deselect the data series, and click Save.**

The modified column chart is saved in the FormatGraphs worksheet. Keep the workbook open for the next lesson, or close the workbook and exit Excel.

Exam Note: Changing Other Chart Elements

In this lesson, you made changes to four areas in a chart: the Y-axis, the chart title, background, and a data series. You started the change process by positioning the pointer on the area and right-clicking. You can use the same steps to initiate changes in any area of a chart, such as the legend or X-axis.

 Inside Stuff: Alternatives to Shortcut Menus

Right-clicking a chart area displays a context-sensitive shortcut menu that enables you to clear or modify the selected area. You can access chart dialog boxes and modify settings in other ways as well. Double-clicking a chart area bypasses the Clear option and opens the dialog box for formatting that area. You can also access Chart options from the menu bar after you select the entire chart.

 Exam Note: Ways to View a Chart

If you scroll through the worksheet to view a chart, you can view the chart in its own window. First, select the chart; then choose View, Chart Window. You can edit the chart while it is open in the window.

If you select a chart before clicking the Print Preview button, Excel displays only the chart instead of the worksheet data and the chart. You can view, but not change, a chart displayed in Print Preview mode.

Lesson 7: Adding, Reordering, and Deleting a Data Series

Even a relatively small set of data can be charted in a variety of ways. Look at the range A4:E7 in Figure 6.21. In that example, a data series can be a column of data, such as the sales for each year from 1997 through 2000. A data series can also be a row of data, such as the four-year sales pattern for each city.

Each column can be a data series

Each row can be a data series

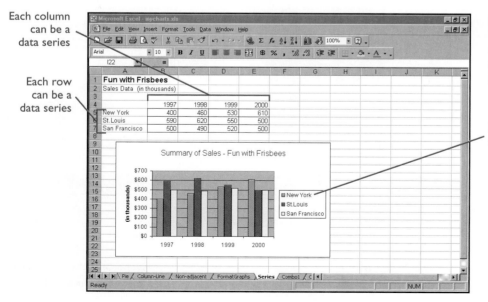

Figure 6.21
You can add, delete, or change the order of data series without recreating a chart.

First data series charted

You can vary the data presented in a chart by adding a data series, rearranging the order of data series, and deleting a data series. In this lesson, you learn to use all three methods to manipulate data series on an existing chart.

To Add, Reorder, or Delete a Data Series

1 Open the file Mycharts, if necessary, and click the Series sheet tab.
This worksheet contains a column chart showing sales for the New York office of Fun with Frisbees over a period of four years. Dollar amounts are displayed along the vertical axis to the left of the plot area, and a legend to the right of the plot area displays the color assigned to the single data series.

2 Position the mouse pointer on one of the four columns in the chart.
A text box shows the data series (New York), the year, and the value (in thousands) for that year. Next, add the data for St. Louis and San Francisco to the chart. Although there is more than one way to accomplish this, the easiest way is with drag-and-drop.

3 Select cells A6:E7; click the border of the selected cells, drag them to the chart, release the mouse button, and deselect the chart.
The chart displays data for all three cities as shown in Figure 6.21. Next, exchange the positions of St. Louis and San Francisco so the cities appear in alphabetical order.

4 Right-click any column in the chart, and select Format Data Series.

5 Select the Series Order tab in the Format Data Series dialog box, and select San Francisco in the Series order list box (see Figure 6.22).

Figure 6.22
Use the Series Order tab in the Format Data Series dialog box to view and change the order of data series.

The current order displays in the Series order list box

The selected data series

Click here to move a selected series up

Click here to move a selected series down

The current order displays in the legend

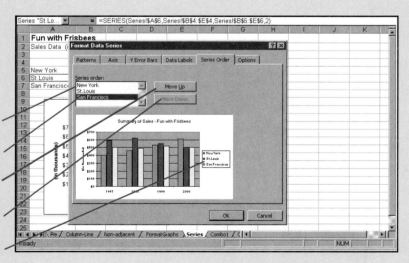

6 Click the Move Up button, and click OK.
The order of the data series changes in both the legend and the plot area. Within the set of columns for each year, San Francisco is now the middle column. Now remove the St. Louis data from the chart.

7 Click any column that represents St. Louis data, and press ⌦.

Any reference to St. Louis data disappears from the plot area and the legend.

8 Click outside the chart to deselect it, and save your changes to the Series worksheet.

You can close the mycharts workbook now or leave it open and continue to the last lesson.

 Inside Stuff: **Alternative Ways to Add or Delete Data Series**

The methods used to add and delete data series illustrated in this lesson are the simplest ways to make those changes to an existing chart—add by dragging a se-lected series and dropping it into the chart; remove by selecting the charted data series and pressing ⌦. You can also make both changes from the Series tab of the Source Data dialog box. Select the chart; choose <u>C</u>hart, <u>S</u>ource Data; and select the Series tab. To add a data series, click the <u>A</u>dd button, and specify the location of the series. To delete a data series, select its name in the <u>S</u>eries list, and click the <u>R</u>emove button.

Lesson 8: Creating and Printing a Combination Chart

A **combination chart** includes two or more chart types, such as showing one data series as a column and another as a line. Create a combination chart if the values in the data series vary widely or if you want to emphasize differences in the data.

The reasons for creating a combination chart do not apply to the Glenn Lakes Golf Course data charted in previous lessons. In this lesson, you chart two data series with widely varying values: the total miles walked, and the average miles per walk.

To Create and Print a Combination Chart

1 Open the file Mycharts, if necessary, and click the Combo1 sheet tab.

The Combo1 sheet illustrates the problem encountered when you chart data series whose values vary widely.

2 Read the Problem and Solution text, and click the Combo2 sheet tab.

The sheet contains only the Year 2000 summary of walking data.

3 Select the range from A3 through E5, and click the Chart Wizard button on the Standard toolbar.

4 Click the Custom Types tab in the Chart Type dialog box, scroll down the <u>C</u>hart type list, and click Line-Column on 2 Axes (see Figure 6.23).

5 Click Next two times to advance to the Chart Options dialog box (Chart Wizard—Step 3 of 4), and click the Titles tab.

6 Type Year 2000 Summary in the Chart <u>t</u>itle text box, and click <u>F</u>inish.

continues ▶

To Create and Print a Combination Chart (continued)

Figure 6.23
Select the Custom Types tab to display variations of standard chart types, including the currently selected chart.

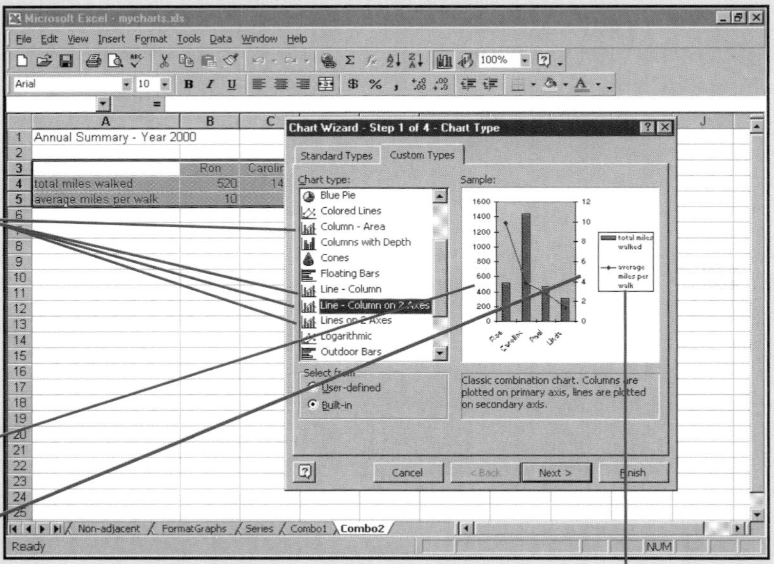

Combination chart types

Y-axis scale related to data in columns

Secondary Y-axis scale, related to data points on the line

Legend identifies the chart type of each data series

❼ **Drag the embedded combination chart below the associated data, as shown in Figure 6.24.**

Figure 6.24
The embedded combination chart includes a second Y-axis at the right side of the chart.

Scale for miles walked (data charted in columns)

Scale for average miles per walk (data charted as points on a line)

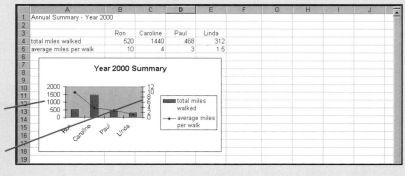

❽ **Click the Save button.**
The embedded combination chart is saved in the Combo2 worksheet. Get in the habit of saving changes before you print to protect against data loss should your system freeze and require a reboot.

❾ **Click any blank area inside the chart to select it, and choose File, Print.**

❿ **Click the Selected Chart option in the Print what area (see Figure 6.25).**

⓫ **Click OK (or click Cancel if you do not want to print at this time).**
This concludes Project 6. Close the workbook, and either continue with the end-of-project activities or exit Excel.

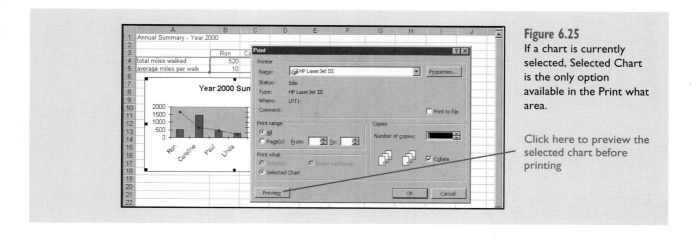

Figure 6.25
If a chart is currently selected, Selected Chart is the only option available in the Print what area.

Click here to preview the selected chart before printing

Summary

In this project, you learned the tasks essential to creating, editing, saving, and printing embedded charts. You used the Chart Wizard to create embedded pie, column, line, and combination charts. You also modified some of the individual elements in a chart: the number format of Y-axis values, font style and size in the chart title, fill effect applied to the background, color assigned to a data series, the number of data series, and the order of data series.

You can extend your learning by experimenting with changes to other elements in a chart. For example, you might remove gridlines, or expand your ability to document a chart by learning how to insert a text box. Change a two-dimensional chart into a 3-D (three-dimensional) one to see if you like the effect. Be sure to browse the extensive coverage of charts available through onscreen Help.

Checking Concepts and Terms

True/False

For each of the following, check *T* or *F* to indicate whether the statement is true or false.

__T __F **1.** After a chart is created, you can choose another chart type if you are not satisfied with the representation of your data. [L4]

__T __F **2.** An embedded chart is a graphical representation of data created as a separate worksheet. [L2]

__T __F **3.** You can print a chart by itself or as part of the worksheet. [L1]

__T __F **4.** You cannot chart data unless the associated data series are entered in rows. [L2]

__T __F **5.** You can chart nonadjacent data series in a worksheet. [L5]

Multiple Choice

Circle the letter of the correct answer for each of the following.

1. Which type of chart is limited to a single data series? [L1]

a. column

b. combination

c. line

d. pie

2. What is the element of a chart that identifies the color, patterns, or symbols assigned to chart data series or categories? [L1]

a. legend

b. data labels

c. X-axis labels

d. chart title

3. What is the horizontal axis of a chart? [L1]

a. Y-axis, which generally appears at the bottom edge of the chart

b. X-axis, which generally appears at the bottom edge of the chart

c. Y-axis, which generally appears at the left edge of the chart

d. X-axis, which generally appears at the left edge of the chart

4. Which Excel feature provides step-by-step assistance to create a line chart? [L2]

a. Drawing Wizard

b. Line Chart Wizard

c. Graph Wizard

d. Chart Wizard

5. Which of the following is a reason for using a combination chart? [L8]

a. A combination chart is more colorful.

b. The values in the data series vary widely.

c. to emphasize differences in the data

d. both b and c

Skill Drill

Skill Drill exercises reinforce project skills. Each skill reinforced is the same, or nearly the same, as a skill presented in the project. Detailed instructions are provided in a step-by-step format.

Each exercise is independent of the others, so you can complete the exercises in any order. Be sure to save the workbook after completing each exercise. If you need a paper copy of the completed exercise, enter your name centered in a header before printing. Other print options have already been set to print compressed to one page and to display the filename, sheet name, and current date in a footer.

Before beginning your first Project 6 Skill Drill exercise, complete the following steps:

1. Open the file named e-0603 and save it as e6drill.

The e6drill workbook contains four sheets: an overview, and exercise sheets named #1-Pie, #2-Column, and #3-Line.

2. Click the Overview sheet to view the organization of the Project 6 Skill Drill Exercises workbook.

If you need more than one work session to complete the desired exercises, continue working on **e6drill** instead of starting over on the original e-0603 file.

1. Creating an Embedded 3-D Pie Chart

You used Excel to create a number of pie charts in the past. For the upcoming Community Volunteer Corps event, however, you'd like to present data in a three-dimensional pie chart.

To create an embedded 3-D pie chart:

1. If necessary, open the **e6drill** workbook, and click the #1-Pie sheet tab.
   You plan to create a pie chart based on the labels and data shown in blue. (The label range A6:A9 and the data range F6:F9 are nonadjacent.)

2. Select the range A6:A9 by clicking cell A6 and dragging the cell pointer to A9.

3. Press and hold down Ctrl.

4. Select the range F6:F9, and release Ctrl.

5. Click the Chart Wizard button in the Standard toolbar to display the Chart Type dialog box.

6. Select Pie as the chart type, and select Pie with a 3-D Visual Effect as the chart subtype.

7. Click Next to display the Chart Source Data dialog box and ensure that the Series is in Columns.

8. Click Next to display the Chart Options dialog box.

9. Deselect Show Legend on the Legend tab, and click Show label and percent on the Data Labels tab.

10. Type `Allocation of 11,340 Volunteer Hours` in the Chart title text box on the Titles tab.

11. Click Finish to accept the default embedded chart and exit Chart Wizard.

12. Move the chart below the data, size as appropriate, and click outside the chart to deselect it.

2. Creating an Embedded Stacked Column Chart

You are looking for a variety of ways to present data on volunteer hours at the upcoming Community Volunteer Corps event. As you look through the subtypes of a column chart, you discover that a *stacked* column chart compares the contribution of each value to a total across all categories. You decide to illustrate the proportion of volunteer hours associated with each volunteer organization in a stacked column format.

To create a stacked column chart:

1. If necessary, open the **e6drill** workbook, and click the #2-Column sheet tab.
   You plan to create a stacked column chart based on the labels and data shown in blue (the range A6:E9).

2. Select the range A6:E9, and click Chart Wizard.

3. In the Chart Type dialog box, select Column as the chart type, and select Stacked Column as the subtype.

4. In the Chart Source Data dialog box, check that Series is in Rows.

5. In the Chart Options dialog box, specify the following titles, and click Finish: Community Volunteer Corps (chart title), Year Just Ended (X-axis title), Volunteer Hours (Y-axis title).

6. Move the chart below the data, size as appropriate, and deselect the chart.

3. Changing Chart Type

As you explore creating a variety of charts for presenting volunteer data, you create a line chart by modifying the chart type of an existing column chart.

To change chart type:

1. If necessary, open the **e6drill** workbook, and click the #3-Line sheet tab.

   The sheet contains a column chart based on the labels and data shown in blue (the range A6:E9).

2. Right-click in a blank area of the column chart, and select Chart Type from the shortcut menu.

3. Select Line as the chart type, and select Line with markers displayed at each data value as the subtype.

4. Click OK, and click outside the line chart to deselect it.

Challenge

Challenge exercises expand on or are somewhat related to skills presented in the lessons. Each exercise provides a brief narrative introduction, followed by instructions in a numbered-step format that are not as detailed as those in the Skill Drill section.

Each exercise is independent of the others, so you can complete the exercises in any order. Be sure to save the workbook after completing each exercise. If you need a paper copy of the completed exercise, enter your name centered in a header before printing. Other print options have already been set to print compressed to one page and to display the filename, sheet name, and current date in a footer.

Before beginning your first Project 6 Challenge exercise, complete the following steps:

1. Open the file named **e-0604** and save it as **e6challenge**.

   The e6challenge workbook contains four sheets: an overview, and exercise sheets named #1-MoveTitle, #2-MoveLegend, and #3-ChangeScale.

2. Click the Overview sheet to view the organization of the Project 6 Challenge Exercises workbook.

If you need more than one work session to complete the desired exercises, continue working on **e6challenge** instead of starting over on the original e-0604 file.

1. Moving a Title

You know that each component of a chart can be moved and sized independently of the other components. You decide to change the Y-axis title on a chart to appear horizontally, above the numbers in the Y-axis scale, instead of appearing vertically to the left of the scale numbers.

To move a title and change its orientation:

1. If necessary, open your **e6challenge** workbook, and click the #1-MoveTitle sheet.

2. Double-click the Y-axis title, and select the Alignment tab on the Format Axis Title dialog box.

3. Drag Orientation to 0 degrees, and close the dialog box.

4. Drag the title to just above the top number on the Y-axis scale.

2. Moving a Legend and Enlarging a Plot Area

Long text descriptions may result in a legend that is quite large in comparison with the plot area of its associated chart. This effect appears in many of the charts that are based on volunteer data. Knowing that the chart's width is nearly twice its height, you decide to move the legend to the bottom of the chart. You also plan to reduce the font size in the legend and enlarge the plot area.

To reposition a legend and enlarge a plot area:

1. If necessary, open your **e6challenge** workbook, and click the #2-MoveLegend sheet.

2. Double-click the legend; click the Placement tab on the Format Legend dialog box, and click Bottom.

3. Click the Font tab on the Format Legend dialog box; click the smallest point size, and close the dialog box.

4. Click the gray background within the plot area, and increase the width and height of the column chart as much as possible to fit within the outside chart border. (Be sure that changes in height are proportional to changes in width.)

3. Changing the Scale Increment

You know that Excel automatically assigns an increment to the numbers displayed on the Y-axis scale. However, you want to change to a lower increment on one of the charts that shows volunteer hours.

To change the Y-axis scale to display in increments of 300 (0, 300, 600, and so on) instead of increments of 500 (0, 500, 1,000, and so on):

1. If necessary, open your **e6challenge** workbook, and click the #3-ChangeScale sheet.

2. Double-click any number on the Y-axis scale, and click the Scale tab on the Format Axis dialog box.

3. Change the Major Unit to 300 instead of 500, and close the dialog box.

Discovery Zone

Discovery Zone exercises require advanced knowledge of topics presented in *MOUS Essentials* lessons, application of skills from multiple lessons, or self-directed learning of new skills.

Each exercise is independent of the others, so you can complete the exercises in any order. Be sure to save the workbook after completing each exercise. If you need a paper copy of the completed exercise, enter your name centered in a header before printing. Other print options have already been set to print compressed to one page and to display the filename, sheet name, and current date in a footer.

Before beginning your first Project 6 Discovery Zone exercise, complete the following steps:

1. Open the file named **e-0605** and save it as **e6discovery**. The e6discovery workbook contains three sheets: an overview, and two exercise sheets named #1-Data and #2-RowCol.

2. Click the Overview sheet to view the organization of the Project 6 Discovery Zone Exercises workbook.

If you need more than one work session to complete the desired exercises, continue working on **e6discovery** instead of starting over on the original e-0605 file.

1. Comparing Data Labels and a Data Table

You want the exact sales figures for baseball bats to be visible in a chart to be presented at the sales meeting next week. A co-worker just told you that Excel supports using data labels or a data table to display the numbers on which a chart is based. However, you're not sure which of the two methods to use. To make up your mind, you created identical column charts, charting the sales of baseball bats. You plan to set up data labels on one and a data table on the other, and compare results. (Make your changes on the sheet named #1-Data in your e6discovery workbook.)

Before you begin, use onscreen Help to learn about showing values as labels and displaying a data table. In the chart on the left in the Data sheet, show the exact number of baseball bats sold that quarter above each column. In the chart on the right, display the associated data table. Which enhancement do you prefer? Would your answer change if you charted all three product lines, instead of only baseball bats?

2. Charting Data Series in Rows or Columns

You know from using the Chart Wizard that you can chart data series in rows or columns. However, you don't have a clear idea what difference that would make in presenting information about sales of baseball bats, tennis racquets, and volleyball nets.

On the #2-RowCol sheet in your e6discovery workbook, create a well-documented clustered column chart that is based on the range A5:E8 (the blue cells). Specify that data series are in rows. Position the chart below the data and size as appropriate. Next, create a well-documented clustered column chart based on the same range and specify that data series are in columns. Position this chart to the right of the first one. (*Hint*: you can quickly create the second chart by copying the first one and changing the source data to columns on the copied chart.) What is the focus of the first chart? What is the focus of the second chart?

PinPoint Assessment

You have completed this project and its associated lessons, and have had an opportunity to assess your skills through the end-of-project questions and exercises. Now use the PinPoint software Evaluation Mode to further assess your comprehension of the specific exam activities you have just learned. You can also use the PinPoint Trainer Mode and the Show Me tutorials to practice these exam activities.

Developing a Multiple-Sheet Workbook

Key terms introduced in this project include

- conditional formatting
- embedded object
- linked object

Objectives	Required Activity for MOUS	Exam Level
➤ Copy Data from Another Application	Import from other applications	Expert
➤ Insert, Move and Rename Worksheets	Insert and delete worksheets; Rename a worksheet; Move and copy worksheets	Core
➤ Edit Multiple Worksheets Simultaneously	Move between worksheets in a workbook	Core
➤ Subtotal Data	Use subtotaling	Expert
➤ Link Worksheets	Link worksheets and consolidate data using 3-D references	Core
➤ Apply Conditional Formatting	Use conditional formatting; Enter functions using the formula palette	Core Expert
➤ Use a Worksheet to Solve a Problem	Preview and print worksheets and workbooks	Core
➤ Save a Worksheet with Chart as a Web Page	Save a worksheet/workbook as a Web page; Use Web Page Preview	Core

Why Would I Do This?

The Excel workbook structure lets you move easily among the different worksheets, add and delete worksheets, move worksheets around, and name each worksheet to make it more identifiable. In addition, you can copy, link, or move cell contents between worksheets, between workbooks, and between applications. With all these tools at your disposal, you can easily manage a workbook of any size.

In this project, you learn to manage workbooks by creating a simple two-sheet workbook. The first sheet provides counts of those planning to attend an event, and the second contains a budget for the event. In the process, you insert a sheet, rename sheets, and apply changes to both sheets at once. You also explore Excel's powerful integration features when you copy data from a Word table to your Excel workbook, link cells between worksheets, and save a worksheet in a format that can be viewed with a Web browser.

Expert Lesson 1: Copying Data from Another Application

Assume that you are responsible for preparing a budget for your Aunt Marie's 90th birthday celebration at the annual family reunion. Your cousin prepared the invitations, tallied the responses, summarized selected data in a Word table, and emailed the information to you this morning. As you look through the table, you realize that you can copy it to a blank Excel workbook and calculate the counts you need to prepare a budget.

Copying from one application to another or copying within an application saves you from having to re-enter data that already exists. You can paste data as either a **linked object** or an **embedded object**. A linked object updates whenever the data in the source file changes; an embedded object does not update when the data in the source file changes.

In this lesson, you copy a Word table to an Excel worksheet as an embedded object. The source file relates to a one-time event and is not updated. You perform the copy by using the Windows Clipboard and task-switching capabilities.

To Copy Data from Another Application

1 Start Excel, if it is not already running, and display a blank worksheet.

2 Start Word, if it is not already running, and open the Word document named e-0701.
Three brief paragraphs and a table display.

3 Click any cell within the Word table.

4 Choose T**a**ble, Sele**c**t, **T**able.
The entire table appears highlighted.

5 Click the Copy button on the toolbar (or select **E**dit, **C**opy).

6 Click Microsoft Excel—Book1 in the taskbar at the bottom of the screen.
The display switches from Microsoft Word to Microsoft Excel.

7 **Click cell A4, and click the Paste button on the toolbar (or choose Edit, Paste).**

Excel copies the Word table to the blank worksheet. Data in each column of the table appears in its own column in the worksheet (see Figure 7.1).

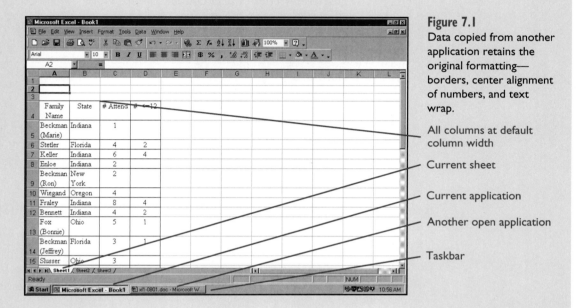

Figure 7.1

Data copied from another application retains the original formatting—borders, center alignment of numbers, and text wrap.

All columns at default column width

Current sheet

Current application

Another open application

Taskbar

8 **Switch to Microsoft Word, and exit Word without saving any changes.**

Excel becomes the active application. The copied data displays unwanted formatting—borders around cells, text wrap in column A, and center alignment in columns C and D.

9 **Select the range A4:D34, and choose Edit, Clear, Formats.**

The unwanted formatting disappears (see Figure 7.2).

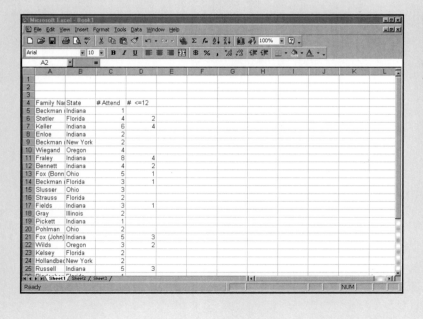

Figure 7.2

Data displays left-aligned (text) or right-aligned (numbers) without borders or text wrap.

continues ▶

To Copy Data from Another Application   (continued)

10 **Widen column A to display long labels.**
Now delete Sheet2 and Sheet3 to prepare the worksheet for the next lesson.

11 **Right-click the Sheet2 tab; choose <u>D</u>elete from the shortcut menu, and click OK.**
Sheet2 is permanently removed from the workbook.

12 **Right-click the Sheet3 tab; choose <u>D</u>elete from the shortcut menu, and click OK.**
Only the Sheet1 worksheet remains.

13 **Save the workbook as Marie90.**
Keep the workbook open for the next lesson, or close the workbook and exit Excel.

Lesson 2: Inserting, Moving, and Renaming Worksheets

You can insert, move, and rename worksheets as well as delete them. Excel positions an inserted worksheet to the left of the current worksheet. You can easily change its position by clicking its sheet name and dragging left or right. Changing the names of worksheets in a multiple-sheet workbook makes it easier to understand the purpose of each sheet.

In this lesson, you insert a sheet, move that sheet, and change the names of both worksheets in the Marie90 workbook. You name one Counts and the other Budget.

To Insert, Move, and Rename Worksheets

1 **Open the Marie90 workbook, if necessary, and double-click the Sheet1 sheet tab.**
Sheet1 displays with a black background, indicating rename mode is active. You could also begin a rename operation by right-clicking the Sheet1 tab and choosing <u>R</u>ename from the shortcut menu.

2 **Type Counts, and press ⏎Enter.**
The sheet is renamed and the worksheet tab displays Counts instead of Sheet1.

3 **Choose <u>I</u>nsert, <u>W</u>orksheet.**
Excel inserts a sheet to the left of the current sheet (see Figure 7.3) and assigns the next available number.

4 **Double-click the Sheet2 sheet tab.**

5 **Type Budget, and press ⏎Enter**
The names of the first two sheets are Budget and Counts, respectively.

6 **Click and drag the Budget sheet to the right of the Counts sheet, and release the mouse button.**
The Counts worksheet is now the first sheet; the blank Budget worksheet is the second sheet.

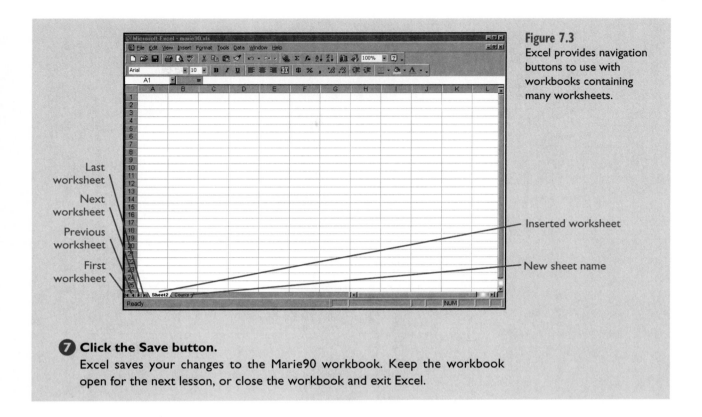

Figure 7.3
Excel provides navigation buttons to use with workbooks containing many worksheets.

Last worksheet

Next worksheet

Previous worksheet

First worksheet

Inserted worksheet

New sheet name

7 **Click the Save button.**
Excel saves your changes to the Marie90 workbook. Keep the workbook open for the next lesson, or close the workbook and exit Excel.

Lesson 3: Editing Multiple Worksheets Simultaneously

Just as you can select multiple cells in Excel, you can select and work with more than one worksheet at a time. This is very helpful if you need to enter the same data or apply the same formatting to more than one sheet.

You can select consecutive sheets by clicking the first sheet, pressing (+Shift), and clicking the last sheet. Select nonadjacent sheets the same way that you select nonadjacent cells— by holding down (Ctrl), and clicking the desired sheets. After selecting multiple worksheets, you can type data and specify settings in any one of the selected worksheets. Excel applies your changes to all the selected worksheets until you ungroup them.

In this lesson, you edit two worksheets simultaneously—the Counts and Budget worksheets of your birthday celebration workbook. After first selecting the worksheets, you enter a title and format the title to display 14-point and bold.

To Edit Multiple Worksheets Simultaneously

1 **Open the Marie90 workbook, if necessary.**
The workbook includes two worksheets: Counts, and Budget.

2 **Click the Counts sheet tab; press and hold down Ctrl, and click the Budget sheet tab.**
The first two sheet tabs display with white backgrounds, and [Group] appears after the filename in the title bar at the top of the screen (see Figure 7.4).

continues ▶

To Edit Multiple Worksheets Simultaneously (continued)

Figure 7.4
Group mode is active, and any change to either selected sheet takes effect on both selected sheets.

Indicates multiple selected sheets

Two selected sheets

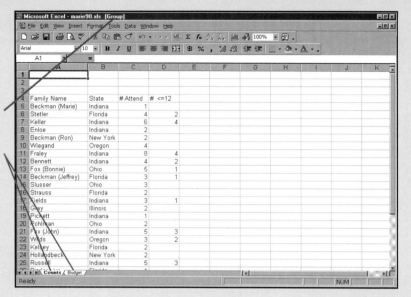

③ Select cell A1 in either selected worksheet, Counts or Budget, and enter the title `Aunt Marie's 90th Birthday Celebration`.

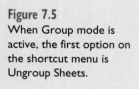

④ On the same sheet, change the font size in cell A1 to 14 point, and click the Bold button on the toolbar.

The title is entered and formatted on both selected sheets. Now, turn off Group mode.

⑤ Right-click either selected sheet tab—Counts or Budget.

The shortcut menu for sheet operations displays (see Figure 7.5).

Figure 7.5
When Group mode is active, the first option on the shortcut menu is Ungroup Sheets.

New font size applied to all selected sheets

Bold applied to all selected sheets

Shortcut menu for sheet operations

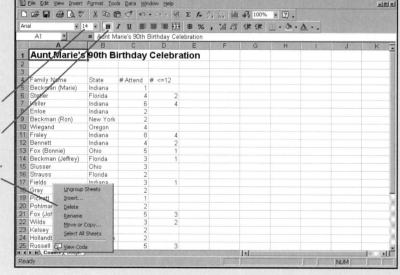

6 **Choose Ungroup Sheets from the shortcut menu.**
Only the current sheet displays with a white background, indicating that it is a selected sheet.

7 **Select each sheet to verify that the title you typed once is entered in both worksheets.**

8 **Click the Save button.**
Excel saves your changes to the Marie90 workbook. Keep the workbook open for the next lesson, or close the workbook and exit Excel.

Inside Stuff: Use Group Mode with Caution
Exercise caution when changing the cell contents of grouped sheets. Any change to the active sheet results in the same change to all other selected sheets, which may result in an unintended replacement of data.

Exam Note: Other Ways to Turn Group Mode On and Off
You can select all sheets in a workbook by right-clicking any sheet tab to display the related shortcut menu, and choosing Select All Sheets.

If some, but not all, of the worksheets in a workbook are selected, you can turn Group mode off by clicking the sheet tab of any unselected worksheet.

Lesson 4: Subtotaling Data

If data is organized in a list and sorted, you can use Excel's automatic subtotaling tool to calculate subtotals and a grand total. You realize that this feature is just one of several ways that Excel could provide the projected attendance totals that you need to prepare the birthday celebration budget. You decide to try this feature, instead of just clicking AutoSum or entering a SUM function, because you think subtotals by state might be of interest to those planning to attend.

In this lesson, you complete the two-step process to automatically subtotal and total data in a list: sort the list on the subtotal field (column), and apply a Data, Subtotals command.

To Subtotal Data

1 **Open the Marie90 workbook, if necessary, and select the Counts worksheet.**

2 **Click any cell in the State column within the list, such as cell B5.**

3 **Click the Sort Ascending button on the toolbar.**
The list of attendees sorts by state (see Figure 7.6).

4 **Click any cell in column A within the range A4:A34.**
The column for the subtotal labels is specified.

continues ▶

To Subtotal Data (continued)

Figure 7.6
Sort a list before
generating automatic
subtotals.

Records in ascending
order by state

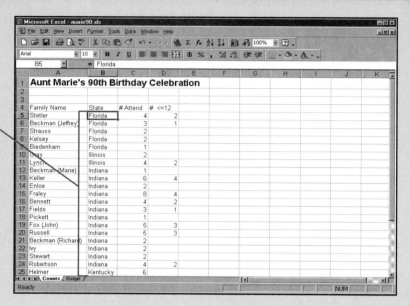

⑤ **Choose Data, Subtotals.**

⑥ **Specify settings in the Subtotal dialog box, as shown in Figure 7.7.**

Figure 7.7
The settings in the
Subtotal dialog box sum
the contents of the #
Attend and # <=12 fields
at each change in state.

Click here to select the field to
subtotal

Click the check box to select or
deselect

Click here to display choices
other than Sum

Scroll to display each field in the
list

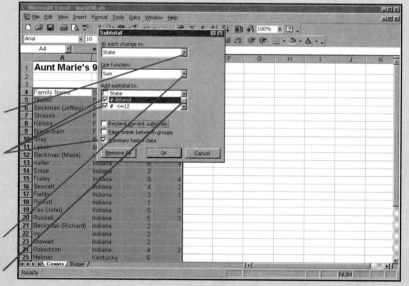

⑦ **Click OK, and widen column B to display the newly inserted subtotal labels.**

⑧ **Scroll down to view the remaining subtotals by state and the grand totals in row 42 (see Figure 7.8).**

⑨ **Click the Save button.**
Excel saves your changes to the Marie90 workbook.

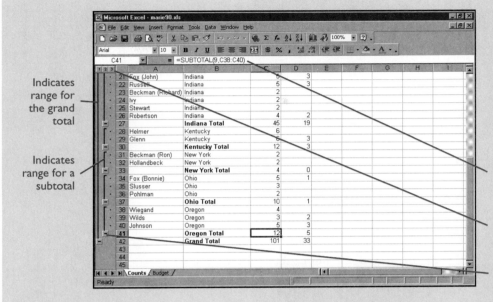

Figure 7.8
Applying a Data, Subtotals command produces the counts for each state and in total, based on two fields: all who plan to attend the celebration (# Attend) and the number of children (# <=12).

Excel automatically inserts Subtotal functions at each change in state

Click 1, 2, or 3 to display varying levels of detail for the entire list

Click a button displaying a minus sign to collapse the view (display less detail)

Indicates range for the grand total

Indicates range for a subtotal

⑩ Close the workbook.
Continue with the next lesson, in which you use an expanded version of the Marie90 workbook, or exit Excel.

Exam Note: **Removing Subtotals**
You can remove subtotals by using a two-step process. Select any cell within the subtotaled list; then choose Data, Subtotals, click the Remove All button, and click OK.

Exam Note: **Collapsing and Expanding Subtotaled Data**
Excel outlines a subtotaled list by grouping detail rows with each related subtotal row and by grouping subtotal rows with the grand total row. You can display the entire list at one of three levels of detail by using small buttons labeled 1, 2, and 3 in the upper-left corner of the worksheet frame (refer to Figure 7.8). Clicking the 1 button displays only the grand total row. Clicking the 2 button displays the subtotal and grand total rows. Clicking the 3 button displays all rows.

You can also collapse or expand the display at the subtotal level by using minus (-) or plus (+) buttons, respectively. At the greatest level of detail, only minus (-) buttons display in the subtotal outline to the left of the row headings in the worksheet frame (refer to Figure 7.8).

Lesson 5: Linking Worksheets

As stated in Lesson 1, when you copy cell contents from one Excel worksheet to another, you can copy as a linked object or an embedded object. Recall that a linked object updates whenever the data in the source file changes.

In this lesson, you open an expanded version of a two-sheet workbook that has preparations for a 90th birthday party. The budget numbers are already entered. To complete the worksheet, you need to enter formulas. First, you copy the count for number of children as a linked object. Next, to calculate the number of adults, you type-and-point a formula that links to cells in another sheet. You then enter a formula to total the planned costs.

To Link Worksheets

❶ **Open the e-0702 workbook, and save the file as Marie90budget.**
The workbook includes sheets named Counts and Budget.

❷ **Click cell D42 in the Counts sheet.**
The cell containing the number of children 12 and under is selected.

❸ **Click the Copy button in the toolbar (or choose Edit, Copy).**

❹ **Click the Budget sheet tab, and click cell B3.**
The second worksheet displays, and the destination for the copied cell contents is selected.

❺ **Choose Edit, Paste Special. (Do not click the Paste button in the toolbar.)**
The Paste Special dialog box opens (see Figure 7.9).

Figure 7.9
Choose the Paste Link button to copy as a linked object.

Click here to create a linked object

Click here to create an embedded object

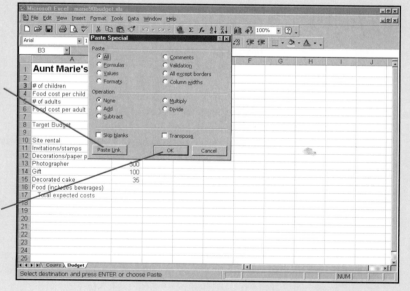

❻ **Click the Paste Link button in the lower-left corner of the Paste Special dialog box.**
The formula =Counts!$D$42 displays in the formula bar. The number 33 displays in cell B3 as the formula result. The Counts! portion of the formula is a reference to the sheet named Counts; the $D$42 portion of the formula is an absolute reference to cell D42 in the Counts worksheet.

You can use Copy and Paste Special to link single cells or ranges of cells. Now, try a linking method that works for one cell only.

7 **Click cell B5 in the Budget sheet, and type an equal sign (=) to start a formula.**

8 **Click the Counts sheet tab, and click cell C42.**

A reference to the cell containing the total number of people expected at the birthday celebration is entered.

9 **Type a minus sign (–); click cell D42, and click the green check mark in the formula bar.**

Excel calculates the number of adults who are expected to attend as the difference between the total expected and the number of children expected (see Figure 7.10).

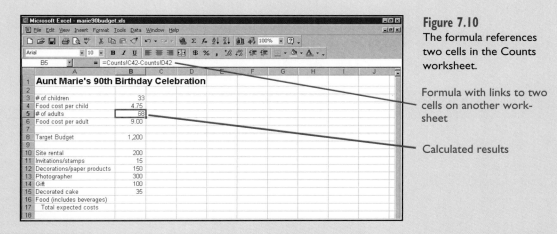

Figure 7.10
The formula references two cells in the Counts worksheet.

Formula with links to two cells on another worksheet

Calculated results

10 **Click the Save button.**

Excel saves your changes to the Marie90budget workbook. Keep the workbook open for the next lesson, or close the workbook and exit Excel.

Lesson 6: Applying Conditional Formatting

Using formats to emphasize cells in a worksheet can call attention to specific data. When you format a cell, however, the formatting remains in effect, even if the data changes.

If you want to accent a cell, depending on the value of the cell, you can use **conditional formatting**. Conditional formats return a result based on whether or not the value in the cell meets a specified condition. Formatting options include specifying font style, font color, shading, patterns, borders, bold, italic, and underlining.

In this lesson, you enter two formulas: one to calculate projected food costs and the other to sum total costs for a birthday celebration. You also format the cell containing the second formula to display results in red and bold if the total costs exceed the target budget.

To Apply Conditional Formatting

1 Open the `Marie90budget` workbook, if necessary, and click cell B16 in the Budget sheet.

2 Enter the formula `=B3*B4+B5*B6` in cell B16.

The formula =B3*B4+B5*B6 displays in the formula bar and the formula results (769) display in cell B16. This formula calculates the expected cost of food, based on values in the range B3:B6. Now use the formula palette to enter a SUM function that computes Total Costs.

3 Click cell B17, and click the Edit Formula button in the formula bar.

The formula palette opens. Buttons to Cancel (a red X) and Enter (a green checkmark) display. The most recently used function appears in the Name Box.

4 Display the Name box drop-down list and select SUM (see Figure 7.11).

=SUM(B10:B16) displays in the formula bar and in the Number 1 text box on the formula palette.

 If You Have Problems...

If the drop-down list does not include the function you want to use, select More Functions to open the Paste Function dialog box and select SUM in the Math & Trig category.

Figure 7.11
Clicking the Edit Formula button provides quick access to the most recently used functions.

Click here to display the most recently used functions

Edit Formula button

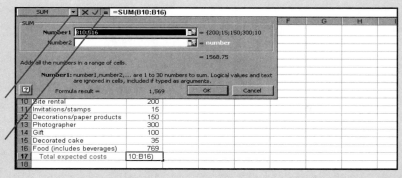

5 Click OK.

The formula results (1,569) display in cell B17. This formula calculates expected total costs.

6 Click cell B17, and choose F**o**rmat, Con**d**itional Formatting.

The Conditional Formatting dialog box opens. Now specify the condition shown in Figure 7.12.

7 Display the comparison options drop-down list, and select greater than (see Figure 7.12).

8 In the window to the right of the comparison option, type =$B$8 (refer to Figure 7.12).

A condition for cell B17 is set with a cell value greater than the contents of cell B8. Now, specify the format of cell B17 if the condition is true—that is, if the total expected costs exceed the target budget.

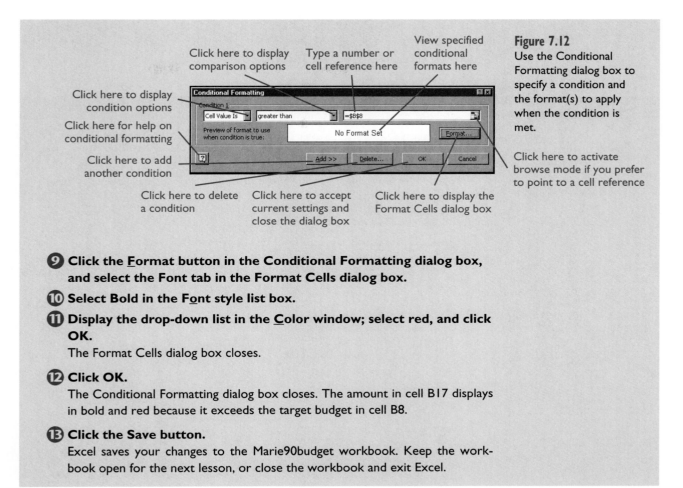

Click here to display comparison options

Type a number or cell reference here

View specified conditional formats here

Figure 7.12
Use the Conditional Formatting dialog box to specify a condition and the format(s) to apply when the condition is met.

Click here to display condition options

Click here for help on conditional formatting

Click here to add another condition

Click here to activate browse mode if you prefer to point to a cell reference

Click here to delete a condition

Click here to accept current settings and close the dialog box

Click here to display the Format Cells dialog box

9 **Click the Format button in the Conditional Formatting dialog box, and select the Font tab in the Format Cells dialog box.**

10 **Select Bold in the Font style list box.**

11 **Display the drop-down list in the Color window; select red, and click OK.**

The Format Cells dialog box closes.

12 **Click OK.**

The Conditional Formatting dialog box closes. The amount in cell B17 displays in bold and red because it exceeds the target budget in cell B8.

13 **Click the Save button.**

Excel saves your changes to the Marie90budget workbook. Keep the workbook open for the next lesson, or close the workbook and exit Excel.

 Exam Note: **Removing Conditional Formatting**
You can remove all conditional formatting from a cell by selecting the cell and choosing Edit, Clear, Formats.

 Inside Stuff: **Specifying More than One Conditional Format**
You can specify up to three conditions, with varying formats for each condition. In the previous exercise, for example, you could specify a second condition to display a blue border around the total expected costs cell if its contents were equal to or less than the target budget.

Lesson 7: Using a Worksheet to Solve a Problem

You are concerned that the total expected costs for the birthday celebration exceed the target budget by more than $350. You are reluctant to change the target budget of $1,200 that was set by the planning committee several months ago. After looking over the list of expenses, you decide that the most likely areas for trimming costs are food and photography. If additional reductions are needed, perhaps you can negotiate a lower site rental fee and spend less on decorations.

In this lesson, you make changes in the budget worksheet to bring the total expected costs within the target budget. As soon as the desired result is achieved, the amount for the total expected costs no longer displays in red and bold.

To Use a Worksheet to Solve a Problem

1 **If necessary, open the Marie90budget workbook and select the Budget sheet.**
Now, enter the reductions in food cost due to changes in the menu that you arranged with the caterer.

2 **Select cell B4 and change Food cost per child to 4.50.**

3 **Select cell B6 and change Food cost per adult to 8.00.**
Total costs drop to just under $1,500. The amount of 1,493 in cell B17 still appears in red and bold. Significant savings can be achieved only by eliminating the professional photographer.

4 **Select cell A13, and replace Photographer with Film/Developing.**

5 **Select cell B13, and replace 300 with 75.**
Total costs drop closer to the target budget of $1,200. The amount 1,268 in cell B17 still appears in red and bold. You negotiate a lower site rental fee, in exchange for increased clean-up responsibilities, and cut the amount allocated for decorations.

6 **Select cell B10, and change Site rental from 200 to 150.**

7 **Select cell B12, and change Decorations/paper products from 150 to 120.**
The 1,188 total expected costs no longer appear in red and bold because they are less than the $1,200 target budget (see Figure 7.13).

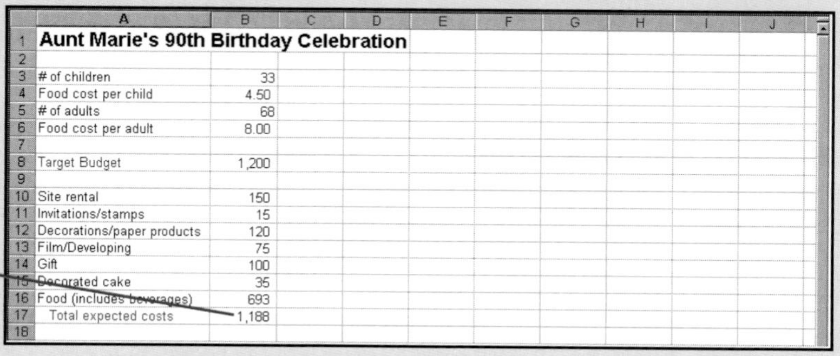

Figure 7.13
Editing the budget achieved the desired results of reducing the total expected costs to a level equal to or less than the target budget.

Conditional formats no longer apply

	A	B
1	**Aunt Marie's 90th Birthday Celebration**	
2		
3	# of children	33
4	Food cost per child	4.50
5	# of adults	68
6	Food cost per adult	8.00
7		
8	Target Budget	1,200
9		
10	Site rental	150
11	Invitations/stamps	15
12	Decorations/paper products	120
13	Film/Developing	75
14	Gift	100
15	Decorated cake	35
16	Food (includes beverages)	693
17	Total expected costs	1,188
18		

8 **Select the Counts worksheet, and click the Save button.**
Excel saves your changes to the Marie90budget workbook. Now preview and print the workbook.

9 **Choose File, Print (do not click the Print button).**
The Print dialog box opens.

10 **Click Entire Workbook in the Print what area.**

⑪ Click the Previe̲w button in the lower-left corner of the Print dialog box.

The Counts worksheet appears in Print Preview mode. The phrase Preview: Page 1 of 2 displays in the lower-left corner.

⑫ Scroll down to view the Budget worksheet.

The phrase Preview: Page 2 of 2 displays in the lower-left corner.

⑬ Click the Prin̲t button (or click C̲lose if you do not want to print at this time).

Excel prints both worksheets in the Marie90budget workbook. Keep the workbook open for the next lesson, or close the workbook and exit Excel.

Lesson 8: Saving a Worksheet with a Chart as a Web Page

Now that you created a workable budget for the birthday celebration, you want to distribute the information to members of the planning committee and anyone else with an interest in the event. You could attach the workbook to an email message, but there's really no need for anyone to edit file contents. You decide instead to save the Budget worksheet as a Web page, to be published later as part of a reunion Web site.

In this lesson, you first embed a pie chart in the Budget sheet to show the percent of each cost in relation to the total expected costs. You then save the worksheet as a Web page on your own computer system (sometimes referred to as a local system). Saving the worksheet to a local system enables you to view it by using a browser such as Netscape or Explorer, prior to publishing it to a Web site.

To Save a Worksheet with a Chart as a Web Page

❶ If necessary, open the Marie90budget workbook, and select the Budget sheet.

❷ Select the range A10:B16, and click the Chart Wizard button on the toolbar.

❸ Specify settings in the Chart Wizard dialog boxes to create a pie chart titled Budgeted Items (show percentages, but do not place the chart on a separate sheet).

❹ Move and size the chart, and move the title box, as shown in Figure 7.14.

❺ Click the Save button.

Excel saves the newly-created pie chart in the Budget.

❻ Choose F̲ile, Save as Web Page.

The Save As dialog box opens, so you can select from the Web-related options (see Figure 7.15).

continues ▶

To Save a Worksheet with a Chart as a Web Page (continued)

Figure 7.14
The pie chart illustrates the proportion of each expected cost in relation to the total budget.

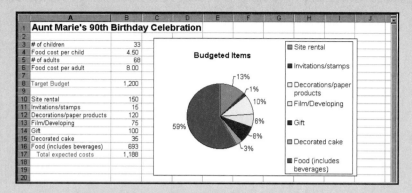

Figure 7.15
Web-related Save options display in the Save As dialog box.

Specify the folder in which to store as a Web page here

Select the entire workbook or only the current worksheet here

If this box is not checked, the Web page can be viewed but not changed

Click here to specify a title to appear in the title bar of your Web browser

Excel assigns the .htm extension to indicate a file stored in HTML format

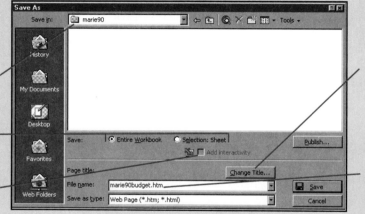

7 **Display the Save in drop-down list, and specify the folder in which you want to store the current worksheet as a Web page.**
Unless you prefer another location, store the page in the same folder as the other files you have been saving.

8 **Click the option to save the current sheet, as opposed to the entire workbook.**
Excel automatically assigns a filename that is the same as the sheet name, followed by the extension .htm, which indicates an HTML file.

9 **Click the Save button in the lower-right corner of the dialog box.**
This completes the process to save a worksheet as a Web page. If you have access to a Web browser, you can choose File, Web Page Preview to see how the worksheet data and chart display on a Web page. Figure 7.16 shows the Budget sheet viewed through the Netscape browser.

This concludes Project 7. You can continue with end-of-project activities or exit Excel.

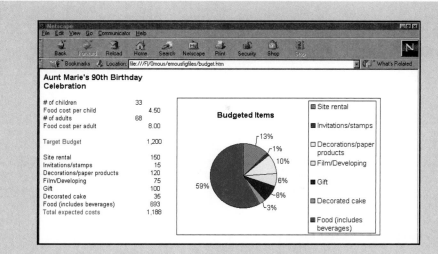

Figure 7.16
The worksheet data and chart display as a Web page in a browser.

Inside Stuff: Before You Publish to a Web Site . . .
Publishing a Web page for general viewing requires that you have an account on a server that is connected to the Internet. Not everyone has this capability. However, before you ever publish a page on the Internet for everyone to see, you should publish it to a local computer and view it with a Web browser. To edit the Web page, return to the worksheet that the page was created from, make any necessary changes, and save the worksheet again as a Web page.

Summary

This project provided opportunities to reinforce existing skills and learn new ones. You demonstrated basic skills by entering formulas, copying, widening a column, sorting a list, creating a pie chart, and varying data entry until you achieved the desired result. New skills included inserting and renaming sheets, editing multiple worksheets simultaneously, creating subtotals, linking worksheets, specifying conditional formatting, and saving a worksheet as a Web page.

You can extend your knowledge by experimenting with variations of skills. Select COUNT or AVERAGE instead of SUM to subtotal a list. You linked cells between worksheets; now try to link cells between workbooks. Specify conditional formatting with two conditions instead of one. Create a chart on a separate sheet in a workbook, and save the chart sheet as a Web page. Don't forget to take advantage of onscreen Help and the many opportunities to learn through end-of-project activities.

Checking Concepts and Terms ✓

True/False

For each of the following, check *T* or *F* to indicate whether the statement is true or false.

__T __F **1.** An embedded object updates whenever the corresponding data in the source file changes. [L1]

__T __F **2.** Renaming worksheets enables you to sort them into ascending or descending order by using the Data, Sort command. [L2]

__T __F **3.** Saving a worksheet to your computer's hard disk as a Web page makes it available for general viewing on the World Wide Web. [L8]

__T __F **4.** Excel inserts a new worksheet to the left of the current worksheet. [L2]

__T __F **5.** To use the Data, Subtotals feature, you must first sort the list on the subtotal field (column). [L4]

Multiple Choice

Circle the letter of the correct answer for each of the following.

1. Which of the following is not a true statement about conditional formatting? [L6]

a. A formatting change occurs when the value or formula in a cell meets a specified condition.

b. Conditional formatting can be based on more than one condition.

c. Conditional formatting can include borders.

d. Choosing Edit, Clear, Formats does not clear conditional formats.

2. Which of the following math operations can be applied when using the Data, Subtotals command? [L4]

a. max

b. average

c. both a and b

d. neither a nor b

3. When you _____ data, you can make a change in the source, and the destination automatically updates. [L5]

a. link

b. embed

c. copy

d. paste

4. Assume that a workbook named Registration.xls includes sheets named Fees and Summary. Which of the following could be a valid formula in the Summary sheet linking to one or more cells in the Fees sheet? [L5]

a. =Registration:Fees!$B$5

b. =Fees!$B$5-Fees!$B$7

c. =Fees:$B$5-Fees:$B$7

d. none of the above

5. Which of the following keys do you press to select nonadjacent sheets in a workbook? [L3]

a. ⬆Shift

b. Ctrl

c. Alt

d. none of the above

Skill Drill

Skill Drill exercises reinforce project skills. Each skill reinforced is the same, or nearly the same, as a skill presented in the project. Detailed instructions are provided in a step-by-step format.

Each exercise is independent of the others, so you can complete the exercises in any order. Be sure to save the workbook after completing each exercise. If you need a paper copy of the completed exercise, enter your name centered in a header before printing. Other print options have already been set to print compressed to one page and to display the filename, sheet name, and current date in a footer.

Before beginning your first Project 7 Skill Drill exercise, complete the following steps:

1. Open the Excel file named **e-0703** and save it as **e7drill**.
   The workbook contains five sheets: an overview, and exercise sheets named #1-Subtotal, #2-LinkAll, #2-LinkOne, and #3-Conditional.

2. Click the Overview sheet to view the organization of the Project 7 Skill Drill Exercises workbook.

If you need more than one work session to complete the desired exercises, continue working on **e7drill** instead of starting over on the original e-0703 file.

1. Subtotaling Data

You use a multiple-sheet workbook to keep track of residential real-estate listings and sales. You want to have a count of the homes available in each area.

To get the information you need by using Excel's Subtotal feature:

1. Open the **e7drill** workbook, and select the #1-Subtotal sheet tab.

2. Click any cell within the Area column of the residential real-estate list, such as cell C6.

3. Click the Sort Ascending button on the toolbar.
   The real-estate listings sort by Area—homes in Autumn Woods first, Cape Cod Village second, and so forth.

4. Check that the current cell is within the residential real-estate list, and choose Data, Subtotals.

5. Specify Area as the At each change in setting in the Subtotal dialog box.

6. Specify Count as the Use function setting in the Subtotal dialog box.

7. Check only the Area box in the Add subtotal to window in the Subtotal dialog box.

8. Click OK.

Excel subtotals at each change in area and provides a count of listings in that area.

2. Linking Worksheets

You are developing a multiple-sheet workbook to keep track of residential real-estate listings and sales. You created a summary worksheet for annual sales and a detail worksheet for one real estate agent. You plan to link the individual's data to the summary sheet. After you set the link and test that it works, you plan to add sheets for other agents.

To link worksheets:

1. Open the **e7drill** workbook, and select the #2-LinkOne worksheet.

2. Select the range B8:B11.
   The quarterly sales for agent Jessica Blair are selected.

3. Click the Copy button on the toolbar (or choose Edit, Copy).

4. Click the #2-LinkAll sheet tab, and click cell B8.
   The screen display switches from the individual worksheet to the summary worksheet, and the first cell in the destination is selected for the copied cell contents.

5. Choose Edit, Paste Special. (Do *not* click the Paste button.)
   The Paste Special dialog box displays.

6. Click the Paste Link button in the lower-left corner of the Paste Special dialog box.
   Excel pastes links to the worksheet containing quarterly data for Jessica Blair. The number 249900 displays in cell B8 as the formula result. The formula ='#2-LinkOne'!B8 displays in the formula bar.

7. Make sure that the formulas in cells B9 through B11 also link to cells on the #2-LinkOne worksheet.

3. Applying Conditional Formatting

You are developing a multiple-sheet workbook to keep track of residential real-estate listings and sales. You want to use Excel's conditional formatting feature to display annual sales of one million or more with a blue border around the cell.

To set up the conditional formatting:

1. Open the **e7drill** workbook and select the #3-Conditional worksheet.

2. Click cell B12.
   The cell containing annual sales for Jessica Blair is selected.

3. Choose Format, Conditional Formatting.
   The Conditional Formatting dialog box opens.

4. In the first text box for condition 1, specify `Cell Value Is`.

5. In the second text box for condition 1, specify `greater than or equal to`.

6. In the third text box for condition 1, type `1000000`.

7. Click the Format button in the Conditional Formatting dialog box.

8. Select the Border tab in the Format Cells dialog box, and select a bright blue color.

9. Choose the Outline preset, and click OK to close the Format Cells dialog box.

10. Click OK to close the Conditional Formatting dialog box, and click a cell other than cell B12.

Cell B12 displays with a blue border because the formula results are greater than or equal to one million dollars.

Challenge

Challenge exercises expand on or are somewhat related to skills that are presented in the lessons. Each exercise provides a brief narrative introduction, followed by instructions in a numbered-step format that are not as detailed as those in the Skill Drill section.

Each exercise is independent of the others, so you can complete the exercises in any order. Be sure to save the workbook after completing each exercise. If you need a paper copy of the completed exercise, enter your name centered in a header before printing. Other print options have already been set to print compressed to one page and to display the filename, sheet name, and current date in a footer.

Before beginning your first Project 7 Challenge exercise, complete the following steps:

1. Open the file named **e-0704** and save it as **e7challenge.**
   The e7challenge workbook contains four sheets: an overview, and three exercise sheets named #1-AvgSubtotal, #2-TwoCondFormat, and #3-InsertGroup.

2. Click the Overview sheet to view the organization of the Project 7 Challenge Exercises workbook.

If you need more than one work session to complete the desired exercises, continue working **e7challenge** instead of starting all over on the original e-0704 file.

1. Subtotaling Data by Using the Average Function

You use a multiple-sheet workbook to keep track of residential real-estate listings and sales. You want to know the average listing price of the homes available in each area.

To get the information you need by using Excel's Subtotal feature:

1. Open your **e7challenge** workbook and select the #1-AvgSubtotal worksheet.

2. Sort the real-estate listings by Area.

3. Choose the option on the <u>D</u>ata menu that displays the Subtotal dialog box.

4. Specify that Excel should use the Average function at each change in Area.

5. Specify the placement of each subtotal only at the Price field, and include summary data at the bottom.

6. Close the dialog box in a way that executes the desired operation.

7. Be sure that the results are accurate before saving your changes.

The average price of a home listed in Autumn Woods is 84,450. The average price in Champions Village is 129,317.

2. Applying Two Conditional Formats to a Cell

You are developing a multiple-sheet workbook to keep track of residential real-estate listings and sales. You want to use Excel's conditional formatting feature to draw attention to quarterly sales greater than or equal to $250,000 or quarterly sales less than $150,000.

To set up the desired conditional formatting:

1. Open your **e7challenge** workbook, and select the #2-TwoCondFormat worksheet.

2. Select the range B10:E13 and choose F<u>o</u>rmat, Con<u>d</u>itional Formatting. (Do not include the totals in row 14.)

3. Specify condition 1 as cell value greater than or equal to 250000.

4. Click the <u>F</u>ormat button, and specify gold shading (not gold text).

5. Restore the display of the Conditional Formatting dialog box, and click the <u>A</u>dd button.

6. Specify condition 2 as cell value less than 150000, and then set up red text as the format.

7. Ensure that conditional formats display as intended, and make changes as necessary.

Cells in the ranges D10:E10 and B12:E12 should display with gold backgrounds. Cell contents should display as red in cells B11, B13, D11, and D13.

3. Inserting Sheets and Editing the New Sheets Simultaneously

You are developing a residential real estate multiple-sheet workbook. The design that you have in mind includes a separate worksheet to track each agent's sales. Because you want identical layouts on these individual sheets, you decide to group new sheets and edit them simultaneously.

To create the desired worksheets:

1. Open your **e7challenge** workbook, and select the #3-InsertGroup worksheet.

2. Insert two blank worksheets, and position them after the #3-InsertGroup sheet.

3. Rename the two new worksheets **#3b** and **#3c**, respectively.

4. Select the three sheets that have names beginning with #3.

5. Reproduce the cell content, alignment, and column widths shown in Figure 7.17.

Figure 7.17
You can select multiple worksheets and edit them simultaneously.

Drag the contents of cell A8 to create the other labels

Selected sheets

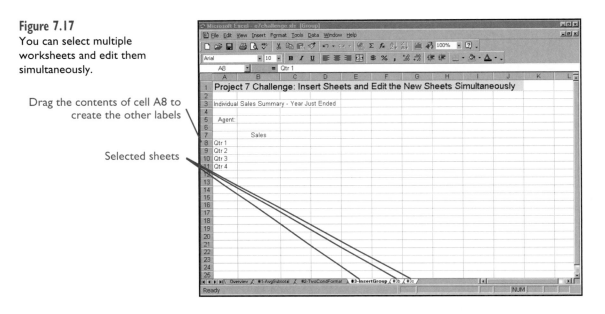

6. Ungroup the sheets.

Discovery Zone

Discovery Zone exercises require advanced knowledge of topics presented in *MOUS Essentials* lessons, application of skills from multiple lessons, or self-directed learning of new skills.

Each exercise is independent of the others, so you can complete the exercises in any order. Be sure to save the workbook after completing each exercise. If you need a paper copy of the completed exercise, enter your name centered in a header before printing. Other print options have already been set to print compressed to one page and to display the filename, sheet name, and current date in a footer.

Before beginning your first Project 7 Discovery Zone exercise, complete the following steps:

1. Open the Excel file named **e-0705**, and save it as **e7discovery**.
   The e7discovery workbook contains three sheets: an overview and two exercise sheets named #1-FindCond and #2-Chart.

2. Click the Overview sheet to view the organization of the Project 7 Discovery Zone Exercises workbook.

If you need more than one work session to complete the desired exercises, continue working on **e7discovery** instead of starting over on the original e-0705 file.

1. Finding Cells with Conditional Formats

Use onscreen Help to learn how to find cells with conditional formats. Open the **e7discovery** workbook, and apply what you have learned to find cells with conditional formatting in the #1-FindCond sheet. Enter a note below the data explaining which cells have conditional formatting and what condition(s) must be present for the formatting to display.

2. Copying from Excel to Another Program

Copying from Excel to another application requires a copy-and-paste operation similar to that for copying *to* Excel from another application. Start Word, open the Word document named e-0706, and save it as **Democopy**. Switch to Excel, open the **e7discovery** workbook, and select the #2-Chart sheet. Select the chart, and copy it to the appropriate place in the Democopy Word document.

PinPoint Assessment

You have completed this project and its associated lessons, and have had an opportunity to assess your skills through the end-of-project questions and exercises. Now use the PinPoint software Evaluation Mode to further assess your comprehension of the specific exam activities you have just learned. You can also use the PinPoint Trainer Mode and the Show Me tutorials to practice these exam activities.

Project 8

Working with Custom Formats, AutoFormats, Styles, and Templates

Key terms introduced in this project include

- AutoFormat
- custom format

- style
- template

Objectives	Required Activity for MOUS	Exam Level
➤ Insert and Delete Cells	Insert and delete selected cells	Core
➤ Replace and Rotate Text	Use Find and Replace; Rotate text and change indents	Core
➤ Create a Custom Format	Create custom number formats	Expert
➤ Apply an AutoFormat	Apply AutoFormat	Core
➤ Create and Use Styles	Define, apply and remove a style	Core
➤ Copy a Worksheet	Move and copy worksheets	Core
➤ Email a Workbook or Worksheet Within Excel	Send a workbook via email	Core
➤ Create and Use a Template	Apply, edit, and create templates	Expert

Why Would I Do This?

Excel provides a variety of features to help you achieve consistency in worksheet content and formatting with a minimum of effort. These features include defining your own formats, creating and storing a model worksheet for repeated use, and applying a predefined combination of formats to an entire worksheet.

In this project, you work with all of these features. You also learn to insert and delete cells, replace multiple occurrences of text in a single operation, rotate text, and email a workbook from within the Excel program.

Lesson 1: Inserting and Deleting Cells

In previous projects, you learned to insert and delete worksheets as well as insert and delete rows and columns. You can also insert or delete a range of cells. Look at a worksheet that illustrates why you might want to insert or delete cells (see Figure 8.1). The worksheet calculates Total Points (column H), Course Percent (column I) and summary statistics (rows 20-22) based on scores entered in the range C7:G18.

Figure 8.1
You can insert and delete cells to make the required changes.

Insert cells for a Project grade between columns F and G and from rows 5 through 22

Delete this cell to shift the Mean, Median, and Mode labels to the proper position

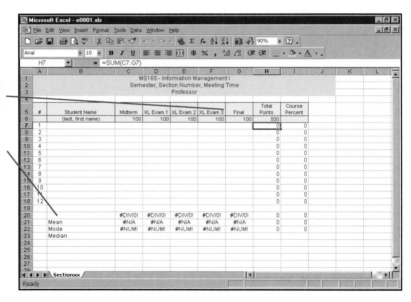

At this point in the worksheet design process, two changes are needed in the model. First you need to make room for a Project grade between the XL Exam 3 grade and the Final grade. If you do this by inserting a column, the background shading in rows 1 through 3 will extend through column K. You would then have to remove the unwanted color from cells K1:K3. If instead you insert cells from G5 through G22, the green shading will still end in column J, and the yellow shading will align below the green.

You must also correct the problem of labels entered in the wrong rows. You could select cells in the range B21:B23 and drag the contents up one cell. Deleting cell B20 would produce the same result. You use the latter method in this lesson.

To Insert and Delete Cells

1 **Start Excel, if it is not already running, and open the e-0801.xls workbook.**

The worksheet shown in Figure 8.1 displays. At this point the workbook contains the single worksheet named Sectionxx.

2 **Save the file using the name MS165grades.**

3 **Select cells G5:G22.**

4 **Choose Insert, Cells.**

The Insert dialog box displays (see Figure 8.2).

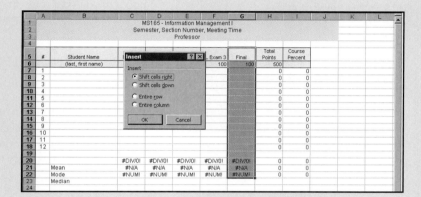

Figure 8.2
Four options display in the Insert dialog box.

5 **Check that Shift cells right is selected, and click OK.**

Excel inserts cells from row 5 through row 22 in column G. The existing cells shift right, and the yellow shading extends through column J. Inserted cells are automatically formatted the same as the corresponding cells to the left (cells F5:F22).

6 **Type Project in cell G5.**

7 **Type 100 in cell G6.**

Excel automatically adjusts the formulas to include the new cells. The Total Points number changes from 500 to 600. Now copy the summary formulas.

8 **Select cells F20:F22, drag the lower-right corner of cell F22 right one cell, and release the mouse button.**

The Mean, Mode, and Median formulas are copied from column F to column G.

9 **Click cell B20, and choose Edit, Delete.**

The Delete dialog box displays (see Figure 8.3).

10 **Check that Shift cells up is selected, and click OK.**

11 **Save the workbook.**

Keep the MS165grades workbook open for the next lesson, or close the workbook and exit Excel.

continues ▶

To Insert and Delete Cells (continued)

Figure 8.3
Four options display in the Delete dialog box.

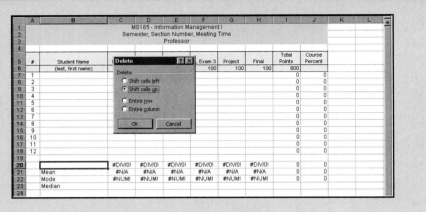

 ## Lesson 2: Replacing and Rotating Text

Excel provides a variety of ways to manipulate both the content and appearance of text. Two options on the Edit menu that can substantially reduce editing time on large worksheets are Find and Replace. Using the Find dialog box, you can search for the next occurrence of the word, number, or phrase you specify. Using the Replace dialog box, you can look for each occurrence of the word, number, or phrase you specify and replace each occurrence or all occurrences.

If column labels in a worksheet are longer than the data they describe, you can rotate the column headings. Text may be rotated up to 90 degrees upward or downward. Changing the orientation of text in a cell can also enhance visual appeal.

In this lesson, you use Excel's Replace feature to substitute the word Test for each occurrence of the word Exam. You then rotate the column headings 45 degrees upward.

To Replace and Rotate Text

1 If necessary, open the MS165grades workbook, and click cell A1.

2 Choose Edit, Replace.
The Replace dialog box opens.

3 Type Exam in the Find what text box.

4 Type Test in the Replace with text box (see Figure 8.4).

Figure 8.4
Use the Replace dialog box to replace multiple occurrences of the word, number, or phrase you specify.

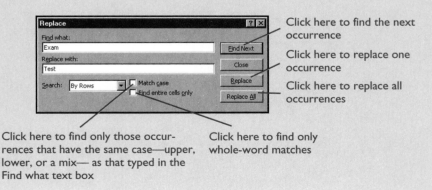

Click here to find the next occurrence

Click here to replace one occurrence

Click here to replace all occurrences

Click here to find only those occurrences that have the same case—upper, lower, or a mix— as that typed in the Find what text box

Click here to find only whole-word matches

5 **Check that your specifications match those in Figure 8.4, and click the Replace All button in the lower-right corner of the dialog box.**

The word Exam in cells D5, E5, and F5 is replaced with the word Test. Now rotate 45 degrees most of the column labels in row 5.

6 **Select cells C5:J5.**

7 **Choose F**o**rmat, C**e**lls, and click the Alignment tab.**

8 **Type 45 in the **D**egrees text box (see Figure 8.5).**

Drag in either direction to change the angle of side-by-side characters

Click here to display each character below the previous character in a label

Click here to check (on) or uncheck (off) wrapping a long label

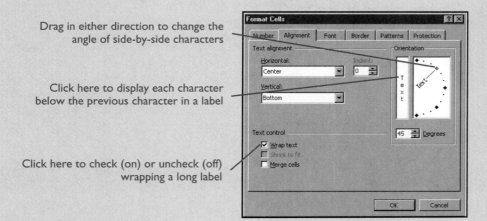

Figure 8.5
Use the Alignment tab in the Format Cells dialog box to specify the orientation of text in selected cells.

9 **Click OK, and click any cell to deselect the rotated range.**

Rotated text does not display well within the cells without an adjustment in row height (see Figure 8.6). Now increase the height of row 5.

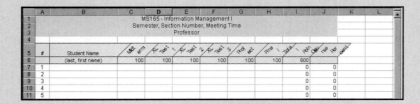

Figure 8.6
Rotated text in row 5 is not readable.

10 **Click any cell in row 5, and choose F**o**rmat, **R**ow, H**e**ight.**

11 **Type 55 in the **R**ow height text box, and click OK.**

All rotated text displays after you increase the height of row 5 (see Figure 8.7).

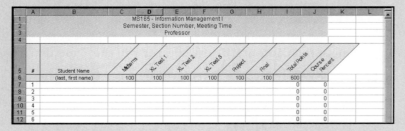

Figure 8.7
Rotated text in row 5 is readable after increasing row height.

12 **Save the workbook.**

Keep the MS165grades workbook open for the next lesson, or close the workbook and exit Excel.

Expert Lesson 3: Creating a Custom Format

Formats are masks that, when applied to a cell, change the display of the content without changing the value in the cell. Excel provides a variety of formats that you can apply using the Number tab in the Format Cells dialog box.

For unique situations in which a predefined format does not meet your needs, you can create your own **custom formats**. To create a custom format, display the Number tab in the Format Cells dialog box, select the Custom category, and type the appropriate codes in the Type text box. These codes are generally separated into two groups—date and time codes, and number and text codes. Excel's onscreen Help offers a substantial coverage of custom formats and the associated codes.

You can also incorporate conditional formatting within a custom format. In this lesson you create and apply a custom format to display a grade in red if the value is less than 70, and to display a grade in blue if it is 70 or greater. Such formatting makes it easy to distinguish between grades equal to or higher than a C (blue) and those lower than a C (red). You create the custom format using the Format, Cells dialog box.

To Create a Custom Format

1 **Open the `MS165grades` workbook, if necessary, and click cell C7 in the Sectionxx worksheet.**

2 **Choose Format, Cells, and select the Number tab.**

3 **Click Custom in the Category list.**
Excel displays the dialog box shown in Figure 8.8.

Figure 8.8
You can create a custom format by entering the appropriate codes in the Type text box.

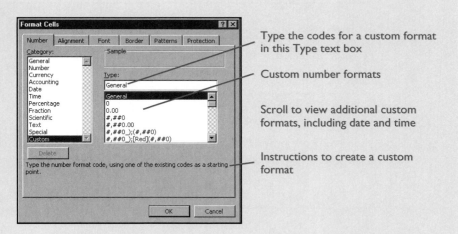

Type the codes for a custom format in this Type text box

Custom number formats

Scroll to view additional custom formats, including date and time

Instructions to create a custom format

4 **Delete the contents, if any, currently in the Type text box.**

5 **Type `[red][<70];[blue][>=70]` in the Type text box, and click OK.**
Your custom format has been saved, and it has also been applied to the current cell C7. Now apply the format to all cells that will contain grades and summary statistics.

6 **Select cells in the range C7:H22.**

7 **Choose Format, Cells, and select the Number tab.**

8 Click Custom in the Category list box.

9 Scroll down the list of custom formats, and select the new custom format, the last one in the list (see Figure 8.9).

The selected custom format →

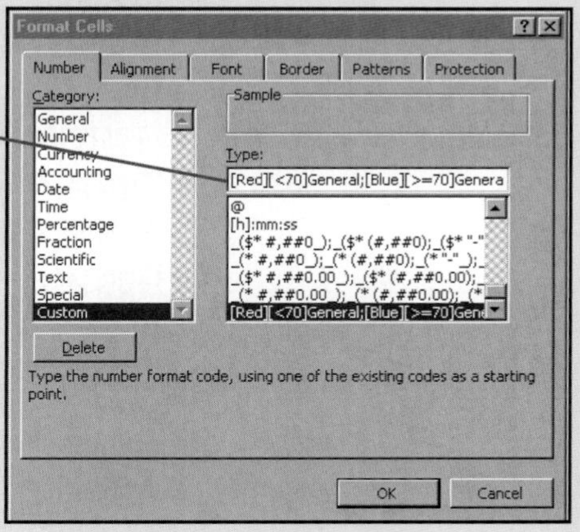

Figure 8.9
Excel inserts General (the default) as the number format because the custom format specified only color based on a condition.

10 Click OK.

The new custom format has been applied to the selected cells. Now test the custom format.

11 Select cell C7, and enter the number 60.

If the custom format was set up properly, the number 60 displays red in cell C7.

12 Select another cell in the range C7:H22, such as cell D10, and enter the number 80.

The number 80 displays blue.

13 Test other numbers in the range C7:H22 as desired; then delete all test entries, and save the workbook.

Keep the MS165grades workbook open for the next lesson, or close the workbook and exit Excel.

 Exam Note: **Explanations of Selected Codes**

You create custom formats by assembling codes. A representative sample of codes is provided in the following two-column list. For additional information and examples, refer to onscreen Help.

d	Day, from 1 to 31
dd	Day, from 01 to 31
ddd	Three-letter day of the week, such as Sun
dddd	Day of the week, such as Sunday
m	Month, from 1 to 12 or minute, from 1 to 60
mm	Month, from 01 to 12 or minute, from 01 to 60
mmm	Three-letter month, such as Jan
mmmm	Month, such as January
yy	Two-digit year

yyyy	Four-digit year
hh	Hour, from 0 to 23
ss	Second, from 00 to 59
am/pm	lowercase am or pm as appropriate
AM/PM	uppercase AM or PM as appropriate
0	Digit placeholder: ensures the correct number of digits (such as 0.250 when the format 0.000 is applied to a cell containing .25)
?	Digit placeholder: similar to 0, but places spaces instead of zeros to the right of the decimal point
#	Digit placeholder: similar to 0, but does not pad a value with extra zeros (such as 19.4 instead of 19.40 when the #,###.## code is applied to a cell containing 19.4)
/	Used with the ? code, converts a decimal to a fraction (such as 14/15 when the ??/?? code is applied to a cell containing .93333)

Lesson 4: Applying an AutoFormat

AutoFormat, located on the Format menu, lets you apply one of sixteen formats to lists and cell ranges. AutoFormats are grouped into five categories; Classic, Accounting, List, 3D Effects, and Colorful. Using the Option button, you decide to apply or reject the AutoFormat's Number, Border, Font, Pattern, Alignment, and Width/Height formats.

In this lesson, you apply the List1 AutoFormat to your grade book. To enhance the readability of the List1 format, you deselect the Font option. After the AutoFormat has been applied, you add another enchancement—in this case, borders.

To Apply an AutoFormat

1 **If necessary, open the MS165grades workbook.**

2 **Select cells A5:J22.**

3 **Choose F̲ormat, A̲utoFormat, and click the Options button in the AutoFormat dialog box.**
The AutoFormat dialog box displays, (see Figure 8.10).

4 **Uncheck the Font check box near the bottom of the dialog box.**

5 **Scroll down and click the List 1 format when it appears. (Format descriptions display below the related format.)**
The dark border surrounding the List 1 display indicates that the List 1 AutoFormat has been selected.

6 **Click OK.**
The List 1 format is applied to the highlighted range, and the range A5:J22 remains selected.

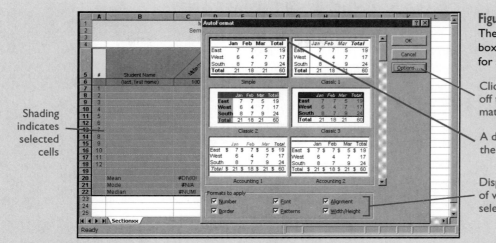

Figure 8.10
The AutoFormat dialog box includes check boxes for six formatting options.

Click here to turn on or off the display of six formats to apply

A dark border indicates the current selection

Display of six formats, all of which are currently selected

Shading indicates selected cells

If You Have Problems...
If you apply the wrong AutoFormat, and want to immediately reverse this action, use the Edit, Undo command or click the Undo button on the toolbar.

7 **Choose Format, Cells, and select the Border tab.**

8 **Select the Outline and Inside Presets.**
The border colors from the applied AutoFormat are maintained (see Figure 8.11).

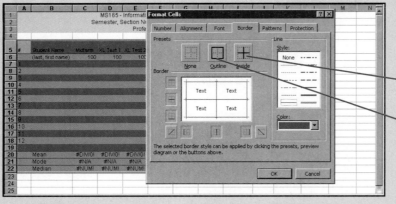

Figure 8.11
The color applied through the AutoFormat carries over to the border color.

Inside border is active

Outline border is active

9 **Click OK, deselect the highlighted range, and save the workbook.**
Borders surround the selected cells. This concludes Lesson 4. You can close the `MS165grades` workbook and exit Excel, or proceed with the next lesson.

Exam Note: Removing an AutoFormat
To remove an AutoFormat, execute the steps to apply an AutoFormat, and select the last AutoFormat named None.

Lesson 5: Creating and Using Styles

A **style** is a means of combining more than one format, such as font type, size, and color, into a single definition that can be applied to one or more cells. Use styles to maintain a consistent look to a worksheet. If you want to change that look, you can change the style once and reapply it, rather than edit individual cell attributes in each location that you used the style.

You may be surprised to know that you already use styles. When you create a new workbook, each cell is formatted using the Normal style containing Excel's default formats.

The easiest way to define a style is to apply all of the desired formats to a cell; select Format, Style; and give the current style a new name. You can also define a new style in the same manner as you edit a style—by selecting Format, Style; giving the current style a new name; and modifying the current formats as necessary.

Complete four steps to apply a style: select the cell range to receive the new style; select Format, Style; select the appropriate style from the Style name list; and click OK. To remove a style, select the appropriate cell range, and apply a different style or the Normal style.

In this lesson, you define a style named comic14gold. The style includes settings for applying a 14-point bold Comic Sans MS font in a gold color. You create the style, apply it in another location, and remove the style from one location.

To Create and Use Styles

❶ If necessary, open the MS165grades workbook.

❷ Select cell B20.
You are ready to create a style by first applying several formats to cell B20.

❸ Choose Format, Cells, and select the Font tab.

❹ Specify the Comic Sans MS font, bold font style, 14-point size, and gold color settings shown in Figure 8.12.
You have now defined all of the settings you want to include in this style, which specifies only font-related attributes. Now create the style.

Figure 8.12
You can create a style by first applying multiple settings to a single cell, and then defining those settings as a style.

Select a different font

Specify a predefined font style

Select a color from the drop-down list

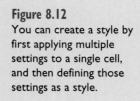
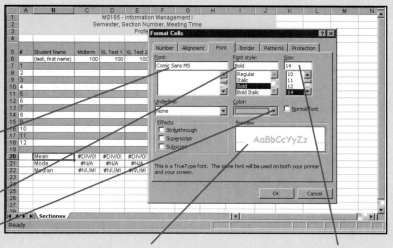

Preview the effects of multiple settings here   Increase the font size

⑤ Check that cell B20 is the current cell, and choose F̲ormat, S̲tyle.

The Style dialog box opens. Normal displays in the Style name text box. The font assigned to the Normal style—Arial 10pt—is listed in the `Style in-cludes` section.

⑥ Type `comic14gold` to replace Normal in the Style name text box.

Excel automatically displays the newly applied font settings—Comic Sans MS 14, Bold Color 44—to the right of the Font check box (see Figure 8.13).

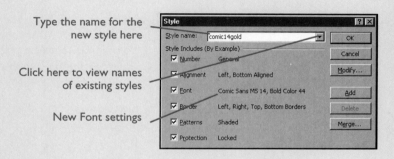

Type the name for the new style here

Click here to view names of existing styles

New Font settings

Figure 8.13
Use the Style dialog box to add or modify styles.

⑦ Click the A̲dd button, and click OK.

Excel adds the comic14gold style to other defined styles. Now apply the new style.

⑧ Select the range A1:A3, and choose F̲ormat, S̲tyle.

⑨ Display the Style name drop-down list; select the comic14gold style, and click OK.

The labels centered across the range A1:J3 display with attributes defined in the selected style—Comic Sans MS bold 14-point font in a gold color. Now remove the style applied to cell B20.

⑩ Click cell B20, and choose F̲ormat, S̲tyle.

⑪ Select Normal from the Style name drop-down list, and click OK.

Excel removes the elements of the comic14gold style from cell B20 (see Figure 8.14).

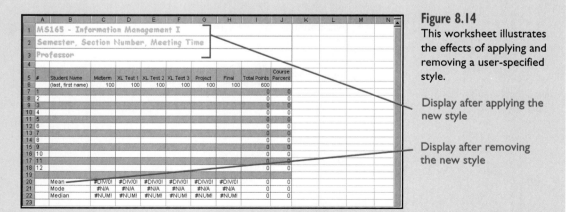

Figure 8.14
This worksheet illustrates the effects of applying and removing a user-specified style.

Display after applying the new style

Display after removing the new style

⑫ Click cell A1, and save your changes to the MS165grades workbook.

This concludes Lesson 5. You can close the workbook and exit Excel, or continue with the next lesson.

Inside Stuff: **Creating a Library of Styles**

User styles are unique to a worksheet but can be shared between worksheets by choosing Format, Style, and selecting Merge. The Merge option merges styles from any open worksheet that you select. If you use styles frequently and share them among worksheets, consider creating a template to store commonly used styles. (You learn about templates in the last lesson of this project.) Then when you want to create a new worksheet, open the template and merge the styles into the current worksheet.

Lesson 6: Copying a Worksheet

You may want to create a worksheet that is very similar to an existing worksheet. If you copy and edit the existing worksheet, you can create the new one with a minimum of effort.

If you select all cells in a worksheet and copy the selection to another worksheet or workbook, Excel retains cell formats but not the column-width and row-height settings. To make an exact duplicate of a worksheet, use the Move or Copy Sheet option on the Edit menu.

In this lesson you make an exact copy of the Sectionxx worksheet in the MS165grades workbook. You then rename the two worksheets Section01 and Section02 respectively.

To Copy a Worksheet

1 **If necessary, open the MS165grades workbook.**

2 **Choose Edit, Move or Copy Sheet.**
The Move or Copy dialog box displays.

3 **Click the (move to end) option in the Before sheet list box.**

4 **Click the Create a copy check box.**
You have made the selections to duplicate the worksheet Sectionxx in the MS165grades workbook (see Figure 8.15).

Figure 8.15
Use the Move or Copy dialog box to move or copy the current worksheet to a user-specified location in any open workbook.

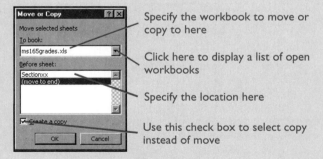

Specify the workbook to move or copy to here

Click here to display a list of open workbooks

Specify the location here

Use this check box to select copy instead of move

5 **Click OK.**
Excel makes a copy of the worksheet and names it Sectionxx(2).

6 **Double-click the Sectionxx sheet tab; type Section01, and press ↵Enter).**

7 **Double-click the Sectionxx(2) sheet tab; type** Section02, **and press** ⏎Enter.

8 **Save your changes to the MS165grades workbook.**

The workbook contains two identical sheets, one named Section01, and the other named Section02.

This concludes Lesson 6. You can close the workbook and exit Excel, or continue with the next lesson.

Lesson 7: Emailing a Workbook or Worksheet Within Excel

Most email programs allow you to attach one or more files to a message. If you have Internet access and an email program that is MAPI (Messaging Application Programming Interface) compliant, such as Outlook, Outlook Express, and most Windows-based email programs, you can also email a workbook or worksheet directly from Excel.

Two options are available: sending the current worksheet as the body of a message, and attaching a workbook to a message. The former method has limited use. The recipient can only view the contents of the worksheet. If you attach the file, however, the recipient can open and edit the workbook if using Excel 97 or a later version.

In this lesson, you attach a workbook to a message. If your computer uses a modem to send and retrieve email, connect to your ISP (Internet Service Provider) before starting this lesson. If you are not able to send email at this time, you can skip the rest of this lesson and proceed to Lesson 8.

To Email a Workbook

1 **If necessary, open the** MS165grades **workbook.**

2 **Choose** **F**ile, Sen**d** To, M**a**il Recipient (as attachment).

3 **Specify yourself as the recipient in the To box, and click Send.**

4 **Switch back to Excel, and close ms165grades.xls.**

5 **Open your email program, and retrieve the message.**

6 **Open the attachment, and check that your worksheet appears.**

7 **Close all open applications.**

Exam Note: Sending a Worksheet as the Message Body

If you choose File, Send To, Mail Recipient, the active worksheet is inserted as text in an email message. This works best if the content of the worksheet is simple and the worksheet is small.

As an alternative to selecting from menus, you can click the E-mail button on the Standard toolbar, and then Send single sheet as message body.

Whichever method you use to start the process, enter recipient names in the To and Cc boxes, set any options you want for the message, and click Send this Sheet.

Lesson 8: Creating and Using a Template

A ***template*** is a workbook saved with the file extension .xlt instead of .xls. It generally contains worksheets, standard text, formulas, functions, styles, and other formatting that you can use to create similar workbooks. For example, in the MS165grades workbook, only the students' names and grades change each semester. If you save the MS165grades workbook as a template, you can use it to create a new workbook each semester.

To save a workbook as a template, select the Save As option on the File menu, and select Template (*.xlt) from the Save as type drop-down list. Excel automatically selects the Templates folder as the storage location (see Figure 8.16). You can, however, specify another location.

Figure 8.16
Use the Save As dialog box to store a workbook as a template.

Specify the storage location here

The default storage location for templates

The .xlt extension indicates a template

The selected file type displays here

Click here to list file types

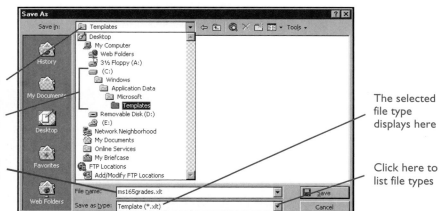

To use a template as the basis for a new workbook, choose File, New from the horizontal menu bar, find the folder containing the desired template and open it, modify labels as needed, and save the file as a workbook.

In this lesson, you save the MS165grades workbook as a template. You then use the template to create a new workbook.

To Create and Use a Template

1 **If necessary, open the MS165grades workbook.**

2 **Choose File, Save As.**

3 **Select Template (*.xlt) from the Save as type drop-down list.**
The settings in the Save As dialog box resemble those shown in Figure 8.16. If you are working in a lab environment, the Templates directory might be on a different drive.

4 **If you are working in a lab environment that doesn't permit saving to the Microsoft Templates folder, specify your own folder location in the Save in text box.**

5 **Click Save, and choose File Close.**
The MS165grades file now exists as both a workbook (.xls extension) and a template (.xlt extension). Now use the template to create a new workbook.

6 **Choose File, New, and click the General tab in the New dialog box.**
The MS165grades template displays to the right of the template for a blank workbook (see Figure 8.17).

Click here to display templates provided by Excel

Click here to select a blank workbook

Click here to select the MS165grades template

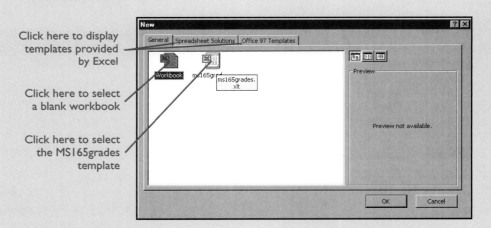

Figure 8.17
Use the New dialog box to select a blank workbook, a user-specified template, or templates provided by Excel.

7 **Select the MS165grades template, and click OK.**
Excel opens the template as a workbook named MS165grades1.xls. Now save the file as a workbook with a name that denotes grades for Fall 2000.

8 **Choose File, Save As.**

9 **Change the workbook name to MS165-f00, specify the desired location, and click Save.**
At this point, you could modify the contents of A1:A3 and the sheet name to reflect Fall 2000, and begin to enter the names of students.

This concludes Lesson 8, the last lesson in Project 8. Close the workbook, and continue with end-of-project exercises or exit Excel.

Exam Note: **Predefined Templates**

Excel provides a few predefined templates for common business needs, including Expense statement, Purchase order, and Invoice. To select one of these templates as the basis for a new workbook, choose File, New and select the Spreadsheet Solutions tab. Click the predefined template of choice, and click OK.

Summary

This project focused primarily on techniques for enhancing worksheets to minimize repetitive tasks. You created a custom format, applied a predefined Autoformat, defined a style combining a number of font-related attributes, and saved a workbook as a template that could serve as the starting point for creating similar workbooks. You also learned to insert and delete cells, replace and rotate text, copy a worksheet, and send an Excel file via email as a body message or an attachment.

To expand your knowledge, explore the many Help screens on custom formats, AutoFormats, styles, and templates. Then experiment with using these features in your worksheets.

Checking Concepts and Terms

True/False

For each of the following, check *T* or *F* to indicate whether the statement is true or false.

__T __F   **1.** When a range of cells is inserted into a worksheet, the user has the option of shifting the existing cells to the right or down. [L1]

__T __F   **2.** When text is rotated in a cell, all necessary formatting such as wrapping text, adjusting row height, and adding borders is done automatically by the alignment feature. [L2]

__T __F   **3.** If you use the Clear, Formats command to remove a formatting mistake you may inadvertently remove other formats you want to keep. [L3]

__T __F   **4.** To undo an AutoFormat, you can use the Undo command or apply the AutoFormat titled "None." [L4]

__T __F   **5.** The easiest way to define a style is to apply all of the desired formats to a cell before you create the style. [L5]

Multiple Choice

Circle the letter of the correct answer for each of the following.

1. Which of the following is a true statement about duplicating the layout and content of a worksheet? [L6]

   a. You can make a copy of a worksheet in the same workbook, but you cannot copy a worksheet to another workbook.

   b. Moving a worksheet requires the use of a different dialog box than that used to specify copying a worksheet.

   c. The two methods of reproducing a worksheet—making a copy of the worksheet, and applying a copy/paste operation to all active cells in a worksheet—produce identical results.

   d. none of the above

2. Which of the following is not an accurate statement about rotating text in a cell? [L2]

   a. Select the cell(s) to be formatted, and choose the Format, Cells, Alignment tab.

   b. You can use the Orientation box on the Alignment tab of the Format Cells dialog box to rotate the text.

   c. You can type the degree of rotation desired in the Degrees text box on the Alignment tab.

   d. You can rotate text in a cell by holding down the (Alt) key and using the mouse to rotate the sizing button in the lower-left corner of the cell.

3. A means of combining more than one format into a single definition that can be applied to one or more cells is a [L5, L8]

   a. style

   b. template

   c. both a and b

   d. neither a nor b

4. Which of the following is a valid statement about AutoFormat? [L4]

   a. You can apply one of sixteen formats to lists and cell ranges.

   b. Remove an AutoFormat by applying the format named None.

   c. AutoFormats are grouped into five design groups; Classic, Accounting, List, 3D Effects, and Colorful.

   d. All of the above are valid statements.

5. Which of the following is not a true statement about emailing Excel worksheets? [L7]

   a. A MAPI-compliant email program, such as Outlook, Outlook Express, and most Windows based email programs, is required.

   b. If you choose File, Send To, Mail Recipient, the active worksheet will be inserted as text in an email message.

   c. If you choose File, Send To, Mail Recipient (as Attachment), the entire workbook is sent as an attached file.

   d. You cannot email a workbook as an attachment if the workbook is currently open.

Skill Drill

Skill Drill exercises reinforce project skills. Each skill reinforced is the same, or nearly the same, as a skill presented in the project. Detailed instructions are provided in a step-by-step format.

Each exercise is independent of the others, so you can complete the exercises in any order. Be sure to save the workbook after completing each exercise. If you need a paper copy of the completed exercise, enter your name centered in a header before printing. Other print options have already been set to print compressed to one page and to display the filename, sheet name, and current date in a footer.

Before beginning your first Project 8 Skill Drill exercise, complete the following steps:

1. Open the file named **e-0802**, and save it as **e8drill**. The workbook contains four sheets: an overview, and exercise sheets named #1-Replace, #2-Reapply, and #3-Compare.

2. Click the Overview sheet to view the organization of the Project 8 Skill Drill Exercises workbook.

If you need more than one work session to complete the desired exercises, continue working on **e8drill** instead of starting all over on the original e-0802.xls file.

1. Replacing Multiple Occurrences of a Misspelled Word

You work for Experienced Wheels, Inc., and your responsibilities include maintaining a worksheet that lists the inventory of used cars. You realize that one of the color descriptions is misspelled. Use Excel's Replace feature to correct all occurrences of the misspelled color in a single operation.

To replace multiple occurrences of a misspelled word:

1. Open the **e8drill** workbook, if necessary, and click the #1-Replace sheet tab.

2. Choose Edit, Replace.

3. Type **Burgandy** in the Find what text box.

4. Type **Burgundy** in the Replace with text box, and choose Replace All.

Excel replaces all occurrences of the misspelled word Burgandy with the correct spelling Burgundy.

2. Applying a Different AutoFormat

The Accounting2 AutoFormat has been applied to an inventory of used cars. Change that AutoFormat to one more colorful.

To apply a different AutoFormat:

1. Open the **e8drill** workbook, if necessary, and click the #2-Reapply sheet tab.

2. Select the range A6:I28, and choose Format, AutoFormat.

3. Scroll down to view AutoFormats with color settings.

4. Select the AutoFormat named List 2, and click OK.

5. Click any cell to deselect the highlighted AutoFormat range.

3. Inserting Cells and Applying a Custom Format

You are constructing a worksheet to display percent, decimal, and fraction equivalents for values between zero and 1. The decimal values are already in place. Shift those values to the right so you can present percentage values in the first column. Copy the decimal values twice, creating values in the percent column the first time, and values in the fraction column the second time. Use a toolbar button to change display in the first column to percents. Apply a custom format to change display in the third column to fractions.

To insert cells and apply a custom format:

1. Open the e8drill workbook, if necessary, and click the #3-Compare sheet tab.

2. Select the range A5:A25, and choose Insert, Cells.

3. Check that **Shift cells right** is selected in the Insert dialog box, and click OK.

4. Type **Percent** in cell A5.

5. Copy the contents of B6:B25 to A6:A25.

6. Copy the contents of B6:B25 to C6:C25.

7. Select A6:A25, and click the Percent Style button in the toolbar.
   Check that 5%, 10%, 15% and so forth displays in the percent column A.

8. Select C6:C25, and choose Format, Cells.

9. Select the Number tab, and click Custom at the bottom of the Category list.

10. Scroll down to view other options in the Type list, select the custom format # ??/??, and click OK.
    Check that 1/20, 1/10, 3/20 and so forth displays in the fraction column C.

11. Right-align, and apply a blue font to the labels in A5:C5.

12. Adjust column widths to eliminate unnecessary white space.

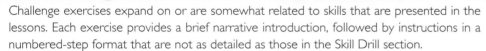

Challenge

Challenge exercises expand on or are somewhat related to skills that are presented in the lessons. Each exercise provides a brief narrative introduction, followed by instructions in a numbered-step format that are not as detailed as those in the Skill Drill section.

Each exercise is independent of the others, so you can complete the exercises in any order. Be sure to save the workbook after completing each exercise. If you need a paper copy of the completed exercise, enter your name centered in a header before printing. Other print options have already been set to print compressed to one page and to display the filename, sheet name, and current date in a footer.

Before beginning your first Project 8 Challenge exercise, complete the following steps:

1. Open the file named `e-0803.xls`, and save it as **e8challenge**.
   The e8challenge workbook contains four sheets: an overview, and three exercise sheets named #1-RotateAlign, #2-Remove2, and #3-EmailSheet.

2. Click the Overview sheet to view the organization of the Project 8 Challenge Exercises workbook.

If you need more than one work session to complete the desired exercises, continue working on **e8challenge** instead of starting all over on the original e-0803.xls file.

1. Changing Rotation and Alignment

You work for Experienced Wheels, Inc., and currently you are trying out various enhancements in a worksheet that lists the inventory of used cars. You want to see if the column headings in row 9 would look better if they were centered vertically within the row, but not rotated.

To change rotation and alignment:

1. Open the **e8challenge** workbook, if necessary, and select the #1-RotateAlign worksheet.

2. Set rotation in cells A9:J9 to zero degrees.

3. Set both vertical and horizontal alignment in cells A9:J9 to Center.

4. Apply bold and the color Blue to the column headings in row 9.

5. Adjust column widths as necessary.

2. Removing a Style and an AutoFormat

You are concerned that too many enhancements have been applied to a worksheet listing the inventory of used cars. You decide to restore the Normal style to data in columns G through J, and to remove the AutoFormat.

To remove a style and an AutoFormat:

1. Open the **e8challenge** workbook, if necessary, and select the #2-Remove2 worksheet.

2. Select the range G9:J31, and apply the Normal style.

3. Select the range A9:J31, access the AutoFormat option, and remove the current AutoFormat.

4. Apply the Comma, zero decimal places format to the values in Column G.

5. Apply the Percent, one decimal place format to the values in Column H.

6. Apply the Currency, two decimal places format to the values in Column J.

3. Sending a Sheet as the Body Message in an Email

Your supervisor is away on vacation and has asked that you email the current inventory of used cars. The supervisor does not need the inventory file itself. You decide to send the requested information from within Excel as the body message in an email.

To send a sheet as a body message in an email:

1. Open the **e8challenge** workbook and select the #3-EmailSheet worksheet.

2. Connect to your Internet Service Provider if necessary.

3. Choose <u>F</u>ile, Sen<u>d</u> To, Mail Recipient. (Do not select the option that includes as Attachment.)

4. Specify a recipient according to directions from your instructor (or specify the email address of a friend).

5. Copy yourself on the email, and send it.

6. Check your copy of the email and verify that the worksheet comprises the body message.

Discovery Zone

Discovery Zone exercises require advanced knowledge of topics presented in *MOUS Essentials* lessons, application of skills from multiple lessons, or self-directed learning of new skills.

Each exercise is independent of the others, so you can complete the exercises in any order. Be sure to save the workbook after completing each exercise. If you need a paper copy of the completed exercise, enter your name centered in a header before printing. Other print options have already been set to print compressed to one page and to display the filename, sheet name, and current date in a footer.

Before beginning your first Project 8 Discovery Zone exercise, complete the following steps:

1. Open the Excel file named **e-0804.xls**, and save it as **e8discovery.xls.** Initially, the e8discovery workbook contains three sheets: an overview and two exercise sheets named #1-Style and #2-Weekly Pay.

2. Click the Overview sheet to view the organization of the Project 8 Discovery Zone Exercises workbook.

If you need more than one work session to complete the desired exercises, continue working on **e8discovery.xls** instead of starting all over on the original e-0804.xls file.

1. Creating and Applying a Style

Create a style in the e8discovery worksheet named **#1-Style**. The style should apply a thick blue outline border, a light yellow fill, wrap text, right-alignment, and Arial Bold Italic 12 point font to selected cells. Name the style **combo1**. Apply the style to the labels in B10:D10.

2. Moving a Workbook and Creating a Template

Move the #2-Weekly Pay worksheet in the e8discovery workbook to a blank workbook. Prepare the moved worksheet for repeated use by making the following changes: Indent the word Average in cell A21 twice; enter in B21:D21 functions to average the Base Pay per Hour, Hours Worked, and Weekly Gross Pay; apply a Classic2 AutoFormat to the range A10:D21; and delete the Hours worked data in C11:C20 and the date in cell B8. Save the worksheet as a template named Weekly Pay in the same location as your other student files.

PinPoint Assessment

You have completed this project and its associated lessons, and have had an opportunity to assess your skills through the end-of-project questions and exercises. Now use the PinPoint software Evaluation Mode to further assess your comprehension of the specific exam activities you have just learned. You can also use the PinPoint Trainer Mode and the Show Me tutorials to practice these exam activities.

Creating Special Effects in a Worksheet

Key terms introduced in this project include

- AutoShape
- callout
- clip art
- graphics file
- grouped objects
- text box
- WordArt

Objectives	Required Activity for MOUS	Exam Level
➤ Create WordArt	Create and modify lines and objects	
➤ Insert and Rotate an AutoShape	Create and modify lines and objects	
➤ Create a Text Box	Create and modify lines and objects	
➤ Group Objects	Create and modify lines and objects	
➤ Add Emphasis with Lines and Arrows	Create and modify lines and objects	
➤ Add Emphasis with Callouts	Create and modify lines and objects	
➤ Insert a Graphics File	Insert, move, and delete an object (picture)	
➤ Embed Sound		

Why Would I Do This?

When you design worksheets for others to use, it is essential that they be aesthetically pleasing. Excel provides a variety of tools to help make worksheets look professional, yet be easy to use. Using Excel's special effects tools to enhance your worksheets is as fun as it is essential.

Excel's toolbox of special effects includes AutoShapes—such as lines, arrows, basic shapes, and callouts—and text boxes, WordArt, pictures and clip art, and sound. You can glimpse the power of Excel's special effects tools by viewing Figure 9.1.

Figure 9.1
Use special effects to draw attention to selected areas of a worksheet.

WordArt

AutoShape: Moon basic shape

Text box

Lines and arrows

AutoShape: Rounded Rectangular Callout

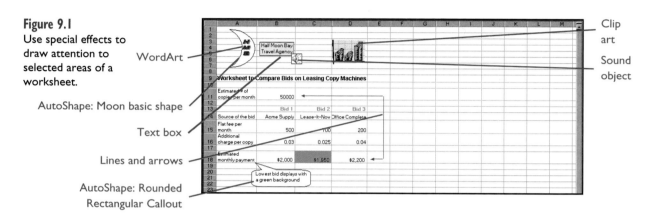

Clip art

Sound object

In this project, you add the special effects shown in Figure 9.1 to a worksheet for the Half Moon Bay Travel Agency. The worksheet computes the expected cost per month of leasing a copy machine—a cost that varies with the expected number of copies made. Consistent with company policy, three bids are being evaluated, each with a different fixed monthly fee and charge per copy.

Lesson 1: Creating WordArt

WordArt displays user-specified text in one of 30 predefined styles (see the WordArt Gallery in Figure 9.2). The styles include curved, slanted, and vertical text. Each style has a predefined color scheme.

Figure 9.2
Use the Insert WordArt button on the Drawing toolbar to add WordArt to your worksheet.

3-D button

Shadow button

WordArt button

Drawing toolbar

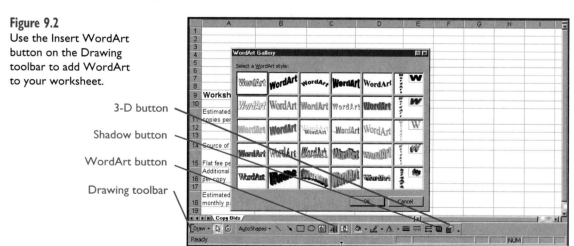

WordArt is not entered in a cell. It is a separate object that can be moved, sized, and edited. For example, you can select a WordArt object and change its color scheme, apply a shadow or 3-D effect, and edit its text.

In this lesson, you create the Half Moon Bay Travel Agency initials HMB using WordArt. You select a vertical WordArt style and size it appropriately. The result will be part of a three-object logo displayed at the top of the Half Moon Bay Travel Agency's worksheet model to analyze copy machine bids (refer to Figure 9.1). You assemble the logo over the course of Lessons 1 through 4.

To Create WordArt

① **Open the e-0901 file and save it as LeaseOptions.**
The file contains a single worksheet named Copy Bids.

② **If the Drawing toolbar does not appear on your screen, select <u>V</u>iew, <u>T</u>oolbars, and click Drawing.**

③ **Click the Insert WordArt button on the Drawing toolbar.**

④ **Select the second vertical style (the last style in the second row), and click OK.**
The Edit WordArt Text dialog box displays.

⑤ **Replace Your Text Here by typing HMB (see Figure 9.3).**

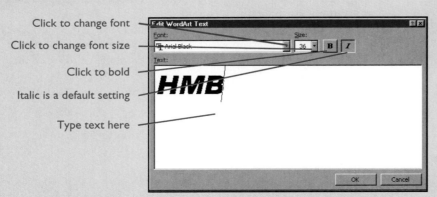

Figure 9.3
Enter WordArt text in the Edit WordArt Text dialog box.

⑥ **Click OK.**
The initials HMB display in the selected word art style in the middle of the screen. The WordArt toolbar displays near the HMB word art.

⑦ **Drag the WordArt object to cell B1.**

⑧ **Select the WordArt object, and use sizing handles to reduce its size similar to that shown in Figure 9.4.**
This is a temporary adjustment. In Lesson 2, you resize the object to fit within a moon shape.

⑨ **Make sure the WordArt object is still selected—that is, the sizing handles are visible—and click the Format WordArt button on the WordArt toolbar.**

⑩ **Apply the Dark Blue fill color to the WordArt object.**

continues ▶

To Create WordArt   (continued)

Figure 9.4
You can use the WordArt toolbar to edit text, select a different WordArt style, and make other changes.

Sizing handles display at the midpoints and corners of the selected object

Drag the yellow handle to change the angle of the letters

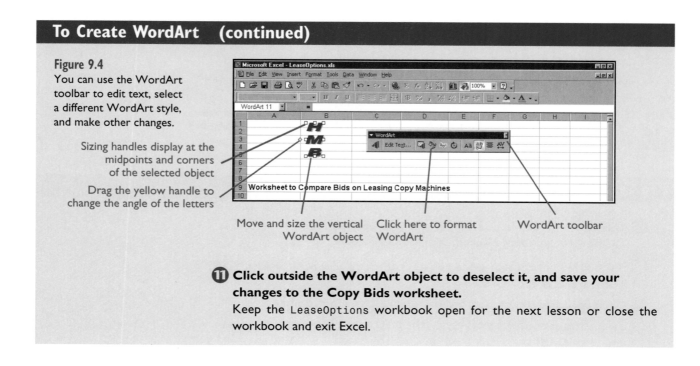

Move and size the vertical WordArt object

Click here to format WordArt

WordArt toolbar

⑪ Click outside the WordArt object to deselect it, and save your changes to the Copy Bids worksheet.

Keep the `LeaseOptions` workbook open for the next lesson or close the workbook and exit Excel.

 Exam Note: **Formatting WordArt**

Use the Format WordArt dialog box to format a shape. You can display this dialog box by right-clicking the WordArt object and selecting Format WordArt from the shortcut menu. You can then work with one or more of the five tabs described below.

Colors and Lines	Add fill color, set the fill as semi-transparent, or choose line color, style, and weight (thickness)
Size	Set height, width, rotation, and scale
Protection	Lock or unlock the object before setting protection
Properties	Specify if an object is to move when the cells under the object move, and disable printing of the object when the worksheet is printed
Web	Add alternative text to an object that appears when the worksheet is loading as a Web page or the object is missing from the Web page

---

 Exam Note: **Deleting an Object**

To delete WordArt or any other object, click within the object to select it, and press (Del).

Lesson 2: Inserting and Rotating an AutoShape

An ***AutoShape*** is a predefined shape that you create using the Drawing toolbar (see Figure 9.5). Categories of AutoShapes include Basic Shapes, Block Arrows, Flowchart, Stars and Banners, and Callouts.

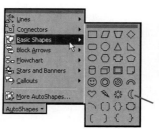

Figure 9.5
Selecting an AutoShape category, such as Basic Shapes, produces a display of related shapes.

Moon shape

To create a shape, select it from the AutoShapes menu, and draw it on the worksheet with the mouse; alternatively, you can click a cell and let Excel draw it for you. You can then move, size, rotate, or flip the shape, and apply a variety of formats.

If you select a shape with some space, such as a banner, circle, star, or block arrow, you can insert text. Lines and connectors show relationships and do not allow messages to be attached.

In this lesson, you create Half Moon Bay's corporate symbol, a half-moon. You select a basic shape and flip it.

To Insert and Rotate an AutoShape

1 Open the `LeaseOptions` workbook and display the Drawing toolbar, if necessary.

2 Click the A**u**toShapes button on the Drawing toolbar, and position the mouse pointer on Basic Shapes.
A display of shapes—four in each row—appears to the right of the AutoShapes menu (see Figure 9.5).

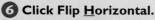

3 Click the Moon shape (the last option in the sixth row).
The shape is a crescent moon curved in the direction of the letter C, or a left parenthesis. The mouse pointer changes to a thin black cross.

4 Click cell A1.
Excel inserts the shape and displays it with sizing handles, indicating the shape is selected.

5 Click the D**r**aw button at the left end of the Drawing toolbar and position the mouse pointer on Rotate or Fli**p**.
Excel displays the draw options that can be applied to the selected object (see Figure 9.6).

6 Click Flip **H**orizontal.
The crescent moon flips to the opposite direction—that is, it curves similar to a right parenthesis.

continues ▶

To Insert and Rotate an AutoShape (continued)

Figure 9.6
Selecting Draw displays
the drawing tools you can
apply to the selected
object.

Selected AutoShape

Draw options when an
AutoShape is selected

Flip options

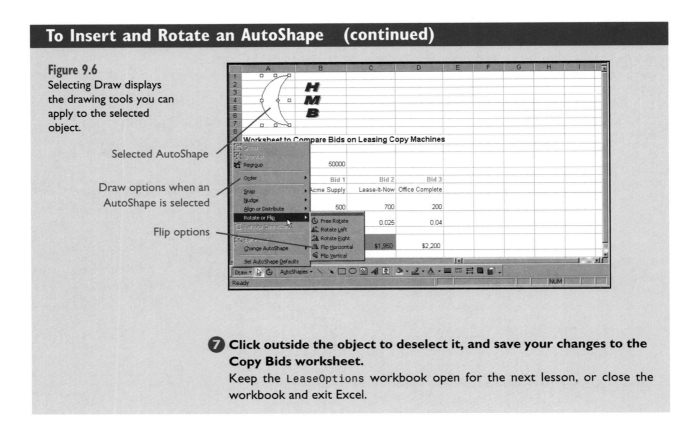

7 **Click outside the object to deselect it, and save your changes to the Copy Bids worksheet.**

Keep the `LeaseOptions` workbook open for the next lesson, or close the workbook and exit Excel.

 Exam Note: **Formatting AutoShapes**

Use the Format AutoShape dialog box to format a shape. You can display this dialog box by right-clicking a shape and selecting Format AutoShape from the shortcut menu. This dialog box includes the five tabs described in the WordArt section: Colors and Lines, Size, Protection, Properties, and Web.

 Inside Stuff: **Replacing One AutoShape with Another**

You can easily change an AutoShape from one style to another. Click the AutoShape to select it, and click D<u>r</u>aw on the Drawing toolbar. Select Change AutoShape, pick a general category, and click the desired style.

 ## Lesson 3: Creating a Text Box

A **text box** is an object that contains words and is shaped like a square or rectangle. Text automatically wraps to fit within the boundaries of the box, and you can make the box larger or smaller by dragging a sizing handle. If you create a text box by dragging the mouse pointer, it displays with a solid border. If instead you click the worksheet to add the box, and then resize it or begin typing, the text does not have a border.

You can edit the words in a text box in the same way you would edit text in a word-processing document (that is, select the text to be changed and type the correction). Some formatting can be done using the toolbar buttons Fill Color, Line Color, Font Color, and Line Style. For other formatting you can choose F<u>o</u>rmat, Text <u>B</u>ox and make selections within the Format Text Box dialog box.

In this lesson, you create a text box containing the name of the Half Moon Bay Travel Agency. You draw the box using the mouse, enter the text using the default font, and apply a light yellow fill (background) to the box (see Figure 9.7).

Selected
text box

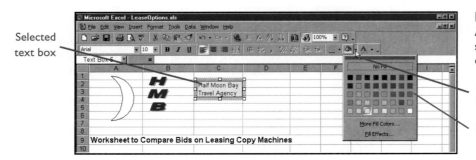

Figure 9.7
A text box resembles a small word-processing document.

Click here to display the Fill color palette

Fill color palette

To Create a Text Box

1 **Open the** `LeaseOptions` **file, if necessary.**

2 **Click the Text Box button on the Drawing toolbar.**

3 **Drag open the text box beginning in cell C2 (similar in size and position to the box shown in Figure 9.7).**

4 **Select the text box, and type** `Half Moon Bay Travel Agency`.

5 **Select the text box border.**

6 **Click the down arrow to the right of the Fill Color button on the Formatting toolbar or the Drawing toolbar. (Figure 9.7 illustrates use of the Formatting toolbar.)**
The Fill Color palette displays.

X ***If You Have Problems...***
If the Fill Color palette is dim, you have not selected the text box border. Text boxes have two selection modes, both of which cause sizing handles to display. A flashing cursor, which indicates text editing mode, displays if you click within a text box. Clicking the border of a text box enables you to edit the text box properties, including fill, border color, and line style.

7 **Select Light Yellow from the Fill Color palette.**

8 **Click outside the text box to deselect it, and save your changes to the Copy Bids worksheet.**
Keep the `LeaseOptions` workbook open for the next lesson, or close the workbook and exit Excel.

Exam Note: Formatting a Text Box
Use the Format Text Box dialog box to format a text box. You can display this dialog box by clicking within the text box, right-clicking a border of the box, and selecting Format Text Box from the shortcut menu. The Format Text Box dialog box includes the same eight tabs as the Format AutoShapes dialog box.

Inside Stuff: **Readability and Linking**

As you add text color and background fill, be mindful of a reader's ability to see the text. Strive for sharp color contrast. For example, yellow text on a white background is nearly impossible to read, and red on green is a problem for people who are color blind.

If the text you want to enter in a text box or AutoShape already exists in a cell, you can set a link to that cell instead of typing the text. Click within the text box or shape, click the formula bar, type an equal sign, click the cell containing the desired text, and press ⏎Enter.

 # Lesson 4: Grouping Objects

Grouped objects consist of two or more objects that can be manipulated as a single object. Prior to grouping, each object has its own set of sizing handles (see Figure 9.8). After grouping, a single set of sizing handles surrounds the objects.

Figure 9.8
The two objects are not grouped. Each has its own set of sizing handles.

Selected AutoShape

Selected WordArt

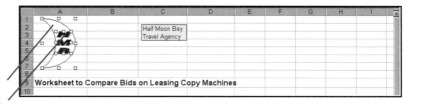

When objects are grouped, any action applied to the group impacts each object in the group. You can, for example, resize all the objects in a group, rotate and flip them, drag them to a different location, and apply attributes such as text, fill, and line color. If you want to change only one object in the group, you can ungroup the objects, make the change, and then regroup the objects.

Stacked objects, such as the moon and the WordArt shown in Figure 9.8, display in layers. You can change the order in which objects display by using an Order option accessed through the Drawing toolbar, or by right-clicking any object in the group and selecting Order from the shortcut menu. Four options are available on the Order menu. Send to Back or Bring to Front places the selected object at the bottom or top of the stack, respectively. If there are three or more layers, use the Bring Forward and Send Backward options to move an object one layer at a time.

In this lesson, you group the moon and the WordArt HMB as one object, and add a third object to the group—the text box containing the company name. You start by adjusting size, location and order of the individual objects—the WordArt initials must fit within the moon shape and the initials must display on top of the moon.

To Group Objects

❶ Open the LeaseOptions file, if necessary.

❷ Drag the WordArt object on top of the moon.
The moon obscures the WordArt object. Now reverse the two objects to get the effect of text inside the moon.

3 **Right-click the moon shape, position the mouse pointer on Order, and select Send to Back.**

4 **Resize the moon, so that it fills cells A1 through A7.**

5 **Resize the WordArt object until it fits inside the moon.**

6 **Hold down ⟨⬆Shift⟩, and select both the moon and the WordArt objects.**

Each object displays its own set of sizing handles (refer to Figure 9.8).

7 **Right-click the selected objects, and position the mouse pointer on Grouping (see Figure 9.9).**

Figure 9.9
Prior to grouping, each selected object displays its own set of sizing handles.

8 **Select Group.**

Now only one set of sizing handles appears because grouped objects take on the characteristics of a single object.

9 **Move the text box to the right of the grouped objects.**

10 **Repeat the procedures described in steps 6 through 8 to include the text box in a grouping of three objects (see Figure 9.10).**

One set of
sizing
handles

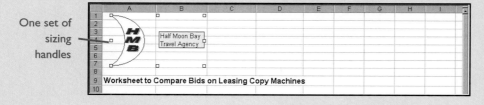

Figure 9.10
Three objects—a text box displaying company name and company initials in a WordArt format superimposed on a moon shape—display as one.

11 **Click outside the grouped objects, and save your changes to the Copy Bids worksheet.**

Keep the LeaseOptions workbook open for the next lesson, or close the workbook and exit Excel.

 Exam Note: Changing the Order of Stacked Objects
Sometimes an object in a stack is hidden by another object. You can press ⟨Tab⇄⟩ or ⟨⬆Shift⟩ + ⟨Tab⇄⟩ to move forward or backward through the objects on a worksheet.

Exam Note: Ungrouping and Regrouping Drawing Objects

To ungroup drawing objects, click within any object in the group, display the D̲raw menu on the Drawing toolbar, and select U̲ngroup.

To regroup drawing objects, select any one of the objects previously grouped, display the D̲raw menu on the Drawing toolbar, and select Regro̲up.

 Inside Stuff: Limitations of Grouping Objects

Grouping works best on drawing objects. Including other objects, such as text boxes, in the group limits what can be done with the group. You can rotate and flip an AutoShape, for example, but the same actions cannot be applied to a text box. Therefore, if one of the objects in a group is a text box, the group cannot be flipped and rotated. When this happens, the affected menu items or buttons appear dimmed.

 # Lesson 5: Adding Emphasis with Lines and Arrows

Use arrows to point to a specific location in a worksheet or to show a connection between two or more related areas or objects on the worksheet. Lines can be used to frame an area, connect or separate areas and objects, or show relationships.

To create an arrow or line, first select the object from the drawing toolbar. Second, drag the line or arrow onto the worksheet using the mouse. Third, apply line styles, such as color, thickness, pattern, and arrow. Figure 9.11 illustrates many of the tools for drawing lines and arrows.

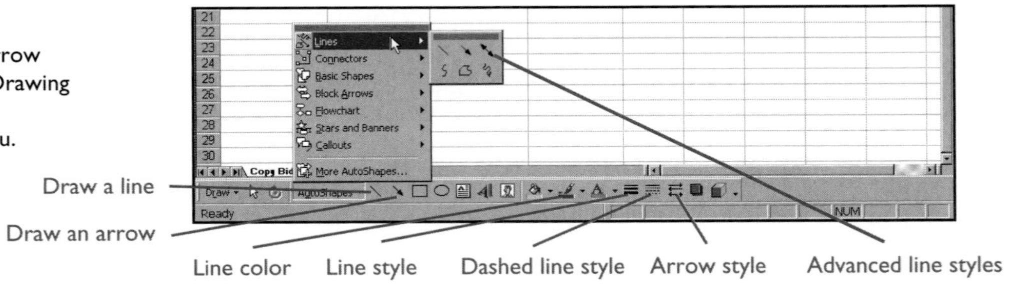

Figure 9.11
Select line and arrow styles from the Drawing toolbar or the AutoShapes menu.

Draw a line

Draw an arrow

Line color   Line style   Dashed line style   Arrow style   Advanced line styles

Lines and arrows are objects that can be moved, copied, resized, and rotated. Clicking anywhere on a line or arrow selects it and displays sizing handles at each end. To move the object to a new location, position the mouse over it until you see the drag and drop symbol—a four headed arrow—and drag the line to its new location. To change length, click a sizing handle, and drag the object longer or shorter, or pivot its angle.

In this lesson, you create objects to show a relationship in the Copy Bids worksheet between the estimated number of copies per month and the estimated monthly payments. You create two left arrows connected with a vertical line (refer to Figure 9.1).

To Add Emphasis with Lines and Arrows

1 Open the LeaseOptions file, if necessary.

2 Click the Arrow button on the Drawing toolbar.

3 Click toward the right end of cell E18, and drag left to create a short arrow pointing left (see the lower of the two arrows in Figure 9.12).

	A	B	C	D	E	F	G	H	I	
9	Worksheet to Compare Bids on Leasing Copy Machines									
10										
11	Estimated # of copies per month	50000								
12										
13		Bid 1	Bid 2	Bid 3						
14	Source of the bid	Acme Supply	Lease-It-Now	Office Complete						
15	Flat fee per month	500	700	200						
16	Additional charge per copy	0.03	0.025	0.04						
17										
18	Estimated monthly payment	$2,000	$1,950	$2,200						
19										

Figure 9.12
Copying an arrow makes it easier to connect the right ends of the arrows with a vertical line.

Copied arrow

Original arrow

⊠ If You Have Problems...
If the object is not drawn as you want, you can select it and press Del to start over, or you can move and size it as necessary.

---

4 Display sizing handles on the arrow, and click the Copy button.

5 Click cell E11, and click the Paste button.
Excel creates a copy of the original arrow (see Figure 9.12).

6 Lengthen the copied arrow by dragging its arrowhead end to cell C11 (refer to Figure 9.1).

7 Click the Line button on the Drawing toolbar.

8 Drag the line so it connects the right ends of the arrows in cells E11 and E18.

9 Hold down ⇧Shift, and click each of the three lines you just created.

10 Click the down arrow to the right of the Line Color button on the Drawing toolbar, select Blue, and deselect the drawn objects.

11 Check your results with Figure 9.13, and make changes as necessary.

	A	B	C	D	E	F	G	H	I	
9	Worksheet to Compare Bids on Leasing Copy Machines									
10										
11	Estimated # of copies per month	50000								
12										
13		Bid 1	Bid 2	Bid 3						
14	Source of the bid	Acme Supply	Lease-It-Now	Office Complete						
15	Flat fee per month	500	700	200						
16	Additional charge per copy	0.03	0.025	0.04						
17										
18	Estimated monthly payment	$2,000	$1,950	$2,200						
19										

Figure 9.13
Three line and arrow objects show the relationship between the input variable for the model (cell B11) and the calculated results (cells B18 through D18).

12 Save your changes to the Copy Bids worksheet.
Keep the LeaseOptions workbook open for the next lesson, or close the workbook and exit Excel.

Exam Note: Setting Line Styles

An arrow is a line with an arrowhead symbol attached to either or both ends. Use the following menus to apply styles to lines and arrows:

Line Style menu. Use the Line Style menu to specify the thickness of a line.

Dash Style menu. Use the Dash Style menu to change lines and arrows from solid to different patterns of lines.

Arrow Style menu. Use the Arrow Style menu to add or change the style of arrowhead attached to a line. You can switch between a line and an arrow using this menu.

Line Color menu. Use the Line Color menu to change the color of a line and its arrowheads.

AutoShape Lines Menu. Use the Lines menu on AutoShapes to select advanced line drawing tools, such as curved, scribble, and freeform lines.

 ## Lesson 6: Adding Emphasis with Callouts

A **callout** is a text-filled object that points to other text or another object. Perhaps you have seen a callout as the balloon or cloud over a cartoon character's head showing what the character is thinking or saying.

You can select among predefined callout styles on the AutoShapes Callouts menu (see Figure 9.14). Positioning the mouse pointer on a callout displays its name.

Figure 9.14
Positioning the mouse pointer on a callout displays its name.

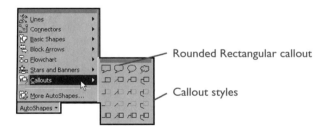

Callout styles are not limited to those shown in Figure 9.14. Any AutoShape except a line, arrow, or connector can be used as a callout. To create a callout, select the style you want to use, click the location on the worksheet where you want to insert the object, type the text, and size the object appropriately. Callouts all have connectors that point to an area or object. You can drag the yellow connector handle to change its direction (see Figure 9.15).

Figure 9.15
Use sizing handles and the connector handle to change the size and direction of a callout.

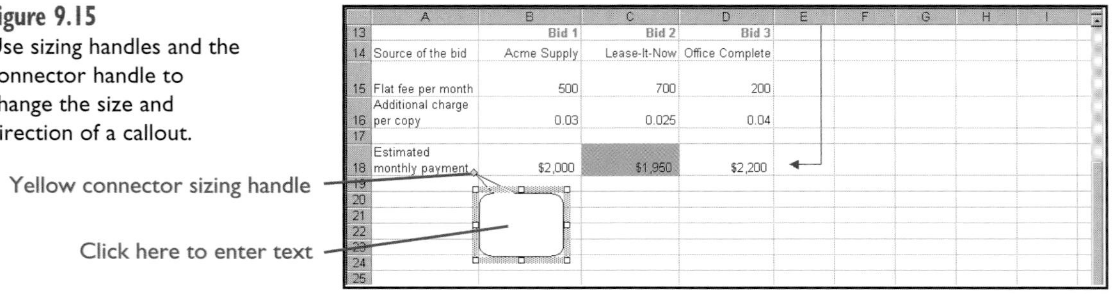

Yellow connector sizing handle

Click here to enter text

	A	B	C	D	E	F	G	H	I
13		Bid 1	Bid 2	Bid 3					
14	Source of the bid	Acme Supply	Lease-It-Now	Office Complete					
15	Flat fee per month	500	700	200					
16	Additional charge per copy	0.03	0.025	0.04					
17									
18	Estimated monthly payment	$2,000	$1,950	$2,200					
19									
20									
21									
22									
23									
24									
25									

In this lesson, you create a Rounded Rectangular callout on the Copy Bids worksheet. You select the callout style, draw it on the worksheet, type the appropriate message in the callout, and then resize and position the callout.

To Add Emphasis with a Callout

1 **Open the LeaseOptions file, if necessary.**

2 **Select <u>C</u>allouts from the A<u>u</u>toShapes menu on the Drawing toolbar (see Figure 9.14).**

3 **Choose the Rounded Rectangular callout.**

4 **Click cell B21, and size the callout appropriately.**
You can resize the callout again later.

5 **Click the yellow diamond-shaped sizing handle, and extend the connector toward cell A18.**

6 **With the callout selected, type Lowest bid displays with a green background.**

7 **Make final adjustments to the size and position of the callout similar to that shown in Figure 9.16.**

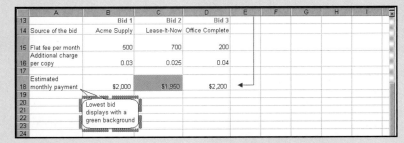

Figure 9.16
The callout points to cell A18.

8 **Save your changes to the Copy Bids worksheet.**
Keep the LeaseOptions workbook open for the next lesson, or close the workbook and exit Excel.

Lesson 7: Inserting a Graphics File

Most people are visual learners, and a picture is truly worth ten thousand words. When you add WordArt, a line, a callout, or other AutoShape in an Excel worksheet, you add a graphic that is available through buttons or menu selections. You can also insert a **graphics file**, an image that is part of a library of images provided by a program or a file stored separately. Graphics files that you can use in a worksheet include an extensive inventory of images provided with Office 2000, other files available online from Microsoft, **clip art** that you can purchase, and files scanned from hardcopy or copied from the Internet.

The Insert ClipArt dialog box provides access to Office 2000 pictures, sounds, and movie clips (see Figure 9.17). From the Pictures tab, you see icons representing groups of related pictures.

Figure 9.17
Select the Pictures tab to access an extensive set of clips.

ClipArt category

Scroll to view other business clips

A thick black border surrounds the selected clip art

Click here to insert the selected clip art

In this lesson, you select a graphics file depicting three stacks of money from the Office 2000 picture library. You insert the image in the Copy Bids worksheet, and then size and position it.

To Insert a Graphics File

1 Open the LeaseOptions file, if necessary.

2 Select cell D3.

3 Choose Insert, Picture, and select Clip Art (or click the Insert Clip Art button on the Drawing toolbar).

4 Select the Picture tab, and click the Business icon.
The Business icon is a picture of a briefcase.

5 Click the Finance picture, and click the Insert clip icon from the pop-up menu (see Figure 9.17).
The finance picture shows three stacks of money.

6 Close the Insert ClipArt dialog box.

7 Select the clip art object, move and size it to fit in cells D3 through D6, and deselect it (see Figure 9.18).

Figure 9.18
Objects in the worksheet include WordArt, an AutoShape, a text box, and clip art.

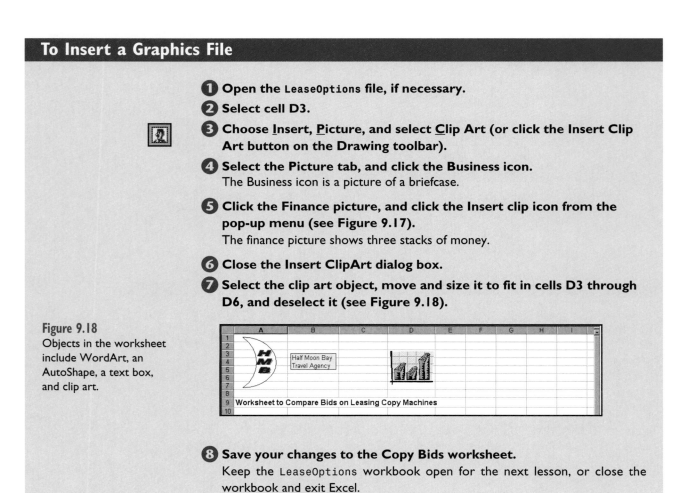

8 Save your changes to the Copy Bids worksheet.
Keep the LeaseOptions workbook open for the next lesson, or close the workbook and exit Excel.

Exam Note: **Graphics File Types Accepted by Excel**
You can insert several graphics file types directly into a worksheet. Some of these are listed next: the three-character file extension is listed in the first column and its explanation in the second column.

.emf	Enhanced Metafile
.gif	Graphics Interchange Format (known as a gif file)
.jpg	Joint Photographic Experts Group (known as a j-peg file)
.bmp	Windows Bitmap (also files with extensions .rle and .dib)
.wmf	Windows Metafile

Other files, including Kodak Photo CD (.pcd), PC Paintbrush (.pcx), and WordPerfect Graphics (.wpg), can be inserted using separate graphics filters. Onscreen Help provides a complete list.

 Inside Stuff: **Copyright Issues**
Pictures, such as print media, recordings, and movies, are intellectual property and are therefore protected by U.S. Copyright laws. Before using a picture, be sure you have clear ownership of the picture and be aware of the copyright laws. Assume that all pictures are copyright-protected unless there is clear written permission to use them or they are original graphics you own. If you use your own pictures for commercial purposes, you should obtain copyrights to protect your interests.

Lesson 8: Embedding Sound

Sound is an integral part of the toolkit for designing a worksheet presented to or used by others. One of the most popular uses for sound is to alert the user when an action is required. Sound can be an excellent form of documentation, such as adding a voice message that provides instructions for using the worksheet.

You can insert a sound file or record your own file onto the worksheet. To record and play sound, your computer must have a sound card, microphone, and speakers. This is basic hardware on most computers sold today.

Several options are available when you add sound to a worksheet. You can record the sound directly into the worksheet. This method is easy, but increases the size of the worksheet significantly and does not enable you to edit the sound file. You can also link your worksheet to an external sound file. The advantage is that you can edit the message and apply recording techniques to reduce the sound file and worksheet size. The disadvantage to linking the worksheet to a sound file is that if the two files are separated, the link is broken and the sound doesn't play. Finally, you can insert the sound file into the worksheet. This has the same advantages of linking but without the risk of losing the sound file.

In this lesson, you attach a brief recorded message to your worksheet. After you embed the sound file, an icon of a speaker displays on the worksheet. To hear the recording, click the icon.

To Embed Sound

1 Open the LeaseOptions file, if necessary.

2 Select cell F4.

3 Choose Insert, Object.
The Object dialog box opens.

4 Select the Create from File tab.

5 Select Browse; select the student file e-0902.wav, and click Insert.

6 Click OK.
The sound icon appears in your worksheet at cell F4.

7 Double-click the sound icon to hear the sound file.

8 Drag the sound icon until it touches the lower-right corner of the Half Moon Bay Travel Agency text box.
The sound message and the text box are related and should appear close together.

9 Click the sound icon once and use a corner sizing handle to reduce the size of the icon (see the Figure 9.1 worksheet at the beginning of the project).
Changing the size of the icon enables you to discretely add short voice messages to any element of your worksheet.

10 Save your changes to the Copy Bids worksheet.
This concludes Project 9. Close the LeaseOptions workbook, and exit Excel or continue with the end-of-project exercises.

Inside Stuff: **Sound Files Are Big!**
You must be aware of the user's environment. Although a recorded message is an effective tool, sound files can be incredibly large. Five seconds of recording can use between 200KB and 2MB of memory, depending on how it is recorded. In addition to the obvious hardware requirements, determine whether the user of your worksheet will be in an office environment where the sound might disturb others.

Summary

In this project, you applied a variety of special effects to a worksheet. As an alternative to entering text in cells, you learned how to create WordArt, callouts, and text boxes. You grouped objects to be manipulated as a unit. You also focused attention on specific areas of the worksheet using lines and arrows, adding a picture, and embedding sound.

To expand your learning, explore the onscreen Help topic About using graphics in Microsoft Excel—if printed, a document of more than 25 pages. Then try features that you have not yet worked with, such as adding a circle or square, drawing a curve or freeform object, and creating a picture of worksheet data or a chart.

Checking Concepts and Terms

True/False

For each of the following, check *T* or *F* to indicate whether the statement is true or false.

__T __F **1.** To edit WordArt text, you must delete the object and reapply it with the correct text. [L1]

__T __F **2.** You can create text within all AutoShapes. [L2]

__T __F **3.** You can link a cell to an AutoShape object so the cell's contents display in the shape. [L3]

__T __F **4.** Callouts are sound files that warn the user when an error is made. [L6, L8]

__T __F **5.** Pictures are intellectual property protected by U.S. Copyright laws. [L7]

Multiple Choice

Circle the letter of the correct answer for each of the following.

1. Which is not a drawing object? [L1, L2]
   a. WordArt
   b. AutoShape
   c. text box
   d. lines and arrows

2. Which is not an AutoShape group? [L2]
   a. block arrows
   b. flowchart symbols
   c. stars and banners
   d. WebArt symbols

3. Which of the following would best improve the readability of a text box? [L3]
   a. Use white text on a yellow background.
   b. Use green text on a red background.
   c. Use text and background with sharply contrasting colors.
   d. all of the above

4. Which is a consideration when adding sound to a worksheet? [L8]
   a. Sound requires a sound card and speakers to play.
   b. Sound files can be very large.
   c. Some user environments, such as libraries, do not permit sound.
   d. all of the above

5. Which action cannot be applied to a group containing a callout and a text box? [L2]
   a. adding fill color
   b. changing line style
   c. rotating and flipping
   d. changing line color

Skill Drill

Skill Drill exercises reinforce project skills. Each skill that is reinforced is the same, or nearly the same, as a skill presented in the project. Detailed instructions are provided in a step-by-step format.

Because these skill drills are a continuous experience developing and using a single worksheet, you may find your experience more beneficial if you work the drills in order. Be sure to save the workbook after completing each exercise. If you need a paper copy of the completed exercise, enter your name centered in a header before printing. Other print options have already been set to print compressed to one page and to display the filename, sheet name, and current date in a footer.

Before beginning your first Project 9 Skill Drill exercise, complete the following steps:

1. Open the file named **e-0903**, and save it as **e9drill**. The workbook contains four sheets: an overview and three sheets named #1-Banner, #2-WordArt, and #3-Block Arrow.

2. Click the Overview sheet to view the organization of the Project 9 Skill Drill Exercises workbook.

If you need more than one work session to complete the desired exercises, continue working on **e9drill** instead of starting over on the original e-0903 file.

1. Creating a Banner

The company's name is Glenn Lakes Blue Ribbon Lawn Care, and you decide that it needs to be on the worksheet. To convey the name graphically, you decide to use one of the ribbons on the AutoShapes menu, type the name in the ribbon, and add a blue fill color to the ribbon. Also, you improve readability by making the text in the ribbon bold and centering it horizontally and vertically.

To add a banner to a worksheet:

1. If necessary, open the **e9drill** workbook, and select the #1-Banner worksheet.
2. Select the Curved Up Ribbon from the AutoShapes Stars and Banners menu.
   If necessary, display the Drawing toolbar.
3. Click cell A3, and drag the lower-right sizing handle to cell C7.
4. Right-click the ribbon object, and select Add Te<u>x</u>t.
5. Type **Glenn Lakes Blue Ribbon Lawn Care**, and turn on Bold.

6. Center the text vertically and horizontally using the Alignment tab in the Format, AutoShape dialog box. To access the Format AutoShape dialog box containing the Alignment tab, you must first click the border around the object. A shadow border made up of dots appears when the object is correctly selected.
7. While the ribbon object is selected, turn on a sky blue fill color.

2. Creating WordArt

You need a title on the worksheet indicating what its purpose is, and you decide to use WordArt. The worksheet's title will be "Loan Payment Analysis" typed into one of the colorful WordArt styles and rotated slightly to give it an upward slant from left to right.

To add WordArt to your worksheet:

1. If necessary, open the `e9drill` workbook; then select the #2-WordArt worksheet.

2. Select Insert WordArt on the Drawing toolbar.

3. Select the WordArt style in the fourth column, third row.

4. Type `Loan Payment Analysis` in the Edit WordArt Text dialog box, and click OK.

5. Move, size, and rotate the word art so it displays above the data in row 12, from column A through column D, with its right end higher than the left. You can select the Rotate button near the left end of the Drawing toolbar and rotate the right end up about 3 rows higher than the left end.

6. Make any final adjustments to size and position, and deselect the object.

3. Adding a Block Arrow Shape

You want to call the user's attention to the monthly payment line and the fact that the cell displaying the lowest payment in the range B18:D18 has a green background. You decide to create a block arrow with a message.

To add a block arrow to your worksheet:

1. If necessary, open the `e9drill` workbook, and select the #3-Block Arrow worksheet.

2. Select AutoShapes from the Drawing toolbar, and access the Block Arrows menu.

3. Select the Up Arrow callout.

4. Click C20 to set the arrow object on the worksheet.

5. Stretch the object until it fills cells B19 to D24.

6. Right-click the arrow object, and select Add Text.

7. Type `Green indicates the lowest monthly payment`.

8. Select the outer border of the object.

9. Using the Alignment tab on the Format, AutoShape menu, center the message horizontally and vertically.

10. Add Light Yellow fill color to the object. You can use the Fill Color button on the Drawing toolbar or make your selections using the Colors and Lines tab on the Format, AutoShapes menu.

Challenge

Challenge exercises expand on or are somewhat related to skills presented in the lessons. Each exercise provides a brief narrative introduction, followed by instructions in a numbered step format that are not as detailed as those in the Skill Drill section.

Each exercise is independent of the others, so you can complete the exercises in any order. Be sure to save the workbook after completing each exercise. If you need a paper copy of the completed exercise, enter your name centered in a header before printing. Other print options have already been set to print compressed to one page and to display the filename, sheet name, and current date in a footer.

Before beginning your first Project 9 Challenge exercise, complete the following steps:

1. Open the file named `e-0904`, and save it as `e9challenge`.
   The workbook contains four sheets: an overview and three exercise sheets named #1-StarText, #2-Oval, and #3-Ungroup.

2. Click the Overview sheet to view the organization of the Project 9 Challenge Exercises workbook.

If you need more than one work session to complete the desired exercises, continue working on `e9challenge` instead of starting over on the original e-0904 file.

1. Adding Text to a Shape

You've added a 16-point star to the worksheet showing budgeted revenues for the year 2001. Now you decide to enlarge the blank space in the center of the star and add text stating that the year 2000 is expected to be the best year yet.

To add text to a star shape:

1. If necessary, open the **e9challenge** workbook; then select the #1-StarText worksheet.

2. Click the star until you see the yellow sizing handle.

3. Drag the yellow handle outward to enlarge the white space in the center. (The space should hold the words Best Year Yet, one word to a line.)

4. Right-click the object to display the shortcut menu, and enter the text described in the previous step.

5. Resize and reposition the object as desired.

2. Circling Text Using an Oval Shape

The focus of the good news in the budget for year 2001 revenues is the Total Revenue in cell F17. You decide to emphasize this value by drawing a circle around it. The shape you draw covers the value, so you need to select the object and turn off the fill color.

To add and edit an oval shape around a cell:

1. If necessary, open the **e9challenge** workbook; then select the #2-Oval worksheet.

2. Select the Oval button from the Drawing toolbar, and drag it over cell F17.
   The shape covers the value in cell F17 so you can't see it. This happens because the fill color is white.

3. Change fill color to No Fill.

4. Change the size and position of the oval as necessary so that it surrounds the value 1,949,100 in cell F17.

3. Ungrouping, Editing, and Regrouping Objects

You've already created an eye-catching grouped object that includes clip art and a callout. You realize that some of the text in the callout does not display, and that an uppercase letter in the callout should be made lowercase. To make the changes, ungroup the objects, select only the callout, edit and resize as necessary, and then regroup the objects.

To ungroup, edit, and regroup objects:

1. If necessary, open the **e9challenge** workbook; then select the #3-Ungroup worksheet.

2. Access onscreen Help, and search for and read information about ungrouping and regrouping objects.

3. Exit Help, and ungroup the cloud callout and clip art.

4. Increase the size of only the cloud callout, so that all text displays.

5. Change the uppercase C in Can't to a lowercase c.

6. Regroup the two objects.

Discovery Zone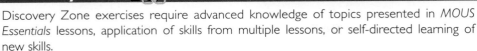

Discovery Zone exercises require advanced knowledge of topics presented in *MOUS Essentials* lessons, application of skills from multiple lessons, or self-directed learning of new skills.

Each exercise is independent of the other, so you can complete the exercises in any order. Be sure to save the workbook after completing each exercise. If you need a paper copy of the completed exercise, enter your name centered in a header before printing. Other print options have already been set to print landscape compressed to one page and to display the filename, sheet name, and current date in the footer.

Before beginning your first Project 9 Discovery Zone exercise, complete the following steps:

1. Open the file named **e-0905**, and save it as **e9discovery**.

   The workbook contains three sheets: an overview, and two exercise sheets named #1-Analyze and #2-Apply.

2. Click the Overview worksheet to view the organization of the Project 9 Discovery Zone Exercises workbook.

If you need more than one work session to complete the desired exercises, continue working on **e9discovery** instead of starting over on the original e-0905 file.

1. Determining Appropriate Use of Special Effects

An important part of the process of creating and maintaining a worksheet in Excel is applying special effects that make the worksheet more readable. To practice the process of determining what special effects to apply, open the #1-Analyze worksheet in the **e9discovery** workbook. Notice the area located just above the worksheet data. In column A is a list of numbers from one to eight. Next to each number is a blank cell for you to write in. Analyze the worksheet carefully, and in the space next to a number describe a special effect you would apply to the worksheet. There is room to describe up to eight improvements. Describe as many as you think would be appropriate.

2. Applying Special Effects to a Worksheet

Assume that you have decided on a number of special effects to apply to a worksheet. Open the **e9discovery** workbook, and select the #2-Apply worksheet. Apply the special effects described in rows four through eight.

PinPoint Assessment

You have completed this project and its associated lessons, and have had an opportunity to assess your skills through the end-of-project questions and exercises. Now use the PinPoint software Evaluation Mode to further assess your comprehension of the specific exam activities you have just learned. You can also use the PinPoint Trainer Mode and the Show Me tutorials to practice these exam activities.

Sorting, Filtering, and Editing Lists

Key terms introduced in this project include

- Advanced Filter
- AND search criteria
- ascending order
- AutoFilter
- data
- database

- data form
- descending order
- field
- filter
- information
- list

- OR search criteria
- record
- sort
- sort field
- sort key

Objectives	Required Activity for MOUS	Exam Level
➤ Use an Excel List as a Database	Use the Office Assistant	Core
➤ Sort Records on the Contents of One Field	Perform single and multilevel sorts	Expert
➤ Sort Records on the Contents of Two or More Fields	Perform single and multilevel sorts	Expert
➤ Use AutoFilter with One Search Condition	Apply data filters	Expert
➤ Use Custom AutoFilter with OR Search Criteria	Apply data filters	Expert
➤ Use Custom AutoFilter with AND Search Criteria	Apply data filters	Expert
➤ Add and Delete Records by Using a Form	Use data forms	Expert
➤ Edit Records by Using a Form	Use data forms	Expert

Why Would I Do This?

n general terms, you can think of a **database** as an organized collection of related data. Many database programs use a table to organize the data contained in a database file. In Excel, this concept is referred to as a **list**, which is simply a worksheet of columns and rows.

The purpose of creating a list is to store data so that it can be viewed in a variety of useful ways. **Data** is unprocessed raw facts or assumptions, stored in a database. Data is transformed into a useful form called **information** when users select the data they need, organize the data in a meaningful order, format the data into a useful layout, and display the results—usually to the screen or a printer.

In this project, you learn to use and maintain a sample database of residential real-estate listings. You start by using onscreen Help to learn about creating a database in a worksheet. In the remaining lessons, you work with the Excel list shown in Figure 10.1.

Figure 10.1
This Excel list consists of nine fields (columns) and 35 records (rows).

Each column is a field

Column headings

Each additional row is a record

Scroll to view additional records

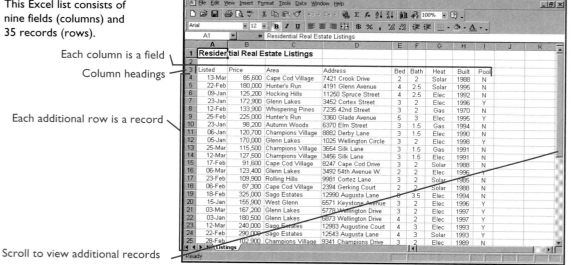

 ## Lesson 1: Using an Excel List as a Database

Each collection of related data in a database is called a **record**. In the Residential Real Estate Listings database (refer to Figure 10.1), the first record relates to property at 7421 Crook Drive in Cape Cod Village (row 4), and the second record relates to property at 4191 Glenn Avenue in Hunter's Run (row 5).

Each record in a database contains several parts, or **fields**. The first four fields in the Residential Real Estate Listings database are the date listed (column A), the asking price (column B), the area (column C), and the address (column D).

Before you begin to work with the Listings database, use Excel's onscreen Help to learn about using a list as a database and the guidelines for creating a list on a worksheet.

To Explore Using an Excel List as a Database

1 **Open the file e-1001, and save it as Listings.**

2 **Click the Office Assistant to display a balloon; type list in the text box, and click the Search button.**
Help topics associated with the word "list" display in the Office Assistant balloon.

3 **Select the topic Guidelines for creating a list on a worksheet.**
Excel displays the selected topic in the Microsoft Excel Help window (see Figure 10.2).

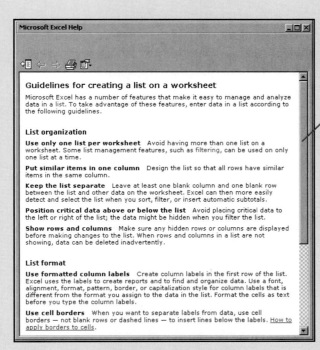

Figure 10.2
This Help topic includes information on list organization and list format.

Scroll down to view more information

4 **Click the link named Use a list as a database.**
Selecting this link near the bottom of the current Help window displays a new topic (see Figure 10.3).

5 **Close the Help window.**
Keep the Listings workbook open for the next lesson, or close the workbook and exit Excel.

continues ▶

To Explore Using an Excel List as a Database   (continued)

Figure 10.3
This Help topic summa-
rizes database tasks—
finding, sorting, or
subtotaling data—and
illustrates the
organization of an Excel
list.

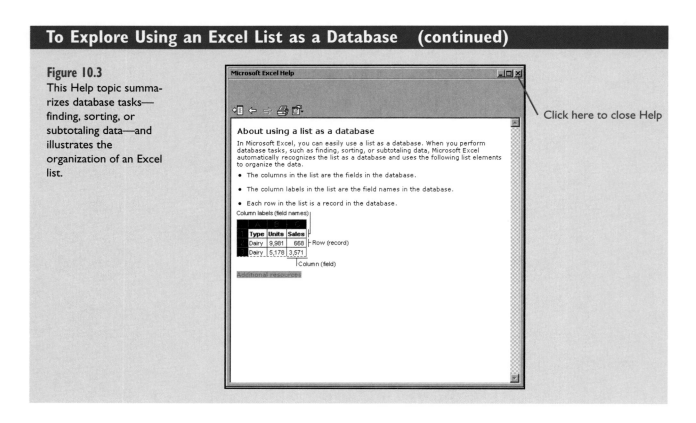

Click here to close Help

Exam Note: **Entering Data in a List**
Every record must have the same fields, but you don't have to enter data into all
the fields for every record. If the data is not available, one or more cells in the
record will be blank.

Expert   Lesson 2: Sorting Records on the Contents of One Field

Now that you have a better understanding of the way an Excel database (list) is organized, you can focus on retrieving data in a useful form. Some information needs can be
met by sorting a list. To **sort** a list means to rearrange the records in the list, based on the
contents of one or more fields. In the Listings database, for example, you might sort
records according to price from lowest to highest. Or you might sort by the date listed—
the most recent first.

Executing a sort involves two selections. First, you must specify the column you want
Excel to use in sorting, known as the **sort field** (sometimes called a **sort key**). You can
also choose the order you want Excel to follow when sorting records: **ascending order**
(A to Z, lowest to highest value, earliest to most recent date, and so on) or **descending
order** (Z to A, highest to lowest value, most recent to earliest date, and so on).

Refer to the list shown in Figure 10.1. The records are not sorted on the contents of any
field. Try sorting those records on a single sort field now by using the Sort Ascending and
Sort Descending buttons on the Standard toolbar.

To Sort Records on the Contents of One Field

1 **Open the** `Listings` **workbook, if necessary.**

2 **Click any cell within column B between row 3 (the field name row) and row 38 (the last record in the list).**

Clicking a cell in column B within the top and bottom boundaries of the list tells Excel that you want to sort on the contents of the Price field.

3 **Click the Sort Ascending button on the Standard toolbar.**

Records appear in order of Price, from lowest to highest (see Figure 10.4). Because there are no blank columns or rows in the database area A3:I38, Excel automatically treats the area as a list and sorts entire records, instead of sorting only the contents in column B.

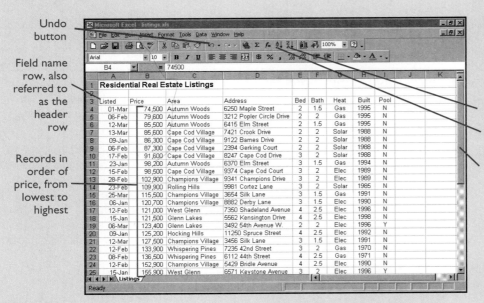

Undo button

Field name row, also referred to as the header row

Records in order of price, from lowest to highest

Figure 10.4
The order of records in the sorted list is determined by the value in the Price field.

Sort Descending button

Sort Ascending button

Scroll to view remaining records in the list

4 **Choose Edit, Undo Sort.**

Excel restores the previous order of records. The list remains selected (see Figure 10.5).

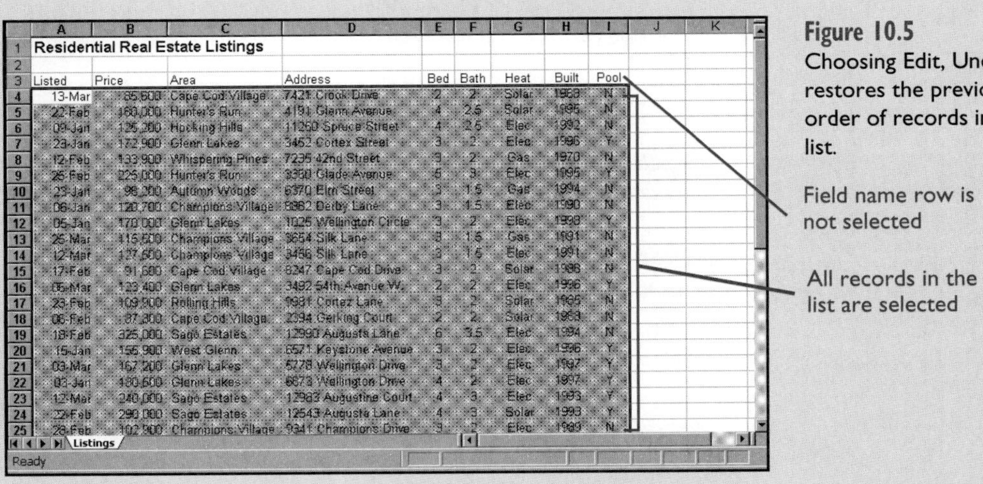

Figure 10.5
Choosing Edit, Undo Sort restores the previous order of records in the list.

Field name row is not selected

All records in the list are selected

continues ▶

To Sort Records on the Contents of One Field (continued)

5 Click any cell within column E, between row 3 and row 38.

Clicking a cell in column E within the top and bottom boundaries of the list tells Excel that you want to sort on the contents of the Bed (number of bedrooms) field.

6 Click the Sort Descending button in the Standard toolbar.

Records appear in order, according to the number of bedrooms, starting with one six-bedroom listing in Sago Estates and followed by two five-bedroom listings—one in Hunter's Run and the other in Sago Estates.

7 Save your changes.

You can close the Listings workbook now, or leave it open and continue to the next lesson.

Inside Stuff: **Restoring the Original Order of Sorted Records**
Usually, there is no need to restore records to their original order. You can quickly rearrange records in any order you choose, and view or print the results.

If you do want the ability to display records in their original order after one or more sorts, design the layout of the list to include an initial column of sequential numbers. For example, specify a column heading of Rec# (for record number), and fill subsequent rows in the column with numbers that increment by one—1, 2, 3, 4, and so forth. After sorting on one or more other columns, you can then restore the original order through an ascending sort on the Rec# column.

 # Lesson 3: Sorting Records on the Contents of Two or More Fields

You can carry out a meaningful sort on two or more fields in a list if there is a relationship or order of importance between the fields. In the Listings database, for example, you can organize records first by area and then by price within each area. Sorting the records in this way enables you to see the price range of homes in various areas quickly.

Try sorting on the contents of two fields now by using Excel's Sort dialog box.

To Sort Records on the Contents of Two or More Fields

1 Open the Listings worksheet, if necessary, and click any cell within the list range A3:I38.

2 Choose Data, Sort.

The Sort dialog box appears, with settings from the most recent sort (see Figure 10.6).

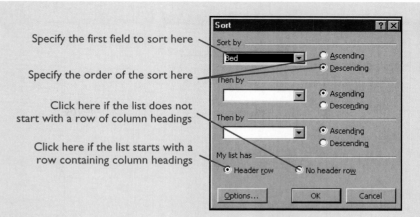

Figure 10.6
Use the Sort dialog box if you want to sort on more than one field.

Specify the first field to sort here

Specify the order of the sort here

Click here if the list does not start with a row of column headings

Click here if the list starts with a row containing column headings

3 **Click the drop-down arrow at the right end of the Sort by window.**
A scrollable drop-down list appears that includes all field names in the database (see Figure 10.7).

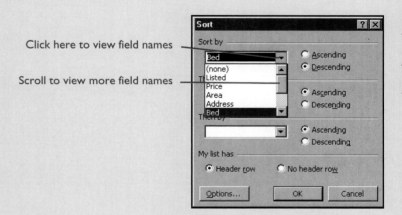

Figure 10.7
The drop-down list displays the names of all fields in the order—left to right—that they appear in the list.

Click here to view field names

Scroll to view more field names

4 **Click Area in the drop-down list, and select Ascending.**
You have specified that Excel should initially sort records in ascending order, based on the contents of the Area column.

5 **Click the drop-down arrow at the right end of the first Then by window, and select Price.**

6 **Select Descending as the sort order.**
You have specified that Excel should execute a second sort after sorting on Area—within each area records are sorted in descending order on the contents of the Price field (see Figure 10.8).

7 **Choose OK.**
Excel closes the Sort dialog box and sorts the records (see Figure 10.9). Within each group of homes in the same area, the records are arranged by price in descending order.

8 **Save your changes, and close the Listings workbook.**
This concludes lessons that focus on sorting records in a list. Continue to the next lesson, or exit Excel.

continues ▶

To Sort Records on the Contents of Two or More Fields (continued)

Figure 10.8
You can sort on up to three fields by using the Sort dialog box.

First (primary) sort field

Next (secondary) sort field

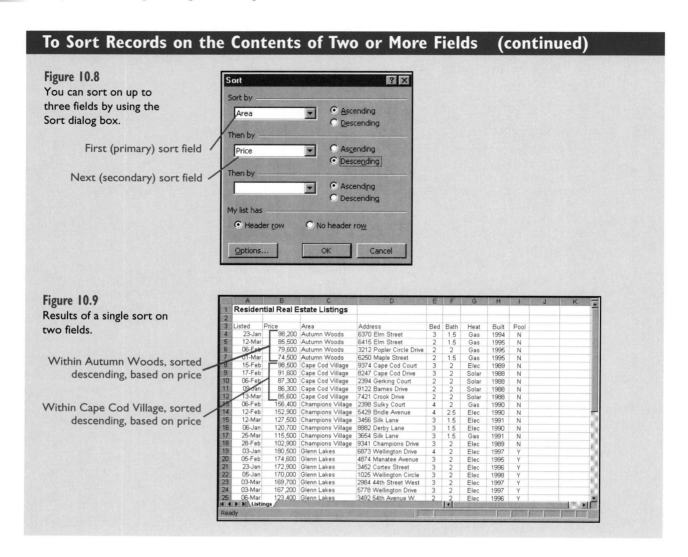

Figure 10.9
Results of a single sort on two fields.

Within Autumn Woods, sorted descending, based on price

Within Cape Cod Village, sorted descending, based on price

 Inside Stuff: Sorting on Multiple Fields by Using Toolbar Buttons
You can also sort on more than one field by executing a series of sorts by using the Sort Ascending and Sort Descending buttons. If you choose this method, you are not limited to sorting on three fields. However, you must perform successive sorts, starting with a sort on the least important field first—which is the opposite of the order in which you specify sort fields in the Sort dialog box.

For example, to sort records first by area and then by price within area by using sort buttons, you execute two sorts. The first sort arranges records in descending order on the contents of the Price field. The second sort then arranges the records in ascending order on the contents of the Area field.

Expert Lesson 4: Using AutoFilter with One Search Condition

Users of large databases with hundreds or thousands of records generally do not want to view all of the records. It's more likely that their information needs focus primarily on finding records that meet one or more conditions.

Filtering data enables you to work with a more manageable set of records. To **filter** a list means to hide all the rows except those that meet specified criteria. This is a temporary view of your list. Canceling the filter operation redisplays all of the records.

Excel provides two filtering commands—AutoFilter and Advanced Filter. You can use **AutoFilter** to limit the display based on simple search conditions. **Advanced Filter** enables you to specify more complex criteria and to copy filtered records to another location.

The Listings database is small and simple for practical reasons—so that you can see the results of your work while you learn Excel. In this lesson, you use AutoFilter to display only those records that match a single search condition. You begin by opening the original student data file and saving it as listings.xls. Working with a copy of the original database ensures that your filters display records in the same order as those shown in figures.

To Use AutoFilter with One Search Condition

1 Open the e-1001 workbook; save it as `listings.xls`, and click any cell in the list range A3:I38.

2 Choose **Data**; point to **Filter**, and click Auto**F**ilter.
Filter arrows appear next to each of the field names in the list (see Figure 10.10). A black filter arrow indicates that AutoFilter is active, but no filter is established.

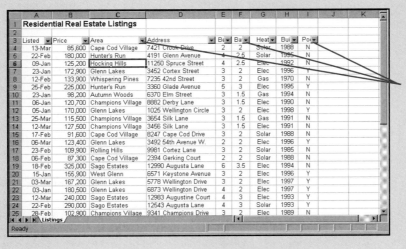

Figure 10.10
Arrows indicate that AutoFilter is active.

Filter arrows

3 Click the filter arrow for the Area field located in cell C3.
A drop-down list of filtering criteria appears (see Figure 10.11).

4 Click **Glenn Lakes** in the AutoFilter options list.
Excel temporarily hides all but the eight records containing Glenn Lakes in the Area field (see Figure 10.12). The filter arrow next to Area is blue instead of black, indicating that there is an active filter on the field.

5 Click the filter arrow for the Bed field located in cell E3.
The drop-down list for the Bed field appears.

continues ▶

To Use AutoFilter with One Search Condition   (continued)

Figure 10.11
The drop-down list displays filter options for the Area field.

Choose (All) to remove filtering criteria

Choose (Top 10) to filter based on the highest values

Select among remaining options to filter based on an exact match

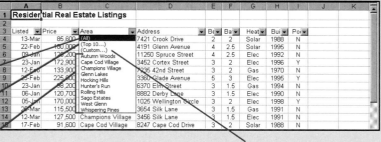

Choose (Custom) to specify two filters and/or comparisons other than an exact match

Figure 10.12
Excel temporarily hides records that do not match the specified search condition Glenn Lakes.

Row numbers of selected records

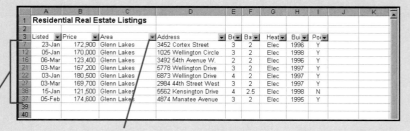

A blue arrow indicates that a filter is active

6 **Click 3 in the AutoFilter options list.**

One-condition filters are now attached to two fields. Fewer records (five) appear because the display is limited to records that meet both conditions: Glenn Lakes area and three bedrooms.

7 **Choose Data, point to Filter, and click Show All.**

The two filters are removed, and all records display. AutoFilter remains active.

8 **Choose Data, point to Filter, and click AutoFilter.**

The arrow at the end of each field name disappears, which indicates that AutoFilter is no longer active. You can close the Listings workbook without saving your changes now, or leave it open and continue to the next lesson.

Lesson 5: Using Custom AutoFilter with OR Search Criteria

Retrieving the information you need from a database quite often requires filtering records based on multiple criteria. In the previous lesson, for example, you set two filters to display only records of three-bedroom homes in the Glenn Lakes area. Each filter required an exact match to data in one field—Glenn Lakes in the Area field and 3 in the Bed field. Both conditions had to be met for a record to display.

Using the Custom filter option within AutoFilter, you can specify two search conditions based on the contents of one field. If you specify that *either* condition must be met, you are using **OR search criteria**. For example, to display only the records of homes for sale in Glenn Lakes or West Glenn, filter for Area equal to Glenn Lakes *or* Area equal to West Glenn. You tell AutoFilter to examine the Area field of each record, and display the record if it contains either Glenn Lakes or West Glenn.

In this lesson, you filter by using OR search criteria. Now, set a filter in the Listings database to find homes for sale in the Glenn Lakes area or the West Glenn area.

To Use Custom AutoFilter with OR Search Criteria

① **Open the `Listings` workbook, if necessary, and click any cell in the list range A3:I38.**

② **Choose <u>D</u>ata, point to <u>F</u>ilter, and click Auto<u>F</u>ilter.**

③ **Click the filter arrow for the Area field in cell C3, and select (Custom).**
The Custom AutoFilter dialog box appears (see Figure 10.13).

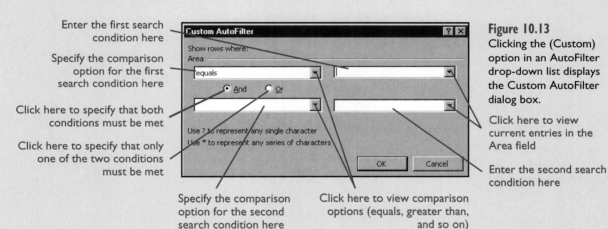

Enter the first search condition here

Specify the comparison option for the first search condition here

Click here to specify that both conditions must be met

Click here to specify that only one of the two conditions must be met

Specify the comparison option for the second search condition here

Click here to view comparison options (equals, greater than, and so on)

Figure 10.13
Clicking the (Custom) option in an AutoFilter drop-down list displays the Custom AutoFilter dialog box.

Click here to view current entries in the Area field

Enter the second search condition here

④ **In the upper-right section of the dialog box, click the arrow to view current entries in the Area field and select Glenn Lakes.**
The search condition Glenn Lakes appears in the dialog box (see Figure 10.14)

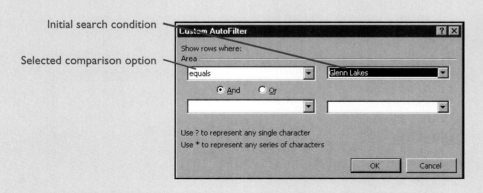

Initial search condition

Selected comparison option

Figure 10.14
Specify the first search condition in the side-by-side windows above the And and Or buttons.

⑤ **Select <u>O</u>r instead of <u>A</u>nd in the Custom AutoFilter dialog box.**

continues ▶

To Use Custom AutoFilter with OR Search Criteria   (continued)

6 **Click the arrow for viewing comparison options in the middle-left section of the dialog box.**
A drop-down list of comparison options appears (see Figure 10.15).

Figure 10.15
Ten comparison options display in the drop-down list.

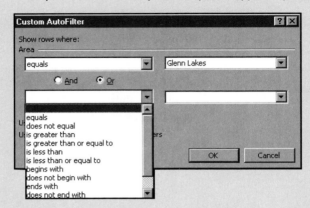

7 **Select equals from the drop-down list.**

8 **In the middle-right section of the dialog box, click the arrow to view current entries in the Area field; scroll down and select West Glenn.**
Check that your criteria match those shown in Figure 10.16 and edit the dialog box, as necessary.

Figure 10.16
Specifications are complete for limiting the display of records to those meeting either one of two conditions, both of which apply to the same field.

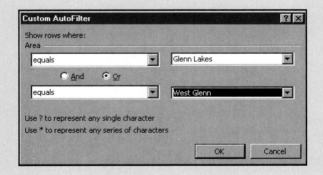

9 **Click OK in the Custom AutoFilter dialog box.**
The current filter limits the display to homes in either Glenn Lakes or West Glenn (see Figure 10.17).

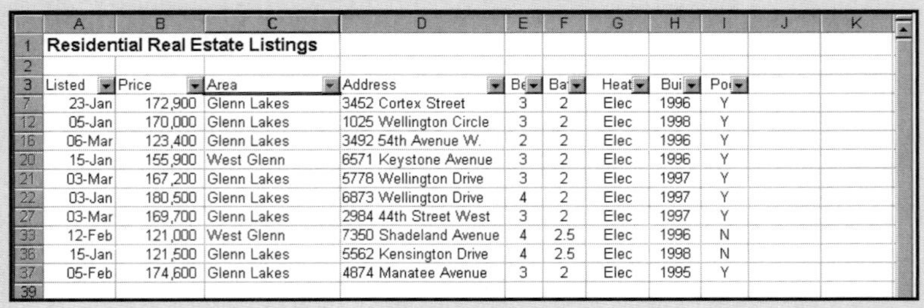

Figure 10.17
Ten records contain either Glenn Lakes or West Glenn in the Area field.

	A	B	C	D	E	F	G	H	I	J	K
1	Residential Real Estate Listings										
2											
3	Listed	Price	Area	Address	Be	Ba	Heat	Bui	Po		
7	23-Jan	172,900	Glenn Lakes	3452 Cortex Street	3	2	Elec	1996	Y		
12	05-Jan	170,000	Glenn Lakes	1025 Wellington Circle	3	2	Elec	1998	Y		
16	06-Mar	123,400	Glenn Lakes	3492 54th Avenue W.	2	2	Elec	1996	Y		
20	15-Jan	155,900	West Glenn	6571 Keystone Avenue	3	2	Elec	1996	Y		
21	03-Mar	167,200	Glenn Lakes	5778 Wellington Drive	3	2	Elec	1997	Y		
22	03-Jan	180,500	Glenn Lakes	6873 Wellington Drive	4	2	Elec	1997	Y		
27	03-Mar	169,700	Glenn Lakes	2984 44th Street West	3	2	Elec	1997	Y		
33	12-Feb	121,000	West Glenn	7350 Shadeland Avenue	4	2.5	Elec	1996	N		
36	15-Jan	121,500	Glenn Lakes	5562 Kensington Drive	4	2.5	Elec	1998	N		
37	05-Feb	174,600	Glenn Lakes	4874 Manatee Avenue	3	2	Elec	1995	Y		
39											

If You Have Problems . . .
It is important to verify that your results are correct. Ensure that all displayed records meet your criteria and that records are not missing that you know are stored in the database. If there is a problem, be sure that you selected the OR logical operator. Also, make sure that you selected the equals comparison option for both criteria.

⑩ Choose Data, point to Filter, and click AutoFilter.
All records display and the arrow at the end of each field name disappears, indicating that AutoFilter is no longer active. You can close the Listings workbook without saving your changes now, or leave it open and continue to the next lesson.

 Exam Note: **Using Wildcards in Search Criteria**
You can use two kinds of wildcards in the Custom AutoFilter dialog box: the asterisk character (*) in place of any sequence of characters and the question-mark character (?) in place of any one character (refer to the lower-left corner of the dialog box in Figure 10.16). For example, a filter for the single search condition *Glenn* in the Area field of the Listings database finds records of homes in Glenn Lakes or West Glenn. The first asterisk indicates that any sequence of characters can precede the word Glenn, such as West Glenn. The second asterisk indicates that any sequence of characters can follow the word Glenn, such as Glenn Lakes.

Lesson 6: Using Custom AutoFilter with AND Search Criteria

If you specify two search conditions in a filter and both conditions must be met, you are using **AND search criteria**. When you use Custom AutoFilter to apply AND search criteria to a single field, Excel displays records that fall within a range. For example, to display the records of homes selling only in the $150,000 to $175,000 range, filter for price less than or equal to $175,000 *and* price greater than or equal to $150,000. To display the records of homes listed only in January 2000, filter for listed greater than 12/31/1999 and listed less than 2/1/2000.

In this lesson, you filter by using AND search criteria applied to a single field. Now, set a filter in the Listings database to find homes for sale in the $150,000 to $175,000 range.

To Use Custom AutoFilter with AND Search Criteria

❶ Open the Listings worksheet, if necessary, and click any cell within the list range A3:I38.

❷ Choose Data, point to Filter, and click AutoFilter.

continues ▶

To Use Custom AutoFilter with AND Search Criteria (continued)

3 Click the filter arrow for the Price field, and then select (Custom) from the drop-down list.

4 Specify the five settings shown in Figure 10.18. (Select the two comparison options from drop-down lists, click **A**nd, and type the numbers 150000 and 175000.)

Figure 10.18
Specifications are complete for limiting the display of records to those that meet two conditions that apply to the same field.

Click here to specify that both conditions must be met

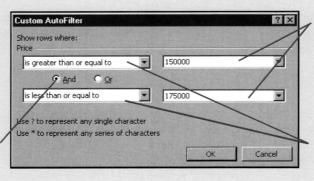

Type values that do not appear in drop-down lists

Comparison options selected from drop-down lists

5 Click OK to close the Custom AutoFill dialog box and execute the filter.

The current filter limits the display to the eight homes priced between $150,000 and $175,000 (see Figure 10.19).

Figure 10.19
Eight properties are listed at prices between $150,000 and $175,000.

If You Have Problems...
It is important to verify that your results are correct. Check that all displayed records meet your criteria. If there is a problem, be sure you selected the **A**nd button. Also ensure that you selected the appropriate comparison options, and typed the upper and lower values correctly.

6 Choose **D**ata, point to **F**ilter, and click Auto**F**ilter.

All records display, and the arrow at the end of each field name disappears, which indicates that AutoFilter is no longer active. You can close the Listings workbook now, or leave it open and continue to the next lesson.

Lesson 7: Adding and Deleting Records by Using a Form

Keeping data current is an essential part of using any database. To add a record to a list, move to the first blank row below the list and type data in each field. To delete a record, find its row and delete the row.

If you work with a large list, you may prefer to add and delete records by using a form that shows all the fields in one record. Excel's **data form** is a dialog box that displays a list one record at a time.

In this lesson, you use a form to add a new listing. You also use a form to find and delete a record.

To Add and Delete Records by Using a Form

① **Open the Listings workbook, if necessary, and click any cell in the list range A3:I38.**

② **Choose Data, Form.**

A dialog box named Listings opens, and displays each field name to the left of the corresponding data in the first record (see Figure 10.20).

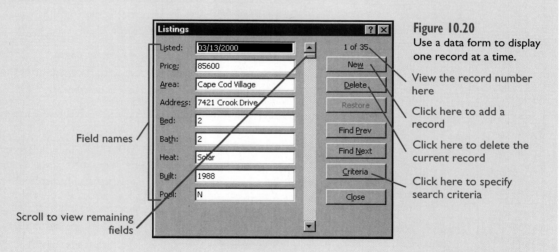

Figure 10.20
Use a data form to display one record at a time.

View the record number here

Click here to add a record

Click here to delete the current record

Click here to specify search criteria

③ **Click the New button in the Listings dialog box.**

④ **Type 1/1/2000 in the Listed field text box, and press Tab.**

Data is entered into the Listed field of the new record. Pressing Tab moves the insertion point to the next field text box. You can press ◆Shift + Tab to move backward to the previous field. You can also move to any field by clicking that field.

❌ **If You Have Problems...**

If you make a mistake while typing, use ◆Backspace or Del to remove unwanted characters and type the correct data. If you press ↵Enter or ↓ instead of Tab to move to the next field, Excel adds the new record to the list and displays a new blank data form. If you did not complete filling out the data form, click the Find Prev button to restore the display of the previous record.

---

continues ▶

To Add and Delete Records by Using a Form   (continued)

⑤ Add remaining data in the new record, as shown in Figure 10.21.

Figure 10.21
You can enter or edit data by using a form.

Indicates that adding a new record is in progress

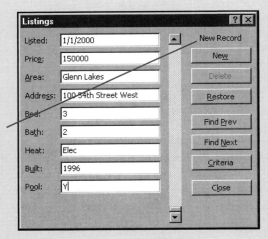

⑥ Click the Close button to add the new record to the list.
Excel adds the new record to the bottom of the list and closes the data form. Now, find and delete the record for a listed property that has been sold.

⑦ Choose Data, Form, and click the Criteria button.
Excel displays a blank data form. The word Criteria appears in the upper-right corner of the dialog box, instead of the record number.

⑧ Click in the Address field, type *Sulky, and click the Find Next button.
The asterisk preceding the word Sulky tells Excel to find records containing Sulky, no matter what characters precede the word. Excel finds the record containing 2398 Sulky Court in the Address field and displays its contents in the Listings data form (see Figure 10.22).

Figure 10.22
Excel displays the next record containing the word Sulky in the Address field.

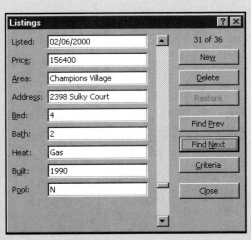

⑨ Click the Delete button.
A dialog box or Help balloon opens with the message Displayed record will be permanently deleted.

⑩ **Click OK, click the Close button, and save your changes to the Listings workbook.**

Excel deletes the record and closes the data form. You can close the Listings workbook now, or leave it open and continue with the final lesson in this project.

Lesson 8: Editing Records by Using a Form

Keeping data current requires more than adding and deleting records. You must be able to revise data in one or more fields of an existing record. If there are many records in a list, you can specify a search condition on a data form to find a record you want to change.

In this lesson, you make two changes to the Listings data: reduce the price for one home and correct the spelling of a street name for another. You use a data form to locate each record.

To Edit Records by Using a Form

❶ **Open the Listings workbook, if necessary, and click any cell in the list range A3:I38.**

❷ **Choose Data, Form, and click the Criteria button.**

❸ **Type 3360 Glade in the Address field, and click the Find Next button.**

Excel displays the record containing 3360 Glade Avenue in the Address field.

❹ **Click in the Price field, change 225000 to 215000, and click the Close button.**

The price of the property at 3360 Glade Avenue has been reduced to 215,000.

❺ **Choose Data, Form, and click the Criteria button.**

❻ **Type 3452 Cortex in the Address field, and click the Find Next button.**

Excel displays the record containing 3452 Cortex Street in the Address field.

❼ **Click in the Address field, and change Cortex to Cortez.**

❽ **Click the Close button.**

The data form closes. The records in rows 7 and 9 reflect the changes you made (see cells D7 and B9 in Figure 10.23).

❾ **Save your changes to the Listings workbook.**

This concludes Project 10. Close the workbook; then either continue with end-of-project activities or exit Excel.

continues ▶

To Edit Records by Using a Form (continued)

Figure 10.23
Changes were made to
two records.

Changed Cortex to Cortez

Changed 225,000 to 215,000

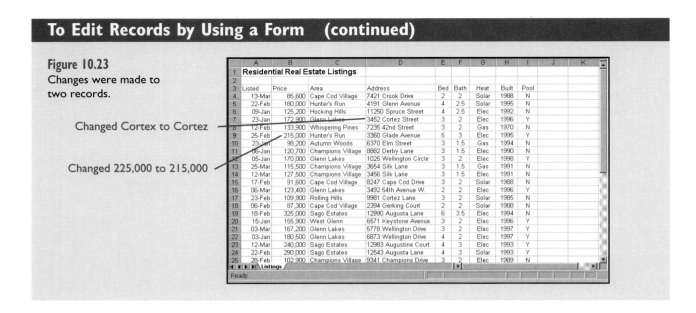

	A	B	C	D	E	F	G	H	I	J	K
1	Residential Real Estate Listings										
2											
3	Listed	Price	Area	Address	Bed	Bath	Heat	Built	Pool		
4	13-Mar	85,600	Cape Cod Village	7421 Crook Drive	2	2	Solar	1988	N		
5	22-Feb	180,000	Hunter's Run	4191 Glenn Avenue	4	2.5	Solar	1995	N		
6	09-Jan	125,200	Hocking Hills	11250 Spruce Street	4	2.5	Elec	1992	N		
7	23-Jan	172,900	Glenn Lakes	3452 Cortez Street	3	2	Elec	1996	Y		
8	12-Feb	133,900	Whispering Pines	7235 42nd Street	3	2	Gas	1970	N		
9	25-Feb	215,000	Hunter's Run	3360 Glade Avenue	5	3	Elec	1995	Y		
10	23-Jan	98,200	Autumn Woods	6370 Elm Street	3	1.5	Gas	1994	N		
11	06-Jan	120,700	Champions Village	8882 Derby Lane	3	1.5	Elec	1990	N		
12	05-Jan	170,000	Glenn Lakes	1025 Wellington Circle	3	2	Elec	1998	Y		
13	25-Mar	115,500	Champions Village	3654 Silk Lane	3	1.5	Gas	1991	N		
14	12-Mar	127,500	Champions Village	3456 Silk Lane	3	1.5	Elec	1991	N		
15	17-Feb	91,600	Cape Cod Village	8247 Cape Cod Drive	3	2	Solar	1988	N		
16	06-Mar	123,400	Glenn Lakes	3492 54th Avenue W.	2	2	Elec	1996	Y		
17	23-Feb	109,900	Rolling Hills	9981 Cortez Lane	3	2	Solar	1985	N		
18	06-Feb	87,300	Cape Cod Village	2394 Gerking Court	2	2	Solar	1988	N		
19	18-Feb	325,000	Sago Estates	12990 Augusta Lane	6	3.5	Elec	1994	N		
20	15-Jan	155,900	West Glenn	6571 Keystone Avenue	3	2	Elec	1996	Y		
21	03-Mar	167,200	Glenn Lakes	5778 Wellington Drive	3	2	Elec	1997	Y		
22	03-Mar	180,500	Glenn Lakes	6873 Wellington Drive	4	2	Elec	1997	Y		
23	12-Mar	240,000	Sago Estates	12983 Augustine Court	4	3	Elec	1993	Y		
24	22-Feb	290,000	Sago Estates	12543 Augusta Lane	4	3	Solar	1993	Y		
25	28-Feb	102,900	Champions Village	9341 Champions Drive	3	2	Elec	1989	N		

Listings

Ready

Summary

You began this project by viewing onscreen Help about using an Excel list as a database. You then learned how to convert data into useful information by sorting and filtering the contents of the sample database of residential real-estate listings. You also practiced basic database maintenance tasks by adding, deleting, and editing records.

You can reinforce your learning if you create your own list and try sorting, filtering, and editing at the simple level demonstrated in the project. You can also use onscreen Help to learn about more advanced sorting and filtering techniques, and apply the more complex techniques to the database of your choice.

Checking Concepts and Terms

True/False

For each of the following, check *T* or *F* to indicate whether the statement is true or false.

__T __F **1.** In a list, data arranged in rows are called fields. [L1]

__T __F **2.** Field names in a list should be unique. [L1]

__T __F **3.** Excel refers to a database as a list. [L1]

__T __F **4.** You can use AutoFilter to arrange data in a particular order by one or more fields. [L4]

__T __F **5.** Excel's data form displays records one at a time. [L7]

Multiple Choice

Circle the letter of the correct answer for each of the following.

1. Each collection of related data in a database is called a [L1]

 a. list

 b. record

 c. field

 d. none of the above

2. Which of the following search conditions would find the name Bellingham? [L5]

 a. Bell*

 b. Bell?

 c. Bell&

 d. none of the above

3. Which of the following would not be a meaningful sort in a student list? [L3]

 a. sort by Student I.D. number, and then by year in school

 b. sort by major, and then by grade point average

 c. sort by last name, and then by first name

 d. all of the above.

4. Which of the following criteria displays records of males old enough to vote (assume that the voting age is 18)? [L5 or L6]

 a. gender equals male and age greater than 18

 b. gender equals male or age greater than 18

 c. gender equals male or age greater than or equal to 18

 d. none of the above

5. Assume that a list contains a field for birth date named Birthday. Data is entered in the form *mm/dd/yyyy*, where *m* = month, *d* = day, and *y* = year. Which of the following criteria limits record display to all individuals born in 1980? [L5 or L6]

 a. birthday is greater than or equal to 1/1/1980 and less than or equal to 1/1/1981

 b. birthday is greater than 12/31/1979 and less than 1/1/1981

 c. birthday is equal to 1980

 d. none of the above

Skill Drill

Skill Drill exercises reinforce project skills. Each skill reinforced is the same, or nearly the same, as a skill presented in the project. Detailed instructions are provided in a step-by-step format.

Each exercise is independent of the others, so you can complete the exercises in any order. Be sure to save the workbook after completing each exercise. If you need a paper copy of the completed exercise, enter your name centered in a header before printing. Other print options have already been set to print compressed to one page and to display the filename, sheet name, and current date in a footer.

Before beginning your first Project 10 Skill Drill exercise, complete the following steps:

1. Open the file named e-1002, and save it as e10drill.
 The workbook contains four sheets: an overview sheet, and exercise sheets named #1-Sort2, #2-FilterAND, and #3-Add.

2. Click the Overview sheet to view the organization of the Project 10 Skill Drill Exercises workbook.

If you need more than one work session to complete the skill drill exercises, continue working on e10drill instead of starting over on the original e-1002 file.

1. Sorting a List by Using Two Fields

You are interested in arranging the data into groups by car size. Within each group, you want to see the data arranged in descending order of the number of days the vehicle was rented.

To sort the data by using two fields of data:

1. If necessary, open the **e10drill** workbook; then click the #1-Sort2 sheet tab.

2. Click any cell in the list range A6:L36.

3. Choose Data, Sort.

4. Display the drop-down list for Sort by and select the Car Size field.

5. Check that Ascending is the selected order for the Car Size field.

6. Display the drop-down list for Then by, and select the Days Rented field.

7. Specify Descending as the sort order.

8. Select OK.

Ensure that records are organized first within groups (Compact, Full Size, and so on), and then within each group by days rented (highest to lowest).

2. Filtering with AND Search Criteria

As you look at your list, you decide to focus on all records of cars rented for periods of between six and ten days, inclusive (that is, including 6 and 10).

To filter for records within a range—days rented more than five and fewer than 11:

1. If necessary, open the **e10drill** workbook; then click the #2-FilterAND sheet tab, and click within any cell in the list.

2. Choose Data, Filter, AutoFilter.

3. Click the filter arrow next to the field name Days Rented.

4. From the drop-down list, select (Custom).

5. Click the drop-down arrow next to the upper-left text box and select **is greater than**.

6. Click the upper-right text box, and type 5.

7. Click the And option (as opposed to Or) in the Custom AutoFilter dialog box.

8. Click the drop-down arrow next to the lower-left text box, and select **is less than**.

9. Click the lower-right text box, and type **11**.

10. Select OK.

Be sure that the display of records is limited to those showing days rented between 6 and 10.

3. Adding a Record by Using a Data Form

You have found a survey document that has not been entered in the list. To add the record:

1. If necessary, open the **e10drill** workbook; then click the #3-Add sheet tab, and click any cell within the list.

2. Choose Data, Form.

3. Click the New button.

4. Type **31** in the ID field text box.

5. Enter the remaining data as follows (remember to press Tab↹ to move from field to field):

Type Use: **Bus**
Type Pmt: **cc**
Car Size: **Mid Size**
Date Rented: **02/01/2000**
Date Returned: **02/15/2000**
Daily Rate: **11.50**
Customer Rating: **5**
Favorite Sport: **tennis**
Favorite Magazine: **WSJ**

6. Select Close to add the record.

Challenge

Challenge exercises expand on or are somewhat related to skills presented in the lessons. Each exercise provides a brief narrative introduction, followed by instructions in a numbered-step format that are not as detailed as those in the Skill Drill section.

Each exercise is independent of the others, so you can complete the exercises in any order. Be sure to save the workbook after completing each exercise. If you need a paper copy of the completed exercise, enter your name centered in a header before printing. Other print options have already been set to print compressed to one page and to display the filename, sheet name, and current date in a footer.

Before beginning your first Project 10 Challenge exercise, complete the following steps:

1. Open the file named **e-1003**, and save it as **e10challenge**.
   The workbook contains four sheets: an overview sheet, and exercises named #1-Sort3, #2-FilterHigh5, and #3-FilterTop10.

2. Click the Overview sheet to view the organization of the Project 10 Challenge Exercises workbook.

If you need more than one work session to complete the desired exercises, continue working on **e10challenge** instead of starting over on the original e-1003 file.

1. Executing a Sort on Three Fields

You have identified three fields on which you'd like to sort. First, you want to display records in two groups by Type Use: first business, and then personal. Within each type, you next want to sort records by car size (ascending order). Finally, within car size, you want to organize records by customer rating in descending order.

To sort your list:

1. If necessary, open the **e10challenge** workbook; then click the #1-Sort3 sheet tab.

2. Display the Sort dialog box.

3. For each text box—Sort by, Then by, and Then by—select the appropriate fields and sort orders.

4. Execute the sort and verify that records appear in the desired order.

2. Filtering for the Highest Five Items

You noticed a Top 10 option using AutoFilter, but you want to find the five highest values in the Rental Cost field. You can modify any of three initial settings in the Top 10 AutoFilter dialog box. Instead of Top, you can specify Bottom. Instead of 10, you can specify the number of your choice. You can also select Percent instead of Items.

To filter your list by using the Top 10 AutoFilter option:

1. If necessary, open the **e10challenge** workbook; then click the #2-FilterHigh5 sheet tab.

2. Turn on AutoFilter.

3. Select the (Top 10) option from the drop-down list for the Rental Cost field.

4. Change the number of items from 10 to **5**, and click OK to activate the filter.

5. Verify that the display is limited to records with the top five values in the Rental Cost field.
    In this case, six records display because two records have the same $182 value.

3. Filtering for the Top 10 Percent

You know that you can use AutoFilter's Top 10 option to display a user-specified number of top or bottom items, but now you want to limit the display to the top 10 percent, based on values in the Rental Cost field.

To set the desired filter:

1. If necessary, open the `e10challenge` workbook; then click the #3-FilterTop10 sheet tab.

2. Turn on AutoFilter.

3. Select the (Top 10) option from the drop-down list for the Rental Cost field.

4. Change settings in the Top 10 AutoFilter dialog box, as necessary, to filter for the top 10 percent.

5. Click OK to activate the filter and verify that only 10 percent (three of 30) of the records display.
    Verify that the records displayed are those with the highest values in the Rental Cost field.

Discovery Zone

Discovery Zone exercises require advanced knowledge of topics presented in *MOUS Essentials* lessons, application of skills from multiple lessons, or self-directed learning of new skills.

Before beginning your first Project 10 Discovery Zone exercise, complete the following steps:

1. Open the file named e-1004, and save it as `e10discovery`.
    The workbook contains three sheets: an overview sheet, and exercise sheets named #1-Wildcard and #2-Filter3on1.

2. Click the Overview sheet to view the organization of the Project 10 Discovery Zone Exercises workbook.

Each exercise is independent of the others, so you can complete the exercises in any order. Be sure to save the workbook after completing each exercise. If you need a paper copy of the completed exercise, enter your name centered in a header before printing. Other print options have already been set to print landscape compressed to one page and to display the filename, sheet name, and current date in a footer.

If you need more than one work session to complete the desired exercises, continue working on `e10discovery` instead of starting over on the original e-1004 file.

1. Using Wildcards to Find Data

From past experience, you know that a variety of software programs support using wildcard characters to locate data or filenames. Open your **e10discovery** workbook, and select the #1-Wildcard sheet. Find information about the word wildcard by using Help's Index feature. Apply what you learned by setting a filter to display only those records containing the letters **news** in the Favorite Magazine field. Inspect the results to see that they meet the criteria you specified. Decide how you might use a wildcard to filter records in at least two other fields. Execute those filters and verify the results.

2. Filtering on Three Criteria (One Field)

You want to display only those records in which car type is Mid Size, Full Size, or Luxury, but you realize that there is a two-condition limit when using AutoFilter's Custom option. You noticed that an <u>A</u>dvanced Filter option appears when you choose <u>D</u>ata, <u>F</u>ilter. Access the Contents tab in onscreen Help and display the subtopic named `Examples of advanced filter criteria`. Focus on the `Multiple conditions in a single column` documentation. (*Hint:* To display the named subtopic, first select Managing Lists, and then select Finding Rows That Meet Specific Conditions.)

You find that specifying three or more search conditions on a single field requires the use of a separate Criteria range. You can apply what you learned through Help in the #2-Filter3on1 worksheet. The worksheet has already been modified to include the field names for a Criteria range in row 6. All fields are included, but you will enter criteria below only the Car Size field. Set up and execute the desired filter and check the results to see that they meet the criteria you specified. Execute another three-condition, one-field filter of your choice (be sure to delete the previous search conditions in the Criteria range), and verify the results.

PinPoint Assessment

You have completed this project and its associated lessons, and have had an opportunity to assess your skills through the end-of-project questions and exercises. Now use the PinPoint software Evaluation Mode to further assess your comprehension of the specific exam activities you have just learned. You can also use the PinPoint Trainer Mode and the Show Me tutorials to practice these exam activities.

Project 11

Documenting and Protecting Worksheets and Workbooks

Key terms introduced in this project include

- comment
- comment indicator
- file property

- password
- range name
- read-only

- unlock
- write access

Objectives	Required Activity for MOUS	Exam Level
➤ Create and Use Range Names	Add and delete a named range; Use a named range in a formula	Expert
➤ Attach Comments to a Cell	Create, edit and remove a comment	Expert
➤ Get Help on Security Features in Excel	Use the Office Assistant	Core
➤ Protect Worksheet Contents and Objects	Add and remove worksheet and workbook protection	Expert
➤ Unlock Cells	Add and remove worksheet and workbook protection	Expert
➤ Unlock Objects	Add and remove worksheet and workbook protection	Expert
➤ View and Set File Properties	Change workbook properties	Expert
➤ Require a Password	Apply and remove file passwords	Expert

Why Would I Do This?

Excel provides a variety of features that you can use to document and protect your work. For example, you can assign a name to a cell or range of cells, and then use that name instead of a cell reference in a formula. User-specified comments can be added to any cell. You can unlock only the cells for which content might change and prevent editing or deleting the contents of any other cells.

In this project, you first work with creating and using English-like names for one or more cells. You continue documenting a worksheet by attaching comments to cells. In the next four lessons you learn to apply cell protection appropriately. Remaining topics include specifying workbook properties and setting a password.

 ## Lesson 1: Creating and Using Range Names

A **range name** is an English-like name applied to a cell or range of cells. The most common use for a range name is to make a formula easier to read and understand. You can also move the cell pointer to another section of a large worksheet by specifying the name assigned to that section instead of a cell reference.

A name must start with a letter or an underscore. The rest of the name can include numbers and letters up to a maximum of 255 characters. Spaces are not allowed, but you can use underscore characters and periods to separate words.

In this lesson, you specify two range names: one to use in a formula and the other to identify a section of the worksheet. You then include one defined name in a formula and use the other to go to the named location in the worksheet.

To Create and Use Range Names

1 **Open the e-1101 file and save it as Protection.**
The file contains a single worksheet named Copy Bids.

2 **Select (click) cell B4, and click the Name box at the left end of the formula bar.**

3 **Type Est_Num_Copies in the Name box, and press ↵Enter.**
This assigns the name Est_Num_Copies to cell B4 (see Figure 11.1).

Figure 11.1
You can enter the range name Est_Num_Copies in a formula instead of a reference to cell B4.

Name box

Newly defined range name

Click here to display a drop-down list of range names

Location defined in the range name

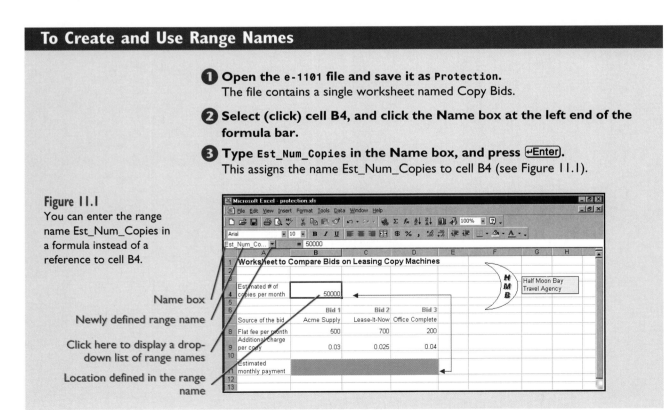

4 **Select the range F20:F34, and click the Name box at the left end of the formula bar.**

5 **Type** ContactVendor **in the Name box, and press** ⏎Enter**.**
The name ContactVendor is assigned to the range F20:F34.

6 **Click cell B11.**

7 **Type** =B8+(B9* **in the cell.**
Do *not* press ⏎Enter yet. This nearly completes a formula to add the flat fee for Bid 1 (cell B8) to the variable cost for Bid 1 (cell B9 times cell B4).

8 **Click cell B4.**
Est_Num_Copies displays in the formula bar in place of cell B4 (see Figure 11.2).

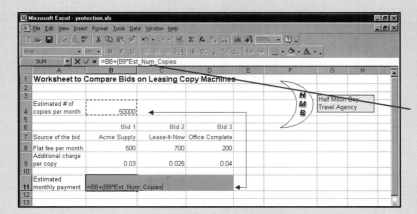

Figure 11.2
Clicking a named cell displays its name instead of its cell reference in the formula bar.

The name assigned to cell B4

9 **Type a right parenthesis to complete the formula, and click the green check mark in the formula bar.**
The formula =B8+(B9*Est_Num_Copies) displays in the formula bar. The $2,000 formula result displays in cell B11.

10 **Copy the formula in cell B11 to the range C11:D11.**
The monthly payments for Bid 2 and Bid 3 are $1,950 and $2,200, respectively. The formula copies correctly because a name uses absolute cell references.

11 **Choose Edit, Go To (or press F5).**
The Go To dialog box opens (see Figure 11.3).

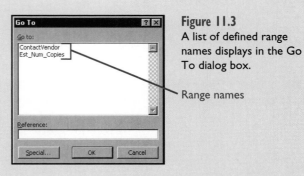

Figure 11.3
A list of defined range names displays in the Go To dialog box.

Range names

12 **Select ContactVendor, and click the OK button.**
Worksheet display shifts to the range containing vendor contact information.

continues ▶

To Create and Use Range Names   (continued)

⓭ Click any cell to deselect the highlighted range F20:F34.

⓮ Save your changes to the Copy Bids worksheet.

Keep the workbook open for the next lesson, or close the workbook and exit Excel.

 Exam Note:*   Deleting a Range Name

You can delete a range name using a three-step process. First select the command sequence Insert, Name, Define. Select the name to delete from the list that appears in the Define Name dialog box, and click the Delete button.

 Inside Stuff:*   Documenting Range Names

If you want to find out what a name refers to without moving the cell pointer to the defined location, select the command sequence Insert, Name, Define, and select the name. Its associated range displays in a Refers to text box in the Define Name dialog box.

You can also create a two-column list of range names and associated ranges in the worksheet. First select a cell in a blank area large enough to hold the list. Then select the command sequence Insert, Name, Paste. Complete the process by selecting the Paste List button in the Paste Name dialog box.

 # Lesson 2: Attaching Comments to a Cell

You can easily attach a comment to any cell in an Excel worksheet. A ***comment*** is an annotation attached to a cell that displays within a box whenever the mouse pointer rests on the cell. If a comment has been attached, you see the ***comment indicator***—a small red triangle—in the cell's upper-right corner. Use the comment feature when you want supplementary information available, but not visible all the time.

You can alter the size of the comment box by dragging the handles on its sides and corners. You can also move a comment, change its text font or color, and hide or display comments and their indicators. The Page Setup dialog box includes options to print comments below the worksheet or where they are displayed on the worksheet.

In this lesson, you set a View option to display only comment indicators. You then create and view three comments, one for each vendor providing a bid for leasing copy machines.

To Attach Comments to a Cell

❶ Open the `Protection` file, if necessary, and select Tools, Options.

The Options dialog box opens.

❷ Select the View tab.

The View tab includes four sections: Show, Comments, Objects, and Window options.

❸ Check that `Comment indicator only` is selected in the Comments section, and click OK.

4 **Click cell B7.**

The cell containing Acme Supply, the provider of the first bid, is selected.

5 **Select Insert, Comment.**

Excel displays a comment box. An arrow extends from the upper-left corner of the box to the comment indicator in cell B7.

6 **Delete existing text in the box, if any, and type the following comment:**

Bid valid for 60 days. Guaranteed service within 24 hours.

7 **Click outside the box to deselect it.**

8 **Position the mouse pointer on cell B7.**

The newly created comment displays (see Figure 11.4).

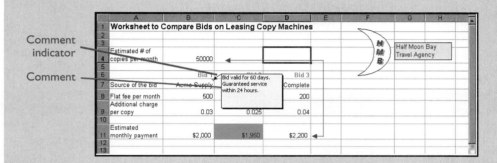

Comment
indicator

Comment

Figure 11.4

If a comment indicator displays in the upper-right corner of a cell, you can see the attached comment by positioning the mouse pointer on the cell.

9 **Click cell C7, and repeat the previous steps to create the following comment:**

Started business 6 months ago. Bid valid for 30 days. Same-day service if call before noon.

10 **Click cell D7, and repeat the previous steps to create the following comment (also drag a sizing handle to enlarge the box as necessary):**

Bid valid for 30 days. Promises service within 4 hours but has not been reliable in the past.

11 **Select View, Comments.**

The three comments and the Reviewing toolbar display. You can click Next Comment or Previous Comment on the Reviewing toolbar to scroll through the comments.

12 **Select View, Comments again to remove the display of the comments.**

13 **Close the Reviewing toolbar, and save your changes to the Copy Bids worksheet.**

Keep the Protection workbook open for the next lesson, or close the workbook and exit Excel.

Exam Note: Editing and Deleting Comments

Right-clicking a cell with an attached comment displays a shortcut menu. Select Edit Comment to revise text. Select Delete Comment to remove it.

If you want to remove all comments, select Go To on the Edit menu, click the Special button, click Comments, and click OK. This highlights all cells with attached comments. Then select Edit, Clear, Comments.

ⓘ **Inside Stuff: Printing Comments**

You can print comments by selecting File, Page Setup, and accessing the Sheet tab. Select the Comments drop-down list, and select At end of sheet or As displayed on sheet.

 # Lesson 3: Getting Help on Security Features in Excel

Excel provides a wide variety of features to control accessing or editing worksheets and workbooks. Use onscreen Help to get an overview of the security features.

To Get Help on Security Features

❶ Open the Protection workbook, if necessary, and display the Office Assistant.

❷ Click the Office Assistant to display a balloon, type security, and click the Search button.
Help topics associated with the word security display in the Office Assistant balloon (see Figure 11.5).

Figure 11.5
Selecting the fourth option provides access to information about a wide variety of protection features.

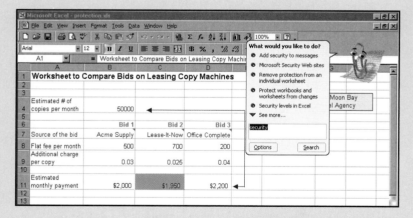

❸ Select Protect workbooks and worksheets from changes.
The Help window includes information in four sections: Limit access, Recommend read-only, Require passwords, and Security.

❹ In the Limit access section, select Limit viewing and editing of an individual worksheet.

❺ Display and read assorted topics related to protecting a worksheet, and press the Back button to reach the Limit access topics.

6 **In the Limit access section, select `Limit changes to an entire work-book`.**

7 **Display and read assorted topics related to protecting a workbook.**

8 **Continue to browse other protection topics of your choice, and then close the Help window.**

Keep the `Protection` workbook open for the next lesson, or close the workbook and exit Excel.

Lesson 4: Protecting Worksheet Contents and Objects

If you protect the contents of a worksheet, you cannot make changes to cells unless you unlock the cells before activating protection. Excel also prevents viewing hidden rows or columns and making changes to items on chart sheets. If you protect objects on a worksheet, you cannot add or edit comments, move or size the objects, or make any changes in formatting.

Protection is an option on the Tools menu. In this lesson, you protect an entire worksheet, and then attempt to modify the worksheet—changing cell contents, moving an object, applying a different color, and selecting another font style—all without success. You then remove the worksheet protection. In the next two lessons, you learn how to unlock selected cells and objects and protect the remaining elements.

To Protect Worksheet Contents and Objects

1 **Open the `Protection` file, if necessary.**
The Copy Bids worksheet includes two range names and comments in cells B7:D7.

2 **Select Tools, Protection, and Protect Sheet.**
The Protect Sheet dialog box displays (see Figure 11.6).

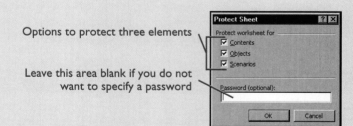

Options to protect three elements

Leave this area blank if you do not want to specify a password

Figure 11.6
Clicking a check mark removes it and turns the feature off. Clicking a blank check box turns the feature on.

3 **Click OK.**
This bypasses entering a password and closes the dialog box. All worksheet elements are protected. Now try to change the contents of cell B4.

4 **Click cell B4 and type 4.**
A message states that the cell is protected. Now try moving the grouped object showing the company's name.

continues ▶

To Protect Worksheet Contents and Objects   (continued)

5 **Click OK to close the message, and click within the half moon shape or within the yellow box displaying the company name.**
Sizing handles do not appear. You cannot select the grouped object because it is protected.

6 **Select the range B6:D6, and display the Font Color drop-down list in the toolbar.**
A grid of sample squares displays without any colors, indicating that you cannot apply a color change.

7 **Display the font style drop-down list, and select Times New Roman.**
You are able to make the selection, but the new font style is not applied because the selected cells are protected.

8 **Select Tools, Protection, and Unprotect Sheet.**
Cell protection is disabled.

9 **Click any cell to deselect the highlighted range B6:D6, and save your changes to the Copy Bids worksheet.**
Keep the `Protection` workbook open for the next lesson, or close the workbook and exit Excel.

 ## Lesson 5: Unlocking Cells

In the previous lesson, you protected every worksheet element. In some situations, however, you may need to modify or delete cell contents. If so, unlock cells for which content might change. As a general rule, all formulas and most labels should remain locked. Cells containing numbers are generally unlocked.

When you **unlock** a cell, you remove the default locked setting that prevents changes when worksheet protection is active. Unlocking a cell requires a four-step process—selecting the element, displaying the Format Cells dialog box, selecting the Protection tab, and clicking the Locked option off.

In this lesson, you unlock several cells prior to activating worksheet protection. You unlock the cell for entering the number of copies and the range of cells related to raw data for three bids—vendor names, flat fees, and charges per copy.

To Unlock Cells

1 **Open the `Protection` file, if necessary, and click cell B4.**

2 **Select Format, Cells, and select the Protection tab (see Figure 11.7).**

3 **Click the box in front of Locked to remove the check mark.**
Cell B4 is unlocked. Now activate worksheet protection and try to change cell B4.

4 **Click OK, and select Tools, Protection, Protect Sheet.**
The Protect Sheet dialog box opens. By default, Excel protects contents, objects, and scenarios, but you can turn off any or all settings.

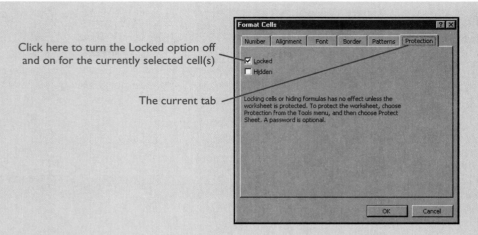

Click here to turn the Locked option off and on for the currently selected cell(s)

The current tab

Figure 11.7
Use the Format Cells dialog box to unlock cells.

5 **Leave the Password text box blank, and click OK.**
This closes the Protect Sheet dialog box. No change is visible, but worksheet protection is now active for all locked cells.

6 **Enter 40000 in cell B4.**
Excel accepts the change because you unlocked cell B4 before enabling worksheet protection. The revised values for estimated monthly payments display in row 11—$1,700 for bids 1 and 2; $1,800 for bid 3.

7 **Click cell B8, and attempt to enter 600.**
Excel displays a message that the cell is protected.

8 **Click OK to close the message, and select Tools, Protection, Unprotect Sheet.**

9 **Select the range B7:D9, and select Format, Cells.**

10 **Check that the Protection tab is active, and click the box in front of Locked to remove the check mark.**
The cells containing vendor names and the two-part vendor bids—flat fee and additional charge per copy—are unlocked.

11 **Click OK, and apply a pale blue fill to cell B4 and to the range B7:D9.**
Shading unprotected cells before protecting a worksheet provides a visual means to identify cells that users can change. Pressing Tab⇆ moves the cell pointer from one unprotected cell to the next in a protected worksheet.

12 **Select Tools, Protection, Protect Sheet, and click OK.**
You can make changes to only cell B4 and cells within the range B7:D9.

13 **Save your changes to the Copy Bids worksheet.**
Keep the Protection workbook open for the next lesson, or close the workbook and exit Excel.

Lesson 6: Unlocking Objects

In the previous lesson, you unlocked selected cells that were subject to change. In some situations, you might need to work with an object after a worksheet is protected. If so, un- lock any object that you might modify, move, or delete. Unlocking an object requires a four-step process—selecting the object, displaying the Format Object dialog box, selecting the Protection tab, and clicking the Locked option off.

In this lesson, you unlock the Half Moon Bay grouped object. After you activate workbook protection, you move the unprotected object.

To Unlock Objects

1 **Open the Protection workbook, if necessary.**

2 **Click within the half-moon shape and try to move it.**
You cannot select the object because its protection status is locked and the worksheet is protected.

3 **Select Tools, Protection, Unprotect Sheet.**

4 **Right-click within the half-moon shape.**
A shortcut menu displays with object-related options.

5 **Select Format Object, and select the Protection tab (see Figure 11.8).**

Figure 11.8
Use the Format Object dialog box to unlock objects.

The current tab

Click here to turn the Locked option off and on for the currently selected object

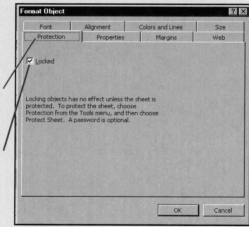

6 **Click the Locked check box to remove the check mark, and click OK.**
The grouped object, showing the company name and logo, is unlocked.

7 **Click outside the object to deselect it, and select Tools, Protection, Protect Sheet.**

8 **Click OK to accept current settings and bypass specifying a pass- word.**
Worksheet protection of all locked cells and objects is activated.

9 **Click within the half-moon shape, and try to move or size it.**
You can now move or size the object even though the worksheet is protect- ed, because the object's protection status is unlocked.

10 **Save your changes to the Copy Bids worksheet.**
Keep the `Protection` workbook open for the next lesson, or close the workbook and exit Excel.

 Exam Note: **Protecting a Workbook**
Excel enables you to protect workbooks as well as worksheets within workbooks. After selecting the two-command sequence <u>T</u>ools, <u>P</u>rotection, you select Protect <u>W</u>orkbook instead of <u>P</u>rotect Sheet.

Protection at this level applies to structure and windows. If you protect structure, users cannot view hidden worksheets. They also cannot insert, delete, move, hide, or rename worksheets. If you protect windows, users cannot move, resize, or close windows.

Lesson 7: Viewing and Setting File Properties

The term ***file property*** describes a characteristic of a file, such as file type, file size, storage location, author's name, and date last revised. You can view the properties of the active workbook by selecting <u>F</u>ile, Proper<u>t</u>ies and choosing one of five tabs in the Properties dialog box: General, Summary, Statistics, Contents, and Custom. You can also view the properties of any Microsoft Excel or Office file through the Open dialog box.

In this lesson, you display the Properties dialog box, view assorted information, and specify your name as the author of the current workbook.

To View and Set File Properties

1 **Open the `Protection` file, if necessary, and select <u>F</u>ile, Proper<u>t</u>ies.**
The Protection.xls Properties dialog box opens.

2 **Select the General tab.**
Excel displays information about the current workbook's name, type, location, and size. You also see the equivalent MS-DOS name (restricted to eight characters) and the dates created, modified, and accessed.

3 **Select the Summary tab, and delete any existing text (see Figure 11.9).**

4 **Click within the Author text box, and type your name.**

5 **Click the Statistics tab.**
Excel displays information about key dates and editing time.

6 **Click the Contents tab.**
Excel lists the sheets in the workbook.

7 **Click the OK button.**
The Properties dialog box closes.

8 **Save your changes to the Copy Bids worksheet.**
Close the Protection workbook, and either continue with the last lesson in this project or exit Excel.

continues ▶

To View and Set File Properties (continued)

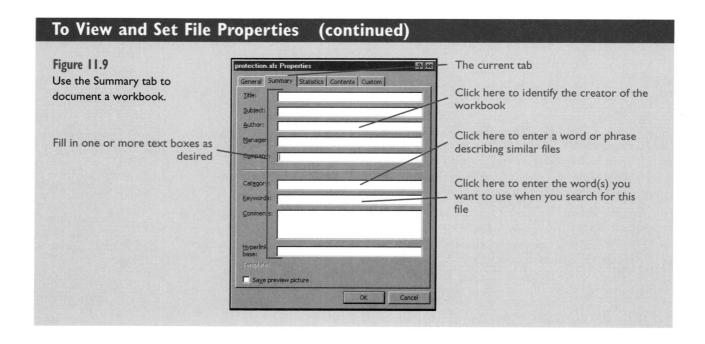

Figure 11.9
Use the Summary tab to document a workbook.

Fill in one or more text boxes as desired

The current tab

Click here to identify the creator of the workbook

Click here to enter a word or phrase describing similar files

Click here to enter the word(s) you want to use when you search for this file

---

 ***Exam Note:* Viewing the Properties of Any Workbook**
In this lesson, you viewed the properties of the active workbook. You can also view the properties of any workbook from the Open dialog box. Select Open from the File menu, display the folder containing the file you want to review, and click the filename to select it (but do not click the Open button yet). Next, click the Tools button in the Open dialog box menu bar and select Properties.

 ## Lesson 8: Requiring a Password

A **password** is a collection of up to 255 case-sensitive characters that must be known to use a password-protected worksheet or workbook. It can contain any combination of letters, numbers, spaces, and symbols.

Excel supports password protection of a workbook at two levels: opening a workbook, and editing a workbook (see Figure 11.10). Each is independent of the other; you can set either one or both. Password protection is set up during execution of a Save As command.

Figure 11.10
You can set only a password to open, only a password to modify, or both password options.

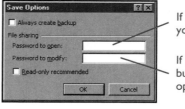

If you forget this password, you cannot open the file

If you know the Open password but forget this one, you can still open the file as read-only

If a password is required to open a workbook, and you don't know the password, you cannot access the file. If you can access a password-protected workbook but a password is required to modify it, you can at least open the file as read-only if you don't know the modify password. A **read-only** file can be viewed but not changed if you save it under the same name. You can, however, modify it if you save it under a different name or save it to a different location.

In this lesson, you set up one password to open a workbook and another to modify that workbook. Because you are just learning this feature, you use a different file from the one you developed in Lessons 1 through 7. That way, if you inadvertently set up a password to open a file that doesn't match the one in the instructions, and you can't remember what you typed, you can start the lesson over at Step 1.

To Require a Password

1 Open the e-1102 file and, save it as Password.
The file reflects the results of Lessons 1 through 7 in this project. Now set passwords for the workbook at two levels.

2 Choose File, Save As, and click the small arrow to the right of Tools near the upper-right corner of the dialog box.
The Tools drop-down list displays.

3 Select General Options.
The Save Options dialog box opens (refer to Figure 11.10).

4 Type abc123 in the Password to open text box.
Be sure to type in the first text box and type the letters in the password in lowercase.

5 Type xyz999 in the Password to modify text box.
Be sure to type in the second text box and type the letters in the password in lowercase.

6 Click OK.
The Confirm Password dialog box opens, with a message to reenter the password to proceed (which is the same as the password to open).

7 Type abc123 in the text box, and click OK.
The Confirm Password dialog box displays again, with a message to reenter the password to modify.

8 Type xyz999 in the text box, and click OK.

9 Complete the steps to save the file and close the workbook.
The workbook is saved with password protection at two levels. Now verify that the passwords work as intended.

10 Open the Password workbook.
The Password dialog box opens with a message that the file is protected.

11 Type abc123, and click OK.
The Password dialog box displays again with a message to enter the password for write access or open as read-only. *Write access* means you can modify a file.

X *If You Have Problems...*
If you do not enter the correct password, which should be abc123, Excel displays a message that the password supplied is not correct. Repeat the process to open the Password file and supply the correct password. (Be sure to use the same capitalization as when you set up the password.) If you still have problems, start the lesson over.

---

continues ▶

To Require a Password   (continued)

 Type xyz999 as the password for write access, and click OK.

X   ***If You Have Problems...***

If you enter text other than xyz999, Excel displays a message that the password supplied is not correct. If ever you cannot remember the modify password, you can open the file as Read-Only and make changes as long as you save the file under another name.

The Copy Bids worksheet in the Password file displays on the screen.

 Close the Password workbook.

This concludes Project 11. You can continue with end-of-project exercises or exit Excel.

    Exam Note: **Changing or Removing a Password**

To change or remove a password, start the process to set up a password—that is, select Save <u>A</u>s from the <u>F</u>ile menu, display the Too<u>l</u>s drop-down list, and select <u>G</u>eneral Options. This displays current passwords in the Save Options dialog box. To change a password, select (highlight) the existing password and type a new one. To remove a password, select the existing password and press Del.

Summary

In this project, you worked with a variety of ways to document and protect worksheets and workbooks. To document your work, you assigned word names to one or more cells, attached comments to cells, and entered summary information as part of the file's properties. You used two approaches to protect your work—one at the cell level and the other at the workbook level. At the cell level, you unlocked cells you wanted to be able to change and enabled protection for all other cells in the worksheet. At the file level, you set up different passwords to open and to modify the workbook.

To expand your learning, try variations of the documentation and protection techniques. Set up an entire formula using range names instead of cell references. Experiment with screen display of comments depending on which of three options you pick in the Comments section of the Options dialog box (<u>T</u>ools, <u>O</u>ptions, View tab). Include in a file's properties one or two key words to describe the workbook, and learn how to search for the file based on key words. Change or modify an existing password. Don't forget to use the extensive onscreen Help feature to support your efforts.

Checking Concepts and Terms ✔

True/False

For each of the following, circle *T* or *F* to indicate whether the statement is true or false.

__T __F   **1.** The most common use for a range name is to make a formula easier to read and understand. [L1]

__T __F   **2.** Before you can set a password to modify a workbook, you must set a password to open it. [L8]

__T __F   **3.** Passwords and range names can contain up to 255 characters. [L1, L8]

__T __F   **4.** If you want to move or size an object on a protected worksheet, the object must be unlocked. [L6]

__T __F   **5.** You can only view the file properties of a workbook if the file is open. [L7]

Multiple Choice

Circle the letter of the correct answer for each of the following.

1. A range name [L1]
   a. displays when you position the mouse pointer on a cell
   b. must start with a letter or underscore
   c. cannot include numbers
   d. none of the above

2. Which of the following is not a valid statement relating to comments? [L2]
   a. Right-clicking a cell with an attached comment displays a shortcut menu through which you can edit or delete the comment.
   b. A small red triangle in a cell's upper-right corner indicates that a comment is attached to the cell.
   c. You can alter the size of a comment box.
   d. You can view comments attached to cells, but you cannot print them.

3. To permit changing the contents of some cells but prevent changing the contents of other cells, [L5]
   a. enable worksheet protection, and unlock the cells subject to change
   b. set a worksheet password
   c. unlock the cells subject to change, and enable worksheet protection
   d. either a or b

4. A password protecting an Excel workbook [L8]
   a. is case-sensitive
   b. can contain any combination of letters, numbers, spaces and symbols
   c. both a and b
   d. neither a or b

5. Which of the following describes a file that can be viewed but not changed if you save it under the same name? [L8]
   a. read-only
   b. write access
   c. locked
   d. none of the above

Skill Drill

Skill Drill exercises reinforce project skills. Each skill reinforced is the same, or nearly the same, as a skill presented in the project. Each exercise includes a brief narrative introduction, followed by detailed instructions in a step-by-step format.

Be sure to save the workbook after completing each exercise. If you need a paper copy of the completed exercise, enter your name centered in a header before printing. Other print options have already been set to print compressed and to display the filename, sheet name, and current date in a footer.

Before beginning your first Project 11 Skill Drill exercise, complete the following steps:

1. Open the file named **e-1103**, and save it as **e11drill**.
   The workbook contains an overview sheet and three exercise sheets labeled #1-Name, #2-Protect, and #3-Comment.

2. Click the Overview sheet to view the organization and content of the Project 11 Skill Drill Exercises workbook.

If you need more than one work session to complete the desired exercises, continue working on **e11drill** instead of starting over on the original e-1103 file.

1. Creating a Range Name and Using It in a Formula

One formula must still be entered in a worksheet that budgets quarterly revenue for the year 2001. The formula calculates the average quarterly revenue expected in a best-case scenario. You decide to assign a name to the range of cells to average, and then use the range name in the formula.

To create a range name and use it in a formula:

1. If necessary, open the **e11drill** workbook.

2. Select the #1-Name worksheet.

3. Select the range B14:E14, and click the Name box at the left end of the formula bar.

4. Type **QtrRev**, and press ↵Enter.
   The name QtrRev is applied to the range B14:E14, the range of cells you now want to average.

5. Enter **=average(QtrRev)** in cell A16.
   The amount 487275 displays in cell A16.

6. Format cell A16 to Comma, zero decimal places.

2. Protecting Formulas and Labels

You have completed a worksheet that budgets quarterly revenue for the year 2001. Now you want to apply worksheet protection appropriately. You decide that you want to be able to change only the numbers used as revenue projections.

To unlock the cells subject to change and protect the rest of the worksheet:

1. If necessary, open the **e11drill** workbook.

2. Select the #2-Protect worksheet.

3. Select the range B10:E12, and choose Format, Cells.

4. Select the Protection tab in the Format Cells dialog box.

5. Click the Locked check box to remove the check mark.

6. Click OK, and apply a light yellow fill to the range B10:E12.
   Applying a fill color is not required, but it does help to show a user which cells are unlocked.

7. Select Tools, Protection, Protect Sheet, and click OK.

8. Check that you can change any estimated quarterly revenue in the range B10:E12.

9. Check that you cannot select the AutoShape, change a label or change a formula.

3. Adding, Editing, and Deleting a Comment

You decide to modify documentation for a budget worksheet by adding, editing, and deleting comments.

To add, edit, and delete a comment:

1. If necessary, open the **e11drill** workbook.

2. Select the #3-Comment worksheet, and click cell B10.

3. Select Insert, Comment.

4. Delete any existing text in the comment box, type **Net of seasonal discounts**, and click outside the comment box.

5. Right-click cell E12, and select Edit Comment from the shortcut menu.

6. Change Christmas Sales to **Holiday Sales** in the comment box, and click outside the box.

7. Right-click cell A16, and select Delete Comment from the shortcut menu.

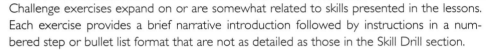

Challenge

Challenge exercises expand on or are somewhat related to skills presented in the lessons. Each exercise provides a brief narrative introduction followed by instructions in a numbered step or bullet list format that are not as detailed as those in the Skill Drill section.

Each exercise is independent of the others, so you can complete the exercises in any order. Be sure to save the workbook after completing each exercise. If you need a paper copy of the completed exercise, enter your name centered in a header before printing. Other print options have already been set to print compressed and to display the filename, sheet name, and current date in a footer.

Before beginning your first Project 11 Challenge exercise, complete the following steps:

1. Open the file named **e-1104** (the password is challenge11) and save it as **e11challenge**.
   The workbook contains three sheets: an overview, and two exercise sheets named #1-DisplayNames and #2-DelChart.

2. Click the Overview sheet to view the organization of the Project 11 Challenge Exercises workbook.

If you need more than one work session to complete the desired exercises, continue working on **e11challenge** instead of starting over on the original e-1104 file. If prompted for a password, enter **challenge11**.

I. Displaying a List of Range Names

You would like to create a list of range names and their definitions in the current worksheet.

To display a list of range names:

1. If necessary, open the **e11challenge** workbook. (If prompted for a password, enter **challenge11**.)

2. Select the #1-DisplayNames worksheet.

3. Position the cell pointer on the upper-left cell of a two-column blank area on the worksheet.
   The blank area needs to be large enough to display all range names in one column and the associated cell references in the next column.

4. Start the process to insert a range name, and select Paste.

5. Make the remaining selection(s) to create the list.
The worksheet contains five named ranges.

2. Deleting an Embedded Chart in a Protected Worksheet

You decide to delete an embedded chart, but it is part of a protected worksheet.

To delete an embedded chart in a protected worksheet:

1. If necessary, open the **e11challenge** workbook. (If prompted for a password, enter **challenge11**.)

2. Select the #2-DelChart worksheet.

3. Disable worksheet protection.

4. Select the column chart below the monthly data, and delete it.

5. Restore worksheet protection.

3. Removing a Password from a Workbook

You decide to remove the password to open a workbook.

To remove a password from a workbook:

1. If necessary, open the **e11challenge** workbook. (The password is **challenge11**.)

2. Display the Save As dialog box.

3. Select General Options from the Tools drop-down list in the Save As dialog box.

4. Delete the password to open, and complete the Save operation.

Discovery Zone

Discovery Zone exercises require advanced knowledge of topics presented in *MOUS Essentials* lessons, application of skills from multiple lessons, or self-directed learning of new skills.

Each exercise is independent of the other, so you can complete the exercises in any order. Be sure to save the workbook after completing each exercise. If you need a paper copy of the completed exercise, enter your name centered in a header before printing. Other print options have already been set to print compressed and to display the file-name, sheet name, and current date in a footer.

Before beginning your first Project 11 Discovery Zone exercise, complete the following steps:

1. Open the file named **e-1105** and save it as **e11discovery**.
The workbook contains three sheets: an overview and two exercise sheets named #1-Protect and #2-Password.

2. Click the Overview sheet to view the organization of the Project 11 Discovery Zone Exercises workbook.

If you need more than one work session to complete the desired exercises, continue working on **e11discovery** instead of starting over on the original e-1105 file.

1. Deciding Which Cells to Unlock and Protecting the Rest

You have completed a worksheet showing monthly and annual revenues, expenses, net income, and gross profit percentages. Now you want to apply protection to the worksheet. Select the #1-Protect worksheet in the e11discovery workbook, and set up worksheet protection so that you can change only raw numbers, date last revised, and the name of the person who revised it.

2. Password-Protecting a Worksheet

You do not want anyone but yourself to have access to data on employees' wage rates per hour. Use onscreen Help to learn how to password-protect a worksheet instead of a workbook. Then password-protect only the #2-Password worksheet in the e11discovery workbook. Use the password `tenwages`.

PinPoint Assessment

You have completed this project and its associated lessons, and have had an opportunity to assess your skills through the end-of-project questions and exercises. Now use the PinPoint software Evaluation Mode to further assess your comprehension of the specific exam activities you have just learned. You can also use the PinPoint Trainer Mode and the Show Me tutorials to practice these exam activities.

Guiding Cell Entry with Data Validation

Key terms introduced in this project include

- data validation
- Error Alert message

- input message
- page break

Objectives	Required Activity for MOUS	Exam Level
➤ Attach an Input Message to a Cell	Use data validation	Expert
➤ Restrict Cell Entries to Data from a List	Use data validation	Expert
➤ Restrict Cell Entries to Numbers within Specified Limits	Use data validation	Expert
➤ Create a User-specified Error Alert Message	Use data validation	Expert
➤ Copy Data Restrictions and Messages to Other Cells	Use data validation	Expert
➤ Use Audit Tools to Find Invalid Data	Work with the Auditing toolbar; Trace errors (find and fix errors)	Expert
➤ Edit Errors Including Validation Settings	Trace errors (find and fix errors); Insert and remove a page break	Expert
➤ Find Cells that have Data Restrictions or Messages	Use data validation	Expert

Why Would I Do This?

You can introduce errors in a worksheet by entering the wrong data or by creating calculations that are not correct. Data in worksheets is used to make decisions. If the data or the calculations in a worksheet are wrong, decisions based on that data are likely to be wrong—often with costly results. Excel provides a variety of **data validation** options to set up data entry instructions, drop-down lists of allowable entries, and error messages.

In this project, you use lists and limits to validate data entry, attach input messages to cells, and set error messages. Other topics include copying, editing, and deleting validation features. To make it easier to focus on individual validation techniques, the data for each lesson is set up on separate worksheets named Message, Drop-down List, Limits, Error Alert, Copy, Find Errors, Fix Errors, and Find Validation. You begin by setting up a message that displays whenever a cell is selected.

 ## Lesson 1: Attaching an Input Message to a Cell

You are setting up a worksheet to hold survey data provided by customers who recently rented vehicles from Indy 500 Motor Works. Staff members will enter the data from the surveys, and you want to give them as much guidance as possible. You decide to include data validation features in the worksheet design.

To apply a validation method to a worksheet, select a cell and open the Data Validation dialog box containing three tabs (see Figure 12.1). These tabs can be used individually or in combination to set up messages and apply a variety of restrictions to a cell.

Figure 12.1
Use the Data Validation dialog box to apply validation techniques to your worksheet.

Select this tab to set up
data restrictions

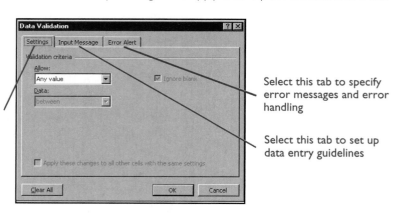

Select this tab to specify
error messages and error
handling

Select this tab to set up
data entry guidelines

In this case, you want to set up an **input message**, a convenient way to display instructions to users when they access a specific cell in a worksheet. The display can have two parts, the heading (optional) and the message itself. Clicking a cell formatted with an input message causes the predefined text to display in a balloon. The balloon is attached to the Office Assistant, if active, or to the corner of the cell.

Use this feature now to provide instructions for entering one of two Type Use codes—Per and Bus. These codes denote whether a rental was for Personal or Business use.

To Attach an Input Message to a Cell

1 **Open the e-1201 file, and save it as Indy500Validation.**
The workbook contains eight worksheets named Message, Drop-down List, Limits, Error Alert, Copy, Find Errors, Fix Errors, and Find Validation.

2 **Select the Message worksheet, and select cell B18.**
Cell B18 is the first cell in the Type Use column of the data area of the Message worksheet.

3 **Select Data, Validation.**
The Data Validation dialog box opens.

4 **Select the Input Message tab, and type Codes for Type Use in the Title text box.**

5 **Type Enter Per (personal) or Bus (business) in the Input message area (see Figure 12.2).**

Click to turn on or off the display of an input message

Type a heading for your input message here

Type your input message here

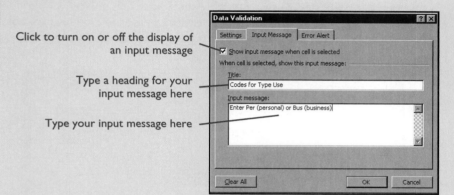

Figure 12.2
Use the middle tab in the Data Validation dialog box to set up an input message.

6 **Click OK, and click cell B18.**
The specified message displays in the Office Assistant's balloon if that feature is active (see Figure 12.3), or in a balloon attached to the corner of cell B18 if the Office Assistant is not active.

Cell containing the input message

Current worksheet

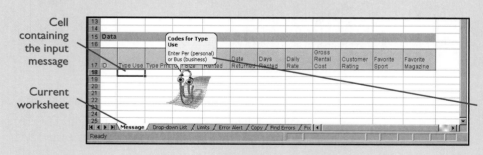

Figure 12.3
The message in the balloon guides data entry.

Input message displayed as a balloon attached to the Assistant

7 **Save your changes to the Message worksheet.**
Keep the Indy500Validation workbook open for the next lesson, or close the workbook and exit Excel.

Inside Stuff: **Positioning an Input Message**

If the Office Assistant is active, an input message displays in its balloon rather than as a balloon attached to a cell. You can, however, drag the Office Assistant closer to the cells where you are entering data.

Expert Lesson 2: Restricting Cell Entries to Data from a List

Options on the Settings tab of the Data Validation dialog box enable you to restrict the type of data that can be entered in a cell. Choices range from allowing any value to allowing only whole numbers, decimals, dates, times, values between two numbers, or values in a list.

The last option, values in a list, is the focus of this lesson. Selecting from a list instead of typing is likely to improve the speed and accuracy of data entry. You decide to use this feature to set up a list of car sizes. Figure 12.4 shows the options for restricting data entry to values in a list. You can create a list right in the Source text box by typing allowable entries separated by commas. However, you may find it easier to type the allowable entries in another area of the worksheet and refer to that range in the Source text box.

Figure 12.4

Select the List option from the Allow drop-down list to restrict data entry to a list of values.

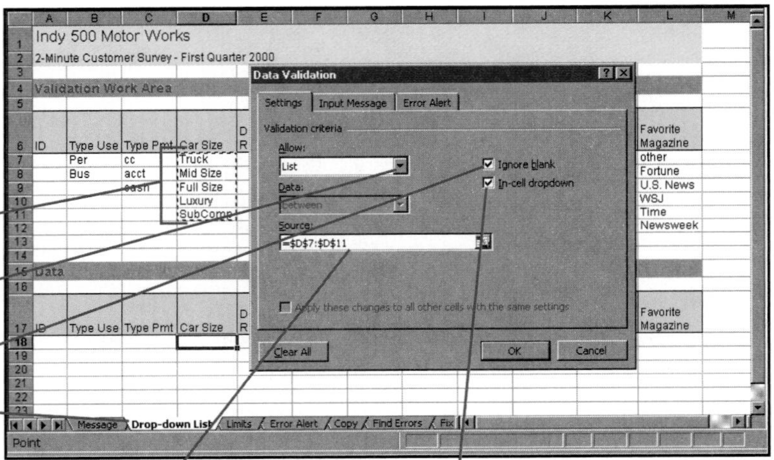

Allowable entries typed in an area outside the database

Click here to display the Allow drop-down list

Check here to allow blank cells

Current sheet

Specify the range of cells that hold the valid entries

Check here to display an in-cell drop-down list

In this lesson, you apply a validation list to the first cell in the Car Size field. Users of the worksheet can then select among Truck, Mid Size, Full Size, Luxury, and SubComp instead of typing each entry. Those allowable entries are already set up for you in a separate area of the worksheet.

To Restrict Cell Entries to Data in a List

1 Open the `Indy500Validation` file, if necessary, and select the **Drop-down List** worksheet.

2 Click cell **D18.**
This selects the first cell below Car Size in the Data area of Indy 500 Motor Works.

3 **Choose Data, Validation, and select the Settings tab.**

4 **Display the Allow drop-down list, and select List.**

5 **Enter =$D$7:$D$11 in the Source text box.**
Be sure to start the entry with an equal (=) sign. The dollar signs make the reference to range D7:D11 absolute—an essential specification if the data validation setting is copied to other cells.

6 **Check that your specifications match those shown in Figure 12.4, including the check mark in the In-cell dropdown check box.**

7 **Click OK.**

8 **Display the drop-down list attached to cell D18 (that is, click the small arrowhead at the right end of cell D18).**

9 **Select Luxury from the drop-down list.**
The word Luxury displays in cell D18.

10 **Save your changes to the Drop-down List worksheet.**
Keep the Indy500Validation workbook open for the next lesson, or close the workbook and exit Excel.

Lesson 3: Restricting Cell Entries to Whole Numbers Within Specified Limits

Controlling data entry through a drop-down list is suitable for selecting among relatively few exact-match entries. Some data, such as whole numbers, decimals, dates, and times, normally would not be validated using a list. For example, if you wanted to allow any date in the year 1999 using a drop-down list, you would have to set up 365 dates. Selecting from such a list would take longer than using no list.

As an alternative, you can specify that data must fit specified criteria, and that any attempt to enter invalid data produces an ***Error Alert message*** in one of three styles—Stop, Warning, or Information. For example, you can require that data be above or below a stated value, within a range of values, or outside a range of values. While this form of validation is not as accurate as restricting entries to a list, it still prevents some errors.

As you continue working with Indy 500 Motor Works survey data, you decide to set up a validation limiting data entry for Customer Rating to a whole number between 1 and 5. Further, you decide to skip using an Input message because you know that Validation automatically generates a Stop Error Alert message if an invalid entry is attempted.

To Restrict Cell Entries to Numbers Within Specified Limits

1 **Open the Indy500Validation file, if necessary, and then select the Limits worksheet.**

2 **Select cell J18, and select Data, Validation.**

3 **Select the Settings tab in the Data Validation dialog box, and select Whole number from the Allow drop-down list.**
The phrase Whole number displays in the Allow text box, and the word between displays in the Data text box.

continues ▶

To Restrict Cell Entries to Numbers Within Specified Limits (continued)

❹ Type 1 in the <u>M</u>inimum text box, and 5 in the Ma<u>x</u>imum text box.
Check that your specifications match those in Figure 12.5, and make changes as necessary.

Figure 12.5
Select the Data *drop-down* list and select between to restrict entry of a value to a range of numbers.

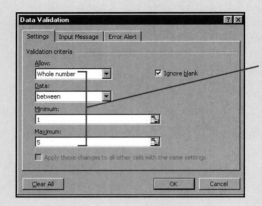

Four settings to specify that valid entries are whole numbers between 1 and 5

❺ Click OK to exit the Data Validation dialog box.

❻ Type 6 in cell J18, and press ⏎Enter.
Notice that an error alert message appears when you try to enter a number that falls outside the allowable range of 1 and 5.

❼ Click <u>R</u>etry in the alert message, type 3, and press ⏎Enter.
The valid number you entered is accepted.

❽ Save your changes to the Limits worksheet.
Keep the Indy500Validation workbook open for the next lesson, or close the workbook and exit Excel.

Expert Lesson 4: Creating a User-Specified Error Alert Message

When validation settings have been specified, Excel displays an Error Alert message when invalid data is entered in the cell. This message is very general and does not explain how to correct the problem. You can specify an Error Alert message that replaces the one generated by Excel.

You can choose from three levels of error alerts: Information, Warning, and Stop. Each style of error message offers different levels of protection. Information messages enable you to accept the invalid data or cancel the entry. Warnings enable you to accept the invalid data, change your data, or cancel the entry. Stop messages prevent invalid data from being entered.

Figure 12.6 illustrates the Error Alert tab of the Data Validation dialog box. Creating a message involves a three-step process. Select the style of Error Alert you want to use, compose your message, and check on the option to display your message.

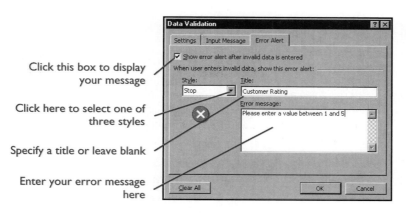

Click this box to display your message

Click here to select one of three styles

Specify a title or leave blank

Enter your error message here

Figure 12.6
Use the Error Alert tab to select from three styles of error messages to display when invalid data is entered in a cell.

In this lesson, you are concerned about entering the Customer Rating code correctly. The setting has already been made to cell J18. However, the Excel-generated error message does not give the user enough information about what the correct data should be. You decide to use the Stop style and display your own message.

To Create a User-Specified Error Alert Message

1 Open the `Indy500Validation` file, if necessary, and select the Error Alert tab.

2 Select cell J18, and select **D**ata, Va**l**idation.

3 Select the Error Alert tab.
Stop displays in the Style text box. The Title and Error message text boxes are blank.

4 Type `Customer Rating` in the Title text box.

5 Type `Please enter a value between 1 and 5` in the Error message text box.
Check that your specifications match those in Figure 12.6, and make changes as necessary.

6 Click **OK** to exit the Data Validation dialog box, type `6` in cell J18, and press ⏎**Enter**.
Notice that the error message is more helpful this time.

7 Click **R**etry in the alert message, type `3` in cell J18, and press ⏎**Enter**.
The valid number you entered is accepted.

8 Save your changes to the Error Alert worksheet.
Keep the `Indy500Validation` workbook open for the next lesson, or close the workbook and exit Excel.

Expert ## Lesson 5: Copying Data Restrictions and Messages to Other Cells

You can apply validation settings and messages to a single cell or an entire range of cells. If you are designing a worksheet and have not yet entered data, you can apply one or more validation settings to the first blank cell of a range, and copy the specifications to the rest of the range. To do this, copy the cell containing the validation restrictions using Copy and Paste commands or drag the Fill handle.

You can also apply validation specifications to existing data by using Paste Special instead of Paste. Paste Special enables you to select among a variety of copy options, one of which is Validation.

The Favorite Sport column in the survey results for Indy 500 Motor Works already contains data. Now you want to create a drop-down list to control data entry for new records and to check the accuracy of records already entered.

To Copy Validation Restrictions and Messages

1 Open the `Indy500Validation` file, if necessary, and select the Copy worksheet.

2 Click cell K18.
A small arrow indicating an in-cell drop-down list displays at the right end of the cell.

3 Click several other cells in column K below cell K18.
A drop-down list has not been applied to remaining cells in the column.

4 Select cell K18 again, and click the Copy button in the toolbar (or choose Edit, Copy).

5 Select (highlight) the range K19:K47.

6 Right-click within the highlighted range K19:K47, and select Paste Special (or choose Edit, Paste Special).

7 Select Validation, click OK, and press Esc.
A validation drop-down list for favorite sport has been copied to all remaining cells in the column that contain data. Pressing Esc removes the marquee from cell K18.

X *If You Have Problems...*
If other displays in all cells, you selected Paste instead of Paste Special. Use Undo to reverse the paste results and start again with Step 6.

8 Display the drop-down list for cell K20.
Options on the copied drop-down list include basketball and golf (see Figure 12.7). Data already entered in column K include two errors in spelling—basketbal in cell K27 and gulf in cell K35. Do not correct the errors now. You learn to audit for such errors in Lesson 6.

9 Save your changes to the Copy worksheet.
Keep the `Indy500Validation` workbook open for the next lesson, or close the workbook and exit Excel.

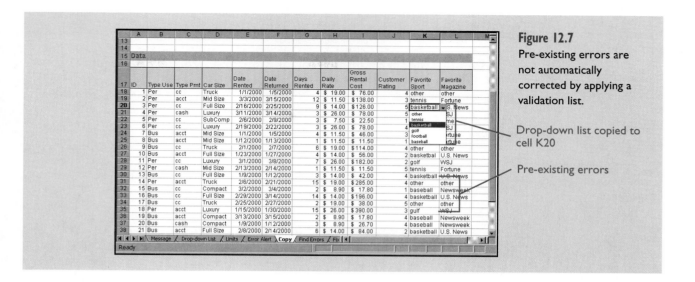

Figure 12.7
Pre-existing errors are not automatically corrected by applying a validation list.

Drop-down list copied to cell K20

Pre-existing errors

 Exam Note: **Applying Validation After Data Entry**
Applying validation restrictions to worksheets after data is already entered is a common situation. Perhaps you entered data manually until you discovered all possible answers. Now you want to turn maintenance of the data over to other staff. It's also possible that you must now maintain a worksheet developed by someone else. If you do apply validation to cells that already contain data, be sure to look for and correct any pre-existing errors.

Lesson 6: Using Audit Tools to Find Invalid Data

Expert

After validation restrictions are applied to a cell they are in effect whenever you enter data in that cell. However, if you apply validation to a cell that already contains data, Excel does not automatically check the existing data for validity. Excel offers a variety of auditing tools, one of which finds cells with errors.

The Auditing toolbar contains a feature to circle invalid data that works in combination with validation. When you select the Circle Invalid Data button on the Auditing toolbar, Excel places a red circle around cells with contents that don't meet the validation rule settings. As you correct the data, the red circles disappear. Corrections are controlled by the new validation settings.

You can display the Auditing toolbar by choosing Tools, Auditing, Show Auditing Toolbar. Use the Auditing toolbar now to find errors in the Indy 500 Motor Works survey data.

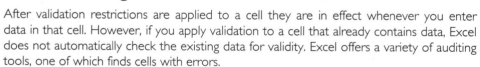

To Use Audit Tools to Find Invalid Data

1 Open the `Indy500Validation` file, if necessary, and select the Find Errors worksheet.

2 Choose Tools, Auditing.

3 Select Show Auditing Toolbar.

continues ▶

To Use Audit Tools to Find Invalid Data (continued)

4 Click the **Circle Invalid Data** button, and scroll to view records in rows 18 through 47.

All invalid data according to validation settings appear circled in red (see Figure 12.8). This data must be corrected or the validation rule changed.

Figure 12.8
Data that violate validation settings are circled in red.

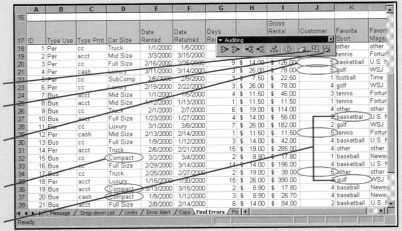

Circle Invalid Data button

Clear Validation Circles button

The range of acceptable entries is erroneously set to between 1 and 4 instead of between 1 and 5

Compact is not one of the options in the Car Size drop-down list

Spelling errors

5 Click the **Clear Validation Circles** button on the Auditing toolbar, and save your changes.

Keep the Indy500Validation workbook open for the next lesson, or close the workbook and exit Excel.

 Inside Stuff: Impact of Saving on Circled Data
Saving or closing a workbook turns off the Circle Invalid Data feature and the red circles around incorrect data disappear. To display the circles again, repeat the process to turn on the Auditing toolbar and select Circle Invalid Data.

If AutoSave is active and it interferes with editing, turn the AutoSave setting off temporarily.

 ## Lesson 7: Editing Errors Including Validation Settings

After you have identified errors in your data, you must investigate each one and make corrections. In this lesson, you correct the three types of errors described in Figure 12.8. In the Car Size field, each occurrence of Compact is circled, which suggests that the word Compact must be missing in the drop-down list set up in the range D7:D11. To correct this problem, you can add Compact to the list and increase the defined range by one cell.

The validation setting for Customer Rating incorrectly limits data to a range of numbers 1 through 4, while the data contains numbers 1 through 5. To correct this problem, you must change the maximum allowed whole number to 5 instead of 4.

The third error involves misspellings in the Favorite Sport column. The data restrictions in the Validation list (K7:K12) are correct. Because these cells use an In-cell drop-down list, you can make corrections by dropping down the list in each cell with a red circle (one at a time) and selecting the correct entry.

After correcting the errors, you insert a page break between the validation work area and the data area, and print the worksheet. A **page break** enables you to end a printed page at a specified point and start a new page. Cell contents below and to the right of a page break print on a new page.

To Edit Errors Including Validation Settings

1 **Open the `Indy500Validation` file, if necessary, and select the Fix Errors worksheet.**

2 **Display the Auditing toolbar, and click the Circle Invalid Data button.**

3 **Select cell D12, and enter `Compact`.**

4 **Select cells D18:D47, and choose Data, Validation.**

5 **On the Settings tab, change the $D$11 entry in the Source text box to $D$12 (see Figure 12.9)**

Expand the source range to include Compact in cell D12

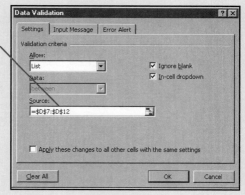

Figure 12.9
You can change one or more current validation settings.

6 **Click OK.**
You have just corrected the Car Size data. The cells containing the word Compact are no longer circled in red. To check this, click the Circle Invalid Data button on the Auditing toolbar.

7 **Select the range J18:J47.**

8 **Display the Data Validation dialog box, and select the Settings tab.**

9 **Type 5 in the Maximum text box, and select OK.**
You have just corrected the Customer Rating field. Remember, check that the errors are corrected by clicking the Circle Invalid Data button on the Auditing toolbar.

10 **Display the drop-down list in cell K27, and select basketball.**
Notice the red circle did not disappear after you made the correction. You must reapply the Circle Invalid Data option to recheck for errors.

continues ▶

To Edit Errors Including Validation Settings (continued)

11 **Display the drop-down list in cell K35, and select golf.**

All errors in the worksheet have now been corrected. You can verify this by reapplying the Circle Invalid Data option one last time. There should be no cells circled in red.

12 **Close the Auditing toolbar, and save your changes to the Fix Errors worksheet.**

Now insert a page break, preview page breaks, move a page break, and print the worksheet. Start by picking a cell immediately below and to the right of where you want to start a new page.

13 **Click cell A14, and choose Insert, Page Break.**

14 **Click the Print Preview button in the toolbar.**

Preview: Page 1 of 4 displays in the lower-left corner of the screen.

15 **Click the Page Break Preview button.**

The Welcome to Page Break Preview dialog box displays if that feature has not been turned off. The welcome message displays in a balloon if the Office Assistant is active (see Figure 12.10). Solid and dashed lines show the current boundaries of printed pages.

Figure 12.10
You can reposition a page break by dragging it to a new location.

A solid blue line indicates a manual page break

A dashed blue line indicates an automatic page break

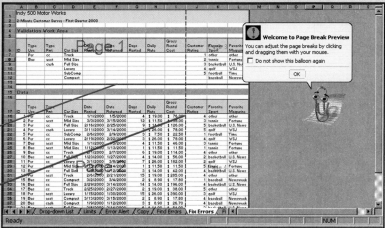

16 **Close the welcome message, if necessary, and drag the dashed blue line to the right edge of column L.**

Specifications to print the worksheet on two pages have been set—Validation Work Area on Page 1 and the Data section on Page 2. Now preview the revised page breaks.

17 **Click the Print Preview button.**

Preview: Page 1 of 2 displays in the lower-left corner of the screen.

18 **Scroll down to display Page 2 of 2.**

Preview: Page 2 of 2 displays in the lower-left corner of the screen.

19 **Click the Normal View button and save your changes. Print the worksheet, if desired.**

Keep the Indy500Validation workbook open for the last lesson in this project, or close the workbook and exit Excel.

Exam Note: **Setting Horizontal and Vertical Page Breaks**
If you click a cell in column A, as you did in this lesson, Excel inserts only a horizontal page break. If you click a cell in row 1, Excel inserts only a vertical page break. If you click a cell in any other location on the worksheet, Excel inserts both a horizontal and a vertical page break.

 Exam Note: **Removing Page Breaks**
You can remove any page break in Page Break Preview mode by dragging its line outside of the print area. You can also remove a manual page break by clicking a cell below the horizontal page break or to the right of a vertical page break and choosing Insert, Remove Page Break.

In Page Break Preview mode you can remove all manual page breaks. Right-click any cell on the worksheet and select Reset All Page Breaks on the shortcut menu.

Lesson 8: Finding Cells That Have Data Restrictions or Messages

You may not know whether the worksheet you are using contains data validation restrictions and messages. This is especially true if you are using a worksheet someone else has designed. Using the Go To Special dialog box (see Figure 12.11) accessed through the Edit menu, you can highlight cells that contain validation restrictions and messages.

Click here to highlight all cells containing data validation restrictions

Click here to highlight those cells with data validation specifications that match those in the current cell

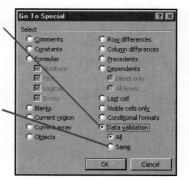

Figure 12.11
Use Edit, Go To, Special to find and highlight cells with data validation settings.

To Find Cells That Have Data Restrictions or Messages

1 Open the `Indy500Validation` file, if necessary, and select the **Find Validation worksheet.**

2 Select cell A1, and then choose **E**dit, **G**o To.

3 Click the **S**pecial button.
The Go To Special dialog box displays.

4 Click the Data **v**alidation option in the lower-right corner, and click All (see Figure 12.10).

continues ▶

To Find Cells That Have Data Restrictions or Messages   (continued)

5 **Check that your settings match those in Figure 12.10, and click OK.**
Use your mouse to scroll around the worksheet. Notice that the Type Use, Type Pmt, Car Size, Gross Rental Cost, Customer Rating, Favorite Sport, and Favorite Magazine fields are all selected (see Figure 12.12).

Figure 12.12
You can click any highlighted cell, such as cell B18, and view a validation message or encounter a data restriction.

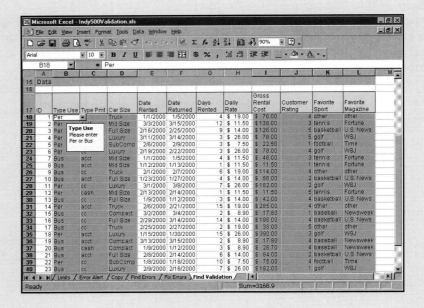

6 **Click any cell that is not highlighted.**
The highlighted cells are deselected.

7 **Click cell B18, and display the Go To Special dialog box.**

8 **Click Data validation, click Same, and click OK.**
The entire Type Use data field displays highlighted, indicating that the data validation in cell B18 is used in all cells in that field.

9 **Save your changes to the Find Validation worksheet.**
This concludes Project 12. You can close the Indy500Validation workbook and exit Excel, or continue with end-of-project exercises.

Summary

This project had a single focus—presenting ways to increase data accuracy by applying data validation techniques. Your experiences ranged from simply displaying a message upon selecting a cell to preventing the entry of data that did not meet predefined restrictions. You learned that you could apply validation settings to blank cells or cells containing data. Remaining topics included using the Auditing toolbar to find invalid data, and highlighting cells that had data restrictions or messages.

You can expand your learning by experimenting with variations of data validation, such as restricting data entry to a time period or to text containing a specified number of characters. Explore related onscreen Help topics, such as Troubleshooting Data Validation.

Checking Concepts and Terms

True/False

For each of the following, circle *T* or *F* to indicate whether the statement is true or false.

__T __F   **1.** Use the Settings tab in the Data Validation dialog box to apply an input message to a cell. [L1]

__T __F   **2.** When the Office Assistant is displayed, all validation messages appear in a balloon attached to the Office Assistant. [L1]

__T __F   **3.** The List setting is used to restrict data to a range between two numbers. [L2]

__T __F   **4.** You can find errors in your data by clicking the Circle Invalid Data check box on the Settings tab in the Data Validation dialog box. [L6]

__T __F   **5.** Error messages should clearly tell the user what the problem is and how to correct it. [L4]

Multiple Choice

Circle the letter of the correct answer for each of the following.

1. Which Data Validation tab would you use to restrict data entry to the values in a list? [L2]

   a. Settings

   b. Error Alert

   c. Input Message

   d. In-cell list

2. Which Error Alert style enables you to enter invalid data? [L4]

   a. Information

   b. Warning

   c. Stop

   d. both a and b

3. Which validation tab can be used to display a message? [L3]

   a. Settings

   b. Input Message

   c. Error Alert

   d. both b and c

4. Which of the following is an accurate statement? [L4]

   a. If you apply validation to a cell that already contains data, the existing data is automatically checked for validity.

   b. You can use a button on the Auditing toolbar to highlight cells that contain validation restrictions and messages.

   c. When you select the Circle Invalid Data button on the Auditing toolbar, Excel places a red circle around cells with contents that don't meet the validation rule settings.

   d. all of the above

5. If you turn off the Office Assistant, an Input or Error Alert message appears in which location? [L1]

   a. as a message in the formula bar

   b. as a balloon callout attached to the appropriate cell

   c. as a balloon callout located where the Office Assistant was last located

   d. none of the above

Skill Drill

Skill Drill exercises reinforce project skills. Each skill reinforced is the same, or nearly the same, as a skill presented in the project. Each exercise includes a brief narrative introduction, followed by detailed instructions in a step-by-step format.

Each exercise is independent of the others, so you can complete the exercises in any order. Be sure to save the workbook after completing each exercise. If you need a paper copy of the completed exercise, enter your name centered in a header before printing. Other print options have already been set to print compressed and to display the filename, sheet name, and current date in a footer.

Before beginning your first Project 12 Skill Drill exercise, complete the following steps:

1. Open the file named **e-1202**, and save it as **e12drill**.
   The workbook contains four sheets: an overview, and three sheets named #1-Data List, #2-Data Limits, and #3-Warning.

2. Click the Overview sheet to view the organization of the Project 12 Skill Drill Exercises workbook.

If you need more than one work session to complete the desired exercises, continue working on **e12drill** instead of starting over on the original e-1202 file.

1. Restricting Data Entry to a List of Values

You decide to control data entry in the Receipt field.

To restrict data entered in a cell to a list of values:

1. If necessary, open the **e12drill** workbook; then select the #1-Data List worksheet.

2. Select cell D19.

3. Choose <u>D</u>ata, Va<u>l</u>idation.

4. Select the Settings tab.

5. Select List from the <u>A</u>llow drop-down list.

6. Enter =$D$5:$D$7 in the <u>S</u>ource text box, and click OK.

7. Type **Lost** in cell D19, and press <u>Enter</u>.
   An **Excel Stop Error** message appears advising you that the entry you just made is invalid.

8. Click Cancel.

9. Select No from the drop-down list attached to cell D19.
   This time the entry was accepted because No was one of the entries on the list.

2. Restricting Data to a Range of Dates

You are concerned that the dates of your contributions fall in the year 2000. Last year at an audit, several of your contributions were dated wrong. The auditor listened to your explanation about typing errors doubtfully. This year you want to apply the Data Validation setting Date to avoid this type of data entry error. You restrict contribution dates to the year 2000. To do this, you must refer to the dates Jan 1, 2000 and Dec 31, 2000.

To limit data to a range of dates:

1. If necessary, open the **e12drill** workbook; then select the #2-Data Limits worksheet.

2. Select cell A19.

3. Choose <u>D</u>ata, Va<u>l</u>idation.

4. Select the Settings tab.

5. Select Date from the <u>A</u>llow drop-down list.

6. Type **01/01/2000** in the <u>S</u>tart date text box and **12/31/2000** in the <u>E</u>nd date text box.

7. Click OK to exit the Data Validation dialog box.
   You should test your validation settings and messages by entering erroneous data.

8. Type **Jul 4, 3000** in cell A19 and press <u>Enter</u>.
   Remember you can type dates in several formats. In this case, you could have typed 07/04/2000. In this example, Excel displays a **Stop Error Alert** message.

9. Select Cancel, type **Jul 4, 2000**, and press <u>Enter</u>.

3. Applying a Warning Error Alert Message

Earlier, you applied a validation setting to the date field in your contributions database. After thinking about it you decide that you want to attach your own Error Alert message to the cell also. The error message advises users that they should enter a year 2000 date.

To add an error message to data validation:

1. If necessary, open the `e12drill` workbook; then select the #3-Warning worksheet.

2. Select cell A19.

3. Choose Data, Validation, and select the Error Alert tab.

4. Select Warning from the Style drop-down list.

5. Type `Contribution Date` in the Title text box.

6. Type `Please enter a date between Jan 1, 2000 and Dec 31, 2000` in the Error message text box.

7. Click OK to exit the Data Validation dialog box.

8. In cell A19, enter an invalid date and check that your validation message works correctly.
   A message should display asking whether you want to continue or not (the choices are Yes, No, and Cancel).

9. Click No in the Contribution Date dialog box, and enter a valid date.

Challenge

Challenge exercises expand on or are somewhat related to skills presented in the lessons. Each exercise provides a brief narrative introduction followed by instructions in a numbered step format that are not as detailed as those in the Skill Drill section.

Each exercise is independent of the others, so you can complete the exercises in any order. Be sure to save the workbook after completing each exercise. If you need a paper copy of the completed exercise, enter your name centered in a header before printing. Other print options have already been set to print compressed and to display the file-name, sheet name, and current date in a footer.

Before beginning your first Project 12 Challenge exercise, complete the following steps:

1. Open the file named `e-1203`, and save it as `e12challenge`.
   The workbook contains four sheets: an overview, and three exercise sheets named #1-Messages, #2-Find and Copy, and #3-Find and Fix.

2. Click the Overview sheet to view the organization of the Project 12 Challenge Exercises workbook.

If you need more than one work session to complete the desired exercises, continue working on `e12challenge` instead of starting over on the original e-1203 file.

1. Applying Validations with Information and Warning Messages

You want to apply validation restrictions and error messages to the Shift and Hire Date fields. Shift data should be limited to whole numbers between 1 and 3, with an input message and an Information Error alert. Hire Date should restrict entries to dates between 1 Aug 1988 and the current date, with an appropriate input message and a Warning Error Alert. This is a little different because you will use the Today() function to determine current date. The date settings will also be stored in cells rather than typed directly into the validation settings.

To apply validations with information and warning messages:

1. If necessary, open the **e12challenge** workbook; then select the #1-Messages worksheet tab.

2. Select the Shift data, and choose Data, Validation.

3. Use the Settings tab to allow whole numbers between 1 and 3.

4. Select the Input Message tab, type `Please enter a number 1, 2, or 3` as the input message, and give the message the title `Shift`.

5. Use the Error Alert tab to display the Information message `You have entered an incorrect number. Please enter a number 1, 2, or 3.`
Check that your Input and Error messages display correctly. You can test your validation by entering an invalid shift such as 0 or 4.

6. Type `8-1-88,` in cell E11, and type `=TODAY(),` in cell F11.

7. Select the Hire Date data in the database area, and choose Data, Validation.

8. Use the Settings tab to allow Dates, and refer to cell E11 as the start date and cell F11 as the end date.

9. Use the Input Message tab to inform users that they must enter a date between August 1, 1988 and the current date.

10. Use the Error Alert tab to display a Warning message with two messages:

`Please enter a date between August 1, 1988 and the current date.`

`Select Yes to accept the date, No to enter another date, or Cancel to quit.`

11. Test your Hire Date validation settings. Try entering the date 1-1-1980 or a date in the future.

2. Finding and Copying Validation Restrictions and Messages

You have just looked at your worksheet for the first time in several days and can't remember whether you finished entering validation restrictions and messages. The first thing to do is use Go to Special and find all validations in the worksheet. You will find that validations are applied to the Position, Department, Shift, and Hire Date fields of the first record only. You must copy the validations to all records in the database.

To find and copy validation restrictions and messages:

1. If necessary, open the **e12challenge** workbook; then select the #2-Find and Copy worksheet.

2. Choose Edit, Go To, and click the Special button.

3. Select the Data validation and All options.
Notice that there are validation restrictions in the Position, Department, Shift, and Hire Date fields of the first record only.

4. Copy the entire first record (cells C29:I29).

5. Paste special only the validations to the remaining records in the database (cells C30:I139).
Now verify that the Validation restrictions were copied correctly.

6. Repeat steps 2 and 3.

If validation settings copied correctly, all data in the Position, Department, Shift, and Hire Date fields displays highlighted.

3. Finding and Fixing Errors Using the Auditing Toolbar

Having applied validation restrictions and messages to the existing data in your worksheet, you need to check that no data violates these restrictions. Using the Auditing toolbar, you find errors. For example, two entries in the Position field use abbreviations that are not in the drop-down list. You must reenter that data.

All Marketing entries in the Department field are in error. This indicates that the Marketing department is not on the drop-down list and must be added. This requires that you add marketing to the Database Work Area and change the Validation settings.

Shift data also contains two errors. These can be fixed by entering correct data. Both employees should be on the first shift.

To find and fix errors using the Auditing toolbar:

1. If necessary, open the `e12challenge` workbook; then select the #3-Find and Fix worksheet.

2. Display the Auditing toolbar, and click the Circle Invalid Data button.
    All errors should appear circled in red.

3. In the Position data field, select each of the fields circled in red, and select the correct entry from the drop-down list.

4. Click the Circle Invalid Data button.

5. Select the range D15:D17, and move the selected cells down one cell.

6. Enter `Marketing` in the blank cell D15.

7. Select the Department data in the database area (column F).

8. Choose Validation on the <u>D</u>ata menu, and change the Source range on the Settings tab to `=$D$11:$D$18`.

9. Click the Circle Invalid Data button.
    Check that all red circles in the Department field are turned off.

 If You Have Problems...
If marketing entries are still circled, check that you have spelled marketing correctly in the list. Also, test the drop-down list to make sure marketing is one of the choices. If it isn't, check that the cell reference in the Validation Source text box on the Settings tab is correct.

10. Change the data in each of the Shift fields circled in red to `1`.
    As you correct each entry, the red circle should disappear.

Discovery Zone

Discovery Zone exercises require advanced knowledge of topics presented in *MOUS Essentials* lessons, application of skills from multiple lessons, or self-directed learning of new skills.

Each exercise is independent of the others, so you can complete the exercises in any order. Be sure to save the workbook after completing each exercise. If you need a paper copy of the completed exercise, enter your name centered in a header before printing. Other print options have already been set to print compressed and to display the filename, sheet name, and current date in footer.

Before beginning your first Project 12 Discovery Zone exercise, complete the following steps:

1. Open the file named **e-1204**, and save it as **e12discovery**.
   The workbook contains four sheets: #1-Scenario and its related sheet #1-Analyze, and #2-Scenario and its related sheet #2-Validation.

2. Click the #1-Scenario and #2-Scenario worksheets, respectively, to read explanations of the related exercises.

If you need more than one work session to complete the desired exercises, continue working on **e12discovery** instead of starting over on the original e-1204 file.

1. Analyzing Validation Requirements for a Database

An important part of the process of creating and maintaining a database in Excel is to ensure the accuracy of its data. To practice the process of determining what validation restrictions to apply, select the #1-Analyze worksheet in the e12discovery workbook. Notice that there is a Database Work Area located just above the database. Column A contains a list of the field names from the database. Next to each field name is a blank cell. Analyze each field in the database carefully, and in the space next to the field name, describe the validation restriction, Input Message, and Error Alert you would apply to that field. Not every field requires validation. If no validation is required, enter **None**.

2. Applying Validation Restrictions to a Database

After you know what validations you need to use, you must apply them to the database. To practice the process of applying validation restrictions, open the #2-Validation worksheet in the e12discovery workbook. Notice that there is a Validation Instructions area located just above the database. Column A contains a list of the field names from the database. Next to each field name is a description of the validation that should be applied to the field. Follow the instructions and apply the recommended validation to each field.

PinPoint Assessment

You have completed this project and its associated lessons, and have had an opportunity to assess your skills through the end-of-project questions and exercises. Now use the PinPoint software Evaluation Mode to further assess your comprehension of the specific exam activities you have just learned. You can also use the PinPoint Trainer Mode and the Show Me tutorials to practice these exam activities.

Creating PivotTable and PivotChart Reports

Key terms introduced in this project include

- indented format
- nonindented format
- noninteractive table
- pivot table
- PivotTable and PivotChart Wizard
- PivotTable list
- refresh

Objectives	Required Activity for MOUS	Exam Level
➤ Display Help on Pivot Tables and Related Charts	Use the Office Assistant	Core
➤ Create a Pivot Table	Use data analysis and pivot tables	Expert
➤ Expand a Pivot Table	Use data analysis and pivot tables	Expert
➤ Remove, Hide, and Show Data	Use data analysis and pivot tables	Expert
➤ Refresh a Pivot Table	Use data analysis and pivot tables	Expert
➤ Create a Chart from Pivot Table Data	Create PivotChart reports	Expert
➤ Apply a Predefined Format to a Pivot Table	Use PivotTable AutoFormat	Expert
➤ Display Pivot Tables on the Web	Create interactive pivot tables for the Web; Add fields to a pivot table using the Web browser	Expert

Why Would I Do This?

pivot table is an interactive table that summarizes a data source, such as a list or another table. You can also create a chart that plots the data in a pivot table.

Imagine that your responsibilities include maintaining employee data and generating reports based on that data. The annual budget review takes place early next month, and your supervisor has requested information based on current salary levels—total salaries for each department, average salary for each position, and so forth. You have a large amount of data available in an Excel list. Using Excel's powerful PivotTable and PivotChart Report Wizard, you can quickly create the summary information you need.

In this project, you create, expand, edit, and format a pivot table. You also create a chart based on pivot table data and create an interactive pivot table for the Web. Start by viewing related Help topics in Lesson 1.

 ## Lesson 1: Displaying Help on Pivot Tables and Related Charts

Before you begin to create pivot tables and related charts, use Excel's onscreen Help to get an overview of analyzing data interactively. You can find out when to use a PivotTable report, what types of reports are available, and how to create a report.

To Get Help on Pivot Tables

1 **Display the Office Assistant on a blank Excel worksheet.**

2 **Click the Office Assistant to display a balloon, type `pivot tables` in the text box, and click the Search button.**
Help topics associated with the phrase pivot tables display in the Office Assistant balloon.

3 **Select the topic `About PivotTable reports: interactive data analysis`, and click the graphic as instructed in the Help window.**
Excel displays the selected topic in the Microsoft Excel Help window (see Figure 13.1).

4 **Read the remaining information in the Overview, and click the link `Source data`.**
Help displays an example of data for a PivotTable report and provides information on how to set up the source data.

5 **Read the remaining source data information, and click the link `How PivotTable reports organize data`.**
This Help topic includes information about elements of a PivotTable report and summary functions.

6 **Read remaining information on pivot table organization, and click the link `PivotChart reports`.**
This Help topic provides an example of a PivotChart report.

7 **Read other topics of your choice, and close the Help window.**

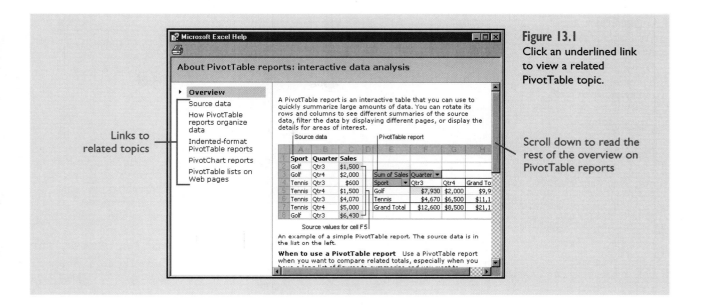

Links to related topics

Figure 13.1
Click an underlined link to view a related PivotTable topic.

Scroll down to read the rest of the overview on PivotTable reports

Lesson 2: Creating a Pivot Table

The **PivotTable and PivotChart Wizard** guides you through the steps to make a custom report from a list of data. The initial steps include specifying the data source, the type of report (PivotTable or PivotChart), and the location of the report (a new worksheet or the existing worksheet). At that point you have two options for completing the design of the pivot table: using a Layout dialog box or making selections directly on the worksheet.

You can easily set up a pivot table directly on the worksheet by dragging the names of fields listed in the PivotTable toolbar to the appropriate areas of a pivot table shell (see Figure 13.2). That way you can view the data while you arrange the fields.

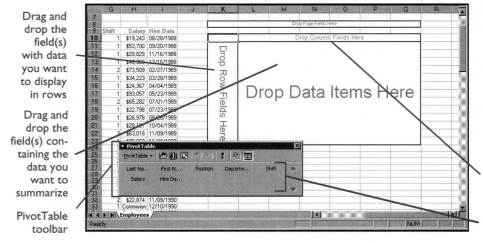

Drag and drop the field(s) with data you want to display in rows

Drag and drop the field(s) containing the data you want to summarize

PivotTable toolbar

Figure 13.2
You can use the PivotTable and PivotChart wizard to specify location and source data, and complete pivot table design by dragging field names to a shell on the worksheet.

Drag and drop the field(s) with data you want to display across columns

Fields listed in the toolbar

If the pivot table you have in mind is very large and complex, the on-sheet layout illustrated in Figure 13.2 can be quite time-consuming. You may prefer to design the pivot table using the Layout dialog box (see Figure 13.3).

Figure 13.3
You can use the PivotTable and PivotChart Wizard to specify location and source data, and then complete pivot table design using the wizard's Layout dialog box.

Instructions for specifying fields

Drag and drop the field(s) with data you want to display in rows

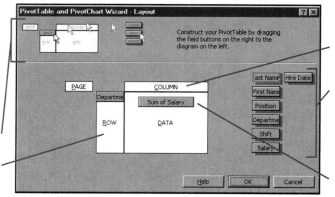

Drag and drop the field(s) with data you want to display across columns

Field buttons

Drag and drop the field(s) containing the data you want to summarize

In this lesson, you design a pivot table directly on the worksheet. You create a simple table that totals salaries by department for Millennium Manufacturing. In the next lesson, you design a more complex pivot table using the Layout dialog box.

To Create a Pivot Table Directly on the Worksheet

1 **Open the file e-1301, and save it as Pivotsalary.**
The workbook contains a worksheet named Employees, which includes employee-related data organized as an Excel list.

2 **Click any cell within the list range C9:I120, and choose Data, PivotTable and PivotChart Report.**
The PivotTable and PivotChart Wizard–Step 1 of 3 dialog box opens, as shown in Figure 13.4.

Figure 13.4
Use the Step 1 of 3 dialog box to select the data source and type of report.

Click here to activate onscreen Help

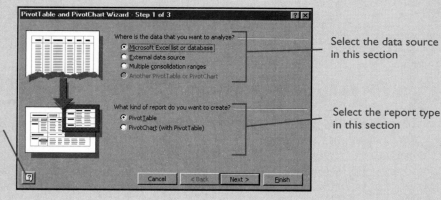

Select the data source in this section

Select the report type in this section

3 **Select Microsoft Excel list or database as the data source.**

4 **Select PivotTable as the kind of report, and click the Next button.**
The PivotTable and PivotChart Wizard–Step 2 of 3 dialog box opens. Because you clicked within the list before activating the Wizard, Excel automatically selects the entire list and displays $C$9:$I$120 in the range window.

5 **Click Next.**
The PivotTable and PivotChart Wizard–Step 3 of 3 dialog box opens. Use this dialog box to specify creating the pivot table in a new worksheet or in the existing worksheet.

6 Select Existing worksheet, and click cell K10.

This tells Excel to position the upper-left cell of the pivot table in cell K10 in the active worksheet. Employees!$K$10 displays in the window below the Existing worksheet option (see Figure 13.5).

Click here to design the pivot table using the Layout dialog box

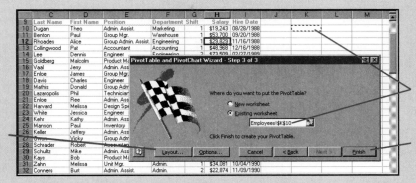

Figure 13.5
Use the Step 3 of 3 dialog box to specify the location of the pivot table.

Specifies the upper-left cell in the pivot table range

Click here to design the pivot table directly on the worksheet

7 Click the Finish button.

Excel creates a shell for a pivot table as shown in Figure 13.3.

8 Drag the PivotTable toolbar below the shell, and position the mouse pointer on the field name Department in the PivotTable toolbar (see Figure 13.6).

Excel displays the complete field name and instructions to drag the field button.

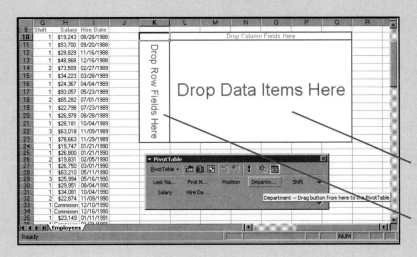

Figure 13.6
If you design a pivot table directly on the worksheet, you can drag fields to one of three areas— Drop Row Fields, Drop Column Fields, and Drop Data Items.

Drag and drop the field Salary here

Drag and drop the field Department here

9 Drag the Department button in the PivotTable toolbar to the Drop Row Fields area.

10 Drag the Salary button in the PivotTable toolbar to the Drop Data Items area.

Excel creates the pivot table (see Figure 13.7). By default, the summary calculation on salary data is a count. Now change the calculation to a sum.

11 Double-click Count of Salary (cell K10).

The PivotTable Field dialog box opens.

continues ▶

To Create a Pivot Table Directly on the Worksheet (continued)

Figure 13.7
The default summary calculation is a count—in this case, for each department and in total.

Description of the calculation

Total number of employees

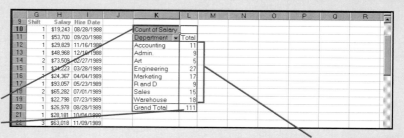

Number of employees in each department

⑫ **Select Sum in the Summarize by list box (see Figure 13.8).**
Sum of Salary replaces Count of Salary in the Name text box.

Figure 13.8
Options in the PivotTable Field dialog box include selecting the type of summary and changing how numbers in a field are formatted.

Click here to accept current settings and close the dialog box

Click here to change the number format

⑬ **Click the Number button to open the Format Cells dialog box, and specify Currency format without the $ sign and with zero decimal places.**

⑭ **Click OK twice to close the Format Cells and PivotTable Field dialog boxes respectively.**
The pivot table reflects the changes in type of summary and number formatting (see Figure 13.9).

Figure 13.9
The numbers in the Total column of the pivot table change from counts to sums.

Description of the calculation

Numbers formatted to display commas and zero decimal places

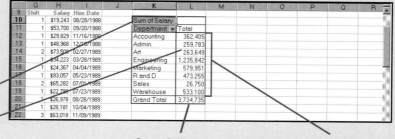

Sum of all salaries   Sum of salaries for each department

⑮ **Save your changes to the Employees worksheet.**
Keep the `Pivotsalary` workbook open for the next lesson, or close the workbook and exit Excel.

Exam Note: Deleting a Pivot Table
Before you can delete a pivot table, you must select it using a three-step
process. Right-click within the pivot table, choose ¨S̱elect from the shortcut
menu, and click Entire Ṯable. After selecting the table, choose Ḏdit, Cle̱ar, Ḏll.
When you delete a pivot table, the source data is not affected.

Lesson 3: Expanding a Pivot Table

You can greatly expand a pivot table by dragging more fields to a pivot table on the worksheet or to the row, column and data areas of the Layout dialog box. For example, instead of displaying a single column with total salary for each Millennium Manufacturing
department, you can add columns that provide totals for each shift within a department.
You can also add rows that provide totals for each position within a department. In this
lesson, you make these changes using the PivotTable and PivotChart Wizard's Layout dialog box.

To Expand a Pivot Table Using the Layout Dialog Box

1 **If necessary, open the `Pivotsalary` workbook, and select the
Employees sheet.**

2 **Click any cell in the pivot table located in the range K10:L20, and
click the PivotTable Wizard button in the PivotTable toolbar.**
The PivotTable and PivotChart Wizard–Step 3 of 3 dialog box opens.

3 **Click the Ḻayout button in the lower-left corner of the dialog box.**
The current pivot table specifications display—the Department in the Row
area and Sum of Salary in the data area.

4 **Drag the Position button to the Ṟow area below Department.**

5 **Drag the Shift button to the C̱olumn area.**
Check that layout specifications match those in Figure 13.10.

Drag the Shift field button
to the column area of the
diagram

Drag the Position field
button to the row area
of the diagram

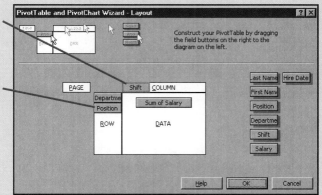

Figure 13.10
The current settings
specify that data in rows
will be organized first by
department, and then by
position within
department.

6 **Click OK to close the Layout dialog box, and click the F̱inish button.**
Excel expands the pivot table as shown in Figure 13.11. Notice that the information in the table has more than doubled as a result of these changes.

continues ▶

To Expand a Pivot Table Using the Layout Dialog Box (continued)

Figure 13.11

Adding a row field (Position) and a column field (Shift) greatly expands the pivot table.

The first row specification

The second row specification

The column specification

Sum of salaries for one position

Sum of salaries for one department

Example of expanded data: Sum of salaries for engineering technicians who work the 2nd shift

Columns added by the column specification

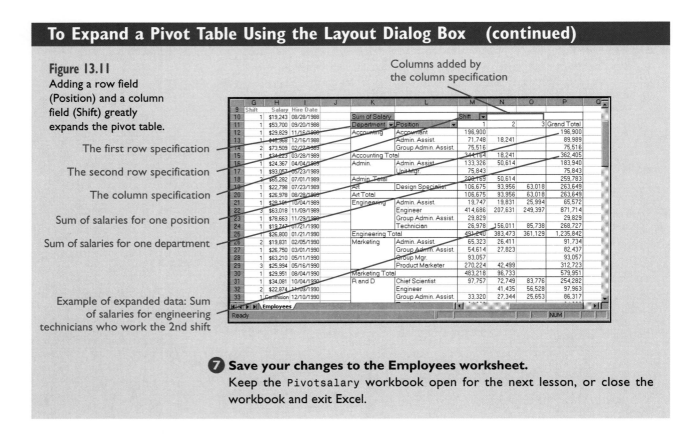

7 **Save your changes to the Employees worksheet.**
Keep the Pivotsalary workbook open for the next lesson, or close the workbook and exit Excel.

 Exam Note: **Changing the Order of Summary Data**
The order in which the field buttons appear in the Row, Column, and Data boxes of the Layout Dialog box determines the order in which data displays in the pivot table. To change the order, open the Layout dialog box and drag a field button to the desired location.

 ## Lesson 4: Removing, Hiding, and Showing Data

As your information needs change, you may want to display more or less summary data in a pivot table. The process for removing a field is opposite that of adding a field—drag the field away from the pivot table on the worksheet or drag the field away from the Row, Column, or Data area in the Layout dialog box. Showing or hiding detail in a field is as easy as pulling down a list of items in a field on the pivot table and checking or unchecking the field.

In this lesson, you modify the pivot table in preparation for creating a chart. You remove the Shift field, and hide data for the Engineering, R and D, and Warehouse departments. When you are done, only the Accounting, Administration, Art, Marketing, and Sales summary data display.

To Remove, Hide, and Show Data

❶ If necessary, open the `Pivotsalary` **workbook and select the Employees sheet.**

❷ Click the Shift button in the pivot table (cell M10), and drag it upward off the pivot table.

The three columns of Shift summary data are removed from the pivot table. Excel keeps the removed field button accessible by positioning it just above the pivot table.

❸ Display the Department drop-down list (cell K11).

Check marks in front of department names indicate the pivot table currently displays summary data for all departments (see Figure 13.12). Clicking a check mark deselects the box and temporarily hides the related data in the pivot table.

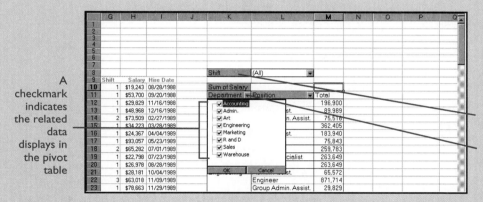

A checkmark indicates the related data displays in the pivot table

Figure 13.12
Click a checkmark to remove it and temporarily hide the associated data; click a blank box to show previously hidden data.

Field removed from the pivot table

Click here to display the field's drop-down list

❹ Uncheck the Engineering, R and D, and Warehouse items in the Department drop-down list.

❺ Click OK.

Summary data for the Engineering, R and D, and Warehouse departments does not display in the pivot table (see Figure 13.13).

	G	H	I	J	K	L	M	N	O	P	Q
7											
8					Shift	(All)					
9	Shift	Salary	Hire Date								
10	1	$19,243	08/28/1988		Sum of Salary						
11	1	$53,700	09/20/1988		Department	Position	Total				
12	1	$29,829	11/16/1988		Accounting	Accountant	196,900				
13	1	$48,968	12/16/1988			Admin. Assist.	89,989				
14	2	$73,509	02/27/1989			Group Admin. Assist.	75,516				
15	1	$34,223	03/28/1989		Accounting Total		362,405				
16	1	$24,367	04/04/1989		Admin.	Admin. Assist.	183,940				
17	1	$93,057	05/23/1989			Unit Mgr.	75,843				
18	2	$65,282	07/01/1989		Admin. Total		259,783				
19	1	$22,798	07/23/1989		Art	Design Specialist	263,649				
20	1	$26,978	08/28/1989		Art Total		263,649				
21	1	$28,181	10/04/1989		Marketing	Admin. Assist.	91,734				
22	3	$63,018	11/09/1989			Group Admin. Assist.	82,437				
23	1	$78,663	11/29/1989			Group Mgr.	93,057				
24	1	$19,747	01/21/1990			Product Marketer	312,723				
25	1	$26,800	01/21/1990		Marketing Total		579,951				
26	2	$19,831	02/05/1990		Sales	Group Admin. Assist.	26,750				
27	1	$26,750	03/01/1990			Sales	0				
28	1	$63,210	05/11/1990		Sales Total		26,750				
29	3	$25,994	05/16/1990		Grand Total		1,492,538				
30	1	$29,951	08/04/1990								

Figure 13.13
The modified pivot table displays summary data for the Accounting, Administration, Art, Marketing and Sales departments.

❻ Save your changes to the Employees worksheet.

Keep the `Pivotsalary` workbook open for the next lesson, or close the workbook and exit Excel.

Expert Lesson 5: Refreshing a Pivot Table

If you change data in a worksheet and that data impacts a summary calculation in a pivot table, Excel does not automatically update the pivot table. After making changes to the worksheet, you must **refresh** (recalculate) the pivot table.

A word of caution is in order to avoid using invalid data to make decisions. Because you are so used to Excel recalculating a worksheet automatically, it's easy to overlook refreshing any pivot tables that incorporate the changed data. In complex pivot tables, errors in summary amounts are difficult to detect visually. Therefore, acquire the habit of refreshing pivot tables after any change in worksheet data.

In this lesson, you change worksheet data, check for changes in pivot table amounts, refresh the pivot table, and check amounts again.

To Refresh a Pivot Table

1 If necessary, open the `Pivotsalary` workbook, and select the Employees sheet.

2 Scroll the worksheet to display columns H through M, starting with row 9.
Currently the salary for accountant Pat Collingwood is $48,968 (cell H13), and the sum of salaries for accountants is $196,900 (cell M12).

3 Change the contents of cell H13 to $50,968 instead of $48,968.
You changed the salary of an accountant, but the sum of salaries for accountants in the pivot table did not change ($196,900 in cell M12). Just looking at the summary data, it's not apparent that the pivot table contains an error.

4 Right-click anywhere within the pivot table, and choose Refresh Data.
The sum of salaries for accountants increases from $196,900 to $198,900 in cell M12.

5 Save your changes to the Employees worksheet.
Keep the `Pivotsalary` workbook open for the next lesson, or close the workbook and exit Excel.

Inside Stuff: **Other Ways to Select Refresh**
Refresh Data is an option on the shortcut menu that displays when you right-click within a pivot table. You can also choose the menu sequence <u>D</u>ata, <u>R</u>efresh Data or click the Refresh Data button on the PivotTable toolbar.

Lesson 6: Creating a Chart from Pivot Table Data

A pivot table provides informative summary data in rows and columns. Creating a chart based on pivot table data can be an effective means to interpret that data. You can create a chart quickly by right-clicking within an existing pivot table, and selecting Pivot<u>C</u>hart from the shortcut menu. You can also use the PivotTable and PivotChart Wizard to create both a chart and its related table at the same time.

For either method, Excel automatically creates a column chart on a separate sheet. You can then edit the PivotChart report just as you would any Excel chart—adding and deleting data points, changing chart type, applying number formats, and so forth. You can use any chart type except xy (scatter), bubble, and stock.

In this lesson, you create a column chart based on the pivot table in the Pivotsalary workbook. You then hide the Art department salary data, which limits the chart to Accounting, Admin, Marketing, and Sales salaries. You also convert the chart type to Line so you can compare the effectiveness of the two chart types.

To Create and Modify a Chart Based on Pivot Table Data

1 **If necessary, open the Pivotsalary workbook, and select the Employees sheet.**

2 **Right-click any cell in the pivot table (K10:M29), and select PivotChart on the shortcut menu.**

Excel creates a column chart based on the visible data in the pivot table (see Figure 13.14). Department and Position buttons display centered below the chart.

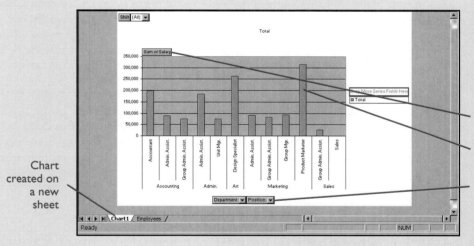

Figure 13.14
Each bar on the chart represents the sum of salaries for a specific position within a department.

Describes the summary analysis

Column chart based on pivot table data

Click a down arrow to add or remove data

Chart created on a new sheet

3 **Display the Department drop-down list, uncheck Art, and click OK.**

Columns depicting Art department data disappear from the chart.

4 **Right-click a blank area within the chart, and select Chart Type from the shortcut menu.**

The Chart Type dialog box opens.

5 **Select Line in the Chart type section of the dialog box, and click OK.**

A line chart replaces the column chart (see Figure 13.15).

6 **Click outside the chart to deselect it, and save your changes to the Pivotsalary workbook.**

Keep the Pivotsalary workbook open for the next lesson, or close the workbook and exit Excel.

continues ▶

To Create and Modify a Chart Based on Pivot Table Data   (continued)

Figure 13.15
You can change from one chart type to another by right-clicking within the chart, selecting Chart Type from the shortcut menu, and selecting a different type.

Data for the Art department is hidden

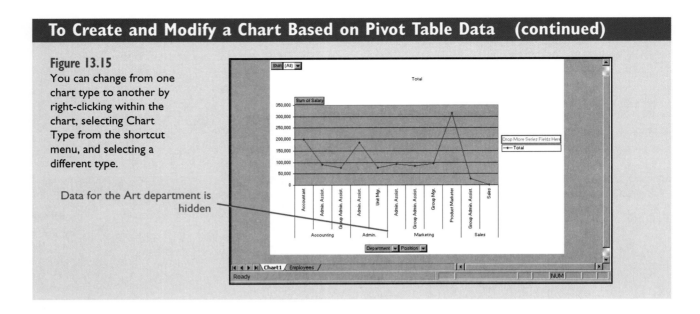

✍️ **Exam Note: How Changes in Pivot Table Data Affect a Related Chart**
If a chart is based on pivot table data—which in turn summarizes worksheet data—you should understand the impact on the chart of a change in underlying worksheet data. Such a chart is updated only when its associated pivot table is refreshed. If you delete a chart's related pivot table, that chart can no longer be modified.

💬 **Inside Stuff: Creating a Static Chart Based on Pivot Table Data**
You can create a static chart—also known as a nonpivoting chart—based on pivot table data. However, you must first copy the pivot table to another area and use Paste Special as Values to make the pivot table data static.

🖊️ Expert Lesson 7: Applying Predefined Formats to a Pivot Table

A variety of predefined formats can be applied to pivot tables. These formats not only improve the aesthetics of a table, they focus the reader's attention on different areas of the table.

Figure 13.16 illustrates three predefined formats. The first is PivotTable Classic, the default format automatically assigned to new pivot tables. The second is Table 1, one of ten table formats, or **nonindented formats**. The third is Report 1, one of ten report formats, or **indented formats**.

Figure 13.16
You can choose from a variety of predefined pivot table formats.

PivotTable Classic format (the default)

Sum of Salary		
Department ▾	Position ▾	Total
Accounting	Accountant	198,900
	Admin. Assist.	89,989
	Group Admin. Assist.	75,516
Accounting Total		364,405
Admin.	Admin. Assist.	183,940
	Unit Mgr.	75,843
Admin. Total		259,783
Marketing	Admin. Assist.	91,734
	Group Admin. Assist.	82,437
	Group Mgr.	93,057
	Product Marketer	312,723
Marketing Total		579,951
Sales	Group Admin. Assist.	26,750
	Sales	0
Sales Total		26,750
Grand Total		1,230,889

Department is a column field

Salary	Department ▾				
Position ▾	Accounting	Admin.	Marketing	Sales	Grand Total
Accountant	198,900				198,900
Admin. Assist.	89,989	183,940	91,734		365,663
Group Admin. Assist.	75,516		82,437	26,750	184,703
Group Mgr.			93,057		93,057
Product Marketer			312,723		312,723
Sales				0	0
Unit Mgr.		75,843			75,843
Grand Total	364,405	259,783	579,951	26,750	1,230,889

Table 1 format (one of 10 nonindented formats)

Department becomes a row field

Department	Position ▾	Salary
Accounting		364,405
	Accountant	198,900
	Admin. Assist.	89,989
	Group Admin. Assist.	75,516
Admin.		259,783
	Admin. Assist.	183,940
	Unit Mgr.	75,843
Marketing		579,951
	Admin. Assist.	91,734
	Group Admin. Assist.	82,437
	Group Mgr.	93,057
	Product Marketer	312,723
Sales		26,750
	Group Admin. Assist.	26,750
	Sales	0
Grand Total		1,230,889

Report 1 format (one of 10 indented formats)

Some formats work better than others, depending on the layout and complexity of the pivot table. You should experiment with different types of formats to see which best presents your data. In this lesson you apply a table format to a pivot table, switch to a report format, and add a field to the table.

To Apply a Predefined Format to a Pivot Table

1 If necessary, open the Pivotsalary workbook, and select the **Employees sheet.**

2 Right-click any cell in the pivot table (K10:M27).

3 Select Forma**t** Report on the shortcut menu.
The AutoFormat dialog box opens (see Figure 13.17).

4 Scroll the gallery of formats.

5 Double-click the Table 1 format (the description displays below the associated format), and then click anywhere outside the table to deselect it.
The pivot table displays in the Table 1 format (see the second of three pivot tables in Figure 13.16).

continues ▶

To Apply a Predefined Format to a Pivot Table (continued)

Figure 13.17
The choices in this AutoFormat dialog box are specific to pivot tables.

Scroll to view other predefined table and report formats

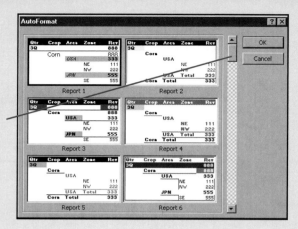

6 Right-click within the pivot table, and select Forma**t** Report on the shortcut menu.

7 Double-click the Report 1 format, and click anywhere outside the table to deselect it.

The pivot table displays in the Report 1 format (see the third of three pivot tables in Figure 13.16).

8 Display the Department drop-down list (cell K10), and uncheck the four fields currently in the pivot table—Accounting, Admin, Marketing and Sales.

9 Check two fields, Engineering and R and D, and click OK.

The pivot table continues to display the Report 1 format.

10 Right-click within the pivot table, and select **W**izard on the shortcut menu.

11 Click the **L**ayout button in the lower-left corner of the PivotTable and PivotChart Wizard–Step 3 of 3 dialog box.

12 Drag the Shift field button to the Row area below the Position field.

Three field buttons are now in the row area in the order—from top to bottom—Department, Position, and Shift.

13 Click OK, and click **F**inish.

The report displays the layered (indented) layout shown in Figure 13.18.

14 Close the PivotTable toolbar, and save your changes to the **Pivotsalary** workbook.

Keep the Pivotsalary workbook open for the next lesson, or close the workbook and exit Excel.

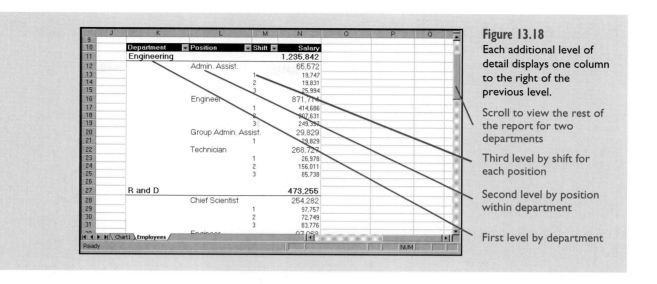

Figure 13.18
Each additional level of detail displays one column to the right of the previous level.

Scroll to view the rest of the report for two departments

Third level by shift for each position

Second level by position within department

First level by department

 Exam Note: **Removing a Predefined Format**

To remove a predefined format, and any other character and cell formats applied manually, display the gallery of predefined formats and choose None. You may not get the results you want, however, because Excel simply removes effects such as borders, shading, italics, and changes in font size. Because cell contents remain in place, the action does not move any fields, change display to *indented* or *nonindented format*, or remove blank lines inserted between items in rows.

You can also reproduce the original layout of a pivot table by saving the workbook just before you apply a predefined format. If using the None option produces unwanted effects, you can close the workbook without saving your changes, and then reopen the workbook as it was before you applied the predefined format.

Lesson 8: Displaying Pivot Tables on the Web

Using Excel 2000, you can make a pivot table accessible to others through the Internet or an intranet site. If you select Excel's Add Interactivity option, users of the Web page can change layout and data fields in the pivot table. This option is only available if users have Office Web Components installed and are using version 4.01 or later of the Microsoft Internet Explorer Web browser. If interactivity is not an option given your computing environment, you can still save the report in HTML format and publish it as a *noninteractive table*—one that can be viewed, but not changed.

An interactive pivot table on a Web page is called a *PivotTable list*. This list does not have worksheet row and column labels, but other features are similar to those available for pivot table reports in Excel. Onscreen Help provides extensive information about feature differences between PivotTable lists on Web sites and PivotTable reports in Excel.

In this lesson, you save a worksheet containing a pivot table as a Web page on your own computer system (sometimes referred to as a local system). You can then view this pivot table using any browser software to see how the table will display on the Web. Your instructor will provide additional directions if your computing environment supports publishing an interactive pivot table.

To Display a Pivot Table on the Web

1 **If necessary, open the Pivotsalary workbook, and select the Employees sheet.**

2 **Choose File, Save as Web Page.**
The Save As dialog box opens, enabling you to select among Web-related options.

3 **Click the Publish Button.**
The Publish as Web Page dialog box opens.

4 **Display the Choose drop-down box, and select Items on Employees.**

5 **In the box below Items on Employees, select PivotTable (see Figure 13.19)**

Figure 13.19
Select the pivot table in the range K10:O32 as the item to publish.

Checking this box allows viewers to make changes in worksheet data and the pivot table if Microsoft Office Web Component and Microsoft Internet Explorer 4.01 or later are available

Specify the location and filename for publishing the pivot table here

Check here to open the Web page using your system's default browser

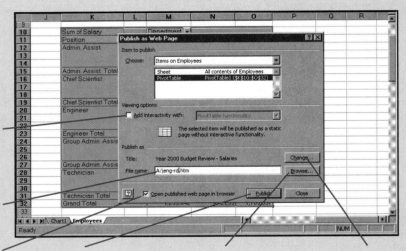

Click here to publish after making other selections

Click here to locate the drive, folder, Web server or FTP location where you want to publish your Web page

Click here to specify a title above the pivot table on the Web page

6 **Make sure the Add interactivity with check box is not checked).**

7 **Click the Change button, type Year 2000 Budget Review - Salaries, and click OK.**
The title you specified displays above the File name text box.

8 **Click the Browse button, specify the filename eng-rd.htm and the location to store the pivot table, and click OK (see Figure 13.19).**
Figure 13.19 illustrates saving to a disk in drive A. You can specify the location where you have been storing your other project files.

9 **Click the Publish button at the bottom of the Publish as Web Page dialog box.**
This completes the process to publish a pivot table that can be viewed but not edited on an Intranet site or the Web. If you have access to a Web browser, complete the remaining steps.

⑩ If your default web browser does not automatically open, and display the pivot table with engineering and R and D summary data, activate your Web browser and use its File, Open feature to see how the pivot table displays. Figure 13.20 shows the pivot table viewed through the Netscape browser.

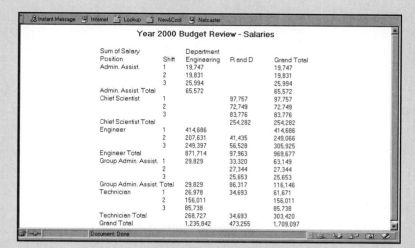

Figure 13.20
The pivot table displays as a Web page in a browser.

⑪ Close your browser, and close the Pivotsalary workbook.
This concludes Project 13. Continue with end-of-project exercises or exit Excel.

 Exam Note: Interactive Pivot Tables
If you check the `Add interactivity with` box on the Publish as Web Page dialog box, you can choose between Spreadsheet functionality (allows change of data and formulas) or PivotTable functionality (allows change in number and location of fields). If PivotTable functionality is active, you can select or deselect field items in a pivot table on a Web page by using drop-down lists, just as you would do if working in Excel. You can also drag and drop fields, and expand or collapse the level of detail provided.

Summary

You began this project by viewing onscreen Help on creating pivot tables and related charts and then started the process of creating a table by using the PivotTable and PivotChart Wizard to specify the data source and location for the table. You completed the table directly on the worksheet by dragging field names from the PivotTable toolbar to the appropriate areas of a pivot table shell. In subsequent lessons, you learned how to add and remove fields, hide and show fields, refresh a pivot table, and create a chart from pivot table data. You completed the project by applying predefined formats and publishing the pivot table as a noninteractive Web page.

You can reinforce and extend your learning by exploring the many onscreen Help topics on creating PivotTable and PivotChart reports and experimenting with those features. For example, you can make a PivotTable report available on the Web, so that others can view and interact with the data. Try displaying the top or bottom items for a field. Learn how to use page fields and sort the data in a pivot table. Find out about grouping and ungrouping data in PivotTable and PivotChart reports.

Checking Concepts and Terms

True/False

For each of the following, check *T* or *F* to indicate whether the statement is true or false.

__T __F   **1.** An interactive pivot table on a Web page can be accessed and modified from any browser. [L8]

__T __F   **2.** A pivot table can be embedded on the current worksheet or created on a separate worksheet. [L2]

__T __F   **3.** The order in which buttons are placed in the row, column, and data areas of a pivot table diagram does not affect the layout of the finished table. [L3]

__T __F   **4.** When working with PivotTable and PivotChart reports, unchecking an item on a field drop-down list hides, but does not delete, that field. [L4]

__T __F   **5.** When you delete a pivot table, the pivot chart remains in the workbook. [L6]

Multiple Choice

Circle the letter of the correct answer for each of the following.

1. Which of the following is a true statement? [L2]

   a. To delete a pivot table, right-click within it and select Delete from the shortcut menu.

   b. To delete a pivot table, click within the pivot table to select it, and press Del.

   c. both a and b

   d. neither a nor b

2. Which of the following chart types cannot be used to chart pivot table data? [L6]

   a. line

   b. xy (scatter)

   c. column

   d. all of the above

3. If you wanted to apply an indented format, which of the following predefined formats would you choose? [L7]

   a. PivotTable Classic

   b. Report 1

   c. Table 1

   d. none of the above

4. Which of the following is a summary calculation available in a pivot table? [L2]

   a. max

   b. average

   c. both a and b

   d. neither a nor b

5. Which of the following is a term associated with up-dating the data in a pivot table after a change in the data source for the table? [L5]

   a. recalculate

   b. redo

   c. refresh

   d. none of the above

Skill Drill

Skill Drill exercises reinforce project skills. Each skill reinforced is the same, or nearly the same, as a skill presented in the project. Detailed instructions are provided in a step-by-step format.

Each exercise is independent of the others, so that you can complete the exercises in any order. Be sure to save the workbook after completing each exercise. If you need a paper copy of the completed exercise, enter your name centered in a header before printing. Other print options have already been set to print compressed to one page and to display the filename, sheet name, and current date in a footer.

Before beginning your first Project 13 Skill Drill exercise, complete the following steps:

1. Open the file named e-1302, and save it as e13drill.
The workbook contains four sheets: an overview sheet and three exercise sheets named #1-NewEdit, #2-Refresh, and #3-MaxMin.

2. Click the Overview sheet to view the organization of the Project 13 Skill Drill Exercises workbook.

If you need more than one work session to complete the desired exercises, continue working on e13drill instead of starting over on the original e-1302 file.

I. Creating and Expanding a Pivot Table

You keep track of your contributions in an Excel list. Now you'd like to find out how much you gave to each agency during the year.

To create a pivot table:

1. If necessary, open the e13drill workbook; then select the #1-NewEdit worksheet.

2. Click any cell in the list range A13:E42.

3. Choose Data, PivotTable, and PivotChart Report, and click the Next button.
The default settings for data and type of report—a pivot table based on an Excel list—are accepted.

4. Verify that the specified range is $A$13:$E$42, and click the Next button.

5. Click Existing worksheet, and select cell G14.

6. Click Layout in the lower-left corner of the wizard's Step 3 of 3 dialog box.

7. Drag the Agency field button onto the ROW area of the pivot table diagram.

8. Drag the Declared field button onto the DATA area. Check that Sum of Declared (or some variation, such as Sum of Declared Val or Sum of Declared V) displays in the DATA area. If another calculation displays, double-click it and change the setting to Sum.

9. Click OK, and click Finish.
A pivot table displaying a summary of contributions by agency displays in the range G14:H22. The Grand Total of contributions is 4685.

10. Right-click any cell in the pivot table.

11. Select Wizard from the shortcut menu, and click the Layout button.

12. Drag the Receipt field button onto the COLUMN area.

13. Click OK, and click Finish.
Two new columns display between the Agency and Grand Total columns. The total of contributions for which no receipt was provided is 685. Contributions confirmed by receipts total 4000.

2. Refreshing a Pivot Table

After creating a pivot table, you discover an error in the amount of a contribution to the Girl Scouts. You need to edit the worksheet data and refresh the pivot table.

To create a pivot table, change data, and refresh the pivot table:

1. If necessary, open the **e13drill** workbook; then select the #2-Refresh worksheet.

2. Click any cell in the list range A13:E42.

3. Choose Data, PivotTable, and PivotChart Report, and click the Next button.

4. Verify that the specified range is $A$13:$E$42, and click the Next button.

5. Click Existing worksheet, select cell G14, and click Layout in the lower-left corner of the wizard's Step 3 of 3 dialog box.

6. Drag the Agency field button onto the ROW area of the pivot table diagram, and drag the Declared field button onto the DATA area.

7. Click OK, and click Finish.
   The total for contributions to the Girl Scouts (100) displays in cell H18 of the pivot table.

8. Click cell B16 in the list of contributions, and change 100 to **200**.

9. Scroll to view the pivot table, and note that cell H18 still displays 100 as the total contributions to the Girl Scouts organization.

10. Right-click any cell in the pivot table, and select Refresh Data from the shortcut menu.
    Now cell H18 displays the correct amount—200.

3. Creating Summary Data Using Max or Min

As you analyze current residential real estate listings, you decide to display the highest selling price for a home in each area. Next you want to switch the display to the lowest price at which someone could buy into each area. To do this you can use Max and Min summary calculations respectively.

To create summary data using Max or Min:

1. If necessary, open the **e13drill** workbook; then select the #3-MaxMin worksheet.

2. Click any cell within the database, and activate the PivotTable and PivotChart Report Wizard.

3. Specify that you want to create a pivot table in the current worksheet to the right of the associated list of homes for sale.

4. Lay out the pivot table to include Area as a row field and Price as the Data item.

5. Double-click Sum of Price in the DATA area, specify Max as the summary calculation on Price, and generate the pivot table.
   Excel creates a two-column pivot table. The second column displays the highest asking price for a home in the corresponding area. For example, the highest asking price for a home in Champions Village is 156400.

6. Change the summary calculation from Max to Min. Excel replaces the prices in the second column with the lowest asking price for a home in each corresponding area. For example, the lowest asking price for a home in Champions Village is 102900.

Challenge

Challenge exercises expand on or are somewhat related to skills presented in the lessons. Each exercise provides a brief narrative introduction, followed by instructions in a numbered-step format that are not as detailed as those in the Skill Drill section.

Each exercise is independent of the others, so that you may complete the exercises in any order. Be sure to save the workbook after completing each exercise. If you need a paper copy of the completed exercise, enter your name centered in a header before printing. Other print options have already been set to print compressed to one page and to display the filename, sheet name, and current date in a footer.

Before beginning your first Project 13 Challenge exercise, complete the following steps:

1. Open the file named **e-1303**, and save it as **e13challenge**.
   The workbook contains four sheets: an overview and three exercise sheets named #1-Modify, #2-PivotChart, and #3-MultiCalc.

2. Click the Overview sheet to view the organization of the Project 13 Challenge Exercises workbook.

If you need more than one work session to complete the desired exercises, continue working on the **e13challenge** workbook instead of starting all over on the original e-1303 file.

1. Changing the Number and Location of Fields

You just created a one-dimension pivot table to display the counts of homes in each area—the list of areas in one column, and the counts in the adjacent column to the right. Now, you'd like to modify the table to display counts based on two dimensions. For each area listed across a worksheet row, you want counts of homes with the same number of bedrooms and further subdivided by type of heat. That way you can easily answer a question such as "How many three bedroom homes in Glenn Lakes have electric heat?"

To change the number and location of fields in a pivot table:

1. If necessary, open the **e13challenge** workbook; then select the #1-Modify worksheet.

2. Right-click any cell within the pivot table (K5:L17), and access the Layout dialog box through the PivotTable and PivotChart Report Wizard.

3. Change Area from a <u>R</u>OW field to a <u>C</u>OLUMN field in the pivot table diagram.

4. Set up two <u>R</u>OW fields, Heat followed by Bed, and close or exit as needed to generate the revised table.
   Excel computes the requested counts in a pivot table that extends across many columns. Scroll to view counts at a detailed level. For example, five 3-bedroom homes have electric heat in the Glenn Lakes area.

5. Apply the Report 6 AutoFormat to the pivot table.

2. Creating a PivotChart Report Using the Wizard

You have already created a chart from an existing pivot table. Now you'd like to create a chart and its associated pivot table at the same time.

To create a PivotChart report:

1. If necessary, open the **e13challenge** workbook; then select the #2-PivotChart worksheet.

2. Click any cell in the list range A5:I40, and activate the PivotTable and PivotChart Wizard.

3. Specify that you want to create a PivotChart report, with the corresponding pivot table located at cell K5, and exit the wizard.
   Excel displays a blank Chart1, with instructions to drag data items, category fields, and series fields as desired.

4. Drag the Price button from the PivotTable toolbar to the Data Item area in the chart.

5. Follow a similar procedure to set up Area as a category field.

6. Change Sum of Price to `Average of Price`.

7. View the corresponding worksheet (#2-PivotChart).
   Excel automatically created the pivot table on which the chart is based.

8. Restore display of the chart and add titles and other documentation as appropriate.

9. Change display of Y-axis values to include commas and dollar signs.

3. Specifying More Than One Summary Calculation

For each area in the residential listings database, you would like to know the number of homes available for sale and the average price of homes.

To specify more than one summary calculation:

1. If necessary, open the `e13challenge` workbook; then select the #3-MultiCalc worksheet.

2. Click any cell within the database, and activate the PivotTable and PivotChart Report Wizard.

3. Specify that you want to create a pivot table in the current worksheet to the right of the associated list of homes for sale.

4. Lay out the pivot table to include Area as a row field and Price as a Data item two times.

5. Specify Count as the summary calculation on the first Price data item, and specify Average as the summary calculation on the second Price data item.

6. Close or exit as needed to generate the pivot table.

7. Change the format of numbers to comma, zero decimal places.
   The table displays in PivotTable Classic format. Eight houses are listed for sale in Glenn Lakes, at an average price of 159,975.

8. Apply a Table 6 predefined format.
   Notice that Excel does not retain number formatting when you apply a predefined format.

9. Change the display of numbers to comma, zero decimal places.

Discovery Zone

Discovery Zone exercises require advanced knowledge of topics presented in *MOUS Essentials* lessons, application of skills from multiple lessons, or self-directed learning of new skills.

Each exercise is independent of the others, so that you can complete the exercises in any order. Be sure to save the workbook after completing each exercise. If you need a paper copy of the completed exercise, enter your name centered in a header before printing. Other print options have already been set to print compressed to one page and to display the filename, sheet name, and current date in a footer.

Before beginning your first Project 13 Discovery Zone exercise, complete the following steps:

1. Open the file named e-1304, and save it as e13discovery.
   The workbook contains three sheets: an overview and two exercise sheets named #1-MultiPivot and #2-Page.

2. Click the Overview sheet to view the organization of the Project 13 Discovery Zone Exercises workbook.

If you need more than one work session to complete the desired exercises, continue working on e13discovery instead of starting over on the original e-1304 file.

1. Creating Multiple Pivot Tables

Your supervisor has asked you to review the shipping data for Great Wilderness Outfitters, Inc (GWO). This analysis already contains a great deal of information about GWO's shipping performance. The list begins in row 10 on the #1-MultiPivot sheet of the e13discovery workbook. It contains data on the day of the week an order was taken and which shift processed the order.

Through PivotTable and PivotChart reports you can determine in more detail the day of the week and which shift has the best or worst performance. Generate and save as many variations of pivot tables as you need to identify the problem areas.

2. Including a Page Field in a Pivot Table

You know how to create two-dimensional pivot tables by setting up row and column fields. Your data analysis can take on a third dimension if you set up a page field. For example, if you are analyzing employees' salary data, you can set up a pivot table to view summary analysis by Position (row) and Shift (column) for each Department (page).

Use onscreen Help to learn about the page dimension, and display the #2-Page worksheet in the e13discovery workbook. Create the three-dimensional pivot table described in the first paragraph (sum on the Salary field). When the table is complete, use the Page pull-down button to page through each department's salary data.

PinPoint Assessment

You have completed this project and its associated lessons, and have had an opportunity to assess your skills through the end-of-project questions and exercises. Now use the PinPoint software Evaluation Mode to further assess your comprehension of the specific exam activities you have just learned. You can also use the PinPoint Trainer Mode and the Show Me tutorials to practice these exam activities.

Creating Consolidated Data, Outlines, Views, and Reports

Key terms introduced in this project include

- Auto Outline
- consolidate
- custom view
- Report Manager
- 3D reference
- worksheet outline
- workspace

Objectives	Required Activity for MOUS	Exam Level
➤ Consolidate Data in Multiple Worksheets	Link worksheets and consolidate data using 3-D references	Core
➤ Consolidate Multiple Workbooks	Link workbooks	Expert
➤ Create an Auto Outline	Use grouping and outlines	Expert
➤ Create a Manual Outline	Use grouping and outlines	Expert
➤ Create and Use Custom Views	Use the Report Manager	Expert
➤ Create Reports Using Report Manager	Use the Report Manager	Expert
➤ Edit and Print Reports Using Report Manager	Use the Report Manager	Expert
➤ Save a Group of Workbooks in a Workspace File	Using a workspace	Expert

Why Would I Do This?

Generating information from spreadsheet data, such as a sales report, can be simple or complex. For example, if you are responsible for only one store in one city, you can enter data in a single worksheet and immediately view or print the results. If, however, you manage multiple stores in several states or countries, you must combine data from many workbooks and communicate the information in a useful format.

Each level of management in an organization needs to view its data in different ways, and usually with little or no detail. For example, a mid-level manager may need to see only subtotals of sales data by a salesperson without looking at all the details. A higher-level manager may need to see that same data summarized by sales region. Still others may only need to see the data as a chart.

In this project, you combine or display data from more than one worksheet or workbook, and create custom views that can be included in custom reports. You also create a file that enables you to open workbooks as a group and to display those workbooks in a predefined arrangement.

Lesson 1: Consolidating Data in Multiple Worksheets

Excel workbooks are often used to record data for different time periods, for different products, for different departments, and for different locations. When this is the case, it is often necessary to **consolidate** data stored in multiple worksheets into a single worksheet. In this lesson, data accumulated for twelve months is summarized using a **3-D reference**, which refers to the same cell or range on multiple sheets.

To Consolidate Data in Multiple Worksheets

1 Open e-1401, and save it as AnnualSales.

2 Click the Jan and Feb monthly worksheets, and note that they have the same structure.

3 Click the AllYear worksheet, and click cell C5.

4 Type =SUM(in cell C5.

5 Click the Jan worksheet tab.

6 Press and hold down ⚹Shift, and click the Dec worksheet tab. Release ⚹Shift.

The sheet tabs named Jan through Dec display with a white background, indicating that they are grouped. Whatever action you apply to one worksheet in the group impacts all the selected worksheets. The last sheet selected (Dec) is the active sheet. Now select the cell whose contents you want to sum across all selected worksheets.

7 Click cell C5, type the closing right parenthesis, and click the green check mark at the left end of the formula bar.

Excel automatically restores the display of the original AllYear worksheet (see Figure 14.1). The completed formula in cell C5 sums the contents of cell C5 for all of the monthly worksheets.

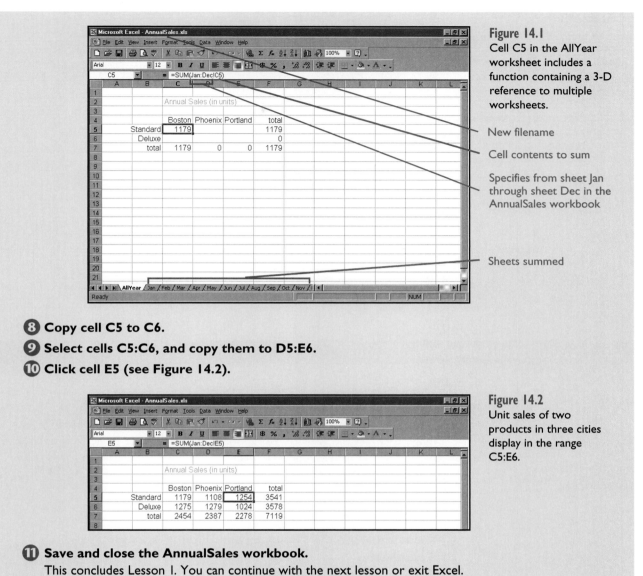

Figure 14.1
Cell C5 in the AllYear worksheet includes a function containing a 3-D reference to multiple worksheets.

New filename

Cell contents to sum

Specifies from sheet Jan through sheet Dec in the AnnualSales workbook

Sheets summed

8 **Copy cell C5 to C6.**

9 **Select cells C5:C6, and copy them to D5:E6.**

10 **Click cell E5 (see Figure 14.2).**

Figure 14.2
Unit sales of two products in three cities display in the range C5:E6.

11 **Save and close the AnnualSales workbook.**

This concludes Lesson 1. You can continue with the next lesson or exit Excel.

Lesson 2: Consolidating Multiple Workbooks

Often, the data to be consolidated is stored in different workbooks that could even be on different computers on a network. For example, sales data for an organization might be maintained at different regional headquarters. Periodically, copies of each region's workbooks are forwarded to a central location, such as a corporate headquarters or accounting center. In these cases, the data in the workbooks must be consolidated.

In this lesson, you use the Consolidate option on the Data menu to combine data about two sales regions. Each region's data is stored in its own file (see Figure 14.3).

Figure 14.3
Data to consolidate must occupy the same cells on each worksheet, such as Units Sold of the Deluxe model in cell D6.

Set of data to consolidate

Additional product

Set of data to consolidate

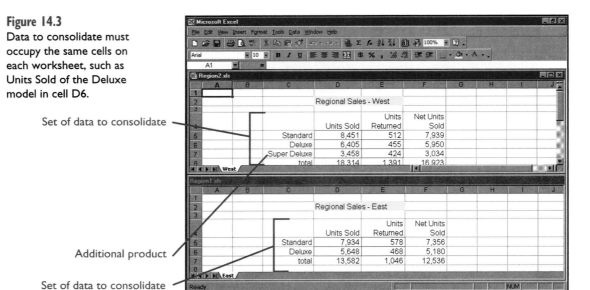

To Consolidate Multiple Workbooks

❶ Open files Region1.xls and Region2.xls.
These are the two workbooks to consolidate in a new workbook (refer to Figure 14.3). Each includes a single named range called Data, defined as the range C4:F7 in the Region1 workbook and C4:F8 in the Region2 workbook. Note that the named ranges contain the same row and column labels; however, the West region includes a product that is not sold in the East region.

❷ Open a new workbook and save it as TotalSales.
Three workbooks are now open—Region1, Region2, and TotalSales.

❸ Select cell B3 in the TotalSales workbook, and choose Data, Consolidate.
The Consolidate dialog box displays. The Sum function is already selected in the Function text box, but other functions are available to use in a consolidation.

❹ Type Region?.xls!Data in the Reference text box.

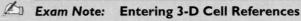

Exam Note: **Entering 3-D Cell References**
The '?' after Region is a wildcard character indicating that you want to use any file that contains a single character after Region—in this case, Region1 and Region2. The '!' character indicates the end of the filename. It is followed by the name of the data range, which must be the same in every file.

In this lesson, the data ranges are named Data, but any name can be used. This example assumes the data files to consolidate are both in the same folder. If the files have different names, different locations or different named ranges, you must enter them individually, clicking the Add button after each entry.

⑤ Select the three check boxes at the bottom of the dialog box.

Figure 14.4 displays the completed Consolidate dialog box settings. Check ⊤op row and ⊾eft column if you want to use the labels in the source data as labels in the consolidated results. Check Create links to ⊇ource data if you want to update the consolidated data automatically each time the source data changes.

Saved blank workbook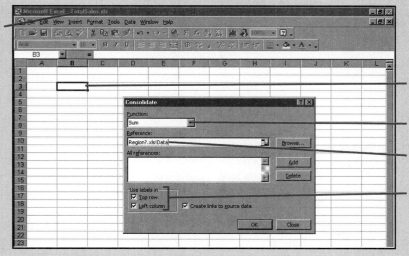

Figure 14.4
Enter the reference source in the Consolidate dialog box.

Starting position for consolidated data

Click here to display other functions for use in consolidation

Specifies the source data

Check to use labels from the source data as labels for consolidated data

⑥ Click OK, and resize columns and format data as necessary to view the consolidated results (see Figure 14.5).

The effects of the consolidation are shown in Figure 14.5. Note that outlining buttons have been added on the left side of the screen. Clicking the + symbol expands the view of collapsed data.

Detail in rows 7 and 8 is hidden

Click here to expand the outline to include rows 7 and 8

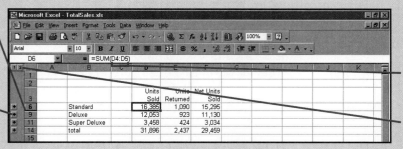

Figure 14.5
Detail rows are hidden in a collapsed outline.

Reference to cells in this worksheet

Click the Row level symbol (2) to expand your view of all consolidated data

⑦ Click the Row level symbol, the 2 button near the upper-left corner of the worksheet frame; then click cell D5.

Rows hidden in the collapsed view are now expanded to reveal detail data (see Figure 14.6). Note also that the reference in the formula bar refers to source data in another workbook. In the expanded view, vertical level bars display to the left of row numbers and horizontal level bars may also display above the column letters. The level bars span groups of data. A + or – symbol displays at an end of each level bar. Clicking the – symbol collapses the view.

⑧ Save and close the TotalSales workbook.

⑨ Close the Region1 and Region2 workbooks without saving changes.

continues ▶

To Consolidate Multiple Workbooks (continued)

Figure 14.6
Detail rows are revealed when you expand the outline.

Vertical level bar

Click here to collapse the outline and hide detail rows 4 and 5

Click here to hide rows 7 and 8

Reference to a cell in another workbook

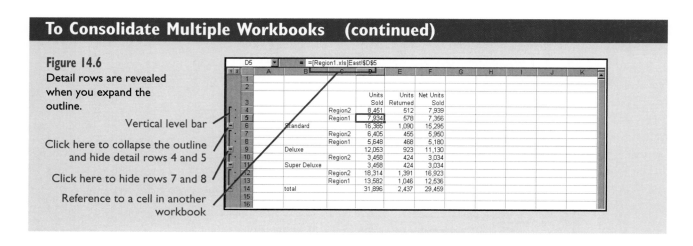

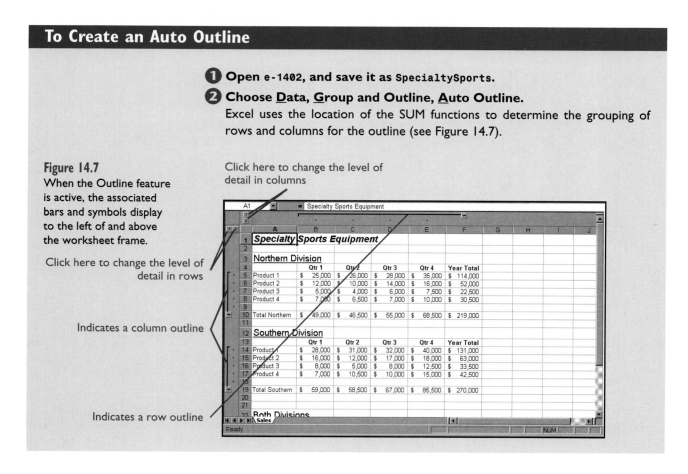

Expert Lesson 3: Creating an Auto Outline

As illustrated in the previous lesson, Data Consolidation creates a **worksheet outline**—a set of buttons and symbols at the top and side of the worksheet that enable you to hide and unhide certain rows and columns. Worksheet outlines can also be created in other contexts and can be very useful in situations where you want to expand and collapse the amount of data displayed.

In this exercise, you create an **Auto Outline** in which Excel examines your worksheet and creates an outline for you. After the outline is created you expand and collapse the data view.

To Create an Auto Outline

1 Open e-1402, and save it as SpecialtySports.

2 Choose **Data, Group and Outline, Auto Outline.**
Excel uses the location of the SUM functions to determine the grouping of rows and columns for the outline (see Figure 14.7).

Figure 14.7
When the Outline feature is active, the associated bars and symbols display to the left of and above the worksheet frame.

Click here to change the level of detail in columns

Click here to change the level of detail in rows

Indicates a column outline

Indicates a row outline

❸ Click the Hide detail symbol (–) to the left of row 10.
The Northern Division data has collapsed, leaving only the summary data in row 10. A Show detail symbol (+) displays to the left of the row number.

❹ Click the '1' Column and Row level symbols at the upper-left corner of the worksheet frame.
Both outlines collapse, leaving only the summary rows and columns. Show detail symbols (+) appear at the left of summary rows and above the summary column.

❺ Click the '2' Column and Row level symbols at the upper-left corner of the worksheet frame.
Both outlines expand to display data in full detail.

❻ Save and close the SpecialtySports workbook.

***Exam Note:*   Removing an Outline**
To remove an entire outline, click any cell on the worksheet, and choose Data, Group and Outline, Clear Outline. Removing an outline does not change any data on the worksheet.

***Inside Stuff:*   Printing Outlined Data**
You can expand or collapse outlined data to vary printed output. Rows or columns that are hidden from view in a collapsed outline do not print.

Lesson 4: Creating a Manual Outline

Auto Outline relies on structural cues such as functions that indicate summary data, or a blank row or column. In the previous lesson, for example, Auto Outline used the SUM functions in the worksheet to determine how to group the data. You can also create your own outlines using a four-step process: sort the data, insert blank rows or columns to separate groups, define each set of data as a group, and activate outlining.

In this lesson, you insert a blank row to separate data that is already sorted by type of use—business or personal. After the data is separated, you define the two data sets as groups, turn on the outline feature, and view various levels of detail.

To Create a Manual Outline

❶ Open e-1403, and save it as `OutlineSurvey`.
Note that the rows are sorted by Type Use. You want to use outlining so you can view either the Business or Personal accounts.

❷ Select row 30, and choose Insert, Rows.
A blank row is inserted between the business use and personal use data.

continues ▶

To Create a Manual Outline   (continued)

③ Select rows 14:29.

④ Choose Data, Group and Outline, Group.

⑤ Select rows 31:44.

⑥ Choose Data, Group and Outline, Group.

⑦ Click the Hide detail symbol (–) to the left of row 45.

Figure 14.8 shows the completed outline with the business accounts expanded and the personal accounts collapsed.

Figure 14.8

Results of manually applying the Group and Outline feature to data.

Rows 31 through 44 are hidden

Click here to collapse Business data

Click here to expand Personal data

ID	Type Use	Type Pmt	Car Size	Date Rented	Date Returned	Days Rented	Daily Rate	Rental Cost	Customer Rating	Favorite Sport	Favorite Magazine
7	Bus	acct	Mid Size	1/1/2000	1/5/2000	4	$ 11.50	$ 46.00	3	tennis	Fortune
8	Bus	acct	Mid Size	1/12/2000	1/13/2000	1	$ 11.50	$ 11.50	1	football	other
10	Bus	acct	Full Size	1/23/2000	1/27/2000	4	$ 14.00	$ 56.00	2	basketball	U.S. News
19	Bus	acct	Compact	3/13/2000	3/15/2000	2	$ 8.90	$ 17.80	4	baseball	Newsweek
21	Bus	acct	Full Size	2/8/2000	2/14/2000	6	$ 14.00	$ 84.00	2	basketball	U.S. News
28	Bus	acct	Compact	3/13/2000	3/15/2000	2	$ 8.90	$ 17.80	4	baseball	Newsweek
29	Bus	acct	Full Size	2/8/2000	2/14/2000	6	$ 14.00	$ 84.00	2	basketball	Time
9	Bus	cc	Truck	2/1/2000	2/7/2000	6	$ 19.00	$ 114.00	4	other	Fortune
13	Bus	cc	Full Size	1/9/2000	1/12/2000	3	$ 14.00	$ 42.00	4	golf	U.S. News
15	Bus	cc	Compact	3/2/2000	3/4/2000	2	$ 8.90	$ 17.80	1	baseball	WSJ
16	Bus	cc	Full Size	2/29/2000	3/14/2000	14	$ 14.00	$ 196.00	4	golf	U.S. News
17	Bus	cc	Truck	2/25/2000	2/27/2000	2	$ 19.00	$ 38.00	5	other	other
20	Bus	cc	Compact	1/9/2000	1/12/2000	3	$ 8.90	$ 26.70	4	football	Time
23	Bus	cc	Luxury	2/9/2000	2/16/2000	7	$ 26.00	$ 182.00	1	golf	WSJ
26	Bus	cc	Truck	2/25/2000	2/27/2000	2	$ 19.00	$ 38.00	5	other	Newsweek
30	Bus	cc	Full Size	1/9/2000	1/12/2000	3	$ 14.00	$ 42.00	4	golf	Time

⑧ Save and close the OutlineSurvey workbook.

 Exam Note: Ungrouping Segments of an Outline

To ungroup a segment of an outline, first select the columns or rows you want to ungroup. Choose **D**ata, **G**roup and Outline, **U**ngroup.

You can select the segment to ungroup by highlighting the columns or rows, or by holding down and clicking the appropriate Show detail symbol, Hide detail symbol, or level bar.

Expert Lesson 5: Creating and Using Custom Views

When you use a workbook on a daily basis, you probably find yourself clicking particular worksheets and scrolling through them in order to find cells that are of special interest. By creating **custom views**, you can save the views you use most often and recall them when you need them. You can also include custom views in custom reports, as illustrated in the next lesson.

Settings that remain in effect in a custom view include column widths, display options, Group and Outline settings, window size and position, split and frozen window settings, the active worksheet, selected cell ranges at the time a view is created, hidden rows and columns, filters and sorts, and print settings. You must apply all settings to the workbook and its worksheets before you create the custom view. Custom views apply to the entire workbook.

In this lesson, you create a custom view and add it to the list of other custom views. Then, you practice displaying the different views.

To Create and Use a Custom View

1 **Open e-1404, and save it as** `NewViews`**.**

2 **Click each worksheet tab, and return to the Sales worksheet.**
The workbook contains a worksheet with sales data and another worksheet with percentages—both containing outlines. There is also a chart sheet.

3 **Check that the current sheet is Sales; and choose _V_iew, Custom _V_iews, and click _A_dd.**
The Add View dialog box is displayed.

4 **Type** `Home` **in the _N_ame text box, and click OK.**
You have just added a custom view to the menu of existing custom views. This new Home view provides quick access to all the data on the first sheet in the workbook. The purpose of the Home view is to give you a standard starting place because you will be creating several other views.

5 **Click the Hide detail symbol (–) above column F in the Sales worksheet.**

6 **Choose _V_iew, Custom _V_iews, and click Add.**

7 **Type** `Sales by Product within Division` **in the _N_ame text box and click OK.**

8 **Choose _V_iew, Custom _V_iews.**
Figure 14.9 shows the Custom Views dialog box with each of the views you added. One view named Sales Percentages by Quarter had already been defined.

Custom views created by the user

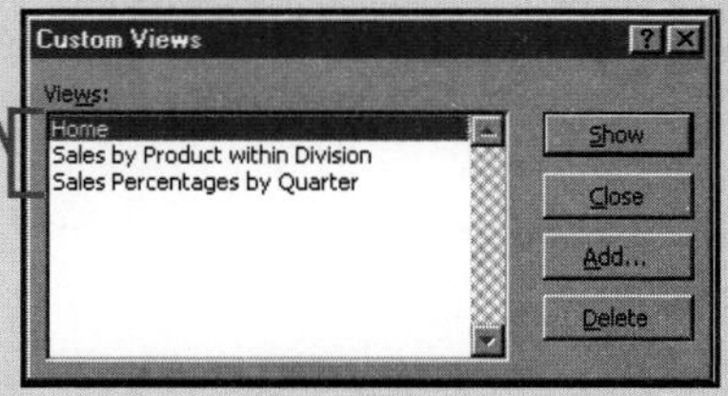

Figure 14.9
Custom views are created and accessed through the Custom Views dialog box.

9 **Select Sales Percentages by Quarter, and click the _S_how button.**
The view changes to display the sales percentages by quarter.

10 **Choose _V_iew, Custom _V_iews.**

11 **Select the Home view, and click _S_how.**
Selecting the Home view returns the display to the first worksheet in the workbook.

12 **Save and close the NewViews workbook.**

> *Exam Note:* **Deleting a Custom View**
> To remove a custom view, choose <u>V</u>iew, Custom <u>V</u>iews. Then select the view you want to remove and click the <u>D</u>elete button.

 # Lesson 6: Creating Reports Using Report Manager

Complex worksheets and workbooks nearly always mean printing several different views of the data. Using the example of a store manager, think about keeping records for four stores. Data for each store are entered on a separate worksheet in one workbook. The manager frequently needs at least two views of each worksheet. This means creating and printing as many as eight reports. One means of making this job easier is to create and store custom views of your data. You can also use Excel's ***Report Manager*** to combine and save multiple custom views into a single report. Printing complex reports is as easy as selecting a desired report from a list.

In this lesson you create one custom report that includes several custom views.

To Create a Report Using Report Manager

1 **Open e-1405, and save it as** NewReport.
Four custom views have been stored with this workbook.

2 **Choose <u>V</u>iew, <u>R</u>eport Manager.**
The Report Manager dialog box displays (see Figure 14.10).

Figure 14.10
Use the Report Manager dialog box to create, edit, print, or delete a report.

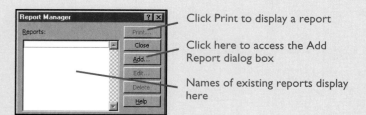

> **X** *If You Have Problems...*
> The Report Manager is not an intrinsic part of Microsoft Excel—it is an add-in. If your <u>V</u>iew menu does not list Report Manager, you need to install it. Choose <u>T</u>ools, Add-<u>I</u>ns. Scroll until you find Report Manager, select the check box, and click OK. When the dialog box asks whether you want to install, select <u>Y</u>es. You will probably need your Microsoft Office CD.

3 **Click <u>A</u>dd.**
The Add Report dialog box displays.

4 **In the <u>R</u>eport Name text box, type** Sales Report.

5 **In the Section to Add area, click the <u>S</u>heet drop-down list and select Sales.**

6 **Click the View drop-down list, select Sales by Product within Division, and click the Add button.**
The Sales by Product within Division view is added as a section in the report.

7 **Click the View drop-down list, select Sales Chart, and click Add.**
Note that chart sheets do not appear in the Sheet drop-down list. They must be selected in the View drop-down list.

8 **Select the Use Continuous Page Numbers check box.**
Selecting this option numbers all pages in the report consecutively instead of restarting the numbering at the beginning of each section. The Sections in this Report list box should show two views: Sales by Product within Division and Sales Chart (see Figure 14.11).

Enter the name of the report here

Specify the name of the worksheet containing data to include in the report

Specify the name of a custom view to add to the report

Specify the name of a scenario to add to the report

Click here to specify continuous page numbering when printing multiple-page reports

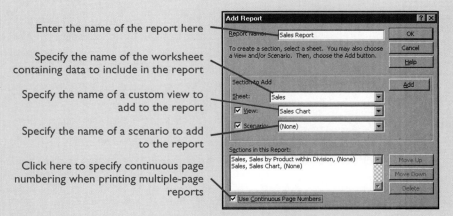

Figure 14.11
Use the Add Report dialog box to define sections of the report.

9 **Click OK to exit the Add Report dialog box.**

10 **Click Close to exit the Report Manager dialog box.**

11 **Save and close the NewReport workbook.**
In the next lesson, you edit and print the report.

Lesson 7: Editing and Printing Reports Using Report Manager

Now that you have a custom report created in Report Manager, you may notice that the report is not quite what you want. Sometimes you overlook something or your needs may change. When that happens, you need to edit the custom report. In this lesson, you add an additional section to the Sales Report. You also change the order of the sections to be printed, and print the report.

To Edit and Print a Report Using Report Manager

1 **Open the e-1406 workbook and save it as EditReport.**
The workbook is a duplicate of the one used in the previous lesson. It contains one report.

continues ▶

To Edit and Print a Report Using Report Manager   (continued)

② **Choose View, Report Manager.**
The Report Manager dialog box displays.

③ **In the Reports list, select Sales Report, and click the Edit button.**
The Edit Report dialog box displays. Now add the Sales Percentages by Quarter view as a new section in the report.

④ **Select the Sheet drop-down list, and choose Percents.**

⑤ **Select the View drop-down list, and choose Sales Percentages by Quarter.**

⑥ **Click Add.**
Sales Percentages by Quarter is added to the sections in the report. Now you want to change the order of the report sections.

⑦ **In the Sections in this Report list box, select the Sales Percentages by Quarter report section, and click the Move Up button two times.**
The sections are listed in the order they will print. You can make additional changes to the report order by selecting a section name and clicking the Move Up or Move Down buttons to change the order. To delete a section—from the report only—select the section and click the Delete button.

⑧ **Click OK.**
The Edit Report dialog closes and the Report Manager dialog box appears on the screen.

⑨ **In the Report Manager dialog box, click the Print button.**
The Print dialog box displays.

⑩ **Click OK (or click Cancel if you prefer not to print).**
The report prints on the default printer using the default settings. Three sections print, one per page. The order is determined by the order displayed on the Add Report or Edit Report dialog box.

⑪ **Save and close the EditReport workbook.**
This concludes Lesson 7. You can exit Excel, or continue with the final lesson in this project.

 ## Lesson 8: Saving a Group of Workbooks in a Workspace File

If you frequently display more than one workbook on the screen, and specify approximately the same window sizes and screen positions for those multiple workbooks, Excel's workspace feature can save the startup time needed to open and arrange multiple workbooks. A **workspace** file saves information about all open workbooks, including filenames, screen positions, and window sizes. It does not contain the workbooks themselves.

When you are ready to open the group of files defined in the workspace, you execute a File, Open command, and select the associated workspace file from a list of files that have .xlw extensions. The "w" at the end of the extension indicates a workspace file.

In this lesson, you open two workbooks, display one below the other, and save that grouping as a workspace. You then close the two original files, and test that the workspace file functions as intended.

To Save a Group of Workbooks in a Workspace File

1 Open the two workbooks named `Region1.xls` and `Region2.xls`.

2 Choose **W**indow, **A**rrange; then select H**o**rizontal and click **OK** (see Figure 14.12).

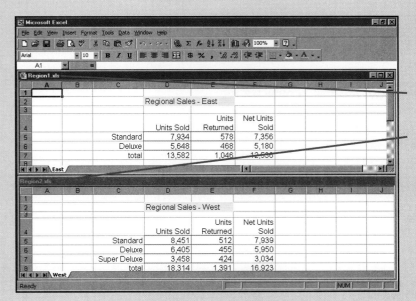

Figure 14.12
One workbook displays below the other.

One open workbook

A second open workbook

3 Choose **F**ile, Save **W**orkspace.
The Save Workspace dialog box opens. The Save as type text box at the bottom displays Workspaces (*.xlw).

4 In the Save **i**n text box, specify the folder in which you are storing completed lesson files.

5 Enter `eastwest.xlw` as the filename (see Figure 14.13).

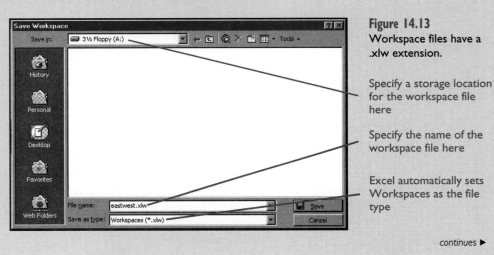

Figure 14.13
Workspace files have a .xlw extension.

Specify a storage location for the workspace file here

Specify the name of the workspace file here

Excel automatically sets Workspaces as the file type

continues ▶

To Save a Group of Workbooks in a Workspace File (continued)

6 Click **Save**, and then close the Region1 and Region2 files.
Now open the newly created workspace file to check that it functions as intended.

7 Choose **File**, **Open**; then specify the location of the eastwest.xlw file in the Look **in** text box.

8 If the eastwest.xlw file does not display in the list of files, specify either **All Microsoft Excel Files** or **Workspaces** files in the Files of **type** text box.

9 Select the `eastwest.xlw` file; then click **Open**.
Excel opens the Region1 and Region2 workbooks, and displays one below the other.

10 Close all open workbooks.
This concludes Project 14. You can continue with end-of-project exercises or exit Excel.

Summary

You started this project by consolidating data within a workbook and from multiple workbooks. As a part of the consolidation process, you learned to group data using the outlining feature. You then learned how to create an Auto Outline and how to take control and make your own outline. Once data were grouped, you learned to expand and collapse your view of the data.

You learned to create custom views of your data, which you could select from a list for later viewing. You then used the Report Manager to collect worksheets and custom views into a report that could be edited and printed. In the last lesson, you opened two workbooks and set each one to display on half of the screen, one below the other. You then saved that combination of files and screen arrangement as a workspace.

Checking Concepts and Terms

True/False

For each of the following, check *T* or *F* to indicate whether the statement is true or false.

__T __F **1.** A workspace saves information about all open workbooks, including filenames, screen positions, and window sizes, but it does not contain the workbooks themselves. [L8]

__T __F **2.** You can delete a report using the Report Manager dialog box, but Excel does not provide a means to delete only a section of a report. [L6, L7]

__T __F **3.** When consolidating workbooks, files with different names or named ranges must be entered individually. [L2]

__T __F **4.** Worksheet outlines are useful for collapsing the amount of data displayed. [L3]

__T __F **5.** After a report has been defined with Report Manager, additional sections cannot be added. [L7]

Multiple Choice

Circle the letter of the correct answer for each of the following.

1. Custom views enable you to [L5]

    a. hide data from other users

    b. save the views you use most often

    c. jump directly to the views you use most often

    d. both b and c

2. The character that indicates the end of a filename in a 3D cell reference is [L2]

    a. ?

    b. :

    c. !

    d. *

3. To use multiple groupings in a manual outline, [L4]

    a. the groups must be adjacent on the worksheet

    b. the groups must be separated by an empty column or row on the worksheet

    c. the groups must be in the same cells on separate worksheets

    d. none of the above

4. Which of the following can be selected from the Report Manager dialog box? [L6]

    a. Use <u>C</u>ontinuous Page Numbers

    b. <u>V</u>iew

    c. Sce<u>n</u>ario

    d. all of the above

5. Workbooks can be consolidated if [L2]

    a. they are stored on the same computer

    b. they are stored on different computers on a network

    c. both a and b

    d. neither a nor b

Skill Drills

Skill Drill exercises reinforce project skills. Each skill reinforced is the same, or nearly the same, as a skill presented in the project. Detailed instructions are provided in a step-by-step format.

The exercises can be worked in any order. Be sure to save the workbook after completing each exercise. If you need a paper copy of the completed exercise, enter your name centered in a header before printing. Other print options have already been set to print compressed to one page and to display the filename, sheet name, and current date in a footer.

Before beginning your first Project 14 Skill Drill exercise, complete the following steps:

1. Open the file named **e-1407**, and save it as **e14drill**.

The workbook contains seven sheets: an overview, and exercise sheets named #1-3D, Data1, Data2, Data3, #2-Consolidation, and #3-Manual Outline.

2. Click the Overview sheet to view the organization of the Project 14 Skill Drill Exercises workbook.

If you need more than one work session to complete the desired exercises, continue working on **e14drill** instead of starting over on the original e-1407 file.

1. Consolidating Data with 3D References

Worksheets Data1, Data2, and Data3 contain sales data for three salespersons. You want to sum the data in these sheets and place the results in the #1-3D worksheet using a 3D formula.

To consolidate data with 3D references:

1. Open the e14drill workbook.
   It would be a good idea to examine worksheets Data1, Data2, and Data3.

2. Select the #1-3D worksheet.

3. Type =SUM(in cell D8.

4. Click the Data1 worksheet tab.

5. Press and hold down ⬆Shift.

6. Click the Data3 worksheet tab, and release ⬆Shift.

7. Click cell C6, and type the closing right parenthesis.

8. Press ↵Enter.
   Pressing Enter returns you to the #1-3D worksheet. Notice that the consolidated value of 899 (model AR353) from the three worksheets appears in cell D8.

9. Copy cell D8 to D9:D10.
   The consolidated values of 363 (model WB-23) and 1109 (model SPR/34-2) display in cells D9 and D10, respectively.

2. Consolidating Multiple Workbooks

This exercise uses the same data as Exercise 1, except the data for the three salespersons are in three separate workbooks. Steps 1 through 3 merely show you the data involved in the consolidation. Step 4 begins the process to implement the consolidation.

To consolidate multiple workbooks:

1. Open files SalesPerson1.xls, SalesPerson2.xls, and SalesPerson3.xls.

2. For each of the files, click the Name box, and click the named range Sold.

3. Close all three SalesPerson files when you are finished.

4. Open the e14drill workbook.

5. Select the #2-Consolidation worksheet, and click cell B4.

6. Choose Data, Consolidate.
   The Consolidate dialog box displays.

7. Type SalesPerson?.xls!Sold in the Reference text box.

8. Select the check boxes for Use labels in Left column and Create links to source data.

9. Click OK, and widen the columns as necessary.

10. Click the outlining buttons and note how they expand the consolidation cells.

3. Creating a Manual Outline

The worksheet for this exercise already contains groupings for business and personal use. Now within each of these categories, you group by type of payment to illustrate how outlining can be nested.

To create a manual outline:

1. Open the e14drill workbook, and select the #3-Manual Outline worksheet.

2. Select row 23, and choose Insert, Rows.

3. Select row 39, and choose Insert, Rows.

4. Select rows 16:22, and choose Data, Group and Outline, Group.

5. Repeat step 4 for rows 24:32, 34:38, and 40:48.
   You now want to see the records of rentals for Personal use charged to a Corporate account.

6. Click the '2' button from the top of the outlining symbols.

7. Click the third '+' from the top.

8. Experiment with the outlining buttons until you can display any combination of Type of Use versus Type of Payment.

Challenge

Challenge exercises expand on or are somewhat related to skills presented in the lessons. Each exercise provides a brief narrative introduction, followed by instructions in a numbered-step format that are not as detailed as those in the Skill Drill section.

Be sure to save the workbook after completing each exercise. If you need a paper copy of the completed exercise, enter your name centered in a header before printing. Other print options have already been set to print compressed to one page and to display the filename, sheet name, and current date in a footer.

Before you begin the challenge exercises, complete the following steps:

1. Open the file named **e-1408**, and save it as **e14challenge**.
The workbook contains three sheets: an overview, and exercise sheets named #1#2-Consolidation and #3-Views.

2. Click the Overview sheet to view the organization of the Project 14 Challenge Exercises workbook.

Exercise 1 must be worked before Exercise 2. If you need more than one work session to complete the desired exercises, continue working on e14challenge instead of starting over on the original e-1408 file.

 Inside Stuff: **Working Challenges in This Project**
Some of the exercises involve linking data in worksheets and workbooks. When you open your practice file, you may see a message telling you that your workbook contains automatic links to other workbooks. This is okay. Respond <u>Y</u>es to update the links and continue to work the Challenge exercises.

1. Consolidating Different Source Files

Workbooks Deluxe and Standard contain sales data across several regions for four quarters. You want to sum the data in the two workbooks and place the results in the e14challenge workbook.

When consolidating data from multiple files, it is good practice to use a consistent file naming convention with the same named range in each file (as illustrated in the lessons and Skill Drill exercises). However, as this exercise demonstrates, you can have different filenames and different named ranges. It is, however, important that the named ranges have the same row or column labels within the ranges because the labels are used to set up the consolidation. The ranges do not need all the same labels, but the areas you want to consolidate must have exactly the same labels.

To consolidate source files:

1. Open **Deluxe.xls** and **Standard.xls**.
The Deluxe workbook contains the Deluxe worksheet. The Standard workbook contains the Standard worksheet.

2. Examine each worksheet, making note of the named ranges.
   The Sales range name in the Deluxe worksheet refers to C6:H11. The Data range name in the Standard worksheet refers to B7:G11. Both worksheets contain the same quarter and annual labels in a row and region labels in a column. There are three regions in the Standard worksheet and four regions in the Deluxe worksheet.

3. Close the Deluxe.xls and Standard.xls files.

4. Open the **e14challenge** workbook, select the #1#2-Consolidation worksheet, and click cell B4.

5. Choose Data, Consolidate.

6. Type **Deluxe.xls!Sales** in the Reference text box, and click Add.

 If You Have Problems...
If your file is not stored in the same folder as your worksheet, use the Browse button to locate the file.

---

7. Type **Standard.xls!Data** as the next Reference, and click Add.

8. Check all three check boxes at the bottom of the Consolidate dialog box, and click OK.

9. Expand the outline and format the table by aligning column headings, adjusting column widths, and applying formats—for example, color—as desired.

10. Collapse the outline.

2. Testing Consolidation Links

When you ran the consolidation challenge in Exercise 1, you specified that you wanted to create links to the source data. This caused the outline to be created but it also allows the consolidation workbook to be updated automatically if changes are made in either of the source files. In this exercise, you view and verify the links.

To test consolidation links:

1. If necessary, open the **e14challenge** workbook, and select the #1#2-Consolidation worksheet.

2. Open **Deluxe.xls** and **Standard.xls**.
   Only three files should be open: Deluxe.xls, Standard.xls, and e14challenge.xls.

3. Choose Window, Arrange; then select Tiled, and click OK.

4. Size the windows, and use the scrollbars to view the data areas of all three workbooks.

5. Click cell C8 within the Standard workbook, and change the Q1 value for the East region from 232 to **274**.
   The change in Q1 data for the East region impacts the Consolidation worksheet. The values 274 and 400 display in cells D6 and D7, respectively.

6. Change some of the other data values in the Standard and Deluxe workbooks, and note the effect in the consolidation workbook.

7. Close all three workbooks without saving your changes.

3. Exploring the Limits of Custom Views

After you realize that custom views exist and are so easy to use, you will find yourself using them frequently. In this exercise, you explore what comprises a view.

To explore custom views:

  1. Open the `e14challenge` workbook and select the #3-Views worksheet.

  2. Add the current worksheet display to the Custom Views menu, naming it **Home**. Remember, when using views, it is usually a good idea to have a home or default view. Otherwise, there is not always an easy way to get back to your original view after selecting some other view.

  3. Make the following display changes to your worksheet.

   ■ Change the zoom factor to 100% using the Zoom toolbar button.

   ■ Remove the gridlines with Tools, Options.

   ■ Select row 14, and choose Window, Split.

   ■ Scroll the bottom window until row 43 is visible.

   ■ Drag the right border of column E, and make the width approximately 30.

  4. Save the current view as a custom view named **Test1**.

  5. Switch between the Home and Test1 views.
   Note that changing column width applies to all worksheets. You changed the width of column E in the Test1 view, but the new width also applies to column E in the Home view. Changing gridline display, however, did not impact all worksheets. You removed display of worksheet gridlines for the Test1 view, but the change had no impact on the Home view.

  6. Go to the Home view, and choose Tools, Options.

  7. Click the View tab, and check Formulas in the Window options area.

  8. Choose View, Custom Views, and add a view named **Formulas**.
   This is a handy way to view cell formulas quickly.

  9. Switch among the Formulas, Home, and Test1 views.

   Note that displaying formulas instead of formula results does not apply to all worksheets. The change impacts only the Formulas view.

  10. Experiment with creating other custom views and note whether changes impact only the current view or all views.

Discovery Zone

Discovery Zone exercises require advanced knowledge of topics presented in *MOUS Essentials* lessons, application of skills from multiple lessons, or self-directed learning of new skills.

Be sure to save the workbook after completing each exercise. If you need a paper copy of the completed exercise, enter your name centered in a header before printing. Other print options have already been set to print compressed to one page and to display the filename, sheet name, and current date in a footer.

Before you begin the discovery zone exercises, complete the following steps:

1. Open the file named `e-1409`, and save it as `e14discovery`.
   The workbook contains three sheets: an overview, and exercise sheets named #1-OutlineChart and #2-OutlineManual.

2. Click the Overview sheet to view the organization of the Project 14 Discovery Exercises workbook.

If you need more than one work session to complete the desired exercises, continue working on the `e14discovery` workbook instead of starting over on the original e-1409 file.

1. Using Outlines with Charts

You wonder whether you can use Excel's outline capability to alter the amount of detail shown in a chart quickly. Access onscreen Help, and look for relevant information. Then open the `e14discovery` workbook, and select sheet #1-OutlineChart. This sheet contains worksheet data and one column chart.

Within the worksheet data, set up data groupings according to the type of order—in-store, phone/fax, Web. Set up the groups in such a way that you can collapse any group to hide the corresponding data in the chart and on the worksheet.

2. Creating and Using a Manual Outline

You are analyzing a representative batch of customer orders, trying to isolate the source of delays in shipping. You've been able to get some counts by developing pivot tables. Now you'd like to organize the data by setting up a manual outline that you can expand or collapse to alter the amount of detail shown. Open the `e14discovery` workbook, if necessary, and select sheet #2-OutlineManual. Set up groups of orders and then subgroups within each group. Remember to sort records before you attempt the grouping required for a manual outline. You might, for example, create an outline that enables you to expand or collapse the outline according to day of the week, and by shift within each day. Remember, your primary focus is viewing the data in such a way that you have a better understanding of data related to late shipments.

PinPoint Assessment

You have completed this project and its associated lessons, and have had an opportunity to assess your skills through the end-of-project questions and exercises. Now use the PinPoint software Evaluation Mode to further assess your comprehension of the specific exam activities you have just learned. You can also use the PinPoint Trainer Mode and the Show Me tutorials to practice these exam activities.

Automating Tasks with Macros

Key terms introduced in this project include

- macro
- macro button
- Personal Macro Workbook

- Visual Basic for Applications (VBA)
- Visual Basic Editor

Objectives	Required Activity for MOUS	Exam Level
➤ Prepare to Record a Macro	Record macros	Expert
➤ Record a Macro	Record macros	Expert
➤ Play a Macro	Run macros	Expert
➤ Record a Macro in a Personal Macro Workbook	Record macros	Expert
➤ Play a Macro from the Personal Macro Workbook	Run macros	Expert
➤ Unhide and Edit the Personal Macro Workbook	Edit macros	Expert
➤ Create a Macro Button in a Workbook	Run macros	Expert

Why Would I Do This?

A *macro* enables you to combine multiple commands and keystrokes, and execute them as a single command. If you perform a particular function or task frequently, creating a macro to perform that function with a single keystroke or a button can be a real time-saver as well as produce consistent results. A macro can be simple, such as one that types a very long company name or prints selected sections of a large worksheet. A macro can also produce more complex results, such as one that creates a chart or calculates and prints a price quote for a customer.

When a macro you've recorded is played back, it is as though an invisible typist were rapidly entering keystrokes. Some early macro recorders literally did just that—recorded keystrokes and played them back on command. However, Excel handles macros differently. Because all Microsoft Office programs are object-oriented, the macro recorder does not look at your keystrokes, but instead looks at the results of your keystrokes. It then creates a subroutine in a language known as *Visual Basic for Applications (VBA),* which produces the same results as your keystrokes.

Macros are viewed and edited using the *Visual Basic Editor*. You can use this editor to fine-tune the macro code or delete lines that resulted from incorrect keystrokes. The Visual Basic Editor is also used to create programs from scratch, which is how many add-in programs, such as data analysis tools, are created.

In this project, you create and run two macros—one that impacts only the associated workbook, and another that can be applied to any workbook. You also edit a macro and add a macro button to a worksheet.

Expert Lesson 1: Preparing to Record a Macro

Before you can record a macro, you need to decide what to name the macro and where to store it. A macro name must start with a letter and can contain letters, numbers, and the underscore character. Spaces are not allowed. You can store your macro in the current workbook or a new workbook. You can also store it in the Personal Macro Workbook so that it is available for use in any existing or future workbook.

In this lesson, you create a macro that copies the contents of a row to the next available blank row in another worksheet before deleting the selected row in the original worksheet. This macro makes it easy to move data about a work order in progress to a database of completed work orders. You store the macro in the current workbook.

To Prepare to Record a Macro

1 **Open the e-1501 file, and save it as** `Project List`.
This workbook contains two worksheets named Current Projects and Completed Projects.

2 **Type** `4/8/2000` **in cell F4 of the Current Projects worksheet, and press** Enter.
The entry indicates that the project described in row 4 has been completed.

3 **Select row 4 by clicking its row heading.**

Specify which row's contents to copy before recording the macro. You cannot specify a specific row to transfer within the macro, because projects may not be completed in order.

4 **Select Tools, Macro, Record New Macro.**

The Record Macro dialog box displays.

5 **Click within the Macro name text box, and type** Completed.

You must name a macro before you record it. If you fail to name the macro, Microsoft Excel gives it a default name of Macro1, Macro2, and so on.

6 **For this macro, leave the Shortcut key text box blank.**

7 **In the** Store macro in **text box, select** This Workbook **from the drop-down list.**

You can enter a description of the macro in the Description text box. If you do not enter a description, Excel enters the current date and author's name.

8 **Type** Switch a record from Current to Completed **in the Description text box (see Figure 15.1).**

Type the macro name here

Enter a single upper- or lowercase letter here to define a shortcut key combination (optional)

You can type a description of the macro's purpose here

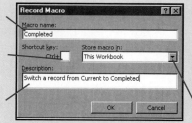

Figure 15.1
Specify the macro's name, storage location, and description in the Record Macro dialog box.

Click here to display available options on the drop-down list

9 **Check that your entries match those shown in Figure 15.1, and click OK.**

The macro recorder is now on. You should see a Stop Recording toolbar and the Recording message at the bottom of the screen (see Figure 15.2).

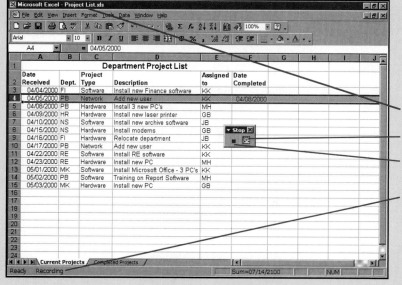

Figure 15.2
When recording mode is active, the Stop Recording toolbar displays, and the word Recording appears in the status bar.

Macro will be stored in this workbook

Relative Reference button

Stop Recording button

Indicates that recording mode is active

You are now ready to record your macro. Keep the Project List workbook open until you complete the next lesson.

> ***Exam Note: Assigning Shortcut Keys to Macros***
>
> You can assign a shortcut key to your macro that can be an upper- or lowercase letter. To do so, type a letter in the Shortcut key text box within the Record Macro dialog box. To run a macro using this shortcut key, press and hold Ctrl and press the letter you assigned to the macro. If your shortcut key is an upper-case letter, press and hold both Ctrl and ⬆Shift with the appropriate key.

 Lesson 2: Recording a Macro

Now that you have established a name and storage location for your macro, you can begin the recording process. The steps to be recorded are copying and pasting the contents of the selected row in the Current Projects worksheet to the first available blank row in the Completed Projects worksheet, and deleting the selected row from the Current Projects worksheet.

To Record a Macro

1 **Check that row 4 is selected in the Current Projects worksheet of the Project List workbook, and that the word Recording displays in the status bar.**

2 **Click the Relative Reference button on the Stop Recording toolbar (see Figure 15.2).**
The Relative Reference button enables you to play the macro anywhere on the worksheet. An absolute reference ties the macro to specific locations.

3 **Click the Copy button on the toolbar.**
The contents of row 4 are copied to the Clipboard. A marquee appears around row 4.

4 **Click the Completed Projects sheet tab.**
Completed Projects is now the active sheet.

5 **Press Ctrl + Home.**
This keystroke combination makes cell A1 the active cell.

6 **Press End, and press ⬇ twice.**
The active cell is now cell A5, the first cell in the first blank row below the data.

7 **Click the Paste button on the toolbar.**
The selected data from row 4 of the Current Projects worksheet is pasted in the first blank row of the Completed Projects worksheet (see Figure 15.3).

8 **Press ⬇, and click the Current Projects sheet tab.**
This action deselects the pasted row and returns the active cell to the Current Projects worksheet. Row 4 should still be selected.

9 **Choose Edit, Delete.**
Row 4 is deleted from the Current Projects worksheet—the last step in transferring a record from the Current Projects worksheet to the Completed Projects worksheet.

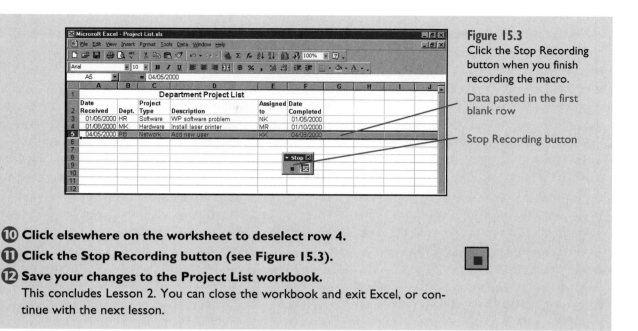

Figure 15.3
Click the Stop Recording button when you finish recording the macro.

Data pasted in the first blank row

Stop Recording button

⑩ **Click elsewhere on the worksheet to deselect row 4.**

⑪ **Click the Stop Recording button (see Figure 15.3).**

⑫ **Save your changes to the Project List workbook.**

This concludes Lesson 2. You can close the workbook and exit Excel, or continue with the next lesson.

Lesson 3: Playing a Macro

After a macro has been recorded, you can run (or play) it at any time. To run the macro, you can either use the Tools, Macro command or the shortcut key, if you assigned one to the macro.

To Play a Macro

❶ **Display the Current Projects worksheet in the Project List workbook, type 5/13/2000 in cell F7, and press ↵Enter.**
You updated the Current Projects worksheet to show that the project in row 7 was completed on 5/13/2000.

❷ **Select row 7.**

❸ **Select Tools, Macro, Macros.**
The Macro dialog box displays.

❹ **Select This Workbook from the Macros in drop-down list.**
A list of all macros defined for the workbook displays. The name of one macro, the newly created Completed, displays in the Macro name list (see Figure 15.4).

❺ **Specify Completed in the Macro name text box, and click Run.**
More quickly than the eye can follow, each action captured in the macro executes. Excel copies the contents of row 7 in the Current Projects sheet to the first blank row in the Completed Projects sheet, and deletes row 7 in the workbook.

❻ **Click the Completed Projects sheet tab.**
Four records display, including the new one in row 6 with a completion date of 5/13/2000 (see Figure 15.5).

continues ▶

To Play a Macro (continued)

Figure 15.4
Use the Macro dialog box
to select and run a macro.

Specify the name of the macro to
run here

Click here to activate the
selected macro

Click here to edit the selected
macro

Click here to delete the selected
macro

Click here to choose among
three sources of macros

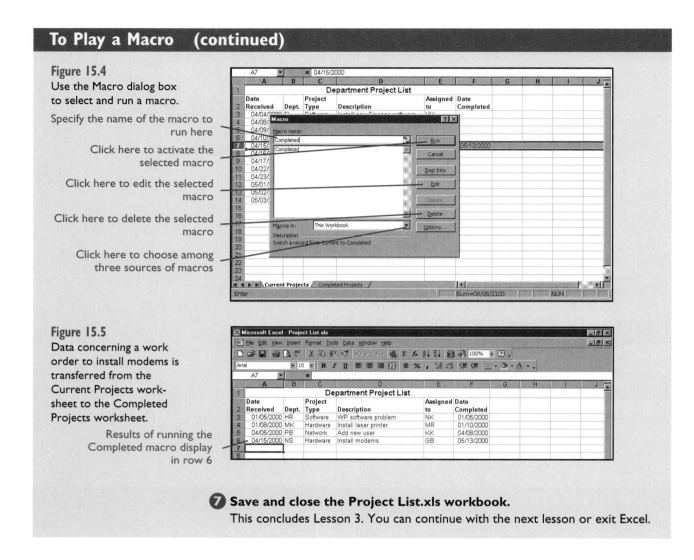

Figure 15.5
Data concerning a work
order to install modems is
transferred from the
Current Projects work-
sheet to the Completed
Projects worksheet.

Results of running the
Completed macro display
in row 6

7 **Save and close the Project List.xls workbook.**
This concludes Lesson 3. You can continue with the next lesson or exit Excel.

 Exam Note: **Deleting a Macro**
To delete a macro, select the macro from the list in the Macro dialog box, and
click the <u>D</u>elete button (see Figure 15.4). If the macro you want to delete is
stored in the Personal.xls workbook, you must first display that hidden workbook by choosing <u>W</u>indows, <u>U</u>nhide.

 ## Lesson 4: Recording a Macro in a Personal Macro Workbook

A *Personal Macro Workbook* is a Microsoft Excel file containing macros that are available to all workbooks. To create a macro that can be used in more than one workbook,
save it to your Personal Macro Workbook.

The macro you created in Lesson 2 was for use with one specific workbook, and you
saved it in that workbook. In this lesson, you create a macro that inserts the page number
code in a footer. The action performed by this macro is one that is useful for any workbook, and you store it in the Personal Macro Workbook.

To Record a Macro in a Personal Macro Workbook

1 Click the New button (or choose **F**ile, **N**ew, and click OK) to open a new workbook.
A blank worksheet displays on the screen.

2 Select **T**ools, **M**acro, **R**ecord New Macro.
The Record Macro dialog box opens.

3 Type `Footer` in the Macro name text box.

4 Type the lowercase letter ⓕ in the Shortcut **k**ey text box.

5 Display the drop-down list for the Store macro **i**n text box, and select Personal Macro Workbook.

> **If You Have Problems...**
> If you do not have permission to save the macro to the Personal Macro Workbook—for example, you are using a network system that protects this file—specify This Workbook instead of Personal Macro Workbook as the storage location. Doing so enables you to create another macro, even though you will not be able to execute it from a different workbook.

6 Type `Page number in footer` in the **D**escription text box (see Figure 15.6).

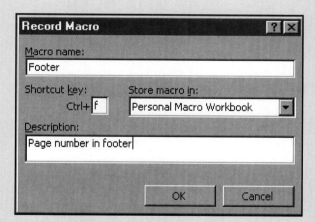

Figure 15.6
Specify Personal Macro Workbook in the Store macro in text box if the macro you are creating is for use in any workbook.

7 Check that your settings match those shown in Figure 15.6, and click OK.
The Record Macro dialog box closes, and the word Recording displays in the status bar.

> **If You Have Problems...**
> If the name of the macro or the letter assigned to the shortcut key is already in use, Excel displays a message that explains the problem and provides instructions to correct it. For example, a message that there is already a macro assigned to the key displays if the upper- or lowercase letter you specify is assigned to another shortcut.

continues ▶

To Record a Macro in a Personal Macro Workbook (continued)

8 **Select File, Page Setup, and click the Header/Footer tab in the Page Setup dialog box.**
The Page Setup dialog box displays (see Figure 15.7).

Figure 15.7
The drop-down lists for the Header and Footer text boxes enable you to select among common entries, such as a page number or current date.

Indicates a new workbook

Click here to display a list of predefined text and codes you can specify in a header

Click here to display a list of predefined text and codes you can specify in a footer

Stop Recording button

Recording mode is active

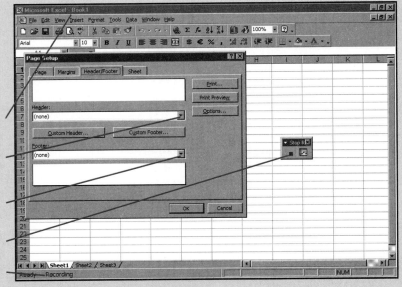

9 **Click the Footer drop-down arrow.**

10 **Select Page 1 from the drop-down list, and click OK.**
The Page Setup dialog box closes.

11 **Click the Stop Recording button.**
This completes recording the macro to insert automatic page numbering in a footer. The macro instructions are stored in the Personal Macro Workbook.

12 **Close the blank workbook without saving your changes.**
This concludes Lesson 4. Continue with the next lesson, in which you run the macro. If you do not have the time now to complete Lesson 5, be sure to work through Lesson 5 on the same computer system you used for Lesson 4.

 Lesson 5: Playing a Macro from the Personal Macro Workbook

In the previous lesson, you created a macro to insert a page number in a footer and stored it in your Personal Macro Workbook. You can play the macro by pressing the key combination you defined as a shortcut, or by selecting it on your Personal Macro Workbook.

In this lesson, you use the shortcut key method. If you stored the Footer macro to a specific workbook instead of the Personal workbook, modify instructions as necessary to reflect the change in location. You start the lesson by opening the Project List workbook.

To Play a Macro from the Personal Macro Workbook

1 Open the `Project List` workbook.

2 If the dialog box shown in Figure 15.8 displays, click **E**nable Macros.

The dialog box displays if macro security is set to Medium or High. (See the Inside Stuff note at the end of the lesson for more information on security.)

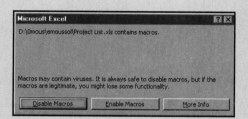

Figure 15.8
Click the option to Enable Macros only if the workbook is from a trusted source.

3 Select the Current Projects worksheet.

4 Click the Print Preview button.

The worksheet displays without a page number in the footer.

5 Click the **C**lose button.

6 Press and hold the Ctrl key, and type the lowercase letter f. (If you assigned a different letter as the shortcut to the macro, substitute that letter in place of f.)

7 Click the Print Preview button.

The worksheet displays with a page number centered in the footer.

8 Click the **C**lose button, and save your changes to the Project List workbook.

This concludes Lesson 5. You can continue with the next lesson or exit Excel.

 Inside Stuff: **Macro Security Levels**

Macros can be carriers of viruses. You can use the **S**ecurity option on the **T**ools, **M**acro menu to set the level of security desired. The security levels are **H**igh (macros from sources not considered trustworthy are automatically disabled), **M**edium (disabling macros is left to the discretion of the user), and **L**ow (all macros are enabled).

Lesson 6: Unhiding and Editing the Personal Macro Workbook

Your Personal Macro Workbook is always open in Excel—it just isn't visible. If you want to edit or delete a macro stored there, you must first unhide the Personal.xls workbook.

You can edit a macro using Microsoft's Visual Basic Editor. Lines of code (such as those for the Footer macro shown in Figure 15.9) display when the Editor is active.

Figure 15.9
The Visual Basic window displays the code for the selected macro.

User-specified name of the macro

User-specified description of the macro

User-specified shortcut assigned to the macro

Line of code to edit

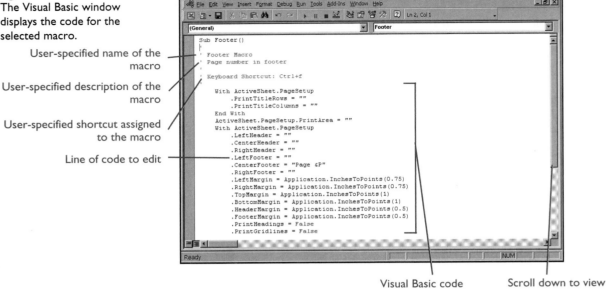

Visual Basic code

Scroll down to view remaining lines of code

To edit a macro, use techniques similar to those you would use to make changes in a word-processed document. In this lesson, you edit the line of code controlling what displays at the left edge of a footer. If you stored the Footer macro to a specific workbook instead of the Personal Macro Workbook, modify instructions as necessary to reflect the change in location.

To Unhide and Edit the Personal Macro Workbook

1 **If necessary, open the `Project List` workbook and select the Current Projects worksheet.**

2 **Choose Window, Unhide.**
The Unhide dialog box displays.

3 **Click Personal from the Unhide workbook list, and click OK.**

4 **Select Tools, Macro, Macros.**
The Macro dialog box lists the names of the macros in the Project List workbook, as well as the Personal Macro Workbook.

5 **Select Footer from the Macro name list, and click Edit.**
The Visual Basic window opens and displays the Visual Basic code for the macro (see Figure 15.9). For your screen to look like Figure 15.9, you may need to maximize the Visual Basic window and/or close other windows (such as Project or Properties).

6 **Locate the line of code `.LeftFooter =""`.**
Now edit this line to add preparer information at the left edge of the footer.

7 **Click between the "" (double quotation marks) symbols, and then type `Prepared by: XXX` (substitute your initials for XXX).**
The revised line of code displays as shown in Figure 15.10.

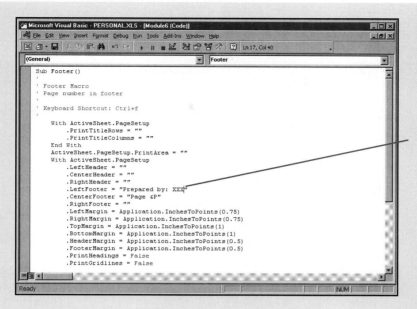

Figure 15.10
The revised macro code now contains instructions to include text at the left edge of the footer.

Modified line of code

⑧ Select File, Save Personal.xls.
The changes to the Footer macro code are saved.

⑨ Select File, Close and Return to Microsoft Excel.
The Visual Basic Editor closes.

⑩ Select Window, Personal.xls; then select Window, Hide.
The Personal.xls workbook is hidden. Now check that the revised macro operates as intended.

⑪ Press Ctrl + f to execute the macro.

⑫ Click the Print Preview button.
The phrase "Provided by: XXX" displays at the left edge of the footer.

⑬ Click the Close button, and save your changes to the Project List workbook.
This concludes Lesson 6. You can continue with the next lesson, or close the workbook and exit Excel.

 Inside Stuff: **Stepping Through a Macro**
If a macro does not perform as intended, and you cannot figure out the problem by looking at the lines of code in the Visual Basic Editor, you can run the macro step by step. To do this, select the Step Into button in the Macro dialog box, and press F8 to see each line as it executes.

Lesson 7: Creating a Macro Button in a Workbook

Excel provides four methods for running a macro: choosing a menu sequence, entering the assigned shortcut keystrokes, clicking a macro button embedded in a worksheet, and clicking a macro button added to a new or existing toolbar.

You work with the third method—creating a macro button in a worksheet—in this lesson. Clicking a **macro button** executes the macro assigned to the button.

To Create a Macro Button in a Workbook

❶ If necessary, open the Project List workbook and select the Current Projects worksheet.

❷ Click cell G2.
Now create a macro button located in cell G2.

❸ Select View, Toolbars and click Forms.
The Forms toolbar displays (see Figure 15.11).

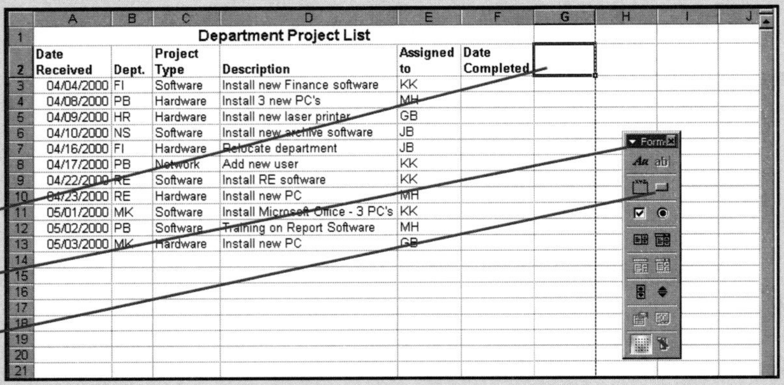

Figure 15.11
Use the Button icon on the Forms toolbar to create a button embedded in the worksheet.

Create the macro button here

The Forms toolbar

The Button icon

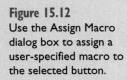

❹ Click the Button icon on the Forms toolbar.
The message Drag in document to create a button displays in the status bar, and the mouse pointer changes to a thin black cross.

❺ Click the upper-left corner of cell G2, and drag the mouse pointer down and to the right; release the mouse when the drawn box fills cell G2.
The Assign Macro dialog box opens and Button 1 displays in cell G2, as shown in Figure 15.12.

Figure 15.12
Use the Assign Macro dialog box to assign a user-specified macro to the selected button.

Macro to be assigned to the button

The newly created button is still selected

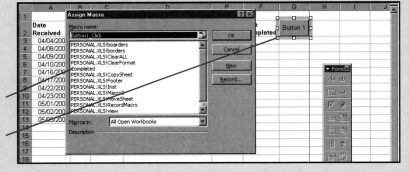

❻ Click Completed in the Macro name list, and click OK.
The Completed macro is assigned to the button in cell G2. Now change the name of the button.

7 **Right-click Button 1.**

A shortcut menu displays. If the option above Grouping in the shortcut menu is Exit Edit Te_x_t, skip the next step because Edit mode is already active.

8 **Choose Edit Te_x_t.**

9 **Replace the phrase Button 1 with the word `Transfer`, and deselect the button.**

Now check that the Transfer macro button works as intended.

10 **Close the Forms toolbar, and click cell F7.**

11 **Enter `05/24/2000` in cell F7, and select row 7.**

The button and selected row display, as shown in Figure 15.13

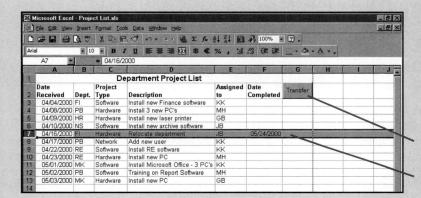

Figure 15.13
Clicking the Transfer button after selecting a row activates the macro that copies selected data to the other worksheet and deletes the selected row.

Renamed macro button

Row selected for transfer to the Completed Projects worksheet

12 **Click the Transfer button.**

Data about the project completed 05/24/2000 is copied to the next available blank row in the Completed Projects worksheet and removed from the Current Projects worksheet.

13 **Close the Project List workbook, saving your changes.**

This concludes Project 15. Continue with the end-of-project exercises, or close the workbook and exit Excel.

 Exam Note: **Modifying, Moving, and Deleting a Macro Button**

If a macro button in a worksheet is too small to contain the descriptive word you specify as its name, you can resize the button by using the handles. If the handles are not in view, press Ctrl while left clicking the button. This activates the handles.

You can change characteristics of a macro button, such as the font, by right-clicking the button and selecting Format C_o_ntrol from the shortcut menu.

A macro button can be relocated anywhere on the worksheet by right-clicking the button and dragging it by its shaded border to the new location.

To remove a macro button in the worksheet, right-click it and select Cu_t_ from the shortcut menu.

Inside Stuff: **Creating a Macro Button on a Toolbar**
If you embed a macro button in a worksheet, the macro assigned to that button can be applied only to that worksheet. You can also create a macro button on a new or existing toolbar that can be applied to any workbook.

Summary

Macros provide a means of automating complex or repetitive tasks. In this project, you created and played two macros—one limited to a workbook, and the other available for use in any workbook. In the process, you learned three ways to run a macro: selecting a menu sequence, using a shortcut key combination, and clicking a macro button embedded in a worksheet. Your experiences also included a brief introduction to Visual Basic for Applications (VBA), the programming language of Excel, as you edited one line of macro code.

Checking Concepts and Terms

True/False

For each of the following, check *T* or *F* to indicate whether the statement is true or false.

__T __F **1.** If a macro is stored in a Personal Macro Workbook, the macro can be run from any workbook. [L4]

__T __F **2.** You can change characteristics of a macro button, such as the font, by right-clicking the button and selecting Format Control from the shortcut menu. [L7]

__T __F **3.** A macro with an absolute reference can be applied anywhere on a designated worksheet. [L1]

__T __F **4.** You must know Visual Basic programming to record a macro. [L1]

__T __F **5.** Right-clicking a macro button executes the macro. [L3]

Multiple Choice

Circle the letter of the correct answer for each of the following.

1. If you want to play a macro in multiple workbooks, you must store it in [L4]

a. the workbook in which it was created

b. a new workbook

c. the Personal Macro Workbook

d. either a or c

2. Which of the following is/are an accurate statement(s) about macro security? [L5]

a. Macros can be carriers of viruses.

b. If you open a workbook containing macros when the macro security level is set to High, all macros in the workbook are automatically disabled.

c. Excel provides only two macro security levels—High and Low.

d. both a and b

3. A macro may be stored in [L2, 4]

    a. a workbook

    b. the Personal Macro Workbook

    c. the Templates workbook

    d. both a and b

4. Which of the following is an accurate statement concerning macros? [L6, L7]

    a. If a macro does not perform as intended, you can try to identify the problem(s) by running the macro step-by-step.

    b. You can edit a macro by inserting, modifying, or deleting a line of Visual Basic code.

    c. When you assign a macro to a button, that button can be embedded in a worksheet, placed on an existing toolbar, or placed on a new toolbar.

    d. all of the above

5. The shortcut key to execute a macro can be [L1]

    a. a lowercase letter

    b. an uppercase letter

    c. both a and b

    d. neither a or b

Skill Drill

Skill Drill exercises reinforce project skills. Each skill reinforced is the same, or nearly the same, as a skill presented in the project. Detailed instructions are provided in a step-by-step format.

The exercises can be worked in any order. Be sure to save the workbook after completing each exercise. If you need a paper copy of the completed exercise, enter your name centered in a header before printing. Other print options have already been set to print compressed to one page and to display the filename, sheet name, and current date in a footer.

Before beginning your first Project 15 Skill Drill exercise, complete the following steps:

1. Open the file named **e-1502**, click <u>E</u>nable Macros, and then save the file as **e15drill**.
The workbook contains four sheets: an overview, and exercise sheets named #1-ColorInOut, #2-Today, and #3-Macro Button.

2. Click the Overview sheet to view the organization of the Project 15 Skill Drill Exercises workbook.

If you need more than one work session to complete the desired exercises, continue working on **e15drill** instead of starting over on the original e-1502 file.

1. Creating a Macro to Apply Font and Border Color

Your responsibilities include reviewing a list of delinquent accounts. You have already determined which accounts should be referred to an attorney at this time. You will be giving the list to another staff member with instructions to call the firm's current attorney, and you want the relevant accounts to be easily identified. You decide to create a macro that applies a red font and border to a user-specified cell.

To create a macro to apply font and border color:

1. Open the `e15drill` workbook; click Enable Macros, if necessary, and select the #1-ColorInOut worksheet.

2. Select cell B14, and choose Tools, Macro, Record New Macro.

3. Name the macro `RedInOut`, and specify `This Workbook` in the Store macro in text box.

4. Type `Apply red font and border` in the Description text box, and click OK.
   The Stop Recording toolbar opens, and the word Recording displays in the status bar. Now start the keystrokes to set up the desired effects.

5. Click Relative Reference in the Stop Recording toolbar.

6. Select Format, Cells, and click the Font tab.

7. Select Red on the Color drop-down list.

8. Select the Border tab; select Red in the Color drop-down list; click the Outline preset, and click OK.

9. Click the Stop Recording button, and click any cell to deselect cell B14.
   The contents of cell B14 display red, and a red border displays around the cell.

10. Save your changes to the workbook.
    Now test the macro.

11. Select cell B18, and choose Tools, Macro, Macros.

12. Select RedInOut, click Run, and click any cell to deselect B18.
    The contents of cell B18 display red, and a red border displays around the cell.

2. Creating a Macro Assigned to a Shortcut Key

Your responsibilities include reviewing a list of delinquent accounts. You want an easy way to enter and format the current date before printing the report. You decide to create a macro activated by a shortcut key that enters the TODAY function in a user-specified cell, followed by formatting the results to display in the form dd-mmm-yyyy (for example, 14-Feb-2000).

To create a macro assigned to a shortcut key:

1. Open the `e15drill` workbook; click Enable Macros, if necessary, and select the #2-Today worksheet.

2. Click cell B5, and select Tools, Macro, Record New Macro.

3. Name the macro `Today`, and specify `This Workbook` in the Store macro in text box.

4. Type the uppercase letter T in the Shortcut key text box.

5. Type `Enter the system date; show as dd-mmm-yyyy` in the Description text box, and click OK.
   If a message appears indicating that the shortcut key is in use, assign another key. The Stop Recording toolbar opens and the word Recording displays in the status bar. Now start the keystrokes to enter and format the desired function.

6. Type `=today()` in cell B5, and click the green checkmark in the formula bar.

7. Choose Format, Cells, and click the Number tab.

8. Select Date in the Category list, and scroll down and select 14-Mar-1998 in the Type list.

9. Click OK, and click the Stop Recording button.
   Now test that the macro works as intended.

10. Click cell B5, and choose Edit, Clear, All.

11. Choose Tools, Macro, Macros.

12. Select Today in the list of macros, and click Run.
    The current date displays in cell B5 in the form dd-mmm-yyyy.

3. Creating a Macro Button

You have been running a macro by selecting from menu options and lists. Now you decide to set the macro up as a button on the worksheet because someone who is not as familiar with Excel as you are is going to take over management of the file.

To create a macro button:

1. Open the `e15drill` workbook; click <u>E</u>nable Macros, if necessary, and select the #3-Macro Button worksheet.

2. Display the Forms toolbar.

3. Create a button in the range F2:F3.

4. Assign the RedBold macro to the button.

5. Delete the Button 1 text, and replace it with `RedBold`.

6. Close the Forms toolbar, and deselect the RedBold button by clicking outside the button's shadow border.

7. Right-click the macro button.

8. Select Format C<u>o</u>ntrol, and click the Properties tab.

9. Make sure a check mark appears in the <u>P</u>rint object check box, and click OK.

10. Deselect the RedBold button.

11. Save the workbook and leave it open.

12. Select cell B5; then click the RedBold macro button.

Contents of cell B5 display bold with a red background.

13. Save and close the workbook.

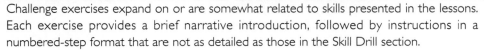

Challenge

Challenge exercises expand on or are somewhat related to skills presented in the lessons. Each exercise provides a brief narrative introduction, followed by instructions in a numbered-step format that are not as detailed as those in the Skill Drill section.

The exercises can be worked in any order. However, if you are working in a lab or on a network, you may not have the ability to create a custom toolbar. If that is the case, you will not be able to do Challenge Exercise 3.

Be sure to save the workbook after completing each exercise. If you need a paper copy of the completed exercise, enter your name centered in a header before printing. Other print options have already been set to print compressed to one page and to display the filename, sheet name, and current date in a footer.

Before beginning your first Project 15 Challenge exercise, complete the following steps:

1. Open the file named `e-1503`; click <u>E</u>nable Macros, and save the file as `e15challenge`.
The workbook contains four sheets: an overview, and exercise sheets named #1-Delete, #2-MacroEdit, and #3-MacroToolbar.

2. Click the Overview sheet to view the organization of the Project 15 Challenge Exercises workbook.

If you need more than one work session to complete the desired exercises, continue working on `e15challenge` instead of starting over on the original e-1503 file.

1. Deleting a Macro and Macro Button

When a macro is no longer needed, it should be deleted. You can delete a macro from a list of macros, and you can delete a macro button in a worksheet. You start this exercise by running two macros, one of which is activated with a macro button. You then delete those two macros, and check that they are no longer available.

To delete a macro and a macro button:

1. Open the **e15challenge** workbook; click Enable Macros, if necessary, and select the #1-Delete worksheet.

2. Click cell D14, and click the Attorney Name/Phone macro button embedded in the worksheet.

   The name and phone number of the firm's attorney display in cell D14.

3. Click cell B5, display the Macro dialog box, and run the BlueInOut macro.

   Cell B4 is surrounded by a blue border, and its contents display in the same color. Now delete both macros, starting with BlueInOut.

4. Display the Macro dialog box; select BlueInOut in the list of macros; click Delete, and click Yes.

5. Right-click the Attorney Name/Phone macro button embedded in the worksheet, and select Cut from the shortcut menu.

   Applying the attorney macro by clicking a button embedded in a worksheet is no longer an option. Now remove the attorney macro itself.

6. Display the Macro dialog box, and delete the Attorney macro.

7. Verify that you no longer can run either macro, and save your changes.

2. Modifying Text in a Macro

If you want to make changes in a macro, you can modify it using the Visual Basic Editor. The editor takes a little practice but is often faster and easier than re-recording the macro. In this exercise, you edit a macro that first writes the name and address of your company in a worksheet, and then widens the column containing the address. You use the Visual Basic Editor to make these changes.

To modify text in a macro:

1. Open the **e15challenge** workbook; click Enable Macros, if necessary, and select the #2-MacroEdit worksheet.

2. Display the Macro dialog box; select the Heading macro, and click Edit.

3. Change the text 5151 Smith Road to reflect the new street address **10 North Sunset Lane**.

   Make sure quotation marks still surround the street address.

4. Save the changes, and exit the Visual Basic window.

5. Select cell D5, and run the macro.

6. Examine the difference between the two addresses to make sure that the change you made in the macro (address) is reflected in the worksheet after running the macro, and then save your changes.

3. Creating a Macro Button on a Custom Toolbar

You know that when you embed a macro button in a worksheet, the macro assigned to that button can only be applied to that worksheet. Now you want to set up a macro button that can be used on many worksheets—one that displays your supervisor's name, Jordan Fields. You have already created the macro, named Supervisor. Now you want to create a macro button on a custom toolbar, as opposed to placing it on one of Excel's toolbars.

You find out that three actions are required if you do not want to put a custom button on an existing Excel toolbar: create a new blank toolbar, create a button on the new toolbar, and assign a macro to the new button.

If you are working in an environment that does not permit you to create a custom toolbar, you will not be able to work through this exercise.

To create a macro button on a custom toolbar:

1. Open the `e15challenge` workbook; click Enable Macros, if necessary, and select the #3-MacroToolbar worksheet.
    Now create the new toolbar.

2. Choose View, Toolbars, and click Customize.

3. Select the Toolbars tab; click the New button; change the name of the new toolbar to `MyTools`, and click OK.
    The New Toolbar dialog box closes, but the Customize dialog box remains open. A new floating toolbar displays. It is quite small at this point, containing room for one button. Now create a button on the new toolbar.

4. Select the Commands tab in the Customize dialog box, and select Macros in the Categories list box.

5. Drag the yellow smiley face in the Commands section to your new MyTools toolbar.
    A copy of the yellow smiley face displays on the new toolbar. A thick black border surrounds it, indicating the new button is selected. Now assign a macro.

6. Right-click the yellow smiley face button on the new toolbar.
    A shortcut menu displays with many options, including Assign Macro near the bottom.

7. Assign the Supervisor macro to the button.

8. Display the shortcut menu again, and change the name and Custom Button to `JF`.

9. Check the Text Only (Always) option in the shortcut menu, and close the Customize dialog box.
    Now test that the new macro button on a custom toolbar operates as intended.

10. Select cell F4, and click the JF button on your custom toolbar.
    Check that the name Jordan Fields displays in red in cell F4.

11. Close the new custom toolbar and save your changes.

Discovery Zone

Discovery Zone exercises require advanced knowledge of topics presented in *MOUS Essentials* lessons, application of skills from multiple lessons, or self-directed learning of new skills.

Be sure to save the workbook after completing each exercise. If you need a paper copy of the completed exercise, enter your name centered in a header before printing. Other print options have already been set to print compressed to one page and to display the filename, sheet name, and current date in a footer.

Before you begin the discovery zone exercises, complete the following steps:

1. Open the file named **e-1504**, click Enable Macros, and save the file as **e15discovery**.
   The workbook contains three sheets: an overview, and exercise sheets named #1-AddButton and #2-ChangeMacro.
2. Click the Overview sheet to view the organization of the Project 15 Discovery Zone Exercises workbook.

If you need more than one work session to complete the desired exercises, continue working on the **e15discovery** workbook instead of starting over on the original e-1504 file.

1. Embedding a Macro Button in a Worksheet

You are a real estate agent and you maintain your own listing of selected properties for sale. You want to create a Hot Property button above the address data in your listing. When you click the button, it should apply a red bold italic 12-point Comic Sans MS font to the user-specified address cell. Create and test this macro button in the #1-AddButton worksheet of the e15discovery workbook.

2. Changing Color by Editing a Macro

Previously, you created a macro named Border that applies a red outline border to a user-specified range of cells. You want to change the color specified in the macro (red), without re-recording the macro. Using the Visual Basic Editor, make the desired change, and test the revised macro by applying it to the range A3:C3 in the #2-ChangeMacro worksheet of the e15discovery workbook.

PinPoint Assessment

You have completed this project and its associated lessons, and have had an opportunity to assess your skills through the end-of-project questions and exercises. Now use the PinPoint software Evaluation Mode to further assess your comprehension of the specific exam activities you have just learned. You can also use the PinPoint Trainer Mode and the Show Me tutorials to practice these exam activities.

Using Auditing Tools, Goal Seek, Data Tables, Scenarios, and Solver

Key terms introduced in this project include

- constraint
- data table
- Goal Seek

- scenario
- Scenario Manager
- Solver

- Trace Dependents
- Trace Precedents

Objectives	Required Activity for MOUS	Exam Level
➤ Use Auditing Tools to Interpret Error Messages	Work with the Auditing toolbar; Trace errors (find and fix errors)	Expert
➤ Use Auditing Tools to Check Worksheet Formulas	Work with the Auditing toolbar; Trace Precedents (find cells referred to in a specific formula); Trace Dependents (find formulas that refer to a specific cell)	Expert
➤ Use Auditing Tools to Reverse Engineer a Worksheet	Work with the Auditing toolbar; Trace Precedents (find cells referred to in a specific formula); Trace Dependents (find formulas that refer to a specific cell)	Expert
➤ Use Goal Seek in Revenue Analysis	Use Goal Seek	Expert
➤ Perform a What-If Analysis with a Data Table	Use data analysis and pivot tables	Expert
➤ Use Scenarios to Perform What-If Analysis	Work with Scenarios	Expert
➤ Use Solver to Maximize Profits	Use Solver	Expert

Why Would I Do This?

Due to their ease of use and versatility, spreadsheets are a primary data analysis tool. Data can be changed to reflect different situations, and analyses can predict outcomes. In this project, you use auditing tools to examine Excel workbooks and verify the accuracy of the formulas in them. You also use four Excel features—Goal Seek, data tables, Scenarios, and Solver—to improve decision making.

Expert ## Lesson 1: Using Auditing Tools to Interpret Error Messages

Important decisions can ride on the results of data analysis and projections, so it is critical to verify that formulas produce accurate results. Excel's Trace Error auditing tool enables you to find errors in your worksheet formulas. You should apply this tool to complex worksheets before making decisions on the basis of formula results.

In this lesson, you open a workbook and select a worksheet that displays #VALUE! in multiple cells. #VALUE! indicates an error that is generally due to a wrong type of argument or operand in a formula. You use the Trace Error button on the Auditing toolbar to find the source of an error. You then fix the error in one cell and copy the revised formula to correct other errors.

To Use Auditing Tools to Interpret Error Messages

1 **Open the e-1601.xls workbook; save it as Analyze-This.xls, and select the Revenue & Expenses worksheet.**
The workbook contains four sheets: Revenue & Expenses, Data Table, Scenario Test and Maximization.

2 **Choose Tools, Auditing, Show Auditing Toolbar.**
The worksheet and Auditing toolbar display, as shown in Figure 16.1.

Figure 16.1
The Auditing toolbar provides access to a variety of auditing techniques.

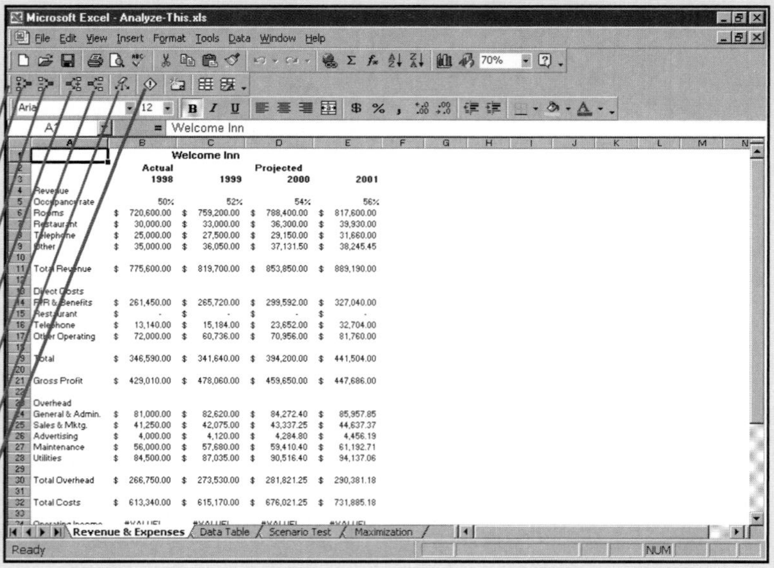

Auditing toolbar

Trace Precedents button

Remove Precedent Arrows button

Trace Dependents button

Remove Dependent Arrows button

Remove All Arrows button

Trace Error button

If You Have Problems...
The Auditing toolbar can be displayed as a floating toolbar within the worksheet instead of a horizontal toolbar anchored near the top of the screen. Figures in the project reflect the horizontal display, but you can change the position of a toolbar if you prefer. To float a toolbar, place the mouse on the vertical bar shaped handle along the top or left edge of the toolbar and drag the toolbar onto the worksheet.

3 **Scroll down to display the rest of the worksheet, and click cell B34.**
You are about to determine the reason for the #VALUE! error message displayed in cells B34:E34 and B39:E39

4 **Click the Trace Error button on the Auditing toolbar (see Figure 16.1).**
A blue border surrounds cells B21:B30, and a blue tracer line with an arrow points to cell B34, as shown in Figure 16.2.

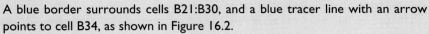

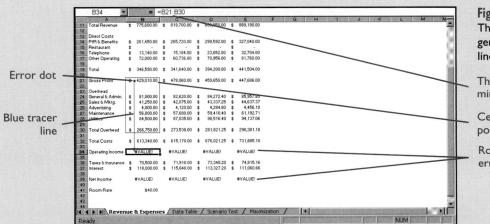

Figure 16.2
The Trace Error button generates a trace error line and an error dot.

The colon should be a minus sign

Cell reference at the point of the error

Rows containing the error message #VALUE!

Error dot

Blue tracer line

5 **Click the formula bar; replace the colon with a minus sign in cell B34, and press ⏎Enter.**
The #VALUE! messages in column B disappear. The number 162,260.00 displays in cell B34, and the negative number (26,240.00) displays in cell B39.

6 **Copy the formula from cell B34 to cells C34:E34.**
The #VALUE! messages in columns C through E disappear.

7 **Save your changes to the Revenue & Expenses worksheet.**
This concludes lesson 1. Continue with the next lesson or close the workbook and exit Excel.

Exam Note: **Error Messages Related to Formulas**

Excel provides a variety of messages to identify a problem in a formula. Common messages are listed and described below.

Error Value	Description
#DIV/0!	The formula is attempting to divide by zero.
#N/A	There is no value in the formula.
#NAME?	Excel doesn't recognize the name in the formula.
#NULL!	An incorrect cell reference or range operator is used in the formula.
#NUM!	There is a problem with a number in the formula.
#REF!	The formula refers to a cell that is not valid.
#VALUE!	The wrong type of operand or argument is used in the formula.

 Inside Stuff: **A Red Tracer Line**

Depending on the type of value you are tracing, a red tracer line may appear. A red tracer line points to a formula that is in error, rather than to the values involved in the error.

 ## Expert Lesson 2: Using Auditing Tools to Check Worksheet Formulas

Trace Precedents and Trace Dependents are auditing tools that enable you to review your worksheets for errors or to help you understand how a worksheet performs its calculations. **Trace Precedents** shows what cells provide data to the current cell, and **Trace Dependents** shows what other cells use the results of the current cell.

In this lesson, you trace precedents and dependents in the Revenue & Expenses worksheet. You discover an error in calculating Total Revenue that is difficult to notice by visual inspection.

To Use Auditing Tools to Check Worksheet Formulas

1 **Open the Analyze-This workbook; select the Revenue & Expenses worksheet, if necessary, and click cell B11.**
Cell B11 contains the first formula in the worksheet.

2 **Click the Trace Precedents button on the Auditing toolbar.**
A blue tracer line connects cell B11 to its related cells, as shown in Figure 16.3. By following the tracer line, you can see that cell B9 was erroneously omitted from the SUM function.

3 **Click cell C11, and click the Trace Precedents button.**
Note that cell C9 was not included in the SUM function in cell C11. Trace Precedents can trace only one cell at a time. If you select multiple cells, Trace Precedents only traces the first cell chosen. You need to check each cell of a formula. If you create a formula and copy it to other cells, those cells should be checked too.

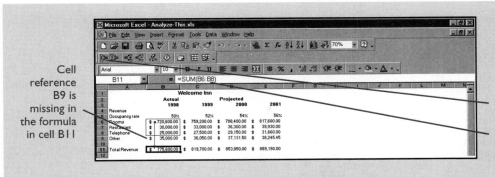

Cell reference B9 is missing in the formula in cell B11

Figure 16.3
Trace Precedents shows the cells used to determine the solution shown in the results cell.

Trace Precedents button

Fix the error by changing B8 to B9

4 **Click cell D11, and click the Trace Precedents button.**
Note that cell D9 was not included in the SUM function in cell D11.

5 **Click cell E11, and click the Trace Precedents button.**
Note that cell E9 was not included in the SUM function in cell E11.

6 **Click cell B11, and edit the formula to sum the range B6:B9 instead of B6:B8.**

7 **Copy the revised formula from cell B11 to cells C11:E11.**
Copying the formula turns off the audit traces. Now that you have corrected the error in row 11, use Trace Precedents to learn how Total Costs in row 32 are calculated.

8 **Click cell B32, and click the Trace Precedents button.**
A blue tracer line points from cell B19 to cell B32. You can see blue dots in cells B19 and B30. These dots indicate that cell B32 uses the values in those cells.

9 **Click the Trace Precedents button again.**
Each time you click the Trace Precedents button, the trace moves to the next level of cells used by the formula.

10 **Click the Remove All Arrows button on the Auditing toolbar.**
All the tracer lines and arrows are removed. Now you can use the Trace Dependents feature to see which cells use the Gross Profit values in row 21.

11 **Click cell B21.**

12 **Click the Trace Dependents button on the Auditing toolbar.**
The tracer line indicates that Gross Profit in cell B21 is used in the calculation of Operating Income in cell B34 (see Figure 16.4).

13 **Click the Trace Dependents button again to see the next dependent cell.**

14 **Click the Remove All Arrows button.**

15 **Save your changes to the Revenues & Expenses worksheet.**
This concludes Lesson 2. Continue with the next lesson, or close the workbook and exit Excel.

continues ▶

To Use Auditing Tools to Check Worksheet Formulas   (continued)

Figure 16.4

Use the Trace
Dependents button to
identify cells that use the
content of the current
cell.

Line tracing dependency

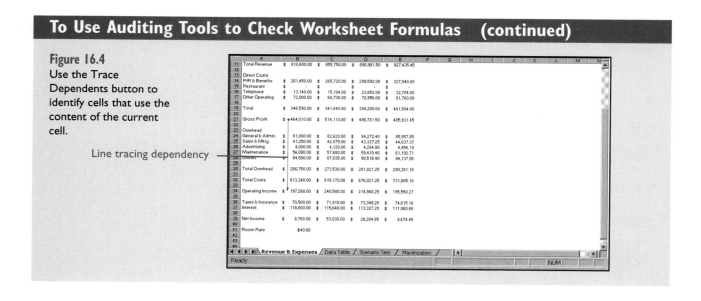

Inside Stuff: **Disappearing Tracer Lines Do Not Ensure**
Correct Formulas

Whenever a change is made to a cell included in a trace, the tracer lines automatically disappear. This does not mean the formula is correct. Retrace the formula to check for accuracy.

 ## Lesson 3: Using Auditing Tools to Reverse Engineer a Worksheet

Often you are faced with the task of understanding a worksheet you did not create.
Determining how someone else's product works by taking it apart and looking at it is
sometimes called reverse engineering.

In this lesson, you use three techniques to learn how the Revenue & Expenses worksheet
is designed. First, you use Trace Precedents to learn how the Taxes & Insurance data is
calculated. Second, you determine which cells are associated with the TaxIns range name.
Finally, you analyze the worksheet by displaying cell formulas rather than values.

To Use Auditing Tools to Reverse Engineer a Worksheet

1 **Open the Analyze-This workbook, select the Revenue & Expenses**
worksheet, if necessary, and click cell C36.

2 **Display the Auditing toolbar if it is not already visible.**

 3 **Click the Trace Precedents button in the Auditing toolbar.**

The tracer line shows that Taxes & Insurance data in cell C36 depends on cell
B36, but in what way? If you look at the formula bar, you see that cell C36
contains a formula that increases the contents of cell B36 by 2 percent. Now
find out what cells are defined in a range name.

4 **Click the Name box drop-down arrow; scroll down the list of range names, and select TaxIns.**

The range B36:E36 is highlighted. Any use of TaxIns in a formula indicates Taxes & Insurance data in the range B36:E36. Now display cell formulas rather than values. This can be done using the Options dialog box or the shortcut key combination Ctrl + ~.

5 **Choose Tools, Options.**

6 **In the Window area on the View tab, check Formulas, and click OK.**

This action provides a quick way to see all the cells that contain formulas. You can use the Trace Precedents and Trace Dependents buttons in formula view. You may need to resize some columns to see complete formulas.

7 **Press the two-key combination Ctrl + ~.**

The shortcut key combination turns formula display off. Pressing this key combination repeatedly toggles between formulas view and regular view.

8 **Turn off the Auditing toolbar, and save your changes.**

This concludes Lesson 3. You can continue with the next lesson or close the workbook and exit Excel.

 Inside Stuff: **Printing Cell Formulas**

When you print a worksheet showing formulas instead of formula results, be sure to set print specifications that make it easy to see which cells are referenced in each formula. Display the Page Setup dialog box, and click the Sheet tab. Check two boxes: Gridlines and Row and column headings. In most worksheets, it is also useful to set Landscape orientation on the Page tab when printing cell formulas.

Lesson 4: Using Goal Seek in Revenue Analysis

Goal Seek is a Microsoft Excel tool that enables you to find a specific result in one cell by adjusting the value in one other cell. In this lesson, you specify that you want to earn $800,000 from Room revenue in the Year 2000. Using Goal Seek, you can determine that an occupancy rate of 54.7945205479452% must occur to reach the desired revenue level. Imagine how difficult it would be to solve for this value using trial and error. With Goal Seek you simply enter a few parameters and Excel provides the solution.

To Use Goal Seek in Revenue Analysis

1 **Open the Analyze-This workbook; select the Revenue & Expenses worksheet, if necessary, and click cell D6.**

This cell contains the projected revenue from room rentals in the year 2000, based on a 54 percent occupancy rate (cell D5) and a $40 room rate (cell B41).

continues ▶

To Use Goal Seek in Revenue Analysis (continued)

2 **Select Tools, Goal Seek.**

The Goal Seek dialog box opens. Cell D6 displays in the Set cell text box.

3 **Click the To value text box, and type 800000.**

The revenue amount you want to produce is set.

4 **Click the By changing cell text box, and click cell D5 in the worksheet.**

Cell D5 is the location of the cell that contains the value you want to change, as shown in Figure 16.5.

Figure 16.5
Three specifications must be entered in the Goal Seek dialog box.

Specify the cell in which to find a specific result

Specify the cell in which to adjust the value

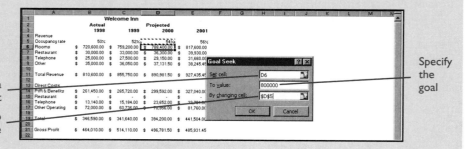

Specify the goal

5 **Click OK.**

The Goal Seek Status dialog box indicates that a solution has been found, as shown in Figure 16.6.

Figure 16.6
Goal Seek parameters display in the Goal Seek Status dialog box.

Occupancy rate needed to achieve the goal of $800,000 room rental revenue in 2000

Target value (goal) in cell D6

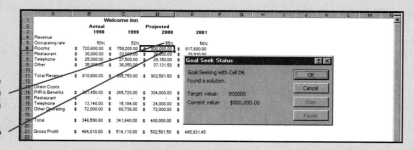

6 **Click OK.**

The Goal Seek Status dialog box closes, and the worksheet reflects the new cell values.

7 **Click cell D5.**

Notice in the formula bar that the occupancy rate to reach the goal set for room revenue is approximately 54.79 percent. An increase of less than 1 percent in occupancy rate can raise room revenue by nearly $20,000.

8 **Save your changes to the worksheet.**

This concludes Lesson 4. You can continue with the next lesson, or close the workbook and exit Excel.

Exam Note: **Restrictions on a Goal Seek Operation**
The variable cell you enter in the By <u>c</u>hanging cell text box must be a value. Goal Seek cannot operate correctly if the cell contains a formula. If the cell contains a formula, Goal Seek displays an alert box.

 Inside Stuff: **Undoing the Results of Using Goal Seek**
To change a worksheet back to its values prior to the Goal Seek operation, click the Undo button on the Standard toolbar.

Lesson 5: Performing a What-if Analysis with a Data Table

A **data table** is a feature that enables you to create a series of results based on one formula. Excel supports creating one- and two-variable tables. The advantage of a data table is that you can view several variations of results at the same time.

In this lesson, you create a one-variable data table that calculates the monthly payment on a loan and the total to be paid back on a loan (the amount of each payment times the number of payments). The variable is the length of the loan—in this case, intervals of 15, 20, 25, and 30 years. You find out that the cost of borrowing $100,000 at 7 percent annual interest is significantly less if you pay the loan off in 15 years instead of 30 years. The table also shows that as total payback increases, the monthly payment decreases.

To Perform a What-If Analysis with a Data Table

1 **If necessary, open the** `Analyze-This` **workbook, and select the Data Table worksheet.**
Most of the worksheet design to create a one-variable table is in place. Explore the layout of the worksheet before creating the one-variable data table.

2 **Click cell B7.**
The formula =PMT(A4/12,A7*12,-A3) displays in the formula bar. This formula calculates the monthly payment assuming a 15 year 7 percent $100,000 loan.

3 **Click cell C7.**
The formula =A7*12*B7 displays in the formula bar. This formula sums all payments across the loan term—years (15 in cell A7) times 12 (the number of payments in a year) times the amount of each monthly payment ($898.93 in cell B7).

4 **Select cells A7:B10.**
The data table range is selected.

5 **Choose** <u>D</u>**ata,** <u>T</u>**able.**
The Table dialog box displays (see Figure 16.7).

6 **Click in the** <u>C</u>**olumn input cell box.**

7 **Click cell A7, and click OK.**
Excel generates the one-variable data table (see Figure 16.8).

continues ▶

To Perform a What-If Analysis with a Data Table (continued)

Figure 16.7

Enter a Row input cell or a column input cell to create a one-variable table.

Enter cell A7 here to generate a data table that calculates monthly payments assuming 20, 25, and 30-year loans

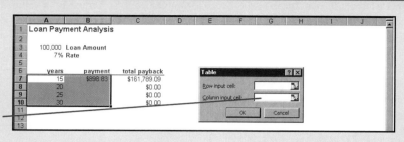

Figure 16.8

The completed data table displays payment and total payback data for four loan terms, assuming a 7 percent $100,000 loan.

Results of specifying a Column input cell when creating a data table

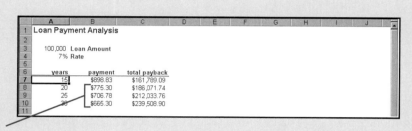

8 Press Ctrl + ~.

Formulas display instead of formula results (see Figure 16.9)

Figure 16.9

The formulas =TABLE(,A7) in column B reflect creation of a one-variable data table based on a column input cell.

Formulas generated by a Data, Table command

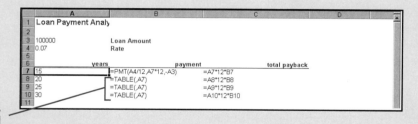

9 Press Ctrl + ~.

The formulas are no longer displayed.

10 **Change the contents of cell A4 from 7% to 8%.**

Payment and Payback amounts update. For example, the monthly payment on a 15-year $100,000 loan is $955.65 for an 8 percent loan, compared to $898.83 for a 7 percent loan.

11 **Save your changes to the Data Table worksheet.**

This concludes Lesson 5. Continue with the next lesson, or close the workbook and exit Excel.

 Exam Note: **Clearing Values Created in a Data Table**

You cannot clear individual values in a data table. To clear only the resulting values, select them (exclude the original formulas and input cell values) and choose Edit, Clear, Contents. To clear the entire data table, select all values (include the original formulas and input cell values), and choose Edit, Clear, All.

Lesson 6: Using Scenarios to Perform a What-If Analysis

Scenario Manager is a feature that enables you to specify multiple input values and save the results. Each combination of input values and the corresponding results is called a **scenario**. Creating scenarios can be useful when you have several what-if assumptions and want to present the results of all of them. For example, you might want to summarize the effects of various combinations of interest rate and loan term on the size of a loan payment.

In this lesson, you analyze loan data similar to that presented in the previous lesson on data tables. You create four scenarios—two loan periods (15- and 20-year) each at two interest rates (7 percent and 8 percent). You also generate a scenario summary. After completing the steps in this lesson and the previous one, you have some basis for deciding which approach—data tables or scenarios—is the better tool for a specific information need.

To Use Scenarios to Perform a What-If Analysis

1 **Open the `Analyze-This` workbook, if necessary, and select the Scenario Test worksheet.**

2 **Choose Tools, Scenarios.**
The Scenario Manager dialog box displays (see Figure 16.10).

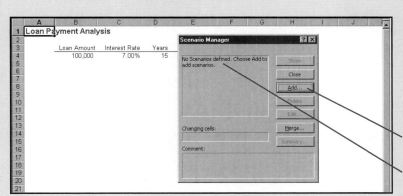

Figure 16.10
Scenarios have not been defined yet. The Scenario Manager dialog box displays a variety of Scenario Manager options.

Add button

Instruction to proceed with creating a scenario

3 **Click the Add button.**
The Add Scenario dialog box displays.

4 **Type `15yr, 7%` in the Scenario name text box.**

5 **Click in the Changing cells text box, and specify cells B4:D4.**

6 **Type `Created by yourname` (substitute your first and last names in place of yourname) in the Comment text box.**
The specifications you entered display in the Edit Scenario dialog box (see Figure 16.11).

7 **Click OK.**
The Scenario Values dialog box displays (see Figure 16.12).

8 **Click the Add button.**
The Add Scenario dialog box displays. Now set up a second scenario.

continues ▶

To Use Scenarios to Perform a What-If Analysis (continued)

Figure 16.11
To create an initial scenario, you must give it a name and specify which cells change. Comments are optional.

Values subject to change (input variables)

Enter a descriptive name for the scenario here

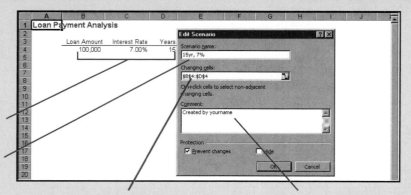

Enter the cells containing input variables here

Enter comments describing the scenario or its update history

Figure 16.12
The Scenario Values dialog box displays the values for the first scenario.

Click here to add another scenario

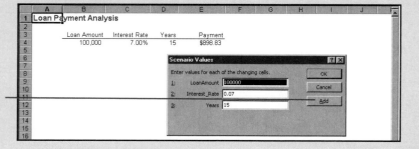

9 Type **15yr, 8%** in the Scenario **n**ame text box; check that **B4:D4** displays in the Changing **c**ells text box; specify comments of your choice, and click **OK**.

10 Type **0.08** in the Interest_Rate text box of the Scenario Values dialog box.

The specifications for the second scenario are complete. Now set up a third scenario.

11 Click **A**dd, type **20yr, 7%** in the Scenario **n**ame text box; check that **B4:D4** displays in the Changing **c**ells text box; specify comments of your choice, and click **OK**.

12 Check that **0.07** displays in the Interest_Rate text box of the Scenario Values dialog box, and type **20** in the Years text box.

The specifications for the third scenario are complete. Now set up a fourth scenario.

13 Click **A**dd, type **20yr, 8%** in the Scenario Name text box; check that **B4:D4** displays in the Changing **c**ells text box; specify comments of your choice, and click **OK**.

14 Type **0.08** in the Interest Rate text box; type **20** in the Years text box, and click **OK**.

Be sure to click OK instead of Add when you complete the last scenario. The Scenario Manager dialog box opens and lists four scenarios (see Figure 16.13).

Figure 16.13
The names of four scenarios display in the Scenario Manager dialog box.

15 **Click the scenario name 20yr, 8%, and click the _S_how button.**
The results of this scenario display on the worksheet—a payment of $836.44 in cell E4. (You may need to move the dialog box to view cell E4.) You can view the results of any other scenario by selecting its name in the Scenario Manager dialog box and clicking _S_how. Now create a summary of the current scenarios.

16 **Click the _S_ummary button in the Scenario Manager dialog box.**

17 **Click the Scenario _s_ummary option, and click within the _R_esult cells text box.**

18 **Specify cell E4, and click OK.**
Excel generates the Scenario Summary shown in Figure 16.14. Notice that the summary output includes outlining symbols. You can click outlining symbols to expand or contract the output.

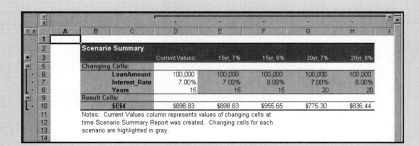

Figure 16.14
The Scenario Summary button generates output summarizing the various scenarios.

19 **Save your changes to the Analyze-This workbook.**
This concludes Lesson 6. Continue with the last lesson in the project, or close the workbook and exit Excel.

**Exam Note: Modifying and Deleting a Scenario**
In this lesson, you used the Add and Show buttons in the Scenario Manager dialog box. You can also use this dialog box to edit or delete a scenario. Select the name of the scenario, and click the _D_elete or _E_dit button as desired.

Lesson 7: Using Solver to Maximize Profits

Solver, like Goal Seek, enables you to manipulate variables to achieve a desired result. The difference is that Solver allows more complex problem solving because you can alter multiple variables and apply constraints. A **constraint** means that there is a limit or maximum value. When manufacturing a product, for example, resources are limited. There is not an infinite amount of time, raw materials, labor, and so on to commit to the manufacturing process.

Constraints are usually stated as some variation of "less than" or "greater than" but there can also be "equal to" constraints. In this lesson, you determine the most profitable product mix for a factory that produces two models of a product: Standard and Deluxe. The Standard and Deluxe models contribute $19 and $24 to profit respectively. Assuming for the moment that there are no constraints on the number of each model that can be sold, we can use Solver to determine how many of each model should be produced to maximize profit. Figure 16.15 illustrates the worksheet that has been set up to solve for the optimal product mix.

Figure 16.15
Use the Maximization worksheet to solve for the most profitable product mix.

Range name defined as cell B5

Range name defined as cell C5

Profit changes if units produced change

Constraints in the range F14:F15

Hours still available

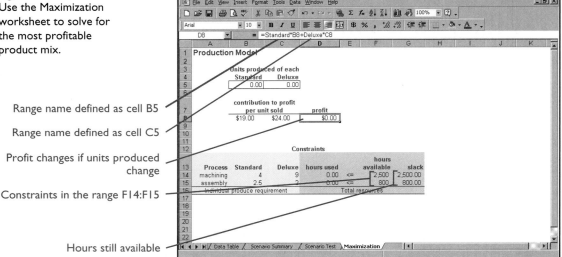

The production requirements display in the range A13:C15. Each model requires two manufacturing operations, machining and assembly. Each Standard model requires 4 hours machining and 2.5 hours assembly. The Deluxe model requires 9 hours machining and 2 hours assembly. The constraints display in the range F14:F15. Each month 2,500 machining hours and 800 assembly hours are available.

Now use Solver to determine the manufacturing mix that will maximize profits.

To Use Solver to Maximize Profits

❶ Open the Analyze-This workbook, if necessary, and select the Maximization worksheet.
The worksheet illustrated in Figure 16.15 displays. Now try to find that combination of units produced that will maximize profits without using Solver.

② **Enter 200 in cell B5 and 100 in cell C5.**

A profit of $6,200 displays in cell D8, and slack hours of 800 (machining) and 100 (assembly) display in cells G14 and G15 respectively.

③ **Enter 100 in cell B5 and 200 in cell C5.**

A profit of $6,700 displays in cell D8, and slack hours of 300 (machining) and 150 (assembly) display in cells G14 and G15 respectively.

④ **Enter 100 in cell B5 and 250 in cell C5.**

A profit of $7,900 displays in cell D8, but the red background (due to conditional formatting applied to cell D14) indicates that the combination of producing 100 standard and 250 deluxe models exceeds the machining hours available. You can continue to vary the content of cells B5 and C5 on your own, hoping to find the optimal combination of units produced by trial and error. Instead, use Excel's Solver feature.

⑤ **Select Tools, Solver.**

The Solver Parameters dialog box opens (see Figure 16.16).

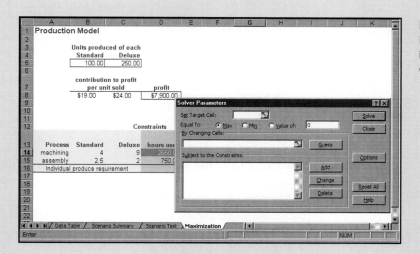

Figure 16.16
Enter Solver specifications in the Solver Parameters dialog box.

⊠ *If You Have Problems...*

Solver is an add-in, meaning that it is not an intrinsic part of Microsoft Excel. If the Solver option does not display on your Tools menu, you need to install the feature. Select Tools, Add-Ins. Scroll down the list of add-ins, select Solver, and click OK. Click Yes if prompted to confirm the install procedure. You will probably need your Microsoft Office CD.

All of the input boxes in the Solver Parameters dialog box should be blank. If not, click the Reset All button, and click OK in the resulting message box.

⑥ **Click within the Set Target Cell text box, and click cell D8.**

Cell D8 calculates profit, the amount you want to maximize. When using Solver, the official name for this cell is the objective function.

⑦ **Click the Max button to the right of Equal To.**

continues ▶

To Use Solver to Maximize Profits (continued)

8 Click within the **B**y Changing Cells text box, and specify the range **B5:C5.**

9 Click within the S**u**bject to the Constraints text box, and click **A**dd.
The Add Constraint dialog box opens. Now specify the first of two constraints.

10 Click within the Cell **R**eference box, and click cell **D14.**

11 In the operator box, the middle box of three boxes, select the less than or equal to operator (<=) if it is not already specified.

12 Click within the **C**onstraint text box, and click cell **F14.**
Settings for the machining hours constraint display, as shown in Figure 16.17.

Figure 16.17
Enter each constraint in the Add Constraint dialog box.

Specify the operator here

Click here to display a list of operators

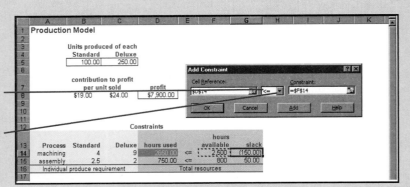

13 Click **A**dd to display a blank Add Constraint dialog box, and specify three settings: **$D$15** as the cell reference, **<=** as the comparison operator, and **$F$15** as the constraint.
The assembly hours constraint is set. Now specify that entries in cells B5 and C5 must be whole numbers (integers).

14 Click **A**dd to display a blank Add Constraint dialog box, and specify **$B$5:$C$5** as the cell reference.

15 Click the drop-down arrow at the right end of the middle box, click **int,** and click **OK.**
The Solver Parameters dialog box reappears. Three constraints are listed in the Subject to the Constraints area of the dialog box (see Figure 16.18).

16 Click the **S**olve button.
The Solver Results dialog box displays, and the values change in cells B5, C5, D14, D15, F14, F15, G14, and G15 (see Figure 16.19).

17 Check that *Keep Solver Solution* is selected, and click **OK.**

18 Save your changes to the Maximization worksheet and close the Analyze-This workbook.
Solver results and parameters remain even after the workbook is saved and closed. This concludes Project 16. Continue with end-of-project exercises, or exit Excel.

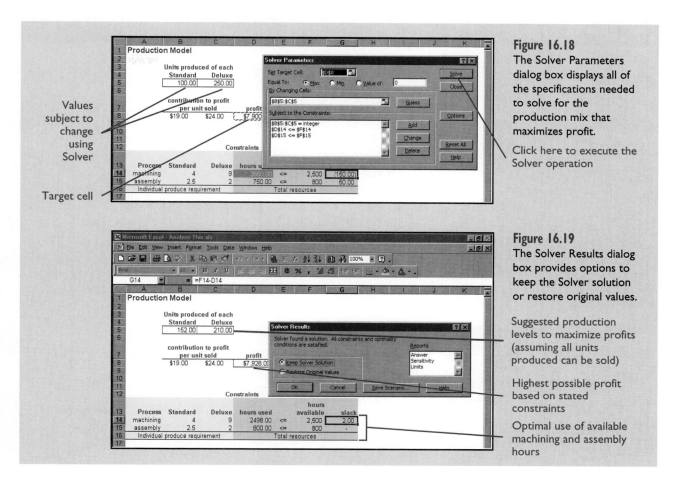

Figure 16.18
The Solver Parameters dialog box displays all of the specifications needed to solve for the production mix that maximizes profit.

Click here to execute the Solver operation

Figure 16.19
The Solver Results dialog box provides options to keep the Solver solution or restore original values.

Suggested production levels to maximize profits (assuming all units produced can be sold)

Highest possible profit based on stated constraints

Optimal use of available machining and assembly hours

Values subject to change using Solver

Target cell

 Inside Stuff: **Saved Solver Solutions Cannot Be Undone**
The Keep Solver Solution option in the Solver Results dialog box is the default option. If you choose to keep the solution, you should know that the change is permanent and cannot be undone. It is a good idea to make a backup copy of your original worksheet in case you want to use it again.

Summary

In the first three lessons of this project, you used Excel's auditing tools to verify the accuracy of worksheet formulas and to understand which cells relate to other cells. You then worked through four lessons providing an introduction to Microsoft Excel tools that support what-if analysis: Goal Seek, data tables, Scenario Manager, and Solver.

Use Goal Seek when you know the desired result, but don't know what some other value must be to achieve that result (for example, finding the occupancy rate that produces a specific amount of room rental revenue). Data tables are appropriate in instances where you want to know the results of changing one or two variables in a formula across a range of data (for example, finding the effect on monthly payment of changes in loan term). Scenario Manager supports creating a variety of analyses, and storing them for later use (for example, determining monthly payment on a loan for an assortment of combinations of loan term and interest rate). Solver enables you to specify a target result (for example, optimizing profit) given constraints (such as limited resources).

Checking Concepts and Terms ✓

True/False

For each of the following, check *T* or *F* to indicate whether the statement is true or false.

__T __F **1.** The Trace Dependents tool shows what cells provide data to the current cell. [L2]

__T __F **2.** Goal Seek can be a useful what-if analysis tool when the desired result is known. [L4]

__T __F **3.** Solutions found through Solver cannot be saved for future use. [L7]

__T __F **4.** Excel supports the creation of one- and two-variable data tables. [L5]

__T __F **5.** A scenario is a combination of input values and the corresponding results that you can select from the Scenario Manager dialog box [L6]

Multiple Choice

Circle the letter of the correct answer for each of the following.

1. Which error value suggests that the wrong kind of operand or argument was used in a formula? [L1]

  a. #NAME?

  b. #REF!

  c. #VALUE!

  d. #N/A

2. Which of the following is not a button on the Auditing toolbar? [L1, L2]

  a. Trace Precedents

  b. Trace Dependents

  c. Remove All Arrows

  d. Fix Error

3. When a solution is found with Solver, [L7]

  a. the worksheet is automatically updated with the solver results

  b. you can keep that Solver solution or restore the original values

  c. and you elect to keep that solution, you can undo the solution

  d. both a and c

4. Which of the following is not an accurate statement about data tables? [L5]

  a. You can clear individual values in a data table.

  b. To clear an entire data table, select all values and then choose Edit, Clear, All.

  c. A data table is a feature that enables you to create a series of results based on one formula.

  d. You can clear only the resulting values in a data table (retaining the original formulas and input cell values) if you select the resulting value cells and choose Edit, Clear, Contents.

5. Which of the following is an accurate statement? [L1, L2, L6]

  a. You can delete one scenario without also deleting other scenarios.

  b. A red tracer line points to a formula that is in error, rather than to the values involved in the error.

  c. When a tracer line disappears, it means that any formula associated with the tracer line is correct.

  d. both a and b

Skill Drill

Skill Drill exercises reinforce project skills. Each skill reinforced is the same, or nearly the same, as a skill presented in the project. Detailed instructions are provided in a step-by-step format.

The exercises can be worked in any order. Be sure to save the workbook after completing each exercise. If you need a paper copy of the completed exercise, enter your name centered in a header before printing. Other print options have already been set to print compressed to one page and to display the filename, sheet name, and current date in a footer.

Before beginning your first Project 16 Skill Drill exercise, complete the following steps:

1. Open the file named **e-1602**, and save it as **e16drill**.
   The workbook contains four sheets: an overview, and exercise sheets named #1-Trace, #2-RoomRate, and #3-DeleteTable.

2. Click the Overview sheet to view the organization of the Project 16 Skill Drill Exercises workbook.

If you need more than one work session to complete the desired exercises, continue working on **e16drill** instead of starting over on the original e-1602 file.

1. Tracing Precedents and Dependents

You have just received a workbook from someone else, and you want to know which cells provide data to a cell containing a formula, and which cells use the results of a formula.

To trace precedents and dependents:

1. Open the **e16drill** workbook, if necessary, and select the #1-Trace worksheet.

2. Display the Auditing toolbar, and click cell B9.

3. Click the Trace Precedents button in the Auditing toolbar.
   Cells B7 and B8 provide data to calculate the Gross Profit in cell B9.

4. Click the Remove Precedent Arrows button.

5. Click the Trace Dependents button.
   Cell B9 was used to determine the contents of cells C9 through N9 and cell B12.

6. Click the Remove Dependent Arrows button.

7. Click cell B10, and click the Trace Precedents button. Cells A15 and B7 provide data to calculate the Commissions in B10.

8. Click cell G10, and click the Trace Precedents button.

9. Click cell B17, and type the cell references of the cells providing data to calculate the Commissions in G10.

10. Save your changes. (The tracer lines disappear when you save a worksheet, but the note you entered in cell B17 is saved.)

2. Using Goal Seek to Find a Room Rate

In Lesson 4 of Project 16, you used Goal Seek to find the occupancy rate needed to generate a desired level of revenue. Now you want to find the room rate required to generate a desired level of revenue assuming a specified occupancy rate.

To use Goal Seek to find a room rate:

1. Open the `e16drill` workbook, if necessary, and se-lect the #2-RoomRate worksheet.

2. Click cell D8, and choose Tools, Goal Seek.

3. Click within the To value text box and type **900000**.

4. Click within the By changing cell text box, type **B43** (the cell reference of the cell containing the room rate), and click OK.
   The Goal Seek Status dialog box indicates that goal seeking with cell D8 found a solution.

5. Click OK, and scroll down to view cell B43. The room rate $45.66 displays in cell B43. All formu-las using room rate data in columns C, D, and E re-calculate to reflect the room rate found by Goal Seek.

6. Save your changes to the #2-RoomRate worksheet.

3. Deleting a Data Table

On some occasions you might want to delete part or all of a data table. You cannot delete an individual cell in a table. You can, however, remove an entire table.

To delete a data table:

1. Open the `e16drill` workbook, if necessary, and se-lect the #3-DeleteTable worksheet.

2. Click cell B11, and press Del.
   Excel displays a message stating that you cannot change part of a table.

3. Click OK; select the range A11:B12, and then press Del.
   Excel again displays a message stating that you can-not change part of a table.

4. Click OK; select the range A10:B12, and press Del.
   This time Excel allows deletion of the values pro-duced by a Data, Table command.

5. Save your changes to the #3-DeleteTable work-sheet.

Challenge

Challenge exercises expand on or are somewhat related to skills presented in the lessons. Each exercise provides a brief narrative introduction, followed by instructions in a numbered-step format that are not as detailed as those in the Skill Drill section.

The exercises can be worked in any order. Be sure to save the workbook after complet-ing each exercise. If you need a paper copy of the completed exercise, enter your name centered in a header before printing. Other print options have already been set to print compressed to one page and to display the filename, sheet name, and current date in a footer.

Before beginning your first Project 16 Challenge exercise, complete the following steps:

1. Open the file named **e-1603**, click No if prompted to update links, and save the file as **e16challenge**.
   The workbook contains five sheets: an overview, and exercise sheets named #1-Data Table, #2-GoalData, #2-GoalChart, and #3-SolverReport.

2. Click the Overview sheet to view the organization of the Project 16 Challenge Exercises workbook.

If you need more than one work session to complete the desired exercises, continue working on **e16challenge** instead of starting over on the original e-1603 file.

1. Creating a One-Variable Data Table

In Lesson 5 of Project 16, you created a one-variable data table in which the rows of the table were varying loan terms. In this exercise, you create a similar data table, except that the rows reflect varying interest rates.

To create a one-variable data table:

1. Open the **e16challenge** workbook, click <u>N</u>o if prompted to update links, and se-
    lect the #1-Data Table worksheet.
2. If values display in the range B10:B21, select B10:B21 and press (Del).
3. Select cells A9:B21, and choose <u>D</u>ata, <u>T</u>able.
4. Select the <u>C</u>olumn input cell, specify cell A9, and click OK.
    Excel automatically calculates all monthly payments in column B associated with the
    varying interest rates in column A.
5. Save your changes to the #1-Data Table worksheet.
6. Experiment with different values for the loan amount and loan term in cells A3:A4.
7. Close the workbook without saving your most recent changes.

2. Updating a Chart with Goal Seek

When Goal Seek finds a solution, changes to data on a worksheet are also reflected in any chart based on that worksheet data. In this exercise, you specify a target revenue in a Goal Seek operation and view the subsequent change in revenue in both the worksheet and its associated chart.

To update a chart using Goal Seek:

1. Open the **e16challenge** workbook, if necessary, click <u>N</u>o if prompted to update
    links, and select the #2-GoalChart tab.
2. Position the pointer on the Year 2000 column.
    Excel displays a message that the value of the Total Revenue point for the year
    2000 is $890,981.50.
3. Select the #2-GoalData worksheet, and click cell D13.
    The amount of Total Revenue for the year 2000 in cell D13 is the same as the
    amount you viewed on the chart.
4. Start a Goal Seek operation, and specify **900000** in the To <u>v</u>alue text box.
5. In the By <u>c</u>hanging cell text box, specify the cell containing the projected occupancy
    rate for the year 2000, and execute the Goal Seek operation.
6. Check that both the worksheet and the chart reflect changes in projected Total
    Revenue given the change in projected occupancy rate entered by Goal Seek, and
    save your changes to the e16challenge workbook.

3. Generating a Solver Report

Solver offers several reports that expand on the results it generates. In this exercise, you generate one of those reports.

To generate a Solver report:

1. Open **e16challenge**, if necessary, click No if prompted to update links, and select the #3-SolverReport worksheet.
   Currently the worksheet shows 100 standard units (cell B7) and 200 deluxe units (cell C7).

2. Activate the Solver, and click the Solve button.

3. View the options in the Reports list box of the Solver Results dialog box.

4. Select the Answer report, and click OK.
   Excel generates a report on a newly created worksheet named Answer Report 1.

5. Select the new worksheet and examine its contents.

6. Save your changes to the e16challenge workbook.

Discovery Zone

Discovery Zone exercises require advanced knowledge of topics presented in *MOUS Essentials* lessons, application of skills from multiple lessons, or self-directed learning of new skills.

Each exercise is independent of the others, so you can complete the exercises in any order. Be sure to save the workbook after completing each exercise. If you need a paper copy of the completed exercise, enter your name centered in a header before printing. Other print options have already been set to print compressed to one page and to display the filename, sheet name, and current date in a footer.

Before beginning your first Project 16 Discovery Zone exercise, complete the following steps:

1. Open the file named **e-1604**, and save it as **e16discovery**.
   The workbook contains three sheets: an overview and two exercise sheets named #1-Invest and #2-Minimize.

2. Click the Overview sheet to view the organization of the Project 16 Discovery Zone Exercises workbook.

If you need more than one work session to complete the desired exercises, continue working on **e16discovery** instead of starting over on the original e-1604 file.

1. Analyzing Investment Options Using Scenarios

You are the president of a homeowners association. The association collects a monthly maintenance fee from each homeowner and in return provides various services including painting, lawn care, and snow removal. The association has a surplus each month and needs to invest part of that in a fund that will provide money needed for replacing roofs on all of the homes. The association tentatively plans to invest $1,000 a month for this purpose, but must have $300,000 at the end of 15 years when the first roofs are scheduled for replacement. There are some reasonably safe fixed interest investments that yield between 6 and 8 percent.

Open the **e16discovery** workbook, and select the #1-Invest worksheet. Create at least six scenarios showing varying interest rates and deposit amounts that might generate the minimum amount needed in 15 years. Generate a summary of your scenarios.

2. Minimizing Costs Using Solver

Solver can be used to minimize costs as well as maximize profits. In this exercise, you use Solver to find the best way to ship from three factories in the United States to six warehouses around the country. The objective is to find the combination that results in the lowest total shipping cost.

Open the **e16discovery** workbook, and select the #2-Minimize worksheet. Take a few moments to understand how the transportation model is organized.

- Cells C6:H8 show the cost per unit of shipping one unit from any factory to any warehouse.

- Cells C15:H17 show the units shipped.

- Cell C22 uses a SUMPRODUCT function to calculate the total shipping cost by multiplying shipping cost times units shipped. This is the objective function that you need to minimize.

- The cells shown in green indicate the capacity of each factory and the requirements of each warehouse. Note that the total capacity is larger than the total warehouse requirement, so the final solution will show some slack.

- The cells shown in yellow represent the actual amount produced/shipped.

The worksheet shows an initial allocation of shipments from the factories to the warehouses. However, the current allocation may not be the best solution ($191,900 total shipping cost). Now start a Solver operation and set up parameters as shown in Figure 16.20. Generate and save the solution.

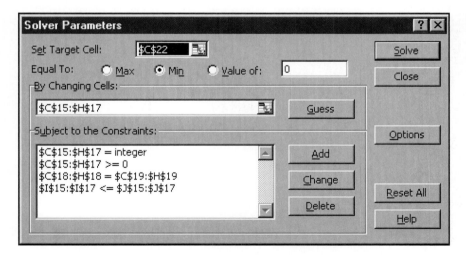

Figure 16.20
The parameters to minimize total shipping costs display in the Solver Parameters dialog box.

Hint: Select the appropriate cell ranges—don't just type them in. As you are creating the constraints, note the purpose of each. The first one makes the quantities integers, and the second one forces non-negative answers. The third constraint sets the warehouse requirements, and the last constraint relates to factory capacity. The optimal solution results in $142,900 total shipping costs.

PinPoint Assessment

You have completed this project and its associated lessons, and have had an opportunity to assess your skills through the end-of-project questions and exercises. Now use the PinPoint software Evaluation Mode to further assess your comprehension of the specific exam activities you have just learned. You can also use the PinPoint Trainer Mode and the Show Me tutorials to practice these exam activities.

Using Collaborative Tools, Extracting Data, and Creating Hyperlinks

Key terms introduced in this project include

- hyperlink
- shared workbook

Objectives	Required Activity for MOUS	Exam Level
➤ Track Changes in a Workbook	Track changes (highlight, accept, and reject)	Expert
➤ Accept or Reject Changes	Track changes (highlight, accept, and reject)	Expert
➤ Edit a Shared Workbook	Create a shared workbook	Expert
➤ Extract Data Using Advanced Filter	Extract data	Expert
➤ Use Hyperlinks within a Workbook	Create hyperlinks	Core
➤ Use a Hyperlink in a Word Document to Reference Excel Data	Create hyperlinks	Core
➤ Use a Hyperlink in a PowerPoint Slide to Reference Excel Data	Create hyperlinks	Core

Why Would I Do This?

Excel provides a feature to track changes that were made since the last time a workbook was saved. Although you may occasionally want to see what you have changed during a session, tracking changes is especially useful when two or more users are sharing (collaborating on) a workbook over a network.

While working with multiple applications and collaborating with others on end products, you are likely to encounter a *hyperlink*—underlined text that you click to jump to another location. Often these links are in Web pages and refer to other Web pages. However, hyperlinks can be embedded in Microsoft Office applications to refer to other application files, other locations within the current file, or Internet links.

Excel also supports extracting data, such as data in selected fields from records in a list that meet specified criteria. You can distribute extracted data to others via email attachment or shared workbooks. All of these features support the collaborative process that promotes working smarter by sharing ideas and information.

[Expert] Lesson 1: Tracking Changes in a Workbook

In a work environment, it is common practice for two or more people to collaborate on developing or editing a workbook. Each user needs to know what changes the others have made. Excel supports this need by providing the ability to track changes.

In this lesson, you work with an office supply inventory model. Imagine that the workbook is available to many users on a network or is distributed among users via email or on disk. After opening the workbook, you save it using a different name. You then turn on the track changes tool and prepare to monitor changes made by different users.

To Track Changes in a Workbook

❶ Open the Excel workbook named e-1701.xls, save it as Tools.xls, and select the Tracking worksheet.
The workbook contains two worksheets named Tracking and Employees. Members of several departments use the Tracking worksheet to monitor items requisitioned from a central supply area.

❷ Choose Tools, Track Changes, Highlight Changes.
The Highlight Changes dialog box displays (see Figure 17.1).

❸ Check the Track changes while editing check box.

❹ Check the When check box, and select All from the drop-down list.
As the name implies, the When check box determines the extent of tracking changes. Selecting All (the default) causes all changes to be tracked. Other options include Since I last saved, Not yet reviewed, and Since date. If you select the last option, Excel provides a prompt to enter the date.

❺ Check the Who check box, and select Everyone from the drop-down list.
Options on the Who drop-down list include Everyone and Everyone but Me. The latter might be used if you were a supervisor or wanted to monitor changes other people in your workgroup made to the workbook.

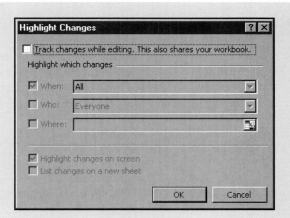

Figure 17.1
Parameters for tracking changes are set from the Highlight Changes dialog box.

Leave the Wh<u>e</u>re check box unchecked. (If you check Wh<u>e</u>re, you can select specific cells to be monitored.)

6 **Check the `Highlight changes on` <u>s</u>`creen` check box, if necessary.**
A cell comment is created for every cell that is changed.

7 **Click OK. If a message box appears asking whether you want to continue the save operation, click OK.**
Note in the Excel title bar that tracking changes automatically shares the workbook even though you may not actually be sharing with anyone yet ([Shared] displays in the title bar). While in shared mode, certain operations are not available. For example, you cannot delete a worksheet while a workbook is shared.

8 **Save your changes to the Tools workbook.**
This concludes Lesson 1. Continue with the next lesson, or close the workbook and exit Excel.

Lesson 2: Accepting or Rejecting Changes

When multiple users revise a tracked document, generally one person makes the final decision on whether to keep or discard the suggested changes. It is a good idea to accept or reject changes on a regular basis to keep the display of changes made to other changes at a minimum.

In this lesson, you continue to work with the Office Supply Inventory model. You use the Accept or Reject Changes option to accept one change and reject another.

To Accept or Reject Changes

1 **Open the Excel workbook named `Tools.xls`, if necessary, and select the Tracking worksheet.**

2 **Enter the number `7` in cell D7.**
Excel automatically displays a border around the cell and inserts a comment, as evidenced by the small triangular comment indicator in the upper-left corner of the cell. In addition, the row heading number, 7, and column heading letter, D, change color.

continues ▶

To Accept or Reject Changes (continued)

③ Position the mouse pointer on cell D7.

The attached comment displays. It identifies the user—by name or computer number—who made the change, specifies the date and time the change was made, and provides a description of the change (see Figure 17.2).

Figure 17.2
Positioning the mouse pointer over a changed cell displays the attached comment.

Indicates a shared workbook

Comment explaining changes to the cell

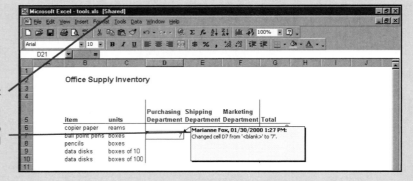

④ Enter the number 5 in cell D9.

⑤ Choose Tools, Track Changes, Accept or Reject Changes.

A message box displays with the following text: This action will now save the workbook. Do you want to continue?

⑥ Click OK.

The Select Changes to Accept or Reject dialog box displays (see Figure 17.3).

Figure 17.3
Changes to be accepted or rejected are identified in this dialog box.

Restrict accepting or rejecting changes to selected cells here

Click here to display When options

Click here to display Who options

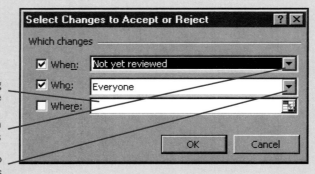

⑦ If necessary, check the When box, and select Not yet reviewed from the drop-down list.

⑧ Check the Who box, and select Everyone from the drop-down list, if necessary, and click OK.

The Accept or Reject Changes dialog box displays (see Figure 17.4).

⑨ Click the Accept button to accept the first change.

Information about the second change displays in the Accept or Reject Changes dialog box.

⑩ Click the Reject button to reject the second change.

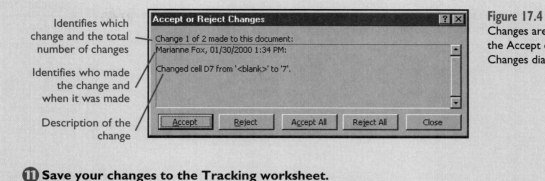

Identifies which change and the total number of changes

Identifies who made the change and when it was made

Description of the change

Figure 17.4
Changes are described in the Accept or Reject Changes dialog box.

⑪ Save your changes to the Tracking worksheet.
This concludes Lesson 2. Continue with the next lesson, or close the workbook and exit Excel.

Lesson 3: Editing a Shared Workbook

Tracking changes is very important when editing a shared workbook. A **shared workbook** enables multiple users on a network to make changes to the workbook at the same time. Changes made by any user can be viewed and edited by any other user as soon as the change is saved.

You can learn how this feature works without actually being one of multiple editors sharing a workbook on a network. In this lesson, you revise the user name on the General tab in the Tools Options dialog box and make and save a change to the Tracking worksheet. After making the change, you revise the user name on the General tab in the Tools Options dialog box again. You then make a second change to the worksheet and check that the comment describing the change correctly identifies which user made the change. As a last step, you reset the user name back to its original specification.

To Edit a Shared Workbook

① Open the `Tools.xls` workbook, and check that its status is still shared.
If the file is shared, the word [Shared] displays after the filename in the title bar.

 If You Have Problems...
If the workbook is not currently shared, choose Share Workbook on the Tools menu, click the Editing tab, and check that the Allow changes by more than one user at the same time check box is selected.

② Select the Tracking worksheet, and choose Tools, Options.

③ Click the General tab, and make note of the current entry in the User name text box.

④ Change the User name to Purchasing, and click OK.

continues ▶

To Edit a Shared Workbook   (continued)

5 **Enter the number 50 in cell D6; save the workbook, and position the pointer on cell D6.**

The comment indicates the change was made by Purchasing. The borders around cells D6 and D7 are different colors, indicating the changes were made by different users.

6 **Choose Tools, Options; click the General tab, change the User name to Shipping, and click OK.**

7 **Enter the number 10 in cell E7; save the workbook, and position the pointer on cell E7.**

Changes are detected only after the file is saved. The comment indicates that the change was made by Shipping. The borders around the three changed cells all have a different color assigned, indicating that three users made the changes.

8 **Choose Tools, Track Changes, Accept or Reject Changes, and click OK.**

The Accept or Reject Changes dialog box displays (see Figure 17.5).

Figure 17.5
Information about the first of two changes made in this work session displays in the Accept or Reject Changes dialog box.

Origin of the change

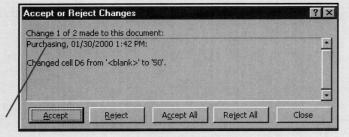

9 **Click Close.**

The Accept or Reject Changes dialog box closes without accepting or rejecting any change. Now restore the original user name.

10 **Choose Tools, Options; click the General tab, change the User name to its original specification, and click OK.**

Now remove the workbook from shared use.

11 **Choose Tools, Share Workbook, and select the Editing tab.**

12 **Make sure that you are the only person listed in the Who has this workbook open now section.**

13 **Remove the check mark from the Allow changes by more than one user at the same time check box, and click OK.**

14 **Click Yes in response to the prompt about effects on other users, and save the Tools workbook.**

This concludes Lesson 3. Continue with the next lesson, or close the workbook and exit Excel.

Exam Note: **Merging Copies of a Shared Workbook**
In a shared workbook, the information maintained about changes in past editing sessions can be viewed through comments on a changed worksheet or viewed on a separate History worksheet.

If you want to merge copies of a shared workbook in which users have made changes, Excel requires that each copy be set up to maintain the history of changes. Generally, change history is specified at the time a shared workbook is established—choose S<u>h</u>are Workbook from the Tools menu; select the Editing tab; check `Allow changes by more than one user at the same time`; click the Advanced tab; click `Keep change history for` under Track changes, and enter the number of days for which a history should be kept.

Actually merging copies of a shared workbook takes only a few steps. Choose Merge <u>W</u>orkbooks from the <u>T</u>ools menu; save the shared workbook if prompted, hold down Ctrl and click the name of each copy of the shared workbook listed in the `Select Files to Merge into Current Workbook` dialog box, and click OK.

Lesson 4: Extracting Data Using Advanced Filter

Decision-makers often need to look at data selectively, focusing only on data relevant to a specific problem. For example, imagine that you are responsible for maintaining a list of employee data—job descriptions, pay rate, and so forth. Filtering a list in-place is useful when you want to see all of the data in records that meet the filter criteria. However, at times you might want to create a list physically located outside your database and perhaps see only selected fields (columns) of data. This is particularly useful if you plan to manipulate the data in a way that may permanently alter the original data and send results to others.

To create a separate list of filtered data, select an Advanced Filter option to copy to another location. If you want to copy selected fields instead of complete records, copy the field names to a separate location before you open the Advanced Filter dialog box. The field names must appear from left to right in the same order as they are arranged in the database.

In this lesson, you copy labels for four fields to an area outside the database; then you use Advanced Filter to extract data to those four fields. The data you extract is limited to records in which Department is Accounting or Admin.

To Extract Data Using Advanced Filter

1 **Open the `Tools.xls` workbook, if necessary, and select the Employees worksheet.**
The worksheet contains a blank criteria range above the database records.

2 **Enter `Accounting` in cell F9.**

3 **Enter `Admin` in cell F10.**

4 **Copy the Last Name, First Name, Department, and Hire Date labels from the database to K17:N17.**
Recall that you can select the nonconsecutive cells C17, D17, F17 and I17 by pressing and holding down the Ctrl key.

continues ▶

To Extract Data Using Advanced Filter (continued)

5 Click any cell within the database area C17:I128, and choose **D**ata, **F**ilter, **A**dvanced Filter.
The Advanced Filter dialog box displays.

6 Check that $C$17:$I$128 is the list range specification.

7 Specify F8:F10 as the criteria range.

8 Select Copy to another location in the Action area of the dialog box.

9 Specify K17:N17 as the Copy to range.
The specifications to copy a filtered list are complete (see Figure 17.6). If you typed the cell ranges, the dollar signs do not display.

Figure 17.6
Using Advanced Filter, you can choose between filtering a list in place and copying it to another location.

Criteria in F8:F10

Select the second option

Specify a Copy to range here

Copied labels

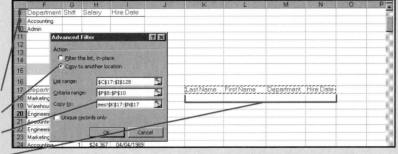

10 Click **OK** to activate the filter, and scroll to view the copied data.
Selected data from records meeting search criteria display in the new location (see Figure 17.7).

Figure 17.7
Copied records display in the same order as they appeared in the original list.

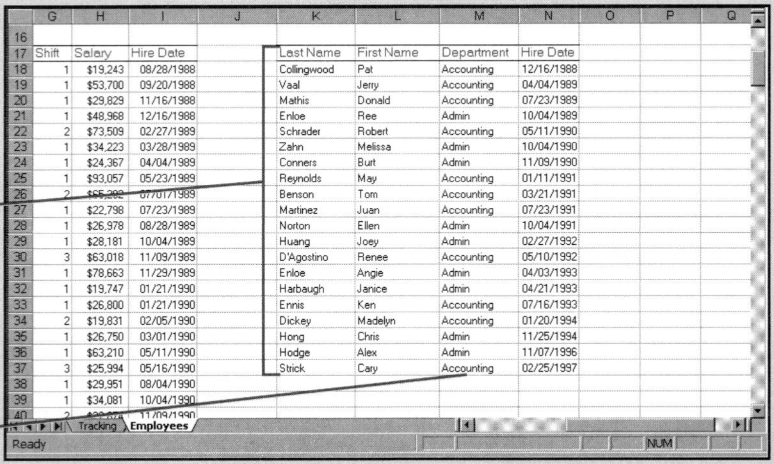

Data from four database fields extracted to the range K17:N37

Data from records for employees in the Accounting or Admin departments

11 Save your changes to the Employees worksheet, and close the workbook.
This concludes Lesson 4. Continue with the next lesson or exit Excel.

Lesson 5: Using Hyperlinks Within a Workbook

A hyperlink is a means for moving from one location to another by clicking the link. If a hyperlink is set up in an Excel worksheet, the connection can be to a position within the same worksheet, to another worksheet in the same workbook, to another workbook, to another application, or to a place within a Web site. When you create a hyperlink, it generally displays as blue underlined text.

In this lesson, you open a workbook containing a very preliminary design for a company's annual report. You set up hyperlinks between the Table of Contents and named ranges in worksheets.

To Use a Hyperlink Within a Workbook

1 **Open the e-1702.xls workbook, click Enable Macros, and save it as AnnualReport.xls.**

This workbook contains the beginnings of a layout for an annual report. The first worksheet is the Table of Contents. Now create a hyperlink to jump to the start of the Balance Sheet and another link to jump back to the top of the Table of Contents worksheet.

2 **Click cell A1 in the Table of Contents worksheet, and name the cell TOC.**

Although you can jump to specific cells, it is easier and less confusing to jump to named cells. Remember, you can quickly name the current cell by clicking the Name box and typing a name for the cell.

3 **Click cell A3 in the Balance Sheet worksheet; name the cell BalSheet, and save the workbook.**

4 **Click cell C10 in the Table of Contents worksheet, and choose Insert, Hyperlink.**

The Insert Hyperlink dialog box displays.

5 **In the Link to area—a column along the left side of the dialog box— click Place in This Document.**

An outline of cell references and defined names displays in the Insert Hyperlink dialog box (see Figure 17.8).

You can type the location to jump to here, or select from the list below this text box

Click here to place the hyperlink in the current worksheet

Click here to establish a link to cell A3 in the Balance Sheet worksheet

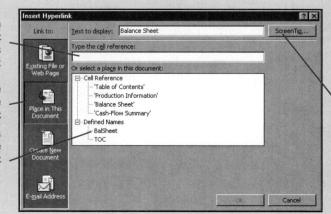

Figure 17.8
Set up specifications for a hyperlink in the Insert Hyperlink dialog box.

Click here to set up a ScreenTip

continues ▶

To Use a Hyperlink Within a Workbook (continued)

6 Click **BalSheet, the first name listed under Defined Names.**

X ***If You Have Problems...***
If you do not see BalSheet, you may need to expand the Defined Names outline by clicking the plus sign (+) outline symbol next to it.

7 Click the **ScreenTip button, and enter** `Click here to see the Balance Sheet` **in the ScreenTip text box.**

8 Click **OK to close the Set Hyperlink ScreenTip dialog box, and click OK to close the Insert Hyperlink dialog box.**
Balance Sheet in cell C10 displays blue and underlined, indicating it is a hyperlink. Now test the link.

9 Click **the hyperlink in cell C10.**
Excel jumps to the destination for the hyperlink, cell A3 in the Balance Sheet worksheet.

10 Click **cell E1 in the Balance Sheet worksheet; enter** `TOC`, **and create a hyperlink in cell E1 to the cell named TOC in the Table of Contents worksheet.**
The steps to complete this step are similar to those described in steps 4 through 8.

11 Click **the new hyperlink.**
If the TOC hyperlink is set up properly, cell A1 in the Table of Contents worksheet becomes the active cell.

12 Save **and close the AnnualReport workbook.**
This concludes Lesson 5. Continue with the next lesson, or exit Excel.

 Exam Note: **Removing and Restoring a Hyperlink**
To remove a hyperlink, right-click the cell containing the hyperlink and select Hyperlink, Remove Hyperlink from the shortcut menu. If you remove a hyperlink in error, you can immediately choose Edit, Undo Remove Hyperlink to restore the link.

 Inside Stuff: **Changing the Appearance of Hyperlinks**
Hyperlinks initially display blue and underlined, which tends to be a standard for links on Web sites, links within email, and so forth. However, the appearance of a hyperlink you create is entirely under your control, and you can apply any formatting—font, color, size, shading, and so on—to it. To change the formatting of a hyperlink, right-click it, and choose Format Cells from the shortcut menu. Make your desired selections from the Format Cells dialog box, and click OK.

Lesson 6: Using a Hyperlink in a Word Document to Reference Excel Data

You can easily set up hyperlinks between Microsoft Office applications. For example, you can create a hyperlink in Excel that jumps to a specific location in a Word document. You can also create a hyperlink in a Word document that jumps to a worksheet cell in an Excel workbook.

Assume you are writing a sales report in Microsoft Word and you want its readers to be able to quickly see data in an Excel worksheet that supports statements made in the report. If the report is a formal one, to be distributed widely throughout the organization, you would probably copy or link the worksheet data to the Word document. Then its readers could view the worksheet data as they read the report online or in hardcopy format. However, if the report is not yet final, or is intended strictly for internal use among a few readers, you might prefer to shorten the word-processed report by placing hyperlinks to only worksheet data within it. If you choose the hyperlink approach, the workbook referenced in the hyperlink must continue to be stored in the location captured in the hyperlink.

In this lesson, you open a Word document containing the initial lines in a sales report and create a hyperlink in that report to supporting data stored in an Excel workbook. You then test the hyperlink to be sure you can easily move between the Word document and the Excel workbook.

To Use a Hyperlink Between Excel and Word

1 **In Word, open e-1703.doc, and save it as DataLink.doc.**

2 **Select the phrase (Click here to see the Excel data).**
Now create the hyperlink to an Excel workbook.

3 **Choose Insert, Hyperlink.**

4 **In the Link to area on the left side of the dialog box, click Existing File or Web Page.**

5 **Click the File button below Browse for, select e1704.xls from the location in which you are storing the student files that accompany this text, and click OK.**

6 **Click the ScreenTip button, type This link will open the Excel file, and click OK.**
Now this ScreenTip will appear whenever the pointer is positioned on the hyperlink.

7 **Click OK again to close the Insert Hyperlink dialog box.**
Now test the hyperlink.

8 **Click the hyperlink in the Word document.**
The Sales Data worksheet displays (see Figure 17.9). When Excel is accessed through a hyperlink, the Web toolbar displays automatically.

9 **Click the Back button.**
The word-processed report displays.

10 **Save and close the Word document, and exit Word.**

continues ▶

To Use a Hyperlink Between Excel and Word (continued)

Figure 17.9
Click the Back button to jump to the Word document.

Web toolbar

Back button

The location of your e-1704.xls workbook displays here

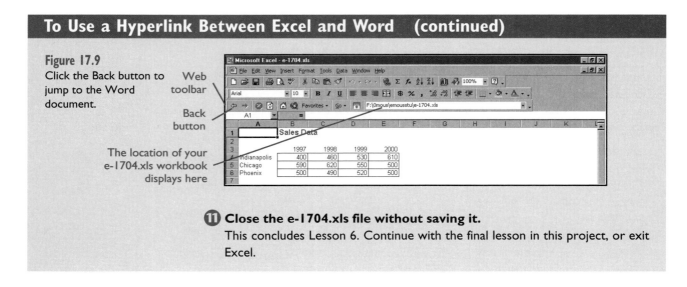

11 **Close the e-1704.xls file without saving it.**
This concludes Lesson 6. Continue with the final lesson in this project, or exit Excel.

 Inside Stuff: **On Hyperlinking to Excel Data**
When you set a hyperlink to an Excel workbook from another Office application, the link accesses the first worksheet of the workbook. Make sure that the Excel data you want to display is in the first worksheet or store it in its own workbook.

 ## Lesson 7: Using a Hyperlink in a PowerPoint Slide to Reference Excel Data

You can create a hyperlink in Excel that jumps to a specific slide in a PowerPoint presentation. You can also create a hyperlink in a PowerPoint presentation that jumps to a worksheet cell in an Excel workbook. The latter situation is far more common. Creating the hyperlink in PowerPoint makes it possible for you to reference Excel data without making it a primary focus of a slide. The worksheet data would not be visible on the slide, but during the presentation, you could activate the hyperlink and display the associated worksheet data in Excel.

In this lesson, you open a PowerPoint presentation file containing a single slide with a chart based on Excel data. The chart is not linked to the corresponding Excel file. You first create a hyperlink from PowerPoint to Excel. You then test the hyperlink, to be sure you can easily move between the PowerPoint slide and Excel worksheet on which the chart is based.

To Use a Hyperlink Between Excel and PowerPoint

1 **In PowerPoint, open e-1705.ppt and save it as pplink.ppt.**
The PowerPoint presentation consists of a single slide—a chart based on data in the e-1704.xls workbook. The two files aren't linked.

2 **Click the PowerPoint chart to select it, and choose Insert, Hyperlink.**

3 **In the Link to area on the left side of the dialog box, click Existing File or Web Page.**

④ **Click the File button below Browse for; select e1704.xls from the location in which you are storing the student files that accompany this text, and click OK.**

⑤ **Click the ScreenTip button; enter** `Click the chart to see the data,` **and click OK.**

⑥ **Click OK to close the Insert Hyperlink dialog box.**

⑦ **Click the Slide Show button near the lower-left corner of the screen.**

The single slide containing a chart displays in Slide Show view.

⑧ **Click within the chart in the slide.**

This activates the hyperlink, and opens the e-1704.xls file in Excel.

⑨ **Use the Back button on the Web toolbar to jump back to the PowerPoint presentation.**

⑩ **Press Esc to end the slide show, save the pplink.ppt file, and exit PowerPoint.**

⑪ **Close the e1704.xls workbook without saving it.**

This concludes Project 17. Continue with end-of-project exercises or exit Excel.

Summary

In this project, you worked with a number of features supporting the collaborative process. In the first three lessons, you explored ways to have more than one person develop and edit a workbook at the same time. Topics included designating a workbook as shared, tracking changes, and accepting or rejecting tracked changes. You then extracted (copied) filtered data from a large worksheet, which makes it easy for multiple users to focus on a smaller subset of data. The three lessons on hyperlinks focused on how to set up jumps from one location to another within a workbook and between Excel and other Microsoft applications.

Reviewing the many onscreen Help pages devoted to these topics can increase your confidence in using the features. The best way to learn, however, is to use the techniques on a regular basis and experiment with additional features.

Checking Concepts and Terms

True/False

For each of the following, check *T* or *F* to indicate whether the statement is true or false.

__T __F   **1.** To remove a hyperlink, right-click the cell containing the hyperlink, and select Hyperlink, Remove Hyperlink from the shortcut menu. [L5]

__T __F   **2.** When using Advanced Filter to extract data from a list, the field (column) labels in the area to copy to must appear from left to right in the same order as they are arranged in the list. [L4]

__T __F   **3.** Assume that a hyperlink to an Excel work-sheet has been set up in PowerPoint presentation. When running that PowerPoint presentation, the worksheet data is automatically visible on the slide. [L7]

__T __F   **4.** Tracking automatically sets up a shared workbook, even though you may not actually be sharing with anyone. [L1]

__T __F   **5.** A hyperlink can only link to named cells. [L5]

Multiple Choice

Circle the letter of the correct answer for each of the following.

1. A hyperlink set up in Excel can be a link to [L5]

a. a Web page

b. another worksheet in the same workbook

c. another application, such as Microsoft Word

d. all of the above

2. Which of the following is not an option when determining the extent of tracking changes? [L1]

a. All

b. Since I last saved

c. Not yet reviewed

d. Between these dates

3. Which of the following is not an accurate statement? [L1]

a. Tracking automatically sets up a shared workbook.

b. You can delete a worksheet if its workbook is currently in shared mode.

c. [Shared] displays in the title bar of a workbook in shared mode.

d. While in shared mode, certain operations are not available.

4. When you choose Tools, Track Changes, Accept or Reject Changes, [L2]

a. Excel prompts that the action will save the workbook, and provides the opportunity for you to continue or not

b. you cannot restrict the changes which display

c. both a and b

d. neither a nor b

5. Which of the following is involved in the process to create a separate list of filtered data? [L4]

a. Select an Advanced Filter option.

b. Copy field labels from the list to set up column headings in the blank extract area.

c. both a and b

d. neither a nor b

Skill Drill

Skill Drill exercises reinforce project skills. Each skill reinforced is the same, or nearly the same, as a skill presented in the project. Detailed instructions are provided in a step-by-step format.

The three Skill Drill exercises can be worked in any order. Be sure to save the workbook after completing each exercise. If you need a paper copy of the completed exercise, enter your name centered in a header before printing. Other print options have already been set to print compressed to one page and to display the filename, sheet name, and current date in a footer.

Before beginning your first Project 17 Skill Drill exercise, complete the following steps:

1. Open the Excel file named `e-1706`, and save it as `e17drill`.

The workbook contains six sheets: an overview, a primary exercise sheet named TOC, and four other sheets involved in setting hyperlinks (Subtotal01, Subtotal02, Pivot01, and Pivot02).

2. Click the Overview sheet to view the organization of the Project 17 Skill Drill Exercises workbook.

If you need more than one work session to complete the desired exercises, continue working on `e17drill` instead of starting over on the original e-1706 file.

1. Creating a Hyperlink Within a Workbook

Hyperlinks make it easy to jump to locations within a document. In this exercise, you create a hyperlink from the TOC sheet to another worksheet in the workbook.

To create a hyperlink within a workbook:

1. Open the `e17drill` workbook, if necessary, and select the TOC worksheet.

2. Click cell D8 containing the phrase Subtotals that Sum Data.

3. Choose Insert, Hyperlink, and click Place in This Document.

4. Click Subtotal01 listed in the Cell Reference area.

5. Click the ScreenTip button, type `Jump to the Subtotal01 worksheet`, and click OK twice.
The hyperlink from the TOC worksheet to the Subtotal01 worksheet is set. Now set a hyperlink in the Subtotal01 worksheet that jumps back to the TOC worksheet.

6. Click cell A2 in the Subtotal01 worksheet.

7. Repeat steps 3 and 4 above, except click TOC in the Cell Reference area.

8. Type `Return to TOC` in the **Text to display** textbox, and click OK.

9. Test the hyperlinks to make sure they work.

10. Save your changes to the e17drill workbook.

2. Setting a Hyperlink in a Workbook to a Word Document

In Lesson 6 of this project, you created a hyperlink in a Word document that jumped to an Excel workbook. Now create a hyperlink in an Excel workbook that jumps to a Word document.

To create a hyperlink to a Word document:

1. Open the `e17drill` workbook, if necessary, and select the TOC worksheet.

2. Click cell D14 containing the word Assignment.

3. Choose Insert, Hyperlink, and click Existing File or Web Page.

4. Click the File button below Browse for; select e-1707.doc from the location in which you are storing the student files that accompany this text, and click OK.

5. Click the ScreenTip button; type `Click here for assignment instructions`, and click OK twice.
The hyperlink from the Excel workbook to the Word document is set up.

6. Test the link to the assignment document, and return to the Excel worksheet using the Back button.

7. Save your changes to the e17drill workbook.

8. Close MS Word without saving e-1707.doc.

3. Removing a Hyperlink

If you no longer need a hyperlink, you can easily remove it by clicking the Remove Link button in the Edit Hyperlink dialog box or selecting an option from a shortcut menu. In this exercise, you use the shortcut method to remove a hyperlink in the TOC worksheet of the e17drill workbook.

To remove a hyperlink:

1. Open the `e17drill` workbook, if necessary, and select the TOC worksheet.

2. Right-click cell D10.

3. From the shortcut menu, choose Hyperlink, Remove Hyperlink.

4. Restore formatting and alignment in cell D10 by applying a 12pt Arial font and centering the contents of the cell.

5. Save your changes to the e17drill workbook.

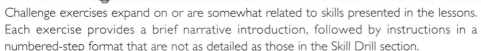

Challenge

Challenge exercises expand on or are somewhat related to skills presented in the lessons. Each exercise provides a brief narrative introduction, followed by instructions in a numbered-step format that are not as detailed as those in the Skill Drill section.

The exercises can be worked in any order. Be sure to save the workbook after completing each exercise. If you need a paper copy of the completed exercise, enter your name centered in a header before printing. Other print options have already been set to print compressed to one page and to display the filename, sheet name, and current date in a footer.

Before beginning your first Project 17 Challenge exercise, complete the following steps:

1. Open the file named `e-1708`, and save the file as `e17challenge`.
   The workbook contains four sheets: an overview, and exercise sheets named #1-Extract, #2-Internet, and #3-Email.

2. Click the Overview sheet to view the organization of the Project 17 Challenge Exercises workbook.

If you need more than one work session to complete the desired exercises, continue working on `e17challenge` instead of starting over on the original e-1708 file.

1. Extracting Data from a List

You are a real estate agent for residential properties. A potential client wants to know what listings are available in the Glenn Lakes or West Glenn subdivisions. You want to provide a printout of the requested data, including only selected fields. For example, you want to include price, number of bedrooms and bathrooms, and so on, but exclude address data. After all, you don't want the client looking at properties without you! Use Excel's Advanced Filter to extract data from selected fields and records.

To extract data from a list:

1. Open the `e17challenge` workbook, if necessary, and select the #1-Extract worksheet.
   The criteria are already entered in the range C6:C8.

2. Copy the field names Listed, Price, Area, Bed, Bath and Heat horizontally across row 13, beginning at cell K13.

3. Enter =NOW() in cell K11.

4. Click within the database, and turn on Advanced Filter.

5. Complete specifications to copy only selected fields from records meeting the stated criteria to the range you set up below the field headings in columns K through P.

6. Save the addition of extracted data in the #1-Extract worksheet.

2. Creating a Hyperlink in Excel to an Internet Site

As more and more users have Internet access, it becomes useful to have Internet links within documents.

To create a hyperlink to an Internet site:

1. Open the e17challenge workbook, and select the #2-Internet worksheet.

2. Click cell A13, and start the process to insert a hyperlink.

3. Select the Existing File or Web Page option on the Insert Hyperlink dialog box.

4. In the Type the file or Web page name text box, type www.indy.org, and click OK.

5. Save your changes to the #2-Internet worksheet.

6. If you are connected to the Internet, click the link to the Indianapolis Web site.

7. Use the Back button in your browser to return to Excel.

3. Creating an Email Hyperlink in Excel

Hyperlinks can also include email addresses. If you find you are frequently sending email while working on a workbook, you can put an email link in the workbook.

To create an email hyperlink:

1. Open the e17challenge workbook, if necessary, and select the #3-Email worksheet.

2. Click cell A14, and start the process to insert a hyperlink.

3. Specify that you want to link to E-mail Address.

4. Enter your personal email address in the E-mail address text box and a subject description, and click OK.
The link to your email address has been established.

5. Save your changes to the workbook, and close it.

6. If you are connected to the Internet, click the email link in the #3-Email worksheet and send a message to yourself.

Discovery Zone

Discovery Zone exercises require advanced knowledge of topics presented in *MOUS Essentials* lessons, application of skills from multiple lessons, or self-directed learning of new skills.

Each exercise is independent of the others, so you can complete the exercises in any order. Be sure to save the workbook after completing each exercise. If you need a paper copy of the completed exercise, enter your name centered in a header before printing. Other print options have already been set to print compressed to one page and to display the filename, sheet name, and current date in a footer.

Before beginning your first Project 17 Discovery Zone exercise, complete the following steps:

1. Open the file named **e-1709**, and save it as **e17discovery**.
   The workbook contains three sheets: an overview and two exercise sheets named #1-SetLinks and #2-AcceptReject.

2. Click the Overview sheet to view the organization of the Project 17 Discovery Zone Exercises workbook.

If you need more than one work session to complete the desired exercises, continue working on **e17discovery** instead of starting over on the original e-1709 file.

1. Creating Hyperlinks within a Large Worksheet

Open the **e17discovery** workbook, if necessary, and select the #1-SetLinks worksheet. Set up seven hyperlinks to make it easier to move from one section to another in the worksheet. Set up four of the links one below the other in the range F3:F6. The links should be defined with names and cell references as follows: Criteria in cell F3, jumping to cell C12; Database in cell F4, jumping to cell C21; Drop-down lists in cell F5, jumping to cell T1; and Extract in cell F6, jumping to cell K134.

Near the side or bottom of the database, the extract area, and the area showing the contents of drop-down lists, set up links that the user can click to return to the top of the jump list (cell F3). Test the links, and save your changes.

2. Accepting or Rejecting Tracked Changes

Open the **e17discovery** workbook, if necessary, and select the #2-AcceptReject worksheet. Turn on tracking of all changes by everyone. Change the shipping cost per unit in cell H8 to **3.40**. Replace all occurrences of Chicago with **St. Louis**. Change the capacity value in cell J17 from 20,000 to **22,000**. Activate accepting and rejecting changes for changes by everyone not yet reviewed. Accept the change in city and shipping cost per unit, but reject the change in capacity. Disable tracking changes while editing, which removes the workbook from shared use. Save your changes.

PinPoint Assessment

You have completed this project and its associated lessons, and have had an opportunity to assess your skills through the end-of-project questions and exercises. Now use the PinPoint software Evaluation Mode to further assess your comprehension of the specific exam activities you have just learned. You can also use the PinPoint Trainer Mode and the Show Me tutorials to practice these exam activities.

Integrating Applications

Key terms introduced in this project include

- destination file
- object
- Object Linking and Embedding (OLE)
- source file

Objectives	Required Activity for MOUS	Exam Level
➤ Link Excel Data to a Word Document	Export to other applications	Expert
➤ Embed Excel Data in a Word Document	Export to other applications	Expert
➤ Link Excel Data to a PowerPoint Slide	Export to other applications	Expert
➤ Link an Excel Chart to a PowerPoint Slide	Export to other applications	Expert
➤ Convert an Excel List to an Access Database	Export to other applications	Expert
➤ Import Data from a Text File	Import data from text files (insert, drag and drop)	Expert
➤ Edit an HTML File Using Excel	Import a table from an HTML file (Insert, drag and drop—including HTML round tripping)	Expert
➤ Get External Data from Access into Excel	Import from other applications; query databases	Expert

Why Would I Do This?

One of the advantages of using Office as an integrated set of programs is that any of the programs can refer to data generated by another program. For example, you can insert an Excel workbook in a Word document but still use Excel to edit and update the workbook. You can export Excel data to an Access database, or get data from an Access database and create an Excel worksheet. You can easily edit HTML files in Excel and retain the HTML format.

Integrating applications is not limited to Microsoft Office programs. You can, for example, import data from a text file or another spreadsheet program. In this project, you sample the powerful integrating opportunities available when using Excel. The lessons focus primarily on integrating Excel data with Word, PowerPoint, and Access data. The procedures, however, are basically the same no matter what objects or programs you use.

Lesson 1: Linking Excel Data to a Word Document

The method of sharing data among Microsoft Office applications is called **Object Linking and Embedding (OLE)**. An **object** in this context has properties and can be referenced and used by another program. In Excel, an object can be as large as an entire workbook or as small as a worksheet cell. Charts, clip art, and WordArt in an Excel workbook are also examples of objects.

You can link or embed an object from a source file to a destination file. The file that contains a link or embedded data is called the **destination file**. The file providing the data to link or embed is the **source file**. For example, if you copy a section of an Excel worksheet to a Word document, the source file is the Excel workbook and the destination file is the Word document.

When you set up the copied object as a link, the object does not become part of the destination file. Instead, a reference to the object appears in the destination file. When files are linked, a change in the source file results in the same change in the destination file.

Think of linking as inserting a picture of the object with a shortcut (that is, *link*) between the destination file and the source of the data. This approach has size-of-file benefits. The destination file is only a few bytes larger than it would have been without the link to data in another application. The primary disadvantage of this approach is that the link will be broken if either of the linked files is moved to a different location.

When you embed an object, it becomes part of the destination file. Thereafter there is no connection to the source file. Changing data in the source file does not change the same data in the destination file.

In this lesson, you link a range of cells containing annual sales data to a sales report in Word. After creating the link, you test it by changing the worksheet.

To Link Excel Data to a Word Document

❶ Open the file `e-1801.xls`, and save it as `SalesData01.xls`.
This file contains worksheet data and a chart. Now copy a range of data to a Word document.

❷ Select cells A3:E6, and choose **E**dit, **C**opy, or click the **Copy** button.

3 **Start Microsoft Word; open the file e-1802.doc, and save it as SalesReport01.doc.**
This file contains the start of a sales report.

4 **Place the insertion point below the single sentence in the document, and choose Edit, Paste Special.**
The Paste Special dialog box displays.

5 **Click the Paste link option, and click Microsoft Excel Worksheet Object in the As list box (see Figure 18.1).**

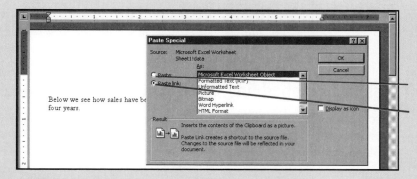

Figure 18.1
Use the Paste Special dialog box to link or embed data.

Click here to embed data

Click here to link data

6 **Leave the Display as icon option unchecked, and click OK.**
The results of the Paste Special operation display in the sales report (see Figure 18.2). Sizing handles indicate the object is selected. Now center the object.

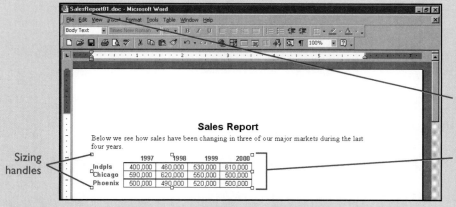

Sizing handles

Figure 18.2
The selected worksheet data becomes a linked object in the Word document.

Name of the current Word document

Results of a Paste Special operation that links the row-and-column data to its source in an Excel workbook

7 **Right-click within the worksheet data; choose Format Object from the shortcut menu; click the Layout tab in the Format Object dialog box; click the Center option in the Horizontal alignment area, and click OK.**
The inserted cells are centered horizontally. Now test the link by changing data in the original worksheet.

continues ▶

To Link Excel Data to a Word Document (continued)

8 **Make sure the worksheet object is selected in the Word document (sizing handles display), and choose Edit, Linked Worksheet Object, Edit Link. (If the object is not already selected, you can double-click it to produce the same results.)**
The original source file displays in Excel.

9 **Change the contents of cell B4 to 600,000 instead of 400,000.**

10 **Check that the change is also reflected in the Word document.**

11 **Save and close both the Word document and the Excel workbook.**
This concludes Lesson 1. Continue with the next lesson, or exit Excel.

Expert Lesson 2: Embedding Excel Data in a Word Document

Embedded data actually becomes a part of the destination file. Initially the results of an embed operation appear to be the same as if a link operation was executed. One major difference, however, is that if the source data in the worksheet changes, the change is not reflected in the destination file. Because embedded data does not have links, you do not have to be concerned about breaking links if a source file is moved or renamed, which is especially important if you send the file(s) to someone else.

In this lesson, you execute the same copy operation as you did in Lesson 1, except that you embed—rather than link—the annual sales data from a worksheet into the sales report. You then access Excel features from within Word, change a value, and verify that the change is not reflected in the linked worksheet.

To Embed Excel Data in a Word Document

1 **Open the Excel file e-1803.xls, and save it as SalesData02.xls.**

2 **Select cells A3:E6, and choose Edit, Copy.**

3 **In Microsoft Word, open the file e-1804.doc, and save it as SalesReport02.doc.**

4 **Place the insertion point below the single sentence, and choose Edit, Paste Special.**

5 **In the Paste Special dialog box, click the Paste option (not the Paste link option).**

6 **Click Microsoft Excel Worksheet Object in the As list.**

7 **Leave the Display as icon option unchecked, and click OK.**
The results display as shown in Figure 18.3. Now center the embedded object.

8 **Right-click within the embedded worksheet; choose Format Object; click the Layout tab; click Center in the Horizontal alignment section, and click OK.**
The embedded object is centered horizontally. Sizing handles indicate the object is still selected. Now access Excel features from within the Word document.

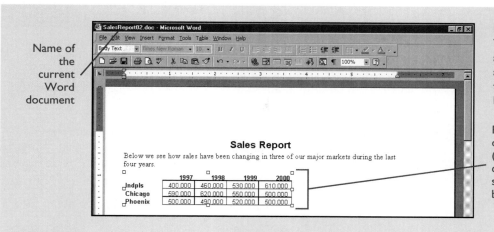

Figure 18.3
The results of copying as an embedded object appear to be the same as the results of copying as a linked object.

Results of a Paste Special operation that copies (embeds) the row-and-column data from its source in an Excel workbook

⑨ Right-click within the embedded worksheet; select Worksheet Object from the shortcut menu, and select Edit.

A miniature Excel worksheet displays, and Word's horizontal menu and toolbars are temporarily replaced with Excel's horizontal menu and toolbars (see Figure 18.4).

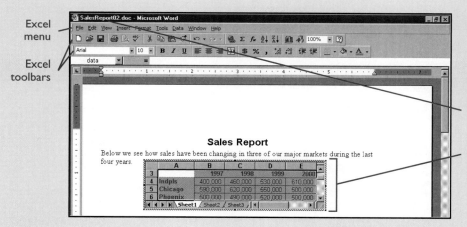

Excel menu

Excel toolbars

Figure 18.4
When you edit an embedded Excel object in another application, it appears as though you are editing directly in Excel.

Word document

Embedded Excel object

⑩ In the Excel window, change the contents of cell B4 to 500,000 instead of 400,000.

⑪ Click an area in the Word document that is outside the Excel window.

The object is deselected, and Word's menus and toolbars reappear.

⑫ Save your changes to SalesReport02.doc, and switch to the SalesData02 workbook.

Making a change to an embedded worksheet in a Word document does not change the corresponding data in the Excel source file. The original value 400,000 still displays in cell B4 of the SalesData02 workbook. Now make a change in the source file.

continues ▶

To Embed Excel Data in a Word Document   (continued)

⑬ Change the contents of cell B4 in SalesData02 to 600,000 instead of 400,000, and check the associated cell in the Word document.
The edited value of 500,000 in SalesReport02 does not change. The two files are not linked in either direction.

⑭ Save and close both the Word document and the Excel workbook.
This concludes Lesson 2. Continue with the next lesson, or exit Excel.

Expert Lesson 3: Linking Excel Data to a PowerPoint Slide

When creating a PowerPoint presentation, you may want to include row-and-column data or a chart that already exists in an Excel worksheet. The two options you worked with in previous lessons—linking in Lesson 1, and embedding in Lesson 2—are available when integrating between Excel and any Microsoft Office application. The procedures are quite similar.

In this lesson, you copy a section of an Excel worksheet to the first of two slides in a PowerPoint presentation. You paste the copied data as a link.

To Link Excel Data to a PowerPoint Slide

❶ Open the Excel file e-1805.xls, and save it as SalesData03.xls.
This file contains the worksheet cells that we want to display in the PowerPoint presentation.

❷ Select cells A3:E6, and choose Edit, Copy.

❸ Open the file e-1806.ppt with Microsoft PowerPoint, and save it as SalesReport03.ppt.
This file contains two slides that are the start of a sales report presentation.

❹ Select the first slide, and choose Edit, Paste Special.

❺ Click Paste link; specify Microsoft Excel Worksheet Object in the As list box, and click OK.
The copied cells display on Slide 1, but the cells are too small to read easily. Now enlarge the worksheet display.

❻ Click one of the corner sizing handles, and hold down the ⬆Shift key while resizing the object (see Figure 18.5).
Holding the ⬆Shift key maintains the object's proportions while resizing. Figure 18.5 shows the completed slide.

❼ Save your changes to the SalesReport03.ppt presentation.
This concludes Lesson 3. Keep both the SalesReport03.ppt and the SalesData03.xls files open for the next lesson, in which you link an Excel chart to the second slide.

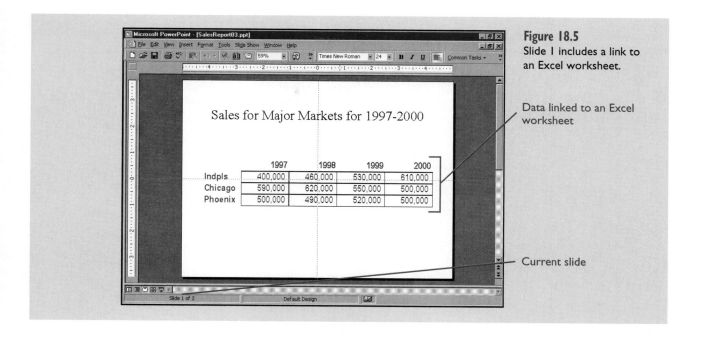

Figure 18.5
Slide 1 includes a link to an Excel worksheet.

Data linked to an Excel worksheet

Current slide

Lesson 4: Linking an Excel Chart to a PowerPoint Slide

Charts and graphics can greatly enhance a presentation. Although you can create charts within PowerPoint, you may already have a chart within an existing Excel workbook. If you link an Excel chart to a PowerPoint slide, the chart on the slide can be updated for any changes in the Excel source file containing the chart.

In this lesson, you link an Excel chart of annual sales to the second slide in a PowerPoint presentation.

To Link an Excel Chart to a PowerPoint Slide

1 Open the `SalesData03.xls` workbook, if necessary.

2 Click within a blank area of the chart to select it, and choose **E**dit, **C**opy.

3 Open the `SalesReport03.ppt` file in PowerPoint, if necessary. (If prompted that the file contains links, select Yes to update the links.)
This file contains the two slides that are the start of a Sales Report presentation. Slide 1 already contains data linked to an Excel worksheet.

4 Display slide 2, and choose **E**dit, Paste **S**pecial.

5 Click Paste **l**ink; select Microsoft Excel Chart Object in the **A**s list box, and click OK.
The chart appears in the slide as shown in Figure 18.6.

6 Save your changes to SalesReport03.ppt, and close the file.

continues ▶

To Link an Excel Chart to a PowerPoint Slide (continued)

Figure 18.6
Slide 2 includes a link to
an Excel chart.

Sizing handles indicate the chart
is selected

Chart linked to an Excel
worksheet

Current slide

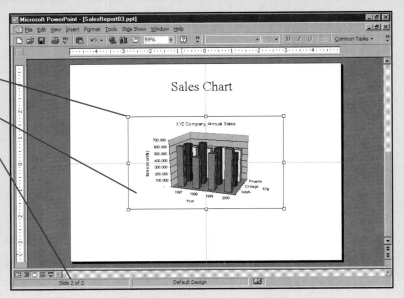

7 **Test the links, as desired, by changing one or more values within the range of charted data in SalesData03.xls.**
When you open SalesReport03.ppt to verify that changes in the Excel source file are reflected on both slides 1 and 2, respond Yes to any prompt asking whether you want to update the links.

8 **Close the SalesReport03.ppt and SalesData03.xls files without saving changes made to verify the links.**
This concludes Lesson 4. Continue with the next lesson, or exit Excel.

 ## Lesson 5: Converting an Excel List to an Access Database

Excel's list or database capability is powerful. However, when data becomes too voluminous or complex it is time to warehouse or store it in a relational database product, such as MS Access. Later the data can be mined or queried and subsets of that data imported back into Excel for analysis.

In this lesson, you use Excel's Convert to MS Access add-in program to convert data about real estate clients into an Access database. A working knowledge of MS Access is useful, but not required, to complete this lesson.

To Convert an Excel List to an Access Database

1 **Open the e-1807.xls workbook, save it as export.xls, and click any cell within the list range A5:K40.**
This file contains the Modern Realty, Inc. client assignments in Excel list format.

2 **Choose Data, and select Convert to MS Access.**

The Convert to Microsoft Access dialog box displays (see Figure 18.7).

> ### ✖ If You Have Problems...
>
> If the Convert to MS Access option does not display when you choose Data, you must install the related add-in program. Choose Tools, select Add-Ins, check Access Links, and click OK. Follow screen instructions to install the add-in (usually the Microsoft Office CD is required).

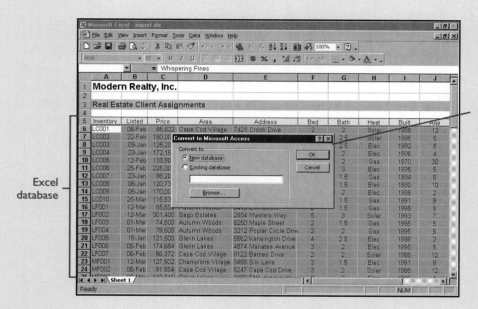

Figure 18.7
You can convert Excel records to a new or existing Access database.

Dialog box to convert Excel data to an Access database

Excel database

3 **Check that New database is selected, and click OK.**

The first of four Import Spreadsheet Wizard dialog boxes displays (see Figure 18.8). You are preparing to export Excel records to Access, but Access opens and generates screens that describe the actions to import spreadsheets.

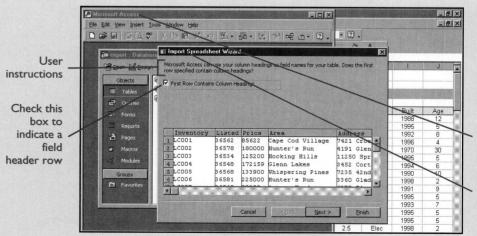

User instructions

Check this box to indicate a field header row

Figure 18.8
In the first Import Spreadsheet Wizard dialog box, specify whether the first row in your Excel list contains column headings.

The conversion automatically opens the Access software

Exporting to Access from Excel is presented as importing Excel data into Access

continues ▶

To Convert an Excel List to an Access Database (continued)

4 **Check the** F**i**rst Row Contains Column Headings **check box.**
A check mark by this setting indicates that the field names row in Excel is not a record. Now proceed to the next dialog box and specify where you want the imported data to be stored.

5 **Click Next; select** In a New Table, **and click Next again.**
The third Import Spreadsheet Wizard dialog box displays. In this box, you can specify information about each of the fields being imported into Access.

6 **Display the Indexed drop-down list.**
Three choices display (see Figure 18.9). To specify that a field can't control the order of the records, click No. To enable the field to control the order of the records but not contain duplicate numbers in the field, click Yes—not duplicates. To enable the field to control the order of the records and contain duplicate numbers in the field click, Yes—duplicates OK. An understanding of Microsoft Access, key fields, indexes, and table relationships is necessary to appreciate this feature.

Figure 18.9
In the third Import Spreadsheet Wizard dialog box, specify whether a field may control the order of records, and indicate whether you want to skip a field.

Specify whether the selected field may control the order of records

Selected field name

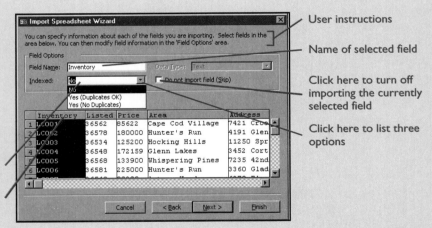

User instructions

Name of selected field

Click here to turn off importing the currently selected field

Click here to list three options

7 **For the Inventory field, select** Yes (No Duplicates).
At this point, before clicking Next, you can select any other field in the table and make it an indexed field, or skip the field. Now advance to the next screen.

8 **Click Next, and select** C**h**oose my own primary key.
The fourth Import Spreadsheet Wizard dialog box displays (see Figure 18.10), in which you specify a primary key. Primary keys are necessary to speed processing data in a table and for setting a relationship between two tables. Relationships link two tables together, so the data from both can be used.

9 **Click Next, and change the Import to Table name from Sheet1 to**
Client Assignments.
The table name Sheet1 was the name of the Excel table being converted.

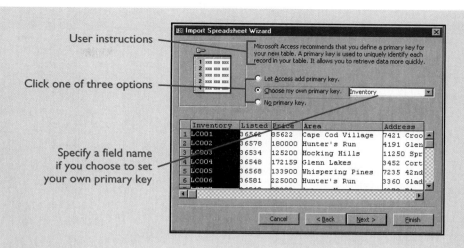

User instructions

Click one of three options

Specify a field name
if you choose to set
your own primary key

Figure 18.10
In the fourth Import
Spreadsheet Wizard
dialog box, choose among
options related to a
primary key.

**⑩ Click Finish, and click OK after the message Finished importing file
displays.**
You have converted the Excel data to a Client Assignments table in the
Access database named export.

**⑪ Close the Access database (which saves your changes); exit Access,
and close the Excel workbook.**
This concludes Lesson 5. Continue with the next lesson or exit Excel.

Lesson 6: Importing Data from a Text File

Data may be stored as a text file, which sometimes happens because it is in the process of
being converted between two products that cannot exchange data directly. Data in text
form appears as a string of characters. Spaces or commas separate (delimit) fields, although other characters are sometimes used to delimit fields in a string. Excel's Text
Import Wizard is available to guide you through the process of importing text data into
the columns and rows of a worksheet.

In this lesson, you use the Text Import Wizard to import data in a text file concerning do-
nations to the Save the Manatee fund.

To Import Data from a Text File

❶ Open a new workbook in Excel.

**❷ Choose File, Open; select Files of type Text Files (*.prn, *.txt, *.csv),
and open the e-1808.txt file.**
The first Text Import Wizard dialog box displays (see Figure 18.11). Records
display in the Preview area across the bottom of the dialog box. Data fields in
each record are separated by commas (name, address, city, and so on).

❸ Select Delimited as the original data type, and click Next.
The Text Import Wizard—Step 2 of 3 displays. An explanation of the screen
is provided at the top of the box.

continues ▶

To Import Data from a Text File (continued)

Figure 18.11
Excel recognizes the file as a text file and displays the Text Import Wizard—Step 1 of 3 dialog box.

Specify original data type here

Preview area

Commas separate fields

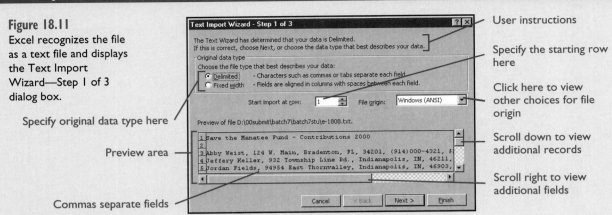

User instructions

Specify the starting row here

Click here to view other choices for file origin

Scroll down to view additional records

Scroll right to view additional fields

❹ **In the Delimiters area, uncheck Tab and check Comma (see Figure 18.12).**

Figure 18.12
Use the Text Import Wizard—Step 2 of 3 dialog box to indicate the characters used to separate fields in the text file.

User instructions

Data aligns in columns

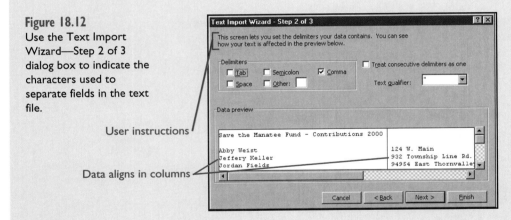

❺ **Click Next.**
The Text Import Wizard—Step 3 of 3 dialog box displays (see Figure 18.13).

Figure 18.13
Use the Text Import Wizard—Step 3 of 3 dialog box to change Excel's initial determination of each column's data format.

User instructions

Specify type of data or skip importing here

Click here to select the next field

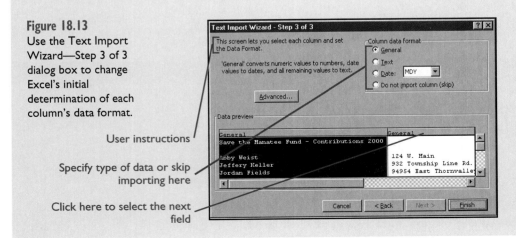

6 **Click Finish to accept current settings.**

Excel imports the data and arranges it in rows (records) and columns (fields) as shown in Figure 18.14. Now make adjustments to the layout and content of the imported data.

Change column widths as needed

Correct spelling of first names

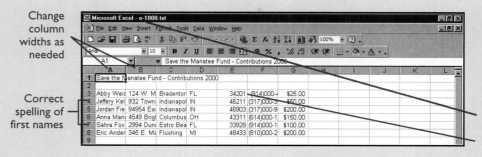

Figure 18.14
Some adjustments, such as changing column widths, must often be made to a new worksheet containing imported data.

Excel assigns the original filename

Remove the extra space

7 **Widen or narrow columns as needed.**

8 **Change Jeffery to `Jeffrey` in cell A4; change Sahra to `Sarah` in cell A7, and remove the extra space at the beginning of the phone number in cell F3.**

9 **Change the name of the sheet to `Contribution List` instead of e-1808.**

This completes initial revisions to imported data. You would also likely revise the worksheet to have separate columns for first and last names, or at least put last name before first name if a single column for name is maintained. Such changes to name data would enable you to sort records alphabetically by last name. Inserting a row below the title and adding field names above the data would complete the conversion of the data into an Excel list format. These additional suggested changes do not have to be made to continue with this project.

10 **Choose File Save As, and select Save as type Microsoft Excel Workbook (*.xls).**

11 **Change the filename to `Save the Manatee.xls`; click Save, and close the workbook.**

This concludes Lesson 6. Continue with the next lesson, or exit Excel.

Lesson 7: Editing an HTML File Using Excel

From your work in previous lessons, you can see that there are several ways to integrate applications. You can also open, edit, and save an HTML document in Excel without converting it to an Excel file type.

To work with integration of applications in this lesson, you open in Excel an HTML Web page containing data about contributions to the Save the Manatee Fund. You make a change to the data, save the HTML document, view it using Microsoft Internet Explorer, access Excel from within Explorer, and make another change to the document.

To Edit an HTML File Using Excel

① **In Excel, open e-1809.htm, and save it as Manatee.htm.**
Excel opens the HTML file containing contribution records (see Figure 18.15).

Figure 18.15
You can open, edit, and save changes to an HTML document using Excel.

HTML file in Excel

Field names in row 5

Records

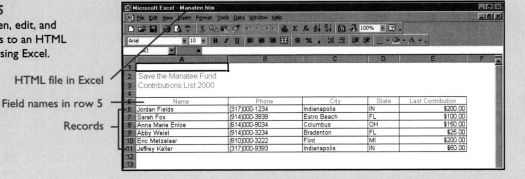

② **Select row 11; choose Insert, Rows, and click cell A11.**

③ **Type the following data in the appropriate fields.**

Name:	Ernie Strauss
Phone:	(914)000-9876
City:	Sarasota
State:	FL
Last Contribution:	$300.00

④ **Save your changes, and close the Manatee.htm file.**

⑤ **Open Microsoft Internet Explorer.**

⑥ **Choose File Open, and use Browse to find and open the Manatee.htm file.**

⑦ **Choose File, Edit with Microsoft Excel for Windows.**
You can also use the Edit button on the Explorer toolbar. Because the two screens look similar, you can check which product you have selected by looking at the left side of the Title bar.

⑧ **Click E11, and change the contribution amount to $500.00.**

⑨ **Save the Manatee.htm file.**

⑩ **Close Microsoft Internet Explorer, and close all files.**
This concludes Lesson 7. Continue with the last lesson in the project, or exit Excel.

 ## Lesson 8: Getting External Data from Access into Excel

When data becomes too voluminous and complex, it is stored in a relational database program like Microsoft Access rather than as a list in Excel. Yet for some information needs—such as producing a chart—Excel may be the better program to use. Excel's Get External Data feature enables you to reach from Excel into an Access database and create or edit a query using data in the Access database.

In this lesson, you work with an Access database that lists properties for sale. You use Excel's Get External Data feature to produce a list in an Excel worksheet of properties available for sale in the Glenn Lakes subdivision.

The lesson is intended to focus only on the mechanics of getting data from an Access database into an Excel worksheet and does not include using the results. The sample Access database has only one table—most databases have multiple tables— which is sufficient to illustrate the process of creating a query prior to extracting data to an Excel worksheet.

To Get External Data from MS Access

1 **Open the e-1810.xls workbook in Excel, and save it as Clients.xls.**

2 **Choose Data, Get External Data, and select New Database Query.**
The Choose Data Source dialog box displays. Click No, Don't provide help now, if the Office Assistant asks whether you want help.

3 **Select MS Access Database, and make sure a check mark displays in the Use the Query Wizard to create/edit queries check box (see Figure 18.16).**

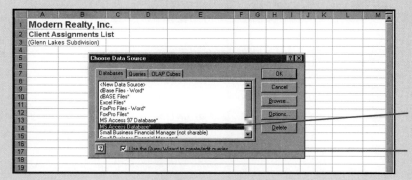

Figure 18.16
Click the Databases tab to view the names of database data sources, and select the appropriate source.

Selected data source

Check here to use the Query Wizard

4 **Click OK.**
The Select Database dialog box displays.

5 **Find and open the e-1811.mdb database.**
The Query Wizard—Choose Columns dialog box displays (see Figure 18.17). A single table named Client Assignments appears in the Available tables and columns list.

Click here to display the field names in the Client Assignments table

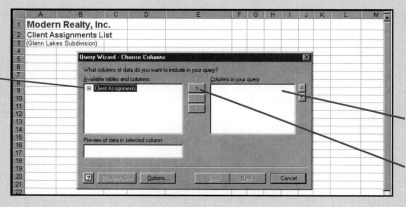

Figure 18.17
Use the Query Wizard— Choose Columns dialog box to specify what columns of data you want to include in your query.

Set up a list of columns in the query here

Click here to copy the selected field name(s) to the list of columns in the query

continues ▶

To Get External Data from MS Access   (continued)

6 Click the + indicator next to the **Client Assignments** table name in the **Available tables and columns** list box.

7 Select the **Client Assignments** table name, and click the **>** button.

When you highlight a table name and click the **>** button, all fields in the table are transferred to the Columns in your query list box (see Figure 18.18). To specify fewer fields, select individual field names instead of selecting the table name. The order in which the fields are selected is the order in which they will appear in your worksheet.

Figure 18.18
The selected table displays in the left side of the dialog box, and the selected fields display in the right side of the dialog box.

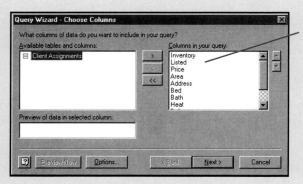

Selected fields in the query

8 Click **Next**.

The Query Wizard—Filter Data dialog box displays.

9 Select **Area** in the **Column to filter** list box.

10 Specify `equals` in the first of two text boxes in the `Only include rows where` area (see Figure 18.19).

Figure 18.19
Use the Query Wizard—Filter Data dialog box to specify which records to include in your query.

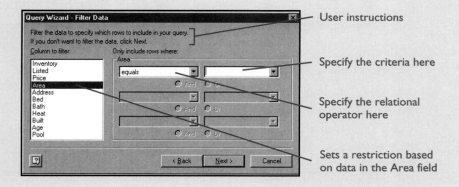

User instructions

Specify the criteria here

Specify the relational operator here

Sets a restriction based on data in the Area field

11 Click the drop-down list in the blank text box to the right of the one in which you specified a relational operator, and select **Glenn Lakes**.

You have set a filter to select only those records from the Access database in which the entry in the Area field equals Glenn Lakes.

12 Click **Next**.

The Query Wizard—Sort Order dialog box displays.

13 Click the **Sort by** drop-down list; select **Inventory**, and click **Ascending**.

Check that your settings match those shown in Figure 18.20.

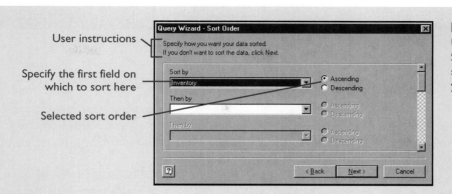

Figure 18.20
Use the Query Wizard—Sort Order dialog box to specify how you want your data sorted.

User instructions

Specify the first field on which to sort here

Selected sort order

⑭ Click Next.
The Query Wizard—Finish dialog box displays.

⑮ Select Return Data to Microsoft Excel, and click Finish.
A dialog box displays asking where you want to put the data.

⑯ Specify Existing worksheet, click cell A5, and click OK.
This completes your Get External Data operation. The records shown in Figure 18.21 are copied from the Access database and placed in Excel's list format beginning in cell A5.

Field names and eight records from an Access database

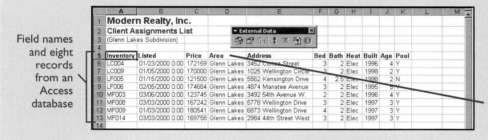

Figure 18.21
The results of querying an Access database display in rows 5 through 13 of the Excel worksheet.

The query limited record selection to listings in the Glenn Lakes area

⑰ Save and close the Clients.xls workbook.
This concludes the last lesson in Project 18. Continue with end-of-project exercises, or exit Excel.

Summary

The first four lessons in this project focused on linking or embedding data from one Microsoft application to another. The result is an object in the destination file that you can move and size. If the result is a linked object, a change in the source data is reflected also in the destination file. If the result is an embedded object, changing the source data does not change data in the destination file.

The remaining four lessons focused on other ways to integrate among applications: converting an Excel list to an Access database, importing data from a text file, editing an HTML file using Excel, and getting data from Access into Excel.

To expand your knowledge, try variations of integrating other applications according to your interests, such as embedding—instead of linking—a portion of an Excel worksheet and/or an Excel chart in a PowerPoint presentation.

Checking Concepts and Terms ✓

True/False

For each of the following, check *T* or *F* to indicate whether the statement is true or false.

__T __F **1.** One of the advantages of using Office as an integrated tool is that any of the programs can refer to data generated by another program. [Why]

__T __F **2.** You can convert an Excel list to an Access database, but you cannot get Access data converted to the Excel list format. [L5, L8]

__T __F **3.** When you link an object, it does become part of the destination file. [L1]

__T __F **4.** Embedding an object is a familiar process of copying the object from the source file and pasting it in the destination file. [L2]

__T __F **5.** Excel's Get External Data feature enables you to reach from Excel into an Access Database and create or edit a query using data in the Access Database. [L8]

Multiple Choice

Circle the letter of the correct answer for each of the following.

1. What is the term that describes sharing data among Microsoft Office applications? [L1]
   a. Object Linking and Embedding (OLE)
   b. Object Sharing and Round-tripping (OSR)
   c. Object Data Sharing (ODS)
   d. none of the above

2. Which of the following can become an Excel linked or embedded object? [L1]
   a. a single cell
   b. a chart
   c. both a and b
   d. neither a nor b

3. What is the term for a file that contains a link or embedded data? [L1]
   a. source file
   b. destination file
   c. application file
   d. object file

4. Which is a true statement about a file containing an embedded object? [L1]
   a. The file is only a few bytes larger than it would have been without the data from another application.
   b. There is no connection between the file containing the embedded object and its source file.
   c. You can edit the connection between the file containing the embedded object and the source file.
   d. both a and b

5. Which of the following is a step in the process to link an Excel chart to a PowerPoint Slide? [L4]
   a. In Excel, select the chart and copy it.
   b. In PowerPoint, select the target slide and click the Paste button.
   c. both a and b
   d. neither a nor b

Skill Drill

Skill Drill exercises reinforce project skills. Each skill reinforced is the same, or nearly the same, as a skill presented in the project. Each exercise includes a brief narrative introduction, followed by detailed instructions in a step-by-step format.

The three Skill Drill exercises can be worked in any order. Be sure to save the workbook after completing each exercise. If you need a paper copy of the completed exercise, enter your name centered in a header before printing. Other print options have already been set to print compressed to one page and to display the filename, sheet name, and current date in a footer.

Before beginning your first Project 18 Skill Drill exercise, complete the following steps:

1. Open the file named **e-1812**, and save it as **e18drill**. The workbook contains four sheets: an overview and three sheets named #1-Client List, #2-Expenses, and #3-Mileage.

2. Click the Overview sheet to view the organization of the Project 18 Skill Drill Exercises workbook.

If you need more than one work session to complete the desired exercises, continue working on **e18drill** instead of starting over on the original e-1812 file.

1. Creating a Link and Viewing Information about Links

Linking Excel worksheet data to an MS Word document is a common business application. In this skill drill, you open a spreadsheet containing data about Modern Realty's clients in the Glenn Lakes subdivision. You have written a memo in MS Word reassigning these properties. Now you want to link the data in the worksheet to the Word memo so that each time the word document is opened, the linked data can be updated. You also want to view information about links in the memo.

To create a link and view information about links:

1. Open the **e18drill** workbook, and select the #1-Client List worksheet.

2. Open the **e-1813.doc** Word document, and save it as **Glenn Lakes.doc**.

3. Switch to the #1-Client List worksheet; select cells A8:K16, and click the Copy button.

4. Switch to the Glenn Lakes document, and position the pointer below the last sentence.

5. Choose Edit, Paste Special.

6. Select Paste link, specify pasting as a Microsoft Excel Worksheet Object, and click OK.
The range of data from an Excel workbook has been linked within the Word document. Now view information about the links in the document.

7. Deselect the linked object, and choose Edit, Links. The Links dialog box displays and lists one link. The description of Item #1 near the bottom of the dialog box indicates that the link is a Microsoft Excel worksheet containing data from an Access query.

8. Click OK to close the dialog box.

9. Save your changes to the Glenn Lakes document, and exit Word.

10. If you are not continuing with other Skill Drill exercises, close e18drill without saving your changes.

2. Importing Data from a Text File

You have been keeping a record of the business miles you drive using Notepad, which creates a text file. Now you want to import that text file into Excel as the starting point for a worksheet that computes business expenses.

To import data from a text file:

1. Open the **e18drill** workbook in Excel; select the #2-Expenses worksheet, and click cell A4.
   You will import the mileage data in the text file to this blank worksheet.

2. Choose <u>D</u>ata, Get External Data, and select Import <u>T</u>ext File.

3. Find and select the **e-1814.txt** text file, and click <u>I</u>mport.

4. Select Finish to bypass the remaining Text Import Wizard dialog boxes and accept all default settings.

5. Check that Existing worksheet and $A$4 are the settings for the location of imported data, and click OK. Excel imports the text data, starting in cell A4.

6. Save your changes to the #2-Expenses worksheet.

3. Linking a Pivot Table and Chart to a PowerPoint Slide

A vital part of any PowerPoint presentation is current data and charts. Often this information is maintained in Excel and linked to a slide presentation. In this skill drill, you link an Excel pivot table and associated chart to a PowerPoint slide.

To link a pivot table and chart to a PowerPoint slide:

1. Open the **e18drill** workbook, and select the #3-Mileage worksheet.

2. Open the **e-1815.ppt** PowerPoint file, and save it as **Mileage.ppt**.

3. Page down to display Slide 2.

4. Switch to the #3-Mileage worksheet, and copy cells E8:F13.

5. Switch to PowerPoint, and click within the text box on the left side of Slide 2.

6. Choose <u>E</u>dit, Paste <u>S</u>pecial; click Paste <u>l</u>ink, specify pasting as a Microsoft Excel Worksheet Object, and click OK.

7. Switch to the #3-Mileage worksheet; click within the pie chart, and click the Copy button.

8. Switch to PowerPoint, and click within the graphics box on the right side of Slide 2.

9. Choose <u>E</u>dit, Paste <u>S</u>pecial; click Paste <u>l</u>ink; specify pasting as a Microsoft Excel Chart Object, and click OK.

10. Rearrange and resize the three objects as needed to improve display. (For example, you could reduce the size of the title text box and position it top-right on the slide, reduce the size of the pivot table and display it to the left of the slide title, and enlarge the chart and center it below both of the other objects.)

11. Save your changes to Mileage.ppt, and exit PowerPoint.

12. If you have completed Skill Drill exercises, save and close the e18drill workbook.

Challenge

Challenge exercises expand on or are somewhat related to skills presented in the lessons. Each exercise provides a brief narrative introduction followed by instructions in a numbered step format that are not as detailed as those in the Skill Drill section.

The exercises can be worked in any order. Be sure to save the workbook after completing each exercise. If you need a paper copy of the completed exercise, enter your name centered in a header before printing. Other print options have already been set to print compressed to one page and to display the filename, sheet name, and current date in a footer.

Before beginning your first Project 18 Challenge exercise, complete the following steps:

1. Open the Excel file named **e-1816**, and save the file as **e18challenge**.
   The workbook contains four sheets: an overview, and exercise sheets named #1-Embed, ToAccess, and #3-FromAccess.

2. Click the Overview sheet to view the organization of the Project 18 Challenge Exercises workbook.

If you need more than one work session to complete the desired exercises, continue working on **e18challenge** instead of starting over on the original e-1816 file.

1. Embedding Excel Data in a Word Document

You have prepared a memo to the Accounting department, asking for a review of your monthly expenses. Embed in the memo a copy of those expenses, which are available in an Excel worksheet.

To embed Excel data in a Word document:

1. Open the Word document **e-1817.doc**, and save it as **review.doc**.
2. Open the **e18challenge** workbook, and select the #1-Embed worksheet.
3. Copy cells A7:E21, and switch to the review.doc in Word.
4. Paste the copied Excel data after the last sentence, making sure that you embed (not link) the data as a Microsoft Excel Worksheet Object.
5. Use an option on the Edit menu to verify that there is no link to the #1-Embed worksheet in the document.
6. Save your changes, and close the Word document named review.doc.
7. Deselect the copied range in the #1-Embed worksheet, and close e18challenge.xls unless you are continuing with Project 18 Challenge exercises.

2. Exporting Excel Data to an Access Database

You work in the Marketing department and keep track of expenses in an Excel worksheet. The Accounting department has asked that you convert that data to an Access database. Use a Wizard to guide you through the process.

To export Excel data to an Access database:

1. Open **e18challenge**, and select the ToAccess worksheet.
2. Click within the database area, and select the Convert to MS Access option on the Data menu.
3. Specify that you want to create a new database and that the first row of your Excel data contains column headings.
4. Indicate to the Wizard that your Excel data should be placed in a new table.
5. Accept all fields and default field options.
6. Let Access add a primary key.
7. Specify that the Wizard should import to a table named **Expense List**.
8. Upon completion of the conversion, close the Access database (which saves your changes), and exit Access.
9. Close e18challenge.xls unless you are continuing with Project 18 Challenge exercises.

3. Importing Access Data into an Excel Worksheet

Expense data is currently stored in an Access database and you want to extract all Office and Other category expenses into Excel for analysis. Use Excel's Get External Data feature and specify filtering to produce the desired result.

To import Access data into an Excel worksheet:

1. Open the **e18challenge** workbook; select the #3-FromAccess worksheet, and click cell A9.

2. Open the New Database Query from the Get External Data menu.

3. Choose the MS Access Database option from the Databases tab.

4. Find and open the **e-1818.mdb** database.

5. Choose columns ID, Category, Expense, Date, Amount, and Client (select them in the order given).

6. Filter the data so only Category 1 or 4 records are imported.
   To do this, you must use two filter lines and specify the OR button between the two specifications.

7. Sort the data by the Expense field in Ascending order.

8. Select the <u>R</u>eturn Data to Microsoft Excel option, and complete the process to import data into Excel.
   Imported data should display starting in cell A9 of the #3-FromAccess worksheet. The client column is blank because Category 1 and 4 type expenses do not have clients.

9. Reformat as needed, including changes in column widths.

10. Save your changes to the #3-FromAccess worksheet.

11. Close e18challenge.xls.

Discovery Zone

Discovery Zone exercises require advanced knowledge of topics presented in *MOUS Essentials* lessons, application of skills from multiple lessons, or self-directed learning of new skills. Each exercise is independent of the others, so you can complete the exercises in any order.

1. Checking Sizes of Linked Versus Embedded Files

In Lesson 1, you created SalesReport1.doc, within which you linked a worksheet range. In Lesson 2, you created SalesReport2.doc, in which you embedded the same range. Use Windows Explorer to find the sizes of these two files. You should find that SalesReport1.doc is smaller than SalesReport2.doc, because it contains only the link, not the actual worksheet data.

2. Inserting a Non-Microsoft-Office Object

Expand your knowledge of how Excel can integrate with other programs. Create a new Excel workbook, and choose <u>I</u>nsert, <u>O</u>bject. Scroll through the object types, and experiment with inserting objects other than those associated with Microsoft Word, PowerPoint, and Access. You might work with Microsoft Note-It or Microsoft Drawing, if available on your system. Other suggestions include inserting an Adobe Acrobat document or a Netscape hypertext document.

PinPoint Assessment

You have completed this project and its associated lessons, and have had an opportunity to assess your skills through the end-of-project questions and exercises. Now use the PinPoint software Evaluation Mode to further assess your comprehension of the specific exam activities you have just learned. You can also use the PinPoint Trainer Mode and the Show Me tutorials to practice these exam activities.

Using the MOUS PinPoint 2000 Training and Testing Software

Objectives

➤ Install and Start the PinPoint Launcher

➤ Start and Run PinPoint Trainers and Evaluation

➤ View Trainer and Evaluation Results

➤ Recover from a Crash

➤ Remove PinPoint from Your Computer

Introduction to PinPoint 2000

PinPoint 2000 is a software product that provides interactive training and testing in Microsoft Office 2000 programs. It is designed to supplement the projects in this book and will aid you in preparing for the MOUS certification exams. PinPoint 2000 is included on the CD-ROM in the back of this text. PinPoint 2000 Trainers and Evaluations currently run under Windows 95, Windows 98 and Windows NT 4.

The MOUS PinPoint software consists of Trainers and Evaluations. Trainers are used to hone your Office user skills. Evaluations are used to evaluate your performance of those skills.

PinPoint 2000 requires a full custom installation of Office 2000 to your computer. A full custom installation is an option you select at the time you install Microsoft Office 2000, and means that all components of the software are installed.

The PinPoint 2000 Launcher

Your PinPoint 2000 CD contains a selection of PinPoint 2000 Trainers and Evaluations that cover many of the skills that you may need for using Word 2000, Excel 2000, PowerPoint 2000 and Access 2000.

Concurrency

PinPoint 2000 Trainers and Evaluations are considered "concurrent." This means that a Trainer (or Evaluation) is run simultaneously with the Office 2000 application you are learning or being tested in. For example, when you run a Pinpoint Excel 2000 Trainer, the Microsoft Excel 2000 application is automatically started and runs at the same time. By working directly in the Office 2000 application, you master the real application, rather than just practice on a simulation of the application.

Today's more advanced applications (like those in Office 2000) often allow more than one way to perform a given task. Concurrency with the real application gives you the freedom to choose the method that you like or that you already know. This gives you the optimal training and testing environment.

Trainer/Evaluation Pairs

Trainers and Evaluations come in pairs. For example, there is a Trainer/Evaluation pair for Word 2000 called "Expert Creating a Newsletter." This means that there is both a Trainer and an Evaluation for "Expert Creating a Newsletter."

Pinpoint Word 2000, Excel 2000, PowerPoint 2000, and Access 2000 all have such sets of Trainers and Evaluations.

Tasks

Each Trainer/Evaluation pair, or *module*, is a set of tasks grouped according to level (Core or Expert) and skill set.

Trainers

If you need help to complete the task you can click the Show Me button and activate the Show Me feature The Show Me will run a demonstration of how to perform a similar task.

After you attempt the task, the program checks your work and tells you if you performed the task correctly or incorrectly. In either case you have three choices:

- Retry the task.
- Have the Trainer demonstrate with the task's Show Me an efficient method of completing the task.
- Move on to the next task.

After you have completed all of the tasks in the module, you can study your performance by looking at the report that appears when you click the Report tab on the Launcher. Reports are covered in Lesson 7.

You may take a Trainer as many times as you like. As you do so, the Launcher keeps track of how you perform, even over different days, so that when you run a Trainer another time, the Trainer is set up to run only those tasks that were performed incorrectly on all of your previous run(s).

Evaluations

Since an Evaluation is really a test, it does not give you immediate feedback. You also cannot go back to a previous task or watch a demonstration of how to do the current task. You simply move from task to task until you have attempted all of the tasks in the Evaluation.

When you have finished, you can look at the report in the Reports section to see how you performed.

You can take an Evaluation as many times as you like. While you do so, the Launcher program keeps a record of how you have performed. As a result, if you take a Trainer after the corresponding Evaluation has been taken, the Trainer will set up to run only those tasks that were performed incorrectly on the Evaluation.

System Requirements

Table A.1 shows the system requirements to run PinPoint 2000 software on your computer.

Table A.1   PinPoint 2000 System Requirements

Component	Requirement
CPU	Minimum: Pentium
	Recommended: 166 MHz Pentium or better
Operating System	Windows 95, Windows 98 or WindowsNT 4.0 sp5
Installed Applications	Full Custom Installation of Office 2000*
	Printer
RAM	Minimum: 16 MB
	Recommended: 32 MB or higher

*Office 2000 must be installed before installing PinPoint 2000. If a Full Custom Installation of Office 2000 has not been performed, some tasks will not be available, because the components required for those tasks will not have been installed. The tasks will not be counted as right or wrong but recorded as N/A.

Table A.1   PinPoint 2000 System Requirements   (continued)

Component	Requirement
Hard Drive Space	Minimum: Installing PinPoint 2000 software requires about 4 MB of hard drive space.
	Recommended: For efficient operation, however, you should make sure you have at least 100 MB of unused drive space after installing PinPoint 2000.
CD-ROM Drive	4X speed or faster
Video	Minimum: Color VGA video display running at 640x480 resolution with 16 colors.
	Recommended: Color VGA video display running at 800x600 (or higher) resolution with 16 colors.
	Note for Gateway computer users: If running a P5 90 (or less) Gateway computer, obtain the latest ATI "Mach 64" video driver from Gateway. This can be downloaded from Gateway's web site.

Running PinPoint 2000

Now that you know what PinPoint 2000 is and what is required to use it, you now see how to install and use the Launcher, and start and run Trainers and Evaluations. You also see how to view Trainer and Evaluation reports. Lastly, you find out how to recover from a crash of PinPoint 2000, one should occur.

Lesson 1: Installing the Launcher to Your Computer

To run the PinPoint 2000 Trainers or Evaluations, you must first install the Launcher program.

To Install the Launcher

❶ **Start Windows on your computer.**

❷ **Be sure that Office 2000 has already been installed to your computer with a Full Custom Install. If this is not the case, perform this installation before you continue with step 3.**

❸ **Insert the PinPoint 2000 CD into your CD-ROM drive.**

❹ **From the Start menu, select Run.**

❺ **In the Run dialog box, enter the path to the SETUP.EXE file found in the root directory of the CD. For example, if your CD-ROM drive has been assigned the letter D, you would enter D:\setup.exe as shown in Figure A.1.**
Note: If your CD-ROM drive has been assigned a letter different from D, use that letter to begin the path in this dialog box. For example, if your CD-ROM drive has been assigned the drive letter E, enter E:\setup.exe in this dialog box.

❻ **Click OK.**

❼ **When the Setup Type screen appears, select Normal Single-User Installation.**

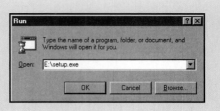

Figure A.1

8 **Click Next to continue.**

You are given a choice concerning the location of the PinPoint 2000 folder

The recommended location of the PinPoint 2000 folder is shown as the default. (*Note:* Two files that initially take up only 109 KB will be placed in this folder.)

If you prefer to use a different path or name for the `PinPoint 2000` folder click the B̲rowse button and navigate to the location you prefer, or rename the folder.

Click N̲ext to continue.

After the installation is complete, the PinPoint 2000 program group window appears.

9 **Close the PinPoint 2000 program group window.**

If the installation has occurred correctly, the following changes have been made to your computer:

- A PinPoint 2000 shortcut icon has been installed that will enable you to run the Launcher program via the Start menu.

- A new folder called PinPoint 2000 has been created on the hard drive of your computer (see Figure A.2).

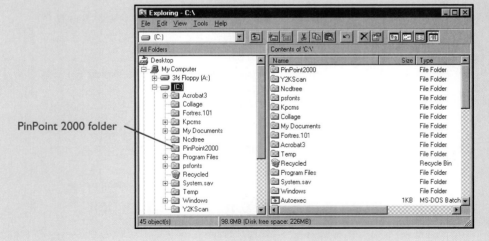

Figure A.2

PinPoint 2000 folder

The PinPoint 2000 folder contains:

- An empty database file, CC_Admin.mdb. As you run Trainers and Evaluations, this file records your performance.

- A small file, Uninst.isu, that is used for removing PinPoint 2000 from your computer.

Note: If your computer is configured so that file extensions are turned off, the CC_Admin.mdb file will appear without the .mdb extension.

Some files necessary for database access have been added to the Windows\System folder.

Lesson 2: Preparing to Run the PinPoint 2000 Launcher

Before running the PinPoint 2000 Launcher, it is necessary to initialize each of the Microsoft applications (Word 2000, Excel 2000, PowerPoint 2000 and Access 2000) at least one time. If you have already used each of these applications, you can ignore this section.

Initializing these applications enables PinPoint training and testing to run in a more stable environment. You will need to provide user information in the first application that you run.

Preparing to Run PinPoint 2000

1. **Start Microsoft Word 2000.**
2. **When the User Name dialog box appears type your Name and Initials.**
3. **Click OK to confirm.**
4. **When the Word window is completely set up and ready for use, you can close the application.**
5. **Start Microsoft Excel 2000.**
6. **When the Excel window is completely set up and ready for use, you can close the application.**
7. **Start Microsoft PowerPoint 2000.**
8. **When the PowerPoint window is completely set up and ready for use, you may close the application.**
9. **Start Microsoft Access 2000.**
10. **When the Access window is completely set up and ready for use, you can close the application.**

You are ready to run the Launcher program and begin Trainers and Evaluations.

Lesson 3: Starting the PinPoint 2000 Launcher

The Launcher program enables you to run Trainers and Evaluations. It also gives you a performance report after you have taken a Trainer or Evaluation.

To Start the PinPoint 2000 Launcher

1 **Select Start, Programs, PinPoint 2000, PinPoint 2000 (see Figure A.3).**

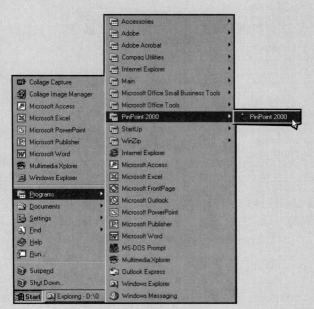

Figure A.3

2 **Enter a user name and password (see Figure A.4).**

Figure A.4

The user name and password can consist of any characters, as long as neither of them exceeds 50 characters. They are NOT case sensitive: It doesn't matter if you use upper- or lowercase letters.

If more than one person will be running PinPoint 2000 from your computer, each person must enter a different user name. However, passwords can be the same.

3 **Click OK in the Logon dialog box.**
If you are logging on for the first time, you need to enter some information in the User Information dialog box.

4 **Enter the requested information and click OK.**
The PinPoint 2000 Launcher screen appears (see Figure A.5).

continues ▶

To Start the PinPoint 2000 Launcher   (continued)

Figure A.5

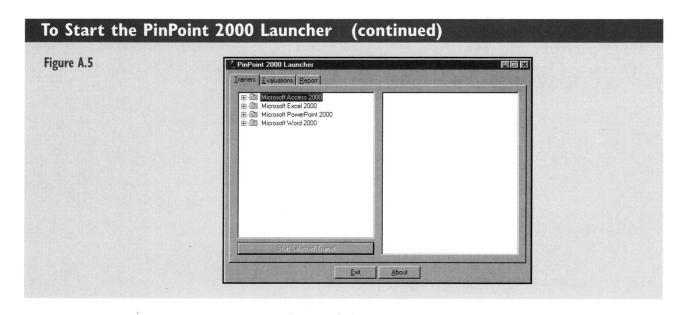

You are now ready to run PinPoint Trainers and Evaluations.

Lesson 4: Starting PinPoint 2000 Trainers and Evaluations

To Start Trainers and Evaluations

1 **From the PinPoint Launcher, click the _Trainers_ tab if you want to start a Trainer, or the _Evaluations_ tab if you want to start an Evaluation (see Figure A.6).**

Figure A.6

Trainer tab

Evaluation tab

Report tab

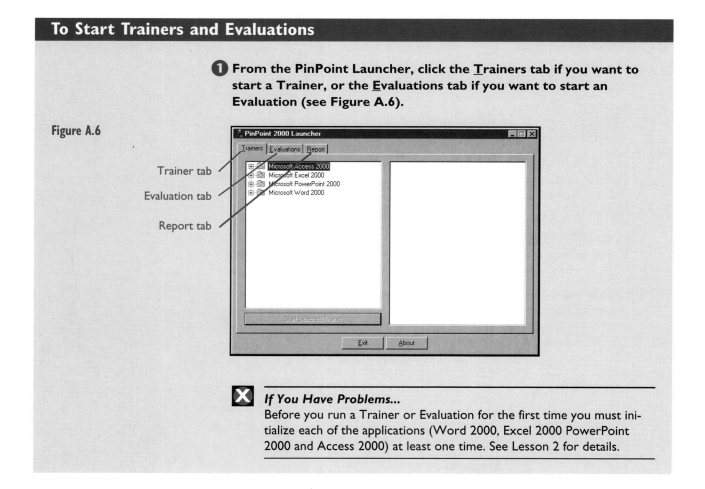

> **✖** **_If You Have Problems..._**
> Before you run a Trainer or Evaluation for the first time you must ini-
> tialize each of the applications (Word 2000, Excel 2000 PowerPoint
> 2000 and Access 2000) at least one time. See Lesson 2 for details.

② **Click the plus sign (+) to open an application's Core and Expert modules and exams. The plus sign becomes a minus sign (–), as shown in Figure A.7.**

Click here to open and close the Core and Expert modules and exams

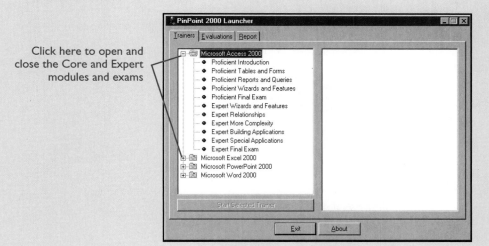

Figure A.7

③ **Select the module or exam that you want to run.**

The individual tasks that are part of the Trainer or Evaluation appear in the pane on the right.

④ **If you are running a Trainer without an Evaluation, you can select or deselect individual training tasks by clicking on the box beside the task name (see Figure A.8).**

The tasks that are deselected will not run during the Trainer. This enables you to adjust your training to include only those tasks that you do not already know how to do.

When running an Evaluation, however, you cannot deselect individual tasks. All tasks will run.

Select or deselect tasks here

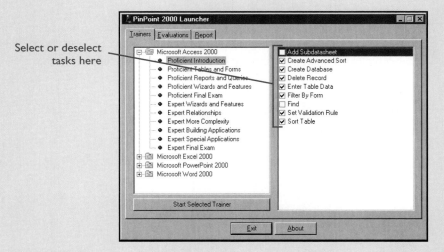

Figure A.8

continues ▶

To Start Trainers and Evaluations (continued)

5 Click **Start Selected Trainer** button if you are starting a Trainer. Click the **Start Selected Evaluation** button if you are starting an Evaluation.

The PinPoint 2000 Launcher dialog box with your name and module selection appears (see Figure A.9).

Figure A.9

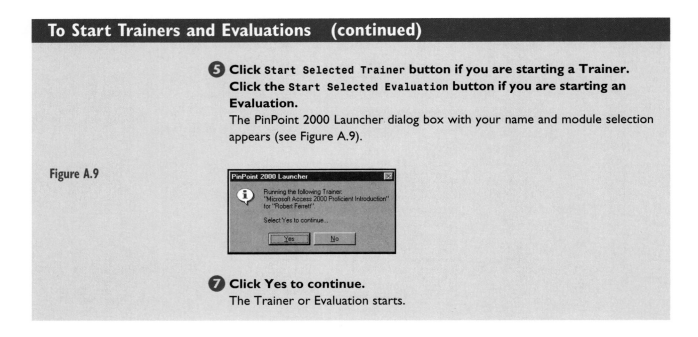

7 Click Yes to continue.

The Trainer or Evaluation starts.

Proceed to the next two sections to see how to run Trainers and Evaluations.

Lesson 5: Running a Trainer

This lesson shows you how to run a Trainer. It also details how to handle some of the situations you might encounter during a Trainer.

To Run a Trainer

1 When you start the Trainer, you might encounter a warning message instructing you to change your computer's Taskbar settings (see **Figure A.10**).

If this message appears, follow its instructions before proceeding. Changing your taskbar settings in this way is necessary for proper functioning of a PinPoint Trainer. You can carry out the instructions given without canceling the box.

Figure A.10

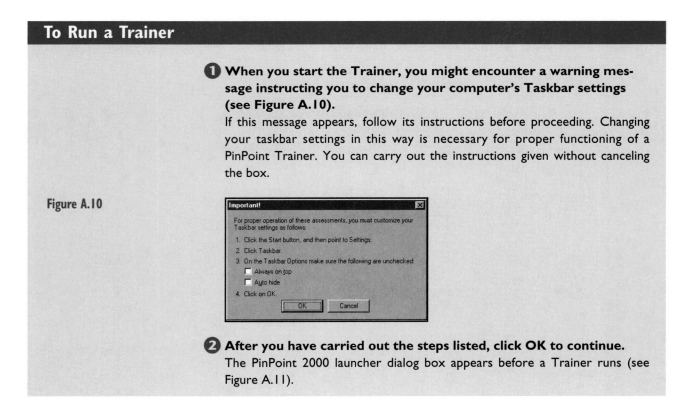

2 After you have carried out the steps listed, click **OK** to continue.

The PinPoint 2000 launcher dialog box appears before a Trainer runs (see Figure A.11).

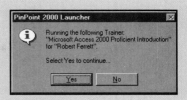

③ Click Yes to continue.
The first thing you see is an introduction to how all PinPoint 2000 Trainers work. If you want to see the demonstration of how a PinPoint Trainer works and how to use the PinPoint 2000 controls, press any key or click the mouse to continue.

④ Skip through the introduction for now and go directly to a task.
After initializing, the Trainer opens the first selected task.

 Inside Stuff: **Exiting the Introduction**
You can exit the introduction at any time by pressing Esc and moving straight to the training.

The task instructions display in a moveable instruction box that hovers over the application (see Figure A.12).

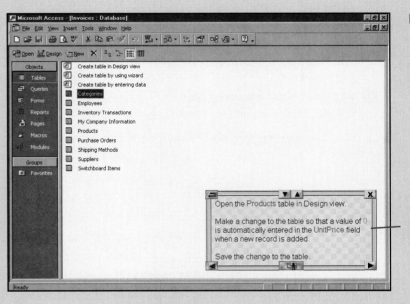

Figure A.12

The instruction box can be moved to different parts of the screen

 If You Have Problems...
If the instruction box is blocking your view of something, you can drag it to another part of the screen. To instantly move the box to the other side of the screen, right-click the instruction box.

Notice the PinPoint control buttons that appear on the perimeter of the instruction box. Use these buttons to interact with the Trainer according to your needs (see Figure A.13).

continues ▶

To Run a Trainer (continued)

Figure A.13

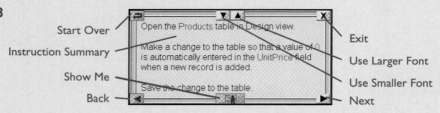

Start Over

Instruction Summary

Show Me

Back

Exit

Use Larger Font

Use Smaller Font

Next

The features of the instruction box in Figure A.13 and their descriptions are listed here:

- The Instruction Summary displays the task to be completed. Instructions remain visible during the task.
- The Start Over button starts the current task again.
- The Back button returns you to the previous task.
- The Show Me button gives you a step-by-step demonstration using a similar example.
- The Use Larger Font and Use Smaller Font buttons enlarge or reduce the size of the box and text.
- The Quit button ends the current training session and returns you to the Launcher.
- The Next button checks a finished task for correct performance and moves you to the next task.

5 **Try to do the task exactly as instructed in the PinPoint instruction box.**

6 **Click the Next button (refer to Figure A.13).**
PinPoint 2000 gives you feedback in the Results dialog box.

Whether you performed the task correctly or not, you now have three choices:

- Click the Show Me button to display a step-by-step demonstration using a similar example.
- Click the Try Task Again button to set up the task so you can attempt it again.
- Click the Next Task button to move on and attempt the next task.

If you click the Show Me button, a demonstration of how to perform a similar task is given. This demonstration, called a Show Me, begins with a summary of the steps required to perform the task.

7 **Press any key or click the mouse to advance the next Show Me box.**
Usually the key concept behind the particular skill is explained during the Show Me.

After the instruction summary (and possibly a key concept), each of the instructions in the summary is explained and demonstrated in detail.

 Inside Stuff: **Exiting Show Me Demonstrations**
If you want to exit from the Show Me demonstration at any point, press Esc to return to the PinPoint task.

During the Show Me demonstration, the mouse pointer moves and text is entered automatically when appropriate to the demonstration, but whenever the description or action is completed the demonstration halts until the user prompts it to continue with either a mouse click or a key stroke.

After the demonstration is complete, you can perform the task yourself.

8 **Continue through the PinPoint Trainer at your own pace, attempting each task and watching Show Me demonstrations when you need help.**

When you have finished with the training session, the Trainers screen of the Launcher is visible again. You can see a report of your performance by clicking the Report tab in the Launcher (viewing reports is covered in Lesson 7).

 Inside Stuff: **Exiting Trainers**
You are free to exit from the training at any time by clicking the Exit button (refer to Figure A.13). When you attempt to exit a Trainer before it is finished, you are asked to confirm this decision (see Figure A.14).

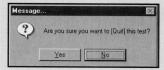

Figure A.14

If you want to exit from the trainer at this point, click Yes.

Lesson 6: Running an Evaluation

This lesson shows you how to run an Evaluation. It also details how to handle some of the situations you might encounter during an Evaluation.

To Run an Evaluation

1 **When you start the Evaluation, you might encounter a warning message instructing you to change your computer's Taskbar settings (refer to Figure A.10).**

If this message appears, follow its instructions before proceeding. Changing your taskbar settings in this way is necessary for proper functioning of a PinPoint Trainer. You can carry out the instructions given without canceling the box.

2 **After you have carried out the steps listed, click OK to continue.**

The Pinpoint 2000 Launcher dialog box appears before an Evaluation runs (refer to Figure A.11).

3 **Click Yes to continue.**

The first thing you see is an introduction to how all PinPoint 2000 Evaluations work. If you want to see the demonstration of how an Evaluation works and how to use the PinPoint 2000 controls, press any key or click the mouse to continue past each screen. If you do not need to see the demonstration, press Esc to go straight to the testing.

continues ▶

To Run an Evaluation   (continued)

Like a Trainer, an Evaluation presents you with a task to perform. In an Evaluation, however, the Start Over, Back, and Show Me buttons are all disabled. Therefore, you cannot restart a task, return to a previous task, or run a Show Me demonstration of how to perform the task.

4 **After attempting a task, click the Next button to continue to the next task.**

Normally, you would attempt all of the tasks in the Evaluation. But if you need to finish early and click the Exit button before you have attempted all of the tasks, the message box in Figure A.14 will display. Click the <u>Y</u>es button if you want to exit the Evaluation and go back to the Launcher program.

5 **You can view a report of your performance by clicking the <u>R</u>eport tab in the Launcher.**

See the next section for details about viewing reports.

Inside Stuff: **What to Avoid While Running Trainers and Evaluations**

Keep the following in mind for PinPoint 2000 Trainers and Evaluations to run properly:

- Only perform actions that the PinPoint task instructions ask you to perform.

- Do not exit from the Microsoft Office 2000 application in which you are training or testing unless you are told to do so.

- Do not close the example document (the document that PinPoint opens for you when you begin a task) unless you are told to do so.

- Do not run other programs (such as email, Internet browsers, virus shields, system monitors, and so on) at the same time as running PinPoint, unless you are asked to do so.

- Do not change views in one of the Office 2000 applications unless you are asked to do so.

- Do not change the way your Windows operating system or Office 2000 applications are configured by default.

- Do not turn off your computer in the middle of a PinPoint Trainer or Evaluation. Instead, first exit from the Trainer or Evaluation, then exit from Windows and then turn off your computer.

Lesson 7: Viewing Reports in the Launcher

After you have taken at least one PinPoint 2000 Trainer or Evaluation, you can view detailed reports at any time concerning your performance on any of the modules that you have taken.

To View Reports in the Launcher

1 **If the Launcher is not running, click Start, Programs, PinPoint 2000, PinPoint 2000 to run it. Then log on.**

2 **Click the Report tab.**
The Report screen appears (see Figure A.15).

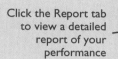
Click the Report tab
to view a detailed
report of your
performance

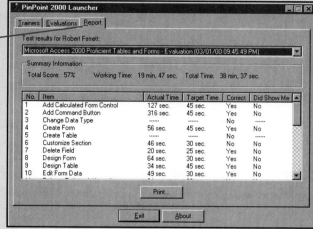

Figure A.15

The very last Trainer or Evaluation that you ran displays onscreen. The information displayed in the Report screen is as follows:

- *Total Score*—The percentage of the correctly performed tasks out of the total number of tasks set to run.

- *Working Time*—The total time you actually spent working on all of the tasks in the Trainer or Evaluation.

- *Total Time*—The total time you spent running the entire Trainer or Evaluation.

- *Item*—The name of the task.

- *Actual Time*—The time you took to perform the task.

- *Target Time*—A reasonable amount of time required to perform the task by an efficient method.

- *Correct*—Displays Yes if you performed the task correctly; No if you did not.

- *Did Show-Me*—Displays Yes if you ran a Show Me demonstration for that task; No if you did not.

Note: A blank or dotted line running through the task line, or N/A, indicate that the task was not taken.

3 **If you want to print a report, click the Print button.**

4 **If you want to see a report for a Trainer or Evaluation that you took previously, select it from the Test results for <your name> drop-down list.**
The reports are listed in the order in which they were taken.

Note: You will see only your own reports on the Reports screen and not the reports for anyone else using PinPoint on your computer.

 ***Inside Stuff:*   User History**

An important feature of the PinPoint 2000 Launcher is its capability to keep track of your history of running Trainers and Evaluations. The Launcher uses your history to reconfigure a Trainer each successive time you run it. To "re-configure" means to change the tasks that will run.

The Launcher does not reconfigure an Evaluation the same way it does a Trainer. No matter which tasks you have performed correctly in the past (on either a Trainer or Evaluation), all tasks are automatically selected to be run when you attempt to take an Evaluation.

Lesson 8: Recovering from a Crash During a Trainer or Evaluation

If your computer crashes while you are running a Trainer or Evaluation, all the work you have already done is not wasted. You do not need to start the Trainer or Evaluation over again from the beginning. To recover from a crash during a Trainer or Evaluation, follow these simple instructions.

To Recover from a Crash

1 **Reboot your computer.**

2 **Start the Launcher again and log on as usual.**

3 **When a message like the one in Figure A.16 appears, close the Office application you were working on (if it's still running in the background) by clicking the Close button in the top right corner of the application window.**

Figure A.16

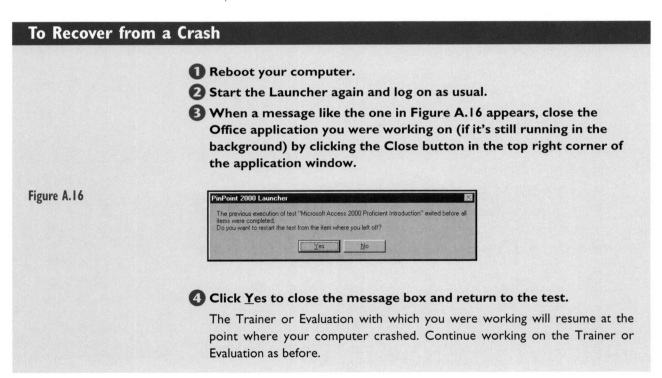

4 **Click Yes to close the message box and return to the test.**

The Trainer or Evaluation with which you were working will resume at the point where your computer crashed. Continue working on the Trainer or Evaluation as before.

Removing PinPoint 2000

When you have finished training and testing with PinPoint 2000, you may want to remove the Launcher program from your computer. PinPoint 2000 can be removed using the procedure for removing most other applications from your computer.

Lesson 9: Removing PinPoint 2000

To Remove PinPoint 2000

❶ From the Start menu, select Settings, Control Panel.

❷ Double-click the Add/Remove Programs icon.
The Add/Remove Programs Properties dialog box displays.

❸ Select PinPoint 2000.

❹ Click the Add/Remove button.

❺ Confirm the removal of PinPoint 2000 by clicking Yes in the dialog box.

❻ When the Remove Shared File? dialog box appears, click the Yes To All button (see Figure A.17).

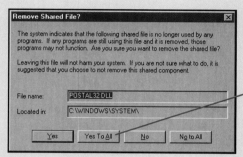

Figure A.17

Click here to uninstall PinPoint 2000

❼ When the Remove Programs From Your Computer dialog box reports Uninstall successfully completed, click OK.

❽ Click OK in the Add/Remove Programs Properties dialog box.

❾ Close the Control Panel window.
PinPoint 2000 has now been completely removed from your computer.

Summary

PinPoint 2000 is a very valuable tool for preparing yourself for a MOUS Exam. You've learned how to install and start the PinPoint Launcher. You can now run Trainers and Evaluations, and view a report of their results. You also know what to avoid while running Trainers and Evaluations. You've seen how to recover if PinPoint crashes. And finally, you've learned how to uninstall PinPoint when you no longer need it. You are now equipped to take full advantage of the PinPoint 2000 training and testing software.

Preparing for MOUS Certification

This appendix gives you information that you need regarding the certification exams—how to register, what is covered in the tests, how the tests are administered, and so on. Because this information may change, be sure to visit www.mous.net for the latest updates.

What This Book Offers

This text is certified for both levels of certification:

- Core—You are able to manage a wide range of real world tasks efficiently.
- Expert—In addition to the everyday tasks at the Core level, you are able to handle complex assignments and have a thorough understanding of a program's advanced features.

In addition to the Core and Expert levels, Microsoft now offers a Master certification, which indicates that you have a comprehensive understanding of Microsoft Office 2000 and many of its advanced features. A Master certification requires students to successfully pass all five of the required exams: Word, Excel, PowerPoint, Access and Outlook.

Each exam includes a list of tasks you may be asked to perform. The lessons in this book identify these required tasks with an icon in the margin. You can also review the MOUS Skill Guide in the front of this book to become familiar with these required tasks.

In addition to these icons, this book contains various study aids that not only help you pass the test, but also teach you how the software functions. You can use this book in a classroom or lab setting, or you can work through each project on your own using the PinPoint CD-ROM. You don't have to move through the book from front to back as each project stands on its own. Each project is broken down into lessons, which are then broken down into step-by-step instructions.

The PinPoint CD-ROM includes Project Review Tests for each MOUS Exam skill set. The coverage has two parts: a Task and a Show Me. The Task requires you to do something, (for example, format a document) and the Show Me demonstrates how to perform that task. In addition, each PinPoint has a practice test that mirrors the actual MOUS exams.

Follow the steps within each of the lessons, and use the PinPoint software as an evaluation of your comprehension. If you get stuck, be sure to use the Show Me demonstration.

Registering for and Taking and the Exam

All MOUS exams are administered by a MOUS Authorized Testing Center (ATC). Most MOUS ATCs require pre-registration. To pre-register contact a local ATC directly. You can find a center near you by visiting the MOUS Web site at www.mous.net. Some ATCs accept walk-in examination candidates, allowing on-the-spot registration and examination. Be sure to check with a specific ACT to make certain of their registration policy.

The exam is not written and there are no multiple choice or true-false questions. You perform the required tasks on a computer running the live Microsoft application. A typical exam takes 45 to 60 minutes to complete. You must work through each task in the exam as quickly as you can.

All examination data is encrypted, and the examination process is closely monitored so your test scores are completely confidential. Examination results are provided only to the candidate and to Microsoft.

The Day of the Exam

Bring the following items with you to the testing center on exam day:

- Picture ID—driver's license or passport
- Your MOUS identification number (if you have take a previous MOUS certification exam)
- ATC Student ID, if applicable

At the exam center, you can expect to first complete the candidate information section, which provides the information necessary to complete your MOUS certificate.

After confirming your ID, the administrator will seat you at the test computer, log you onto the test system, and open your test module. You are now ready to begin.

To start the test, click the "Start Test" button and you're ready to begin your certification exam.

The Exam Itself

Instructions are displayed in a separate window on the screen. You can close the instruction window by clicking on it. You can restore it by clicking "Instructions" on the test information bar at the bottom of the screen. Read the test instructions carefully. Once you have started, a box in the bottom right corner of the screen indicates the question on which you are currently working. (For example, "question 3 of 50".)

If anything abnormal happens during the exam, or if the application "crashes," stop immediately and contact the administrator. The administrator will restart the test from where you left off. You will not be penalized any time for this.

When you have completed your exam, the computer will calculate your score. The scoring process takes a short time, and you will be notified onscreen whether you passed or failed. You may then ask the administrator to give you a printed report.

If you complete the exam successfully, your MOUS certificate will be delivered within 2-3 weeks.

General Tips

Unlike earlier MOUS exams, the results of the Office 2000 MOUS exams are expressed as a value on a 1000-point scale, rather than a percentage.

Each activity or question on the Office 2000 MOUS exams is comprised of several individually scored subtasks. A candidates's score is derived from the number of subtasks successfully completed and the "weight" or difficulty assigned to each.

Pay close attention to how each question is worded. Answers must be precise, resolving the question exactly as asked.

You can use any combination of menus, toolbars and short-cut keys to complete each assigned task. Answers are scored based on the result, not the method you use or the time taken to complete each required task. Extra keystrokes or mouse clicks will not count against your score as long as you achieve the correct result within the time limit given.

Remember that the overall test is timed. While spending a lot of time on an individual answer will not adversely affect the scoring of that particular question, taking too long may not leave you with enough time to complete the entire test.

Answers are either right or wrong. You do not get credit for partial answers.

Important! Check to make sure you have entirely completed each question before clicking the NEXT TASK button. Once you press the NEXT TASK button, you will not be able to return to that question. A question will be scored as wrong if it is not completed properly before moving to the next question.

Save your Results Page that prints at the end of the exam. It is your confirmation that you passed the exam.

Take note of these cautions:

- DON'T leave dialog boxes, Help menus, toolbars, or menus open.
- DON'T leave tables, boxes, or cells "active or highlighted" unless instructed to do so.
- DON'T click the NEXT TASK button until you have "completely" answered the current question.

Lastly, be sure to visit the mous.net Web site for specific information on the Office 2000 exams, more testing tips, and to download a free demo of the exams.

All key terms appearing in this book (in bold italic) are listed alphabetically in this Glossary for easy reference. If you want to learn more about a feature or concept, turn to the page reference shown after its definition. You can also use the Index to find the term's other significant occurrences.

3-D reference   Refers to the same cell or range on multiple sheets. [pg. 308]

absolute reference   Specifies that the row and/or column cell references do not change as a formula is copied. For example, copying the formula =$A$1*A5 in cell A6 to cells B6 and C6 results in the formulas =$A$1*B5 and =$A$1*C5, respectively. You can create an absolute reference by placing a dollar sign ($) in front of the part(s) of the cell reference that you do not want to change during the copy operation (see also **relative reference**). [pg. 41]

active cell   See current cell.

Advanced Filter   A database feature that enables you to specify complex criteria and to copy filtered records to another location (see also **filter**). [pg. 227]

AND search criteria   Two or more search criteria of which all conditions must be met to select a record. [pg. 231]

annuity   Fixed payments at equal intervals (see also **FV function**). [pg. 106]

argument   A specific component in a function, such as a range of cells. For example, the function =SUM(B5:B20) has one argument—the range of cells from B5 through B20. The function =IF(B5>B2,"Goal Met","   ") has three arguments within parentheses, separated by commas. [pg. 98]

arithmetic operator   A symbol in a formula that specifies the type of calculation; symbols include +, -, *, and / (to add, subtract, multiply, and divide, respectively). [pg. 15]

ascending order   A sort in which items are arranged from smallest to largest (1, 2, 3) or from first to last (A to Z). [pg. 222]

Auto Outline   A feature that examines a worksheet and creates an outline (see also **worksheet outline**). [pg. 312]

AutoComplete   A feature that compares text you are typing into a cell with text already entered in the same column and automatically completes the word or phrase if a match is found. You can accept the suggested entry or continue typing. [pg. 6]

AutoCorrect   A feature that corrects common errors as you type, such as changing **adn** to **and**. [pg. 42]

AutoFill   A feature that enables you to automatically fill in a series of numbers, dates, or other items in a specified range. [pg. 34]

AutoFilter   Limits the display of records in a list, based on simple search conditions. [pg. 227]

AutoFormat   Applies one of sixteen predefined formats to lists and cell ranges. [pg. 182]

AutoShape   A predefined shape that you create using the Drawing toolbar. [pg. 39]

AutoSum   Inserts a formula that sums a range of cells automatically. Excel suggests a formula that you can accept or edit. [pg. 39]

AVERAGE function   A predefined formula that calculates the average of specified values. [pg. 98]

border   A solid or dashed line that is applied to one or more sides of a cell, or to a range of cells. [pg. 60]

callout   A text-filled object that points to other text or another object. [pg. 208]

cell   The intersection of a column and a row. You can enter text, a number, or a formula in a cell. [pg. 2]

cell address   Describes which column and row intersect to form the cell; for example, A1 is the address for the cell in the first column (column A) and the first row (row 1). [pg. 4]

chart   A graphical representation of data that makes it easy to see trends and make comparisons. [pg. 124]

clip art   An image that is part of a library of images provided by a program (see also **graphics file**). [pg. 209]

Clipboard   A temporary storage area for data that you want to copy or move to another location. [pg. 38]

clustered column chart   A chart subtype that presents multiple data series as side-by-side columns. [pg. 133]

column chart   A chart in which each data point is reflected in the height of its column, in relation to the scale shown on the Y-axis. [pg. 126]

column letter   Identifies a column in a worksheet. Columns are lettered A through Z, AA through AZ, and so on through IV, up to 256 columns. [pg. 4]

combination chart   Includes two or more chart types, such as showing one data series as a column and another as a line. Create a combination chart if the values in the data series vary widely or you want to emphasize differences in the data. [pg. 143]

comment   An annotation attached to a cell that displays within a box whenever the mouse pointer rests on the cell. (see also **comment indicator**) [pg. 246]

comment indicator   A small red triangle in the upper-right corner of a cell; indicates a comment is attached to the cell. (see also **comment**) [pg. 246]

comparison operator   Used to test the relationship between two items, such as finding out whether the items are equal (=) or if one is greater than (>) the other. [pg. 72]

concatenation operator   The & symbol in a formula that joins one or more text entries to form a single entry. [pg. 72]

conditional formatting   Used to accent a cell, depending on the value of the cell. Conditional formats return a result that is based on whether the value in the cell meets a specified condition. Formatting options include font style, font color, shading, patterns, borders, bold, italic, and underlining. [pg. 161]

consolidate   To summarize data stored in multiple worksheets into a single worksheet. [pg. 308]

constant   A text value (also called a label), a numeric value (number), a date value, or a time value entered in a worksheet cell. Constants do not change unless you edit them. [pg. 6]

constraint   A limit or maximum value. (see also **Solver**) [pg. 360]

current (or active) cell   The selected cell where the next action you take happens, such as typing. An outline appears around the cell to indicate that it is the current cell. [pg. 4]

custom format   A format you create and store for future use. Used for unique situations in which a predefined format does not meet your needs (see also **format**). [pg. 180]

custom views   Allow you to save the views of worksheets you use most often and recall them when you need them. [pg. 314]

data   Unprocessed raw facts or assumptions that are stored in a document such as a worksheet or database. [pg. 220]

database   An organized collection of related records. (see also **list**) [pg. 220]

data form   A dialog box that displays a list one record at a time. If you work with a large list, you may prefer to add and delete records by using this form, which shows all the fields in one record. [pg. 233]

data series   A range of values entered in a row or column and plotted on a chart. [pg. 124]

data table   The result of an Excel procedure that calculates multiple results from a formula containing one or two variables. [pg. 355]

data validation   Options to guide data entry and prevent common data entry errors. [pg. 264]

default   A setting that a program uses unless you specify another setting. [pg. 2]

descending order   The order that is opposite of ascending order. Descending order is 3, 2, 1; or Z to A. [pg. 222]

destination file   A file that contains linked or embedded data (see also **source file**). [pg. 390]

embedded chart   A graphical representation of data created within the worksheet rather than as a separate worksheet. [pg. 124]

embedded object   An object in a destination file that does not update when the data in the source file changes (see also **linked object** and **object**). [pg. 152]

Error Alert message A user-specified informational, stop, or warning message that is displayed when invalid data are entered in a cell (see also **Stop Error Alert**). [pg. 267]

field A data item in each database record, such as an order number or order date in a database that tracks catalog sales. In an Excel list, each **field** is set up in a column. [pg. 220]

file property Describes a characteristic of a file such as file type, file size, storage location, author's name, and date last revised. [pg. 253]

fill handle A small black square in the lower-right corner of the current cell or a selected range. Dragging the fill handle copies the contents of the current cell or selected range to adjacent cells. [pg. 34]

filter A database feature that enables you to hide all the rows except those that meet specified criteria. [pg. 227]

font The type style, type size, and type attributes that you apply to text and numbers. [pg. 56]

footer Contains text or graphics that repeat at the bottom of each page in a multiple-page printout. [pg. 16]

format To apply attributes to cells that alter the display of cell contents. For example, you can format a worksheet by italicizing text and displaying a border around a cell or group of cells. [pg. 52]

Formatting toolbar Provides—in button form—shortcuts to frequently-used commands for changing the appearance of data. The Formatting and Standard toolbars share one row, unless that setting is turned off. [pg. 2]

formula Produces a calculated result, usually based on a reference to one or more cells in the worksheet. The results of a formula change if you change the contents of a cell referenced in the formula. [pg. 6]

formula bar Displays the contents of the current or active cell. [pg. 2]

function A predefined formula in Excel. [pg. 40]

FV function Calculates the future value of an investment based on fixed payments (deposits) earning a fixed rate of interest across equal time periods. [pg. 106]

Goal Seek A Microsoft Excel tool that enables you to determine a value of a formula variable that would be required to yield a given result. [pg. 353]

graphics file An image that is part of a library of images provided by a program or a file stored separately. (see also **clip art**) [pg. 209]

grouped objects Two or more objects that can be manipulated as a single object. [pg. 204]

header Contains text or graphics that repeat at the top of each page in a multiple-page printout. [pg. 16]

HLOOKUP function Used when comparison values are located in a row across the top of a table of data, and you want to look down a specified number of rows. [pg. 114]

hyperlink Underlined text that is clicked to jump to another location. [pg. 372]

IF function Used to perform one of two operations in a single cell, based on the evaluation of some condition being true or false. [pg. 108]

indented format One of ten predefined report formats applied to a pivot table. [pg. 297]

information Data transformed into a useful form; created when you select the data that you need, organize the data in a meaningful order, format the data into a useful layout, and display the results—usually to the screen or a printer. [pg. 220]

input message A convenient way to display instructions to users when they access a specific cell in a worksheet. [pg. 264]

landscape orientation Produces a printed page that is wider than it is long. [pg. 16]

legend Displays the colors, patterns, or symbols that identify data categories in a chart. [pg. 124]

line chart Plots one or more data series as connected points along an axis. [pg. 125]

linked object An object in a destination file that updates whenever the data in the source file changes (see also **embedded object** and **object**). [pg. 152]

list An Excel database in which columns are fields and rows are records. [pg. 220]

long label Text that exceeds the width of its cell. Overflow text displays if the adjacent cells are blank. [pg. 6]

macro Multiple commands or keystrokes that are executed as a single operation. [pg. 328]

macro button A button that executes a macro when it is clicked. [pg. 338]

MAX function Displays the largest value among specified values. [pg. 98]

menu bar The screen area under the title bar that contains command options that, when activated, display a list of related commands. The File menu, for example, includes Open, Close, Save, and Print commands. [pg. 2]

MIN function Displays the smallest value among specified values. [pg. 98]

mouse pointer The moving arrow (or other object) onscreen that represents the location of the mouse. It is used to select items, activate objects and programs, and position the insertion point in text. [pg. 5]

name box Displays the cell address of the current cell, or the name of a cell or range of cells. [pg. 2]

nonindented format One of ten predefined table formats applied to a pivot table. [pg. 297]

noninteractive table A pivot table on a Web page that can be viewed, but not changed. [pg. 297]

NOW function Enters the serial number of the current date and time—numbers to the left of the decimal point represent the date, and numbers to the right of the decimal point represent the time. [pg. 113]

object Anything that has properties and can be referenced and used by another program. An object may be as small as a character or as large as an Excel workbook. [pg. 390]

Object Linking and Embedding (OLE) A means to share data among Microsoft Office applications by linking or embedding data from the source file to the destination file (see also **embedded object** and **linked object**). [pg. 390]

Office Assistant A component of onscreen Help in the form of an animated graphic image that can be turned on or off; brings up a list of subjects related to a question you type. [pg. 2]

OR search criteria Two or more search criteria of which only one condition must be met to select a record. [pg. 229]

order of precedence The order in which Excel performs calculations. For example, multiplication and division take place before addition and subtraction. [pg. 72]

page break Ends a printed page at a specified point and starts a new page. Cell contents below and to the right of a page break print on a new page. [pg. 273]

password A collection of up to 255 case-sensitive characters that must be known to use a password-protected worksheet or workbook. [pg. 254]

pattern Repeats an effect, such as a horizontal, vertical or diagonal strips. [pg. 60]

Personal Macro Workbook A Microsoft Excel file designed to contain macros which are available to all workbooks. [pg. 332]

pie chart A circular chart in which each piece (wedge) shows a data segment and its relationship to the whole. [pg. 124]

pivot table An interactive table that summarizes a data source such as a list or another table. [pg. 284]

PivotTable and PivotChart Wizard Guides you through the steps to create a pivot table, or a chart based on pivot table data. [pg. 284]

PivotTable list An interactive pivot table on a Web page. [pg. 297]

PMT function Calculates the payment due on a loan, assuming equal payments and a fixed interest rate. [pg. 99]

point A unit of measurement used in printing and publishing to designate the height of type. There are roughly 72 points in an inch. The default type size in an Excel worksheet is 10 points. [pg. 56]

portrait orientation Produces a printed page that is longer than it is wide. [pg. 16]

range One or more adjacent cells that form a rectangule. [pg. 32]

range name An English-like name applied to a cell or range of cells. [pg. 244]

read-only A file attribute that specifies a file can be viewed, but not changed, if you save it under the same name. [pg. 254]

record Each collection of related data in a database. In an Excel list, each row is a record. [pg. 220]

reference operator Used to combine cell references in calculations. The colon (:), which connects the first and last cells of the range to be summed, is an example of a reference operator. [pg. 72]

refresh Recalculate a pivot table after making changes to worksheet data. [pg. 292]

relative reference   Specifies that the row and/or column cell references change as a formula is copied. For example, copying the formula =A1+A2 in cell A3 to cells B3 and C3 results in the formulas =B1+B2 and =C1+C2, respectively (see also **absolute reference**). [pg. 41]

Report Manager   Used to combine and save multiple custom views into a single report to facilitate printing complex worksheets. [pg. 316]

row number   Identifies a row in a worksheet. Rows are numbered 1 through 65,536. [pg. 5]

scenario   A unique set of input values stored for use in "what-if" analyses. [pg. 357]

Scenario Manager   An Excel procedure for saving multiple sets of input values and results. [pg. 357]

scrollbars   Enable you to move the worksheet window vertically and horizontally so that you can see other parts of the worksheet. [pg. 3]

select   To highlight or click an item so you can make changes to it. [pg. 32]

shared workbook   Enables two or more users to have simultaneous access to a workbook. [pg. 375]

shortcut menu   A menu activated by placing the pointer over an object or in text, and then clicking the right mouse button. [pg. 37]

sizing handle   A small black square at the corner or midpoint of a selected object. Dragging a sizing handle increases or decreases the size of the object. [pg. 129]

Solver   An Excel add-in designed to handle complex problem-solving with mathematical models and constraints. [pg. 360]

sort   To rearrange the records in a list, based on the contents of one or more fields. [pg. 222]

sort field   The column that you want Excel to use in sorting (sometimes called a *sort key*). [pg. 222]

sort key   The column you want Excel to use in sorting (sometimes called a *sort field*). [pg. 222]

source file   A file providing the source data linked to, or embedded in, a destination file (see also **destination file**). [pg. 390]

Spelling checker   Checks the spelling of words in the current worksheet or selected range, and enables you to change or ignore any word not found in its dictionary. [pg. 42]

spreadsheet   A work area—called a **worksheet** in Excel—comprised of rows and columns. [pg. 2]

stacked column chart   Displays multiple data series as stacked components of a single column instead of as side-by-side columns. The stacked column subtype is appropriate if the multiple data series total to a meaningful number. [pg. 133]

Standard toolbar   Provides—in button form—shortcuts to frequently used commands including Save, Print, Cut (move), Copy, and Paste. The Standard and Formatting toolbars share one row unless that setting is turned off. [pg. 2]

status bar   The bar at the bottom of a window that gives additional information about the window. [pg. 2]

style   A means of combining more than one format—such as font type, size, and color— into a single definition that can be applied to one or more cells. [pg. 184]

template   A document with features such as boilerplate text, styles, and Form controls that are applied to any document created from the template. [pg. 188]

text box   An object shaped like a square or rectangle that contains words. [pg. 202]

title bar   The line at the top of a window that contains the name of the application and document, along with the Minimize, Maximize/Restore, and Close buttons. [pg. 2]

Trace Dependents   An auditing tool that shows what other cells use the results of the current cell. [pg. 350]

Trace Precedents   An auditing tool that shows what cells provide data to the current cell. [pg. 350]

typeface—A style of print such as Arial, Courier, or Times New Roman. The default font in an Excel worksheet is Arial. [pg. 56]

unlock   To remove the default locked setting that prevents changes when worksheet protection is active. [pg. 250]

variable data   Amounts that are subject to change, such as the interest rate or amount borrowed in a loan situation. [pg. 99]

Visual Basic Editor   The Excel method of creating and modifying macros using the VBA language. [pg. 328]

Visual Basic for Applications (VBA)   A programming language that is built into Microsoft Office applications. Recorded macros can create VBA programming code or procedures can be written directly using VBA. [pg. 328]

VLOOKUP function   Used when comparison values are located in a column to the left of a table of data, and you want to look across a specified number of columns. [pg. 114]

WordArt   User-specified text displayed in one of 30 predefined styles. [pg. 198]

workbook   An Excel file that contains one or more worksheets. [pg. 2]

worksheet   Excel's term for a work area comprised of rows and columns; also known as a **spreadsheet**. [pg. 2]

worksheet frame   The row and column headings that appear along the top and left edge of the worksheet window. [pg. 5]

worksheet model   Generally contains labels and formulas, but the cells that hold variable data are left blank. [pg. 99]

worksheet outline   A set of buttons and symbols at the top or side of the worksheet that enable you to hide and unhide certain rows and columns (see also **Auto Outline**). [pg. 312]

worksheet window   Contains the current worksheet—the work area. [pg. 2]

workspace   A file that saves information about all open workbooks, including filenames, screen positions and window sizes, but does not contain the workbooks themselves. [pg. 318]

write access   A file attribute that specifies a file can be edited and saved under the same name. [pg. 255]

X-axis   The horizontal axis of a chart that generally appears at the bottom edge. [pg. 125]

Y-axis   A vertical axis on a chart that usually appears at the left edge. Some chart types support the creation of a second **Y-axis** at the right edge of the chart. [pg. 125]

Index